No Exit from Pakistan

America's Tortured Relationship with Islamabad

This book tells the story of the tragic and often tormented relationship between the United States and Pakistan. Pakistan's internal troubles have already threatened U.S. security and international peace, and Pakistan's rapidly growing population, nuclear arsenal, and relationships with China and India will continue to force it upon America's geostrategic map in new and important ways over the coming decades. This book explores the main trends in Pakistani society that will help determine its future; traces the wellsprings of Pakistani anti-American sentiment through the history of U.S.-Pakistan relations from 1947 to 2001; assesses how Washington made and implemented policies regarding Pakistan since the terrorist attacks on the United States on September 11, 2001; and analyzes how regional dynamics, especially the rise of China, will likely shape U.S.-Pakistan relations. It concludes with three options for future U.S. strategy, described as defensive insulation, military-first cooperation, and comprehensive cooperation. The book explains how Washington can prepare for the worst, aim for the best, and avoid past mistakes.

Daniel S. Markey is a Senior Fellow at the Council on Foreign Relations (CFR), where he specializes in security and governance issues in South Asia. From 2003 to 2007, Dr. Markey held the South Asia portfolio on the Secretary's Policy Planning Staff at the U.S. Department of State. Prior to government service, he taught in the Department of Politics at Princeton University, where he also served as executive director of Princeton's Research Program in International Security. Dr. Markey earned his bachelor's degree in international studies from the Johns Hopkins University and his doctorate in politics from Princeton University. He completed a postdoctoral fellowship at Harvard University's Olin Institute for Strategic Studies. Dr. Markey served as project director of the CFR-sponsored *Independent Task Force Report on U.S. Strategy in Pakistan and Afghanistan* (2010). He has published articles in *Foreign Affairs, The National Interest, The American Interest, Foreign Policy,* and *Security Studies* among other journals. His commentary has been featured in many newspapers, including the *New York Times, Washington Post, Wall Street Journal, Los Angeles Times,* and *International Herald Tribune.* He has been awarded grants from the MacArthur and Smith Richardson foundations to support his research, including regular trips to Pakistan and elsewhere in Asia.

A Council on Foreign Relations Book

The Council on Foreign Relations (CFR) is an independent, nonpartisan membership organization, think tank, and publisher dedicated to being a resource for its members, government officials, business executives, journalists, educators and students, civic and religious leaders, and other interested citizens in order to help them better understand the world and the foreign policy choices facing the United States and other countries. Founded in 1921, the CFR carries out its mission by maintaining a diverse membership, with special programs to promote interest and develop expertise in the next generation of foreign policy leaders; convening meetings at its headquarters in New York and in Washington, D.C., and other cities where senior government officials, members of Congress, global leaders, and prominent thinkers come together with CFR members to discuss and debate major international issues; supporting a Studies Program that fosters independent research, enabling CFR scholars to produce articles, reports, and books and hold roundtables that analyze foreign policy issues and make concrete policy recommendations; publishing *Foreign Affairs*, the preeminent journal on international affairs and U.S. foreign policy; sponsoring Independent Task Forces that produce reports with both findings and policy prescriptions on the most important foreign policy topics; and providing up-to-date information and analysis about world events and American foreign policy on its website, www.cfr.org.

No Exit from Pakistan

America's Tortured Relationship with Islamabad

DANIEL S. MARKEY

A Council on Foreign Relations Book

CAMBRIDGE
UNIVERSITY PRESS

CAMBRIDGE
UNIVERSITY PRESS

32 Avenue of the Americas, New York NY 10013-2473, USA

Cambridge University Press is part of the University of Cambridge.

It furthers the University's mission by disseminating knowledge in the pursuit of education, learning, and research at the highest international levels of excellence.

www.cambridge.org
Information on this title: www.cambridge.org/9781107623590

© Daniel S. Markey 2013

First published 2013
Reprinted 2013

A catalog record for this publication is available from the British Library.

Library of Congress Cataloging in Publication data
Markey, Daniel Seth, 1973– author.
No exit from Pakistan : America's tortured relationship with Islamabad / Daniel S. Markey.
    pages : maps ; cm
Includes bibliographical references and index.
ISBN 978-1-107-04546-0 (hardback : alkaline paper) – ISBN 978-1-107-62359-0 (paperback)
1. United States – Foreign relations – Pakistan. 2. Pakistan – Foreign relations – United States. 3. Anti-Americanism – Pakistan. 4. Pakistan – Politics and government. 5. Pakistan – Strategic aspects. I. Title.
E183.8.P18M375 2013
327.7305491–dc23   2013019456

ISBN 978-1-107-04546-0 Hardback
ISBN 978-1-107-62359-0 Paperback

Contents

Maps   *page* ix

Acknowledgments   xi

1   No Exit   1

2   The Four Faces of Pakistan   29

3   Why Do They Hate Us?   72

4   U-Turn to Drift: U.S.-Pakistan Relations during the
    Musharraf Era   105

5   Great Expectations to Greater Frustrations: U.S.-Pakistan
    Relations after Musharraf   136

6   From the Outside-In: U.S.-Pakistan Relations in the
    Regional Context   169

7   America's Options   200

Index   239

Maps

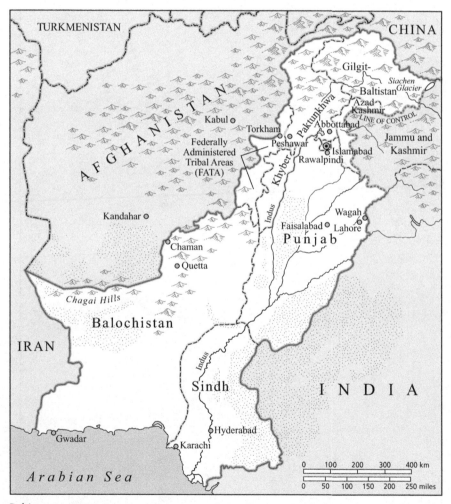

Pakistan.

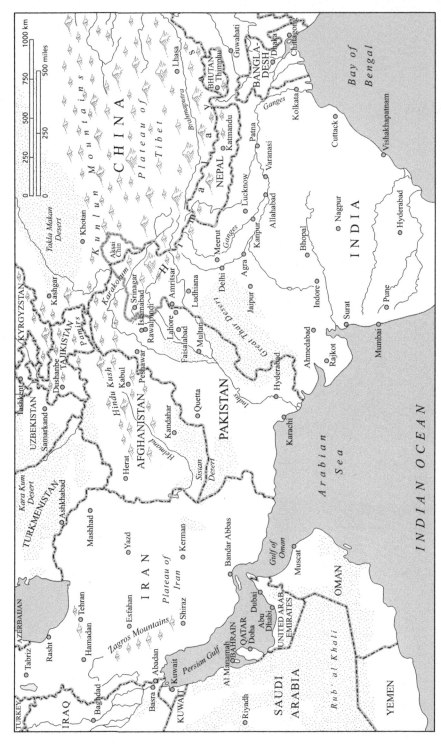

Pakistan and Its Region.

x

Acknowledgments

This book is a hybrid, born of experiences in academia and government. I could only have written it while working at an institution that values both. Few come as close to that ideal as the Washington, D.C., office of the Council on Foreign Relations (CFR). I am forever grateful to CFR President Richard N. Haass, who hired me at the State Department as well as at CFR, and who supported this project from its earliest conceptual stages. Thanks also go to CFR's director of studies, James M. Lindsay, who fulfilled the dream of every author: he freed me to research, think, and write, then offered candid, constructive criticism of every chapter along the way.

Four research associates dedicated their time, energy, and impressive intellectual talents to this book. Daniel Simons and Robert Nelson contributed good ideas and research as the project was just starting to germinate. Later, they graciously made time to read and respond to the entire manuscript despite the demands of new government jobs. The greatest burden of research and editorial assistance fell to Kunaal Sharma, and later, to Kevin Grossinger. Each handled these tasks in his own way, but always masterfully and with good cheer. Kevin's enthusiasm and attention to detail were invaluable down the home stretch. Joining the task for shorter stints were several generations of bright CFR interns: Azmat Khan, Reyad Allie, Arsla Jawaid, Emilie Shumway, Emma Barnes, Bradley Saunders, Jesse Sedler, Edward Krasniewski, Mashal Shah, and Sikander Kiani.

I hope this book reflects well the lessons I have learned from U.S. government colleagues, particularly the policy planning directors, staffers, and officers of the embassies and consulates in Pakistan, India, and China. U.S. embassy Islamabad, in particular, has welcomed and assisted me during various research trips. If this book also reveals a measure of academic wisdom, it is because I have benefited from my time at Johns Hopkins and Princeton, and especially from the teaching and guidance of Professors Steven David and Aaron Friedberg.

As part of the editorial process, I was fortunate to convene a group of top experts on Pakistan and U.S. foreign policy chaired by George Perkovich. Their responses to the manuscript, as well as those of two outstanding reviewers, Stephen Cohen and Ashley Tellis, helped me to revise and strengthen the final product. The help of Dennis Kux and Alan Kronstadt was invaluable as I pulled together the historical threads in U.S.-Pakistan relations. Others, including many U.S. officials from administrations past and present, generously agreed to sit for interviews but were not always able to be cited by name in the text. Thanks to all, and also to my colleagues at CFR and elsewhere, including Paul Stares, Michael Krepon, Dick Sokolsky, Howard and Teresita Schaffer, Anita Weiss, Lisa Curtis, Amanda Catanzano, Patricia Dorff, Amy Baker, Janine Hill, Elliott Abrams, Jakub Grygiel, Edward Lacey, Eric Lupfer, and Gary Samore. Many other intellectual debts are paid in footnotes.

My gratitude is even deeper for the many Pakistanis who have so generously opened their offices and homes to me over the years. Whatever troubles may ail Pakistan, many of its people remain unfailingly hospitable and willing to share their perspectives. Numerous prominent Pakistanis are profiled in this book, but my appreciation of their political significance was informed by hundreds of conversations with knowledgeable Pakistani diplomats, politicians, scholars, journalists, officers, civil servants, and concerned citizens from across the political spectrum. For many reasons, I will not name them here. However, one of my guides to Pakistan deserves special mention: Tariq Zaheen. Tariq is an idealist of boundless energy and patience. I know I still have much more to learn from him.

Thanks to Cambridge University Press and to my editor, Lewis Bateman, for his quick and unstinting support of this project. The entire team at Cambridge deserves great credit for managing the publication process with impressive speed and skill. The book was made possible with financial support from the Rockefeller Foundation, Starr Foundation, and other generous donors. If not for these sorts of institutions and the people who sustain them, serious and policy-relevant research would be an American hobby, not a profession.

Thank you to my parents, who have always been a vital source of love and strength, and to my grandmother, Sophie Fischer, who at one hundred years of age expresses her affection by urging me to stay closer to home. The joy of spending time with family and close friends provides the greatest incentive to heed her advice. This is especially true for my wife, Robyn, and our children, Zachary and Chloe. Fortunately, Robyn understands my devotion to this line of work. For that understanding and her love, I thank her most of all.

I

No Exit

During the final dark days of the Second World War, the French philosopher Jean-Paul Sartre first staged his play, *Huis Clos*, in Nazi-occupied Paris. In English, the title is usually translated as *No Exit*.

Sartre's drama featured three sinners, all dead to the world, who learn to their surprise that hell is not a land of fire, brimstone, and devils, but an oddly furnished living room where they are subjected to eternal torment by each other. The more they interact, the more the sinners come to appreciate that they are perfectly suited to the task, each vulnerable to precisely the psychological torture meted out by the others, and each capable of inflicting similarly devastating punishment in return.

In a moment of epiphany, one of Sartre's characters exclaims, "Hell is other people!" And yet, when the living room door swings open and the three have a chance to make a run for it, they cannot. The moment the escape option is presented, the sinners recognize it as an illusion. The only possible path to salvation is through struggle against their special tormentors. And that means there is truly no exit; they are stuck "for ever, and ever, and ever."

For American and Pakistani diplomats, policymakers, military officers (and a handful of think tank analysts like this author) who have been condemned to work with one another, this vision of perpetual mutual torment strikes close to home. For much of the past decade, Pakistan has been rocked by internal turmoil and exceptional levels of violence. Over the same period, relations between Washington and Islamabad have run from frustrating to infuriating.

This is nothing new. Well before Pakistan so routinely made headline news in America, the relationship was also a tortured one. Like Sartre's sinners, the United States and Pakistan have tormented each other for decades, if in very different ways. Both sides believe they have been sinned against. Even at high points in the relationship, there were still underlying irritations and disagreements that got in the way of building any sort of strong, sustainable cooperation.

In the early Cold War era, when Pakistan joined America's global effort to contain the Soviet Union, contentious negotiations over the scale of U.S. assistance nearly derailed the nascent alliance. Later, during the 1980s when the two sides worked hand in glove to assist the Afghan mujahedeen in their war against the Soviet Union, the Pakistanis secretly pursued a nuclear weapons program that Washington opposed. When the Cold War ended, Pakistan's nuclear program moved ahead at full steam as the U.S.-Pakistan relationship fell into a disastrous, decade-long tailspin.

At the lowest points in the relationship, such as the late 1970s, the two sides behaved more like adversaries than allies. When Pakistani student protesters ransacked the U.S. embassy in Islamabad in 1979, Pakistan's ruling general Zia-ul-Haq cynically decided to let the protest burn itself out rather than to venture a serious rescue attempt. Two Americans died that day, and only the stout walls of the embassy vault and some lucky timing allowed another 139 American and Pakistani personnel to escape the smoldering embassy grounds alive.[1] Had the story ended differently, an already tense relationship between Washington and Islamabad might have collapsed into outright hostility.

Few Americans or Pakistanis now recall that episode in 1979, but many young Pakistanis are taught to recite a litany of other low points in the relationship. These include several instances of what they call American "abandonments," such as when the United States did not adequately rise to Pakistan's defense in its wars with India in 1965 or 1971, or in 1990 when Washington slapped sanctions on Pakistan for pursuing a nuclear weapons program. American historians describe these events differently. They correctly observe that Pakistan's own choices – to go to war and to build a nuclear arsenal – led to predictable American responses, not betrayals.

Thus, Pakistanis and Americans tell conflicting versions of their shared history. There is at least a nugget of truth to the Pakistani lament that America has used their country when it suited the superpower's agenda and then tossed it away when inconvenient. Ever since Pakistan gained independence from British India in 1947, Washington has viewed the country as a means to other ends, whether that meant fighting communism or terrorism. When Pakistan was helpful, it enjoyed generous American assistance and attention. When Pakistan was unhelpful, the spigot was turned off.

Yet, for all the Pakistani complaints about how the United States has never been a true friend, the fact is that Pakistan also used America. Pakistani leaders dipped into America's deep pockets to serve their purposes, sometimes

[1] For a full account of the attack on the Islamabad embassy, see Steve Coll, *Ghost Wars* (New York: Penguin, 2004), pp. 21–37.

parochial or corrupt, oftentimes driven by persistent geopolitical conflict with neighboring India.

Above all, the Pakistani military viewed relations with the United States as a means to balance against India, Pakistan's larger sibling with which it has maintained a more or less hostile relationship since birth. The Indo-Pakistani relationship explains a great deal about how the Pakistani state views the world, and more than a little about how it functions at home as well. When the United States failed to provide money, diplomatic backing, or equipment that would be useful against India, Pakistan hardly reconsidered its hostile stance. Islamabad simply looked elsewhere to meet its perceived needs: to nearby China, to an independent nuclear weapons program, and even to nurturing violent anti-Indian insurgents and terrorists. Pakistan took these steps even when it knew full well that they would anger Washington and threaten the basis of any lasting alliance with the United States.

In short, the United States has been the more fickle partner, its approach to Pakistan shifting dramatically across the decades. Pakistan, however, has been guilty of greater misrepresentation, claiming support for American purposes while turning the U.S. partnership to other ends. As a consequence, both sides failed repeatedly to build a relationship to serve beyond the immediate needs of the day. Theirs was neither a special relationship of the sort that exists between America and Britain, nor a mature alliance like the United States has developed with countries such as Japan and South Korea.

Worse, the on-again, off-again pattern of U.S.-Pakistan cooperation resulted in growing mistrust. That historical pattern and its implications for anti-American sentiment in Pakistan is the central theme of the third chapter in this book. In Pakistan, mistrust of the United States extended well beyond the foreign policy elite. Today, Pakistanis high and low wade in a swamp of anti-Americanism. The muck seeps into every debate over how best to manage relations with the United States, but it does not stop there. In their public and private conversations, Pakistanis routinely hold America responsible for an enormous range of events inside their country, sometimes by way of tangled conspiracy theories. Whether the conversation turns to government corruption, suicide bombers, or routine electrical blackouts, the United States usually takes a share of the blame.

Differences of perception and interest, not to mention a litany of historically bound grievances, now divide the two countries. No U.S. public relations campaign, no matter how sophisticated, will redefine Pakistani attitudes. That said, few Pakistanis hate Americans for who they are or what they believe. Tens of millions of Pakistanis would gladly live in a society that allowed the personal freedoms and opportunities afforded in America. This leaves a narrow but important space for hope. Pakistani anti-Americanism is a noxious by-product of the interplay between U.S. foreign policies, wider trends within the Muslim world, and Pakistan's own domestic politics. If some or all of these dynamics were to shift, it is conceivable that America would find new allies and partners in Pakistani society.

Pakistanis are not, however, the only aggrieved party in this relationship. A decade after 9/11, the U.S.-Pakistan relationship also has very few fans left in Washington. In the corridors of U.S. power, from the White House and State Department to the Pentagon and CIA, a gallows humor hangs over most Pakistan policy debates. Best-laid plans and high hopes have been dashed too often for anyone to champion costly new agendas.

Having spent billions of dollars in military and civilian assistance to Pakistan, many representatives and senators have reached the conclusion, as Gary Ackerman, a Democratic congressman from New York, put it in May 2012, that "Pakistan is like a black hole for American aid. Our tax dollars go in. Our diplomats go in, sometimes. Our aid professionals go in, sometimes. Our hopes go in. Our prayers go in. Nothing good ever comes out."[2]

Whereas the Obama administration spent its first two years seeking a grand transformation in the U.S. relationship with Pakistan, most of 2011 and 2012 were devoted to salvaging a minimal degree of cooperation. By early 2011, analysts in American government and academic circles began to contemplate how a total rupture in the U.S.-Pakistan relationship might look, and whether, for instance, the threats posed by terrorists and Pakistan's nuclear arsenal could be contained within its borders if the official relationship turned completely hostile. They conducted a range of "contingency planning exercises" to assess how hypothetical crises in and around Pakistan might escalate into full-scale wars.

Underneath those bloodless planning drills and calculations, passions ran deep. Increasingly, Washington's top policymakers felt a personal animus toward Pakistan. After reading scores of incriminating intelligence reports and experiencing firsthand the frustrations of dealing with Pakistani counterparts, many concluded that Pakistan's military and intelligence forces were guilty of a cruel, immoral, and deceptive strategy that helped Afghan Taliban insurgents kill hundreds of U.S. troops and made another major terrorist attack against Americans and their allies more likely.

In addition to poisoning cooperation in the short run, such experiences leave lasting scars. In the tumultuous years immediately after 9/11, American officials tended to give their Pakistani counterparts the benefit of the doubt, hoping that over time the relationship would mature and improve. A decade later, the opposite is true. The generation of U.S. officers who served in the Afghan war is likely to emerge from that conflict perceiving Pakistan as an enemy more than an ally. Their views are already influencing policymakers and legislators in Washington.

[2] Ackerman, quoted in Richard Leiby, "Pakistan's Power Crisis May Eclipse Terrorist Threat," *Washington Post*, May 27, 2012, http://www.washingtonpost.com/world/asia_pacific/pakistans-power-crisis-may-eclipse-terrorist-threat/2012/05/27/gJQAPhOSuU_story.html.

In May 2011, America closed the first chapter of the post-9/11 era by killing Osama bin Laden. U.S. and allied leaders have resolved to withdraw the lion's share of their troops from Afghanistan in 2014. Frustration and disgust with Pakistan shows little sign of abating. Perhaps now is the moment for the world's sole superpower to escape from this particular torment. The situation feels a lot like the dramatic point in Sartre's play when the living room door swings open, offering his sinners the chance to make a run for it. Can't America simply leave Pakistan behind?

No. However appealing it might seem for America to wash its hands of Pakistan, to move on and let Pakistanis, or someone else, pick up the mess, it would be little more than wishful thinking to believe that neglecting the challenges posed by Pakistan will make them go away. This is the essential meaning of "No Exit."

Unfortunately, this does not mean the United States has any easy solutions. The situation is troubling and, in a deep sense, tragic. It requires Americans to appreciate that some problems may be too big to solve, and yet still too important to avoid.

MUTUAL VULNERABILITY

The U.S. experience of the twentieth century, from two world wars to the Cold War, convinced most American policymakers that the world was shrinking. One could no longer trust that the United States would be insulated by its surrounding oceans from the repercussions of decisions in far-off places like Berlin, Tokyo, or Moscow.

The twenty-first century has only accelerated the speed and density of global interconnections. Threats of disease, climate change, economic crisis, terrorism, and war routinely spill across countries and leapfrog continents. All countries, including the United States, are vulnerable. By this logic, even though Pakistan is on the other side of the world, America is not necessarily protected from what happens there.

Yet, even if world is shrinking, some places matter more to the United States than others. As an extreme example, in the late 1990s, a brutal war started in the Congo. Neighboring states were sucked into the conflict that brought death, displacement, and destruction to millions of Africans over the subsequent decade. The suffering went almost entirely unnoticed in Washington. One can debate the morality of this fact, but it is necessary to recognize that states are typically moved to action by what they perceive to be their own interests. That may or may not lead them to make sacrifices for humanitarian or altruistic purposes. In Pakistan's case, tens of millions of people suffer from poverty, disease, and violence, but none of this necessarily compels the United States to do anything about it.

On close examination, however, it is clear that the U.S.-Pakistan relationship is one of mutual vulnerability. Each side has the potential to threaten the other's interests, even vital ones. This is true in spite of their many other differences in power, wealth, culture, and history.

Pakistan's Vulnerability

Pakistanis, who crave a respite from the exhausting trials of America's post-9/11 campaign against terrorism, find themselves trapped in a humiliating position of dependence upon the United States. Islamabad is addicted to U.S. assistance dollars, whether in the form of grants, projects, or loans. Similarly, Pakistan's military jealously guards its supply of American-made weapons and spare parts, especially its sixty-three F-16 fighter jets, aircraft that rival some of the best in neighboring India's arsenal.

Even if Pakistan were somehow to free itself from these crutches, it would still confront a global economy in which the United States remains the most influential player. It would still confront a regional security environment in which the United States maintains the most powerful military. Unlike nearby China or Russia, Pakistan lacks sufficient strength, wealth, or easily exploited natural resources to insulate itself from American influence.

Pakistanis old enough to recall the 1990s will remember that at the end of the Cold War when relations with the United States took a nosedive, the country's friendships with China and Saudi Arabia failed to save it from a decade of terrible economic and political turbulence. The country cycled through a series of ineffectual and weak governments and ran up an astronomical debt along the way. Today, Pakistan is having an even harder time getting its house in order. This makes the country more vulnerable to outside pressure and more dependent on outside aid.

As has been the case for decades, and as explained at greater length in the second chapter of this book, Pakistani society is dominated by a small, elite class of feudal land barons and industrialists, usually in collusion with the most powerful institution of the land: the army. Together, these power brokers have suppressed radical change, but more and more they are besieged along two fronts.

A relatively small but vocal and violent segment of society favors revolutionary change. These radicals – terrorists, militants, and their ideological sympathizers – who cloak themselves in the garb of Islam, do not enjoy much popular appeal. They are, however, able to intimidate the masses. Some of the most radical voices in Pakistan have also enjoyed the active support of the state, including in the military and intelligence services. Armed, trained, and indoctrinated in the black arts of insurgency and terrorism, these groups now make terrifyingly sophisticated adversaries. It is not surprising that Pakistan's leaders often choose to temporize, negotiate, or at best divide and conquer these extremists rather than to tackle the whole of the problem at once.

Unfortunately, that piecemeal approach also betrays weakness and ambivalence. It has undermined, at times fatally, Pakistanis who might otherwise stand up for a more moderate or progressive society. It fosters an atmosphere of fear and conspiracy. That, in turn, discourages the sorts of investments and entrepreneurial activity that could jumpstart the underperforming economy. Most worrisome, it increases the chance that the guardians of Pakistani national security, including those within the nuclear weapons program, will be compromised from within their own ranks. The greatest threat to Pakistan's stability comes not from the prospect of violent conquest – a virtual impossibility in the face of the army's size and overwhelmingly superior firepower – but from confusion, deterioration, or division within the army itself.

Aside from violent and revolutionary forces of change, Pakistan also faces the pressures and opportunities afforded by massive population growth. By mid-century, Pakistan will almost certainly join India, China, and the United States among the world's four most populous nations. Pakistan's cities are growing fastest of all, and the country's young urbanites are already demanding change. Not surprisingly, their main concerns are jobs and education. Thus far, Pakistan's sclerotic political system has done rather little to meet these needs, but the tide may yet turn. Tens of millions of young Pakistanis are coming of age in a world saturated with new tools of communication and social mobilization, like cell phones and interactive media. These tools may open the door to popular political participation in ways that are entirely new to Pakistan.

Nonviolent, evolutionary change might be the best possible way to unclench the grip on power enjoyed by Pakistan's traditional, repressive elite. For the moment, however, the country's reformers – young and old – are not up to the task. They lack experience and viable allies that can compete in the rough-and-tumble world of Pakistani politics and still remain true to their goals. Pakistan's current crop of reformers is also decidedly inward-looking, which limits its ability to benefit from external support, whether from America or elsewhere.

In short, Pakistan is vulnerable. Its traditional ruling classes and the military are still strong enough to ward off the immediate prospect of revolution or collapse, but the state is stressed by population growth, hamstrung in its reform efforts, and plagued by violence and terror. Change, whether revolutionary and violent or evolutionary and peaceful, looms on the horizon. It is impossible to know when and how the balance of power will tip away from those Pakistanis who favor continuity and toward those who favor change, but all the warning signs are in place.

America's Vulnerability

Americans yearn for the sense of safety that was lost on 9/11 when terrorists turned New York's twin towers to ash. At that time, more al-Qaeda operatives lived in Pakistan than any other country. Washington's first concern when dealing with Islamabad remains the vulnerability of the American people to threats based on Pakistani soil.

Dealing with Pakistan is no straightforward affair. Anyone who claims otherwise has not been paying attention. Pakistan is neither completely aligned with America, nor completely opposed. Some of America's frustrations with Islamabad result from what Pakistan does, others from what Pakistan seems incapable of doing.

The mixed experience of Pakistan's counterterror cooperation with the United States since 9/11 provides one illustration of the point. Some of the greatest American successes in the fight against al-Qaeda, like the arrest of 9/11 organizer Ramzi bin al-Shibh in 2002, came through cooperation with Pakistani authorities.[3] On other occasions, like the raid on Osama bin Laden's compound in May 2011, Washington chose to act unilaterally, fearing that its plans might be compromised if Pakistani officials were informed. In even more troubling circumstances, the United States and Pakistan have worked at cross-purposes. U.S. officials are, for instance, fully convinced that Pakistan employs some terrorist groups as proxy fighters in Afghanistan and India. These groups have American blood on their hands.

Nor is terrorism the only security challenge that the United States has in Pakistan. Prior to 9/11, and again increasingly as al-Qaeda's ranks have been decimated in the years after 2007, many U.S. officials view securing Pakistan's nuclear program as their top concern. Pakistan is expanding its nuclear arsenal and investing in new ways to launch warheads against neighboring India, including tactical (very short range) missiles. Aside from their implications for regional stability, these developments make the program more complicated and more difficult to secure. They also raise the potential costs of internal disorder or a hostile revolutionary turn.

Other American policymakers, focused intently on the endgame of the Afghan war, see Pakistan's role as critical to determining whether Afghanistan emerges as a weak but stable state or reverts to bloody civil war fueled by the enmities of neighboring powers.[4] Of course, Pakistan's regional significance does not end in Afghanistan. Looking ahead to the future – a difficult and speculative business to be sure – Pakistan's most important role is likely to be the one it plays in the geopolitics of Asia, spanning from the energy-rich Persian Gulf and Central Asian states to the thriving economies of the Far East, especially that of China.

Faced with multiple concerns, there is a natural temptation to reduce the challenge of Pakistan to a single issue, to seek a bottom line about what matters to the United States most of all. This impulse to prioritize is admirable and necessary in the context of any single policy decision. But addressing only one of the challenges America faces in Pakistan would not be sufficient, and a

---

[3] David Rhode, "Karachi Raid Provides Hint of Qaeda's Rise in Pakistan," *New York Times*, September 15, 2002, http://www.nytimes.com/2002/09/15/world/threats-responses-karachi-karachi-raid-provides-hint-qaeda-s-rise-pakistan.html?ref=ramzibinalshibh.

[4] For a comprehensive study of Afghanistan's regional context, see Ashley J. Tellis and Aroop Mukharji, eds., "Is a Regional Strategy Viable in Afghanistan?" Carnegie Endowment for International Peace, 2010, http://carnegieendowment.org/files/regional_approach.pdf.

single-track strategy will almost certainly allow other important issues to slip through the cracks.

Worse, policies that serve one set of ends may be counterproductive in other areas. Washington has committed this mistake over and over since the outset of the U.S.-Pakistan relationship. It has swung, pendulum-like, between different bottom line goals in Pakistan. At times, this meant focusing only on Pakistan's role in the Cold War fight against Soviet influence. At other points, Washington was obsessed with Pakistan's nuclear weapons program. Since 9/11, it has focused mainly on Pakistan's cooperation in fighting international terrorists.

To add another layer to this challenge, it is clear that the United States cannot achieve its ends in Pakistan through a strategy of pure cooperation or pure coercion. In some instances the United States will find it exceedingly costly to address its vital security concerns unless it can find a way to work with Pakistan as a partner. Securing Pakistan's nuclear arsenal, for instance, is a project that is best undertaken by Pakistanis themselves, with the United States playing only a supportive role. All things equal, building a close, cooperative relationship with Pakistan's military and nuclear establishment would seem to be the best way for the United States to gain confidence in the security of Pakistan's arsenal.

In other cases, however, achieving U.S. goals in Pakistan may require coercion or confrontation. For example, the experience of the past decade suggests that Pakistan is unlikely to end its support for violent extremist groups unless Washington forces Islamabad's hand. As the more powerful party in the relationship, the United States can put the screws to Pakistan in various ways, but America's power is not always easily turned into useful coercive leverage. If, for instance, Washington were to pressure Pakistan's military and intelligence services, it would be targeting some of the same individuals and institutions responsible for securing the nation's nuclear arsenal.

The effort to balance U.S. goals and avoid contradictory policy prescriptions is further complicated by the regional dimension. Washington cannot afford to deal with Islamabad in a vacuum; it must consider the implications of its policies with respect to other countries, especially India and Afghanistan. These are not always simple calculations. For instance, the more frustrated Washington gets with Pakistan, the more inclined U.S. leaders are to favor a relationship with India, the more stable, democratic partner in South Asia. Of course, an increasingly prosperous India offers ample attraction for the United States in its own right, but there is no escaping the fact that the more Washington tilts toward New Delhi, the more insecurity that inspires in Islamabad.

At times, such insecurity can pay dividends. Immediately after 9/11, Pakistani fears led its leaders to cooperate and compromise with the United States. Throughout 2012, Pakistan energized its diplomatic outreach to India as a means to avoid simultaneous tension with Washington and New Delhi. On many other occasions, however, insecurity has led Pakistan to take counterproductive steps: to build more nuclear weapons, lend support to anti-Indian terrorist groups, or seek a closer relationship with China.

The United States has a full and complicated agenda in Pakistan, fraught with difficult trade-offs. That said, it is possible to disentangle U.S. interests into three primary areas of concern. Each deserves particular attention even as it must be balanced against the others.

First, al-Qaeda remnants, their affiliates, sympathizers, and possible successor organizations based on Pakistani soil pose an *immediate* threat to American security. The threat is an urgent one because innocent American lives are at stake. Successful U.S. military and intelligence operations have diminished, not eliminated, the terrorist threat. It could be reconstituted if Washington takes its eye off the ball.

Second, if Pakistan's nuclear weapons, materials, or know-how end up in hostile or irresponsible hands, they would pose a *vital* threat to the United States. Fortunately, Pakistan's nuclear arsenal does not now pose an existential threat of the sort the United States faced during the Cold War when thousands of nuclear-tipped missiles pointed at America from the Soviet Union. Even so, the possibility that Pakistan's warheads might be smuggled onto U.S. shores or transferred to other states or terrorist groups makes this issue one of Washington's highest security concerns.

Third, Pakistan's size, location, and potential for instability and violence represent an *emergent* geopolitical challenge within the context of Asia's growing importance on the global stage. America's broader economic, political, and strategic interests in Pakistan's neighborhood are less urgent than terrorism and less vital than nuclear weapons. Yet, the United States must still think very seriously about them, especially when it comes to navigating relationships with rising Asian powers like China and India.

All of these U.S. interests are tied up in the fate of Pakistan itself. Pakistan is already a failing state in many ways, but it is not yet a failed one. As explained in Chapter 2, although it is not inevitable or likely in the immediate near term, Pakistan could fail in ways that are far worse than at present. Pakistan's under-performing national institutions could crumble further, its military could fracture, its ethnic and sectarian cleavages could take the country past the point of militancy and into outright civil war.

For the United States, these are scenarios to be feared, for however dangerous Pakistan is today, its collapse or breakup would be disastrous. The human costs, from violence, refugee flows, and internal dislocation would hurt Pakistanis and their neighbors. But the Untied States would also have strategic concerns. Neither Pakistan's resident extremists nor its nuclear arsenal would go quietly into the night. It is hard even to imagine the sort of stabilizing military force required to intervene in a broken Pakistan. In short, for Washington it is better to deal with a single Pakistan than multiple, warring states or, more likely, a morass of feuding fiefdoms.

Pakistanis will decide how to deal with internal threats, how to manage their nuclear program, and how to grapple with regional friends and adversaries. What they decide will have something to do with the character of Pakistan's relationship with the United States, which means that Washington can exert an important influence.

It would be hubristic, however, to argue that Americans can determine the destiny of nearly 200 million Pakistanis. As with many large, complicated societies, Pakistan's future – from the fate of its masses to the character of its leaders – will first depend on internal developments. Washington may be able to shield itself from many of the potential ill effects of these developments, but a healthy Pakistani society and a stable Pakistani state offers the only prospect for achieving all of America's objectives in an enduring way.

THE IMMEDIATE THREAT: TERRORISM

The 9/11 attacks exposed America's vulnerability to the threat posed by a handful of highly motivated terrorists. Armed only with plane tickets, box cutters, and some flight training, the attackers killed thousands of innocents, destroyed billions of dollars of property, and sent a nation of 300 million people into crisis.

Although the United States launched a war in Afghanistan to bring al-Qaeda to justice, many of the terrorist group's top leaders have been found in Pakistan. U.S. drones circling over Pakistan's tribal areas have killed dozens of al-Qaeda operatives. The mastermind of 9/11, Khalid Sheikh Mohammed, was born to Pakistani parents and captured in Rawalpindi in 2003, near Pakistan's capital. Eight years later, and just seventy miles to the north, U.S. Navy SEALs raided Osama bin Laden's compound in the Pakistani town of Abbottabad. No one can doubt that al-Qaeda's roots in Pakistan run chillingly deep.

A central question for U.S. policymakers since 2001 has been how the United States should best defend itself against international terrorism in the future. Heightened American defenses – from closer scrutiny of all the people and goods that come into the United States to greater coordination and vigilance by domestic law enforcement agencies – is a start. Yet shortly after 9/11, the Bush administration also went on the offensive against al-Qaeda. Washington launched the war in Afghanistan and extensive manhunts across the globe. Over time, the United States also relied more heavily on new technologies, such as unmanned drones, to target and kill suspected terrorists in remote locations inside Pakistan, Yemen, and elsewhere. In each of these instances, the goal was to disrupt the safe havens that had permitted al-Qaeda and similar groups to plan and implement their operations.

The Bush administration also called for an even more ambitious American undertaking: the transformation of societies within the Muslim world that had given birth to the violent ideas espoused by al-Qaeda. This push to promote democracy and greater freedom in the Muslim world was driven in large part by the observation that repressive and autocratic regimes were to blame for the alienation and anger behind al-Qaeda's mission. More freedom, the logic ran, would make for less terrorism.

Some aspects of Washington's counterterror campaign have been more successful than others. The combination of homeland defense and overseas disruption of safe havens has so far saved America from another devastating attack. New defenses and procedures make the United States far less likely to suffer from the specific sorts of suicide hijackings it faced on 9/11. U.S. operations inside Pakistan and Afghanistan sent Osama bin Laden to a watery grave and killed or captured many of his top lieutenants. Al-Qaeda in Pakistan and Afghanistan is but a shell of its former self.

Yet, few U.S. security officials rest easily at night because they recognize that terrorist plots against the United States continue to be hatched. Some, like al-Qaeda's 2009 Christmas Day scheme to bring down a Northwest Airlines flight bound for Detroit, have nearly succeeded. Nor did President Obama embrace his predecessor's sweeping agenda of eliminating the political grievances that animate terrorism in Muslim societies. The task was considered too daunting, too costly, and too prone to creating an even greater violent backlash against American intervention.

In Pakistan, the United States still faces the threat posed by al-Qaeda remnants, quite possibly including bin Laden's Egyptian-born successor, Ayman al-Zawahiri, who may have found safe haven along the rugged border between Pakistan and Afghanistan or may, like bin Laden, be more comfortably ensconced in some hideout elsewhere. Either way, as long as the United States maintains a strong virtual presence in Pakistan through drones and intelligence operations, some in coordination with Pakistani authorities, al-Qaeda's remnants are likely to be picked off, one by one, over time.

If, however, U.S. relations with Pakistan rupture, important elements of the U.S. counterterror mission would be jeopardized. Intelligence sharing would cease, and it would be an easy military matter (if not a simple choice) for Islamabad to close its airspace to the slow-moving, low-flying U.S. drones. Under those conditions, al-Qaeda might again take advantage of the remoteness of Pakistan's forbidding mountain ranges or the lawlessness and anonymity of its teeming cities.

Even if al-Qaeda is never able to reconstitute, other like-minded Pakistani terrorist groups have been influenced and strengthened by their contact with al-Qaeda operatives. They have learned new, more sophisticated tactics and adopted aspects of al-Qaeda's worldview, at times trading local and parochial grievances for the rhetoric of global jihad. If the world ever sees the likes of a second Osama bin Laden, there is a very good chance that he would be a Pakistani, raised in a climate of violent anti-Americanism and surrounded by experienced terrorists who command resources from networks of financial support and ideological sympathy.

The Pakistani Taliban (Tehrik-i-Taliban Pakistan, or TTP), founded in 2007 by the ferocious Baitullah Mehsud, has particularly close ties to al-Qaeda. By its own claims and official U.S. statements, the TTP has already struck the United States once. On May 1, 2010, Faisal Shahzad, a Pakistani-born American citizen, drove his dark green Nissan Pathfinder into New York's Times Square, where he left it at the curb, hazard lights on and engine running. Minutes later, nearby street vendors heard the sound of exploding fireworks and noticed smoke drifting from the interior of the SUV. Fortunately, the fertilizer bomb that Shahzad had rigged in the back of the vehicle was an amateurish affair, disarmed by the city's bomb squad without injury. The Federal Bureau of Investigation (FBI) arrested Shahzad days later, just as his Dubai-bound flight from New York was pulling away from the terminal.[5]

In his own court testimony, the American-educated Shahzad admitted to receiving funds to purchase the SUV and bomb materials from a TTP source. In 2009, Shahzad trained briefly in the rugged tribal region along Pakistan's border with Afghanistan, where he translated a bomb-making manual from Urdu to English and received some additional lessons in explosives. In a TTP-produced video released online after the attempted attack, Shahzad menacingly explains his decision to join in a global struggle against those who would oppress Muslims, his desire to bring violent jihad into the United States, and his collaboration with top TTP leaders in conceiving the attack on New York City.[6]

Shahzad was unusual, perhaps even unique, for being an American citizen who chose for his own personal reasons to approach members of the Pakistani Taliban and join their cause. And like al-Qaeda, the ranks of the TTP have been decimated by Washington's relentless drone campaign. So Americans need not fear that a tidal wave of Pakistani-trained bomb makers is about to hit U.S. shores. That said, Shahzad's plot shows that al-Qaeda's Pakistani affiliates are willing to expand the scope of their terrorist activities beyond Pakistan's borders if given half a chance. They are opportunistic and highly motivated.

The TTP is hardly the only al-Qaeda affiliate inside Pakistan with the intent, if not always the means, to attack the United States directly. A range of other terrorist outfits and splinter factions operate throughout Pakistan, from the country's largest city of Karachi to its rural heartland of Punjab. Unlike the sparsely populated Pashtun tribal areas, it is nearly impossible to imagine drones (American or otherwise) raining missiles upon these settled parts of the country. Traditional tools of law enforcement and intelligence collection would

[5] On Faisal Shahzad, see James Barron and Michael S. Schmidt, "From Suburban Father to a Terrorism Suspect," *New York Times*, May 4, 2010, p. A1; James Barron and Sabrina Tavernise, "Money Woes, Long Silences and a Zeal for Islam," *New York Times*, May 5, 2010, p. A1; Andrea Elliott, "For Times Sq. Suspect, Long Roots of Discontent," *New York Times*, May 15, 2010, p. A1.
[6] "Taliban Video of Faisal Shahzad," *New York Times*, September 29, 2010, http://video.nytimes.com/video/2010/09/29/nyregion/1248069111343/taliban-video-of-faisal-shahzad.html.

be more effective and less likely to spark a violent revolt. The United States will have great difficulty conducting these operations without some cooperation or consent from their Pakistani counterparts.

This challenge is magnified and complicated by the fact that Pakistan's own state has a long history of supporting some of country's most sophisticated terrorist groups, envisioning them as proxy forces that advance Pakistan's interests in a hostile region. Since its founding in 1990, Lashkar-e-Taiba (LeT) has been favored by the army and Inter-Services Intelligence directorate (ISI) as a group that brought terror to India, first inside Kashmir, then farther afield. Even though Islamabad officially banned the group in 2002, LeT's humanitarian wing operates openly throughout Pakistan and LeT's founding leader, Hafiz Muhammad Saeed, taunts the United States before television cameras and public rallies.[7]

LeT has won its greatest notoriety for attacking India, but its core ideology and mission is much more global, similar to that of al-Qaeda. In November 2008, LeT launched a paralyzing strike on the Indian metropolis of Mumbai. In a series of coordinated attacks across the city, young LeT commandos methodically gunned down innocent civilians in hotels, the train station, a trendy café, and along the street, while other team members butchered a Jewish family on specific orders from their Pakistani handlers. Six Americans were among those murdered.

To be sure, LeT is no al-Qaeda. Not yet. Its complicated relationship with the Pakistani state offers the organization a degree of protection, but it also imposes constraints upon the group's terrorist activities. If LeT goes too far in attacking American interests, for instance, Islamabad would be unable to protect it from an American reprisal. LeT has still managed to build a far-flung network of sympathizers and operatives, including within the United States. It was an American citizen, David Coleman Headley, born to a Pakistani father and an American mother, who trained for months in Pakistani LeT camps and conducted the surveillance of Mumbai in preparation for the 2008 attacks. Headley also scoped out other sites in India and Europe for possible attacks.[8]

It is not hard to imagine a future in which LeT or a significant faction of the organization decides to strike the United States directly. In an ironic twist, that threat becomes more likely if, under American pressure, Islamabad were to take an unmistakable but only partially effective turn against LeT. In that scenario, the terrorist operatives would have every reason to wreak havoc inside Pakistan

---

[7] Michael Georgy and Qasim Nauman, "With $10 mln Bounty on His Head, Hafiz Saeed Taunts U.S.," *Reuters*, April 5, 2012, http://in.reuters.com/article/2012/04/05/pakistan-usa-hafiz-saeed-mumbai-attacks-idINDEE8330L520120405.

[8] For details on Headley's surveillance role in the 2008 Mumbai attacks, see Stephen Tankel, *Storming the World Stage: The Story of Lashkar-e-Taiba* (New York: Columbia University Press, 2011), pp. 221–30, 248–51. For more on Headley's surveillance of sites in India and in Denmark, including the offices of the Danish paper *Morgenavisen Jyllands-Posten*, see Tankel, *Storming the World Stage*, pp. 249–51.

and activate their international network to strike the United States as well. LeT will be a difficult knot to untangle, under any circumstances.

Unfortunately, Pakistan has taken too little action against groups like LeT and their sympathizers over the past decade. Extreme ideologies have won more adherents. Pakistan's radical Islamists, like their counterparts in other parts of the Muslim world, present themselves as alternatives to the corrupt, ineffective state and the mainstream political parties. LeT-affiliated schools and clinics, not to mention the humanitarian missions it sponsors during times of national crisis like Pakistan's epic 2010 floods, win popular sympathy even if the group's austere interpretation of Islam holds much less appeal for average Pakistanis.

These groups will have no shortage of new recruits if, as anticipated, Pakistan's broken educational system continues to produce millions of young men and women unprepared to contribute to the global economy and millions more who cannot find jobs even if they have skills and training. Frustrated with a Pakistani system that has failed them, indoctrinated in a pervasive anti-Western worldview that blames the United States for the better part of their miseries, and encouraged to devote their energies to global jihad, this rising generation of young radicals will pose a threat to U.S. security.

Some Pakistanis suggest that today's anti-Americanism and violence inside Pakistan is a product of current U.S. policy: the war in Afghanistan and the covert counterterror methods, from drones to Navy SEALs. One of Pakistan's most popular politicians, the charismatic former cricket star Imran Khan, routinely argues that if the United States would simply remove its forces from Afghanistan, the region would settle down and the few remaining terrorists could be more easily targeted.

Reclining behind his office desk on a hot afternoon in May 2012, comfortable in a traditional white cotton tunic, baggy trousers, and sandals, Khan held forth on the terrible mistake Pakistan's President Musharraf made by choosing to side with Washington after 9/11. That error, Khan claimed, was only compounded in 2004 when Musharraf sent the army into Pakistan's tribal areas to root out international terrorists. These moves were the original sins that led to so many of Pakistan's subsequent security troubles.[9]

Khan's arguments, however neatly articulated, put the cart before the horse. The violent extremism and terroristic methods of al-Qaeda, the Taliban, and LeT were spreading inside Pakistan well before 9/11. These trends had their origins in Washington's support for the Afghan mujahedeen during the anti-Soviet war of the 1980s, but to draw a straight line between the 1980s and 2001 would be to skip a critical decade. Throughout the 1990s, Pakistan actively and passively supported al-Qaeda's Taliban hosts, thereby promoting the rise of international terrorism in Afghanistan. The existence of terrorist sanctuaries in Afghanistan prompted America's military intervention in the region after 2001, not vice versa.

9 Author interview with Imran Khan, May 15, 2012.

There is no doubting that for an ailing country like Pakistan, the post-9/11 U.S. military intervention in neighboring Afghanistan and Islamabad's public alignment with Washington against al-Qaeda and its affiliates have been painful. Worse, the treatment has been only partially effective. Al-Qaeda may be nearly beaten. Other groups, however, such as LeT and various Punjab-based terrorist groups, have extended their reach.

Imran Khan and his fellow travelers suffer from wishful thinking when they suggest that an American military withdrawal from the region would in itself bring a quick end to Pakistan's security troubles. Pakistan's immediate pain might dissipate, but so might any serious hope of treating the underlying disease.

America's withdrawal would eliminate the stated raisons d'etre for some of the fighters in the region, but it would almost certainly embolden others. Many tribal militias in Afghanistan and along Pakistan's border are undoubtedly animated by the defensive desire to kick out any foreign invaders. If outside forces leave, some militants would probably be content to go back to their parochial feuds and leave the world alone. Other terrorist groups operating in the region are driven by global visions of jihad. They would be more likely to declare victory, consolidate gains, and rededicate themselves to a wider struggle.

One part of the trouble in U.S.-Pakistan relations has been that the two sides often disagree over the type of threat they face. Islamabad has tended to emphasize the role of local "miscreants" where Washington has been more inclined to see international terrorists. In the early post-9/11 period, it was marginally easier to identify local militant organizations with defensive, rather than global, objectives. Yet even then Islamabad too often whistled past the graveyard, believing it could live and let live or harness such militant groups to suit its purposes. Now, after over a decade of war, many of the regional militants that started with only parochial interests have picked up increasingly sophisticated tactics and jihadist rhetoric. U.S. officials are right not to underestimate the long-term consequences of that transformation.

The United States will have various options for dealing with its own vulnerability to Pakistan-based terrorism. America's choices will depend in large part on the decisions Pakistanis make, above all whether and how they choose to confront the terrorists themselves. Bearing that in mind, Washington might opt to address the threat narrowly, through defensive measures; aggressively, through a persistent and expanded counterterror campaign inside Pakistan; holistically, by attempting to address the underlying grievances that are believed to fuel violent extremism in the first place; or by some combination of all these approaches. Even under the best of circumstances, however, the problem of Pakistan-based terrorism is likely to linger for years, possibly decades, to come.

THE VITAL THREAT: NUCLEAR WEAPONS

If Pakistan were a distant country riddled with terrorists, the United States would have cause for concern, as it does with far smaller states like Yemen and

Somalia. But Pakistan is no Yemen: it is far larger and more developed, and it possesses a nuclear arsenal, putting it in the company of only a handful of other states, including its much larger neighbors India and China.

Just because a country has nuclear weapons does not necessarily make it a concern to the United States. Britain and France, for instance, pose no threat. The goals of the nuclear state are nearly as important as the arsenal itself. Unlike Iran or North Korea, at least for the time being, Pakistan is far less likely to use its nuclear weapons against the United States or its treaty allies.

Moreover, in spite of many sensationalistic essays to the contrary, Pakistan's arsenal is not so heedlessly guarded as to make it an easy target for terrorists or other potential thieves.[10] Nuclear weapons are not all that easy to pilfer, and they are usually even harder to detonate without authorization. Moreover, Pakistan has taken pains to improve the security of its entire nuclear program – weapons, labs, and storage facilities – as it has grown larger and more complicated.

Over 20,000 personnel serve to protect that program in one way or another, and all Pakistanis who have contact with nuclear facilities are screened and monitored to reduce the chance of an insider threat.[11] Starting in the early 2000s, the United States also provided the Pakistani nuclear establishment with selective training, limited funds, and technological recommendations to enhance security, and by extension, to open lines of communication with the aim of building confidence on both sides. All of this helps to explain why U.S. officials, including President Obama, have expressed some degree of confidence in the security of Pakistan's nuclear program.[12]

Even so, Americans have good reasons to consider Pakistan's nuclear weapons a vital threat, one that rates among the top U.S. security concerns in the world. Why? Leaving aside real but lesser American concerns about a potential arms race or nuclear crisis between Pakistan and India, the answer has to do with the shadow of Pakistan's alarming past and the nation's uncertain future.

Pakistan's nuclear past is often summarized in one name: Dr. A. Q. Khan. Khan won fame in Pakistan for playing a leading role in the national nuclear program. He won global notoriety for being the world's most successful nuclear proliferator. In 2004, the Pakistani government dismissed Khan from his official position and placed him under house arrest.

Officers inside Pakistan's nuclear establishment today consider Khan ancient history, but Washington will not soon forget or forgive his involvement in

---

[10] See, for instance, Jeffrey Goldberg and Marc Ambinder, "The Ally from Hell," *The Atlantic* (December 2011), http://www.theatlantic.com/magazine/archive/2011/12/the-ally-from-hell/8730/.

[11] This section is based in part on the author's conversation with Lt. General (retired) Khalid Kidwai, Director General of the Strategic Plans Division, Rawalpindi, May 18, 2012.

[12] When pressed by the media in April 2009, Obama stated, "I feel confident that nuclear arsenal will remain out of militant hands, okay?" See Barack Obama, "The First 100 Days Press Conference," Washington, DC, April 29, 2009, http://www.presidentialrhetoric.com/speeches/04.29.09.html.

selling nuclear technologies to the anti-American regimes of Iran, North Korea, and Libya. Despite numerous assurances from the Pakistani military at the time and since, most of official Washington still doubts that Khan's operation could have grown so large and persisted so long without clearance from the very highest ranks.

The scarring experience also raises American doubts about whether Pakistan can ever be trusted, whether its nuclear establishment might again be compromised by an insider, or even whether the state of Pakistan will perceive a vital interest in limiting future nuclear transfers to countries like North Korea, which pose no direct threat to Pakistan but are dangerous to the United States and its allies.

This takes us to the heart of the matter: the main reason for Washington's concern about Pakistan's nuclear arsenal is uncertainty about the future character and intentions of Pakistan's leadership. If Pakistan had a firmly entrenched, moderate, and democratic government in control of its nuclear program, perhaps some of those fears would be mitigated. Unfortunately, Pakistan has never in its history been a stable democracy and its recent civilian leaders have no real say over the nuclear program or its management. Short of the democratic ideal, as long as Pakistan's military remains disciplined, unthreatening, and in firm command of the nuclear arsenal, America will have reasons for confidence, even if nuclear weapons are by their nature risky and dangerous things.

Yet, even the motives, discipline, and capacity of the Pakistani army – undoubtedly the nation's most powerful and professional institution – cannot be taken for granted as we peer into the gloom of Pakistan's future. Pakistan's foxes could take over the henhouse. A country that is riven by a range of internal conflicts, suffers from ever-greater bouts of internal violence, and could well adopt a far more hostile anti-Americanism as its official posture is hardly the sort of place where Washington would prefer to see a significant and growing nuclear arsenal. On the contrary, it is precisely the sort of state that could share nuclear know-how with other dangerous states or find itself vulnerable to "insider" threats from violent extremists who enjoy too-cozy relationships with sympathetic members of an increasingly radical ruling regime.

Most of the present batch of Pakistani generals would never wish to see this scenario unfold. Sadly, they might find themselves powerless to stop it. That prospect turns Islamabad's nuclear program from an issue of serious regional concern into a vital American interest. It should lead U.S. policymakers to appreciate the stakes at risk in Pakistan's long-term stability and political trajectory. When framed in this context, Pakistan's nuclear challenge, like the terrorist threat, is clearly here to stay.

THE EMERGENT THREAT: REGIONAL INSTABILITY

Over the past several years, when American officials spoke of Islamabad's regional role, they were usually referring to the war in Afghanistan. Pakistan has been a conduit for NATO supplies into Afghanistan, and Islamabad has held considerable influence over the stability of the Afghan state as well as the success of the fight against the Taliban insurgency. In this context, by the end of 2011, the consensus in Washington correctly perceived Pakistan's regional role as less than friendly.

The deterioration in relations between the United States and Pakistan over the course of 2011 and 2012 had many different specific causes, but the fact that the two sides mistrusted each other in Afghanistan was the immediate bone of contention. Pakistani officials, particularly the generals who control the country's foreign and defense policies, believed that Washington was insensitive to their concern that the Afghan state being built by NATO was a house of cards poised to collapse into a warring mess once international forces pulled out. Worse than that, they believed Karzai's Kabul was too inclined to play the Pashtun ethnic card in ways that would destabilize Pakistan, and was too susceptible to Indian influence for their tastes.[13]

Given the mixed successes and many missteps in the American-led campaign in Afghanistan since 2001, such Pakistani skepticism was hardly unwarranted. But Pakistan's response was also profoundly unhelpful. Rather than improving upon a flawed American effort, Pakistan contributed to its troubles. Pakistani sanctuaries permitted Afghan Taliban forces, especially the Haqqani network based just inside Pakistan's northwest frontier, to evade NATO forces even when the Obama administration tripled U.S. troop strength to roughly 100,000 by summer's end in 2010. As an irate Ryan Crocker, then U.S. ambassador to Afghanistan, put it after a series of Haqqani-sponsored attacks in April 2012, "We know where their leadership lives and we know where these plans are made. They're not made in Afghanistan. They're made in Miramshah, which is in North Waziristan, which is in Pakistan.... We are pressing the Pakistanis very hard on this. They really need to take action."[14] In September 2012, Washington officially designated the Haqqani network a Foreign Terrorist Organization.[15]

How the Afghan war ends will set the stage for future U.S.-Pakistan relations. If the destructive trends of the present hold, if Washington and Islamabad fail to find a mutually acceptable way to cooperate in Afghanistan, then U.S. officials will blame Pakistan for the deteriorating security and instability that Afghanistan is likely to experience as NATO forces depart. If, as many now fear, Afghanistan then slips back into full-scale civil war, Americans are likely

---

[13] On Pakistan's concerns related to the "Pashtunistan" issue, see Ashley J. Tellis, "Creating New Facts on the Ground," *Policy Brief*, Carnegie Endowment for International Peace, May 2011, http://www.carnegieendowment.org/files/afghan_policy.pdf.

[14] "Pakistan Needs to Act against Haqqani Network: US," *Dawn*, April 20, 2012, dawn.com/2012/04/20/pakistan-needs-to-act-against-haqqani-network-us/.

[15] Hillary Rodham Clinton, "Report to Congress on the Haqqani Network," Press Statement, U.S. Department of State, Washington, DC, September 7, 2012, http://www.state.gov/secretary/rm/2012/09/197474.htm.

to perceive Pakistan's perfidy as the primary cause, discounting many of the other troubling failures of the NATO war effort. This perception would drive the wedge deeper between Washington and Islamabad and raise the political hurdles to cooperation on other matters of American interest, whether counterterrorism or nuclear security.

No matter the significance of the Afghan war, it is important to recognize that Pakistan's regional profile does not begin or end in Afghanistan. Pakistan's connections with India and China are of equal or greater significance to Islamabad. These ties draw Pakistan into a much bigger geopolitical game, the subject of Chapter 6. That game centers on the rise of China and the shift of global power and wealth to Asia.

The United States views the rise of China with at least a little trepidation. The unanswered question is how China will use its newfound wealth and power, and in particular whether it will seek to uproot U.S. influence from Asia. Put simply, Washington's goal is to navigate this shift in global power in a way that least disrupts American interests. If possible, the United States seeks to encourage China to adopt principles at home and abroad that are consistent with, or at least not threatening to, those shared by the United States and its allies.

Although much of the American agenda with China centers on East Asia and the Pacific where the two countries deal with one another most directly, both the George W. Bush and Obama administrations have correctly viewed a good relationship with India as necessary for managing the implications of a rising China. Leaders in both capitals across a wide range of the political spectrum have proclaimed the world's oldest and largest democracies to be "natural allies."[16]

In addition to its own rising power and appeal to American businessmen and policymakers alike, India also offers a pluralist and democratic alternative to the authoritarian Chinese model. Among other common interests, New Delhi shares Washington's interest in at least hedging against the risks associated with China's rising influence. Assuming India's economy grows apace, it will offer an additional wealth-creating engine for a region that might otherwise depend too heavily on Beijing. And in areas where size matters, India delivers: its population is young and growing quickly, likely to surpass China's total by 2025. On the military front, India lags far behind China in many capabilities, but unlike America's allies in East Asia such as Japan, Korea, or Australia (or for that matter, unlike the members of NATO), India's army brings massive manpower, and all of its services are investing billions of dollars in new purchases of equipment and technology.

For all of these reasons, the United States is likely to have an interest in seeing India achieve its ambitions of growth and power. On the whole, this

[16] The term was originally used by Indian Prime Minister Atal Bihari Vajpayee in September 2000. See Malini Parthasarathy, "India, U.S. Natural Allies: Vajpayee," *The Hindu*, September 9, 2000, http://hindu.com/2000/09/09/stories/01090005.htm.

will be true even if New Delhi never seeks or accepts a formal alliance with Washington.

India's rise is likely, but not assured. Many of the primary obstacles to India's rise are internal ones, such as ineffective state institutions, entrenched poverty, insufficient infrastructure, and political corruption. But Pakistan remains the greatest external threat to Indian growth and security. India and Pakistan are locked in a hostile relationship that has nearly spiraled into war on several occasions even after they both tested their nuclear weapons in 1998.

Looking to the future, Pakistan's own weakness and fragility will also pose realistic threats to India. If Pakistan falls into an extended civil conflict, India would face the prospect of millions of refugees, or worse, of energized revolutionary movements aspiring to take their violent struggle beyond Pakistan and into Muslim-majority communities in India. Unless the Indo-Pakistani relationship improves and Pakistan becomes stable enough to make the peace hold, India will be stuck with an albatross around its neck. Like South Korea, India might manage to grow in the shadow of its threatening, nuclear-armed neighbor, but India lacks (and might not even accept) a superpower patron to foot its security bill as the United States has done for South Korea over decades.

Then, there is the open question of how China is likely to play its cards in India and Pakistan. Since the 1960s, Pakistan has been a useful Chinese ally for multiple reasons, not the least of which has been Islamabad's ability to distract and bloody India. Since the 1990s, however, as China's economy has grown and even its trading relationship with India has boomed, Beijing has been more inclined to pursue regional stability to discourage hostility between India and Pakistan, even to the point of placing firm pressure on its ally in Islamabad in times of crisis. China's concern about Uighur separatist groups based in Pakistan has also created some tension between Beijing and Islamabad.

Beijing's relationship with Islamabad might wane in significance as an increasingly mighty China perceives that it has less to gain from such a troubled neighbor. On the other hand, Beijing might continue to see Pakistan as a useful piece in its expanding sphere of influence throughout much of Central Asia. Thousands of Chinese workers, mainly technical staff and engineers, are already hard at work inside Pakistan building power plants and ports, constructing mines, and fulfilling defense contracts. Cheap Chinese goods fill Pakistani markets as they do throughout much of the world. Hundreds of Pakistanis, mainly those with technical educations, have also traveled to China to participate in government-sponsored training programs. Even if China does not have a grand scheme in mind for Pakistan, the steady process of Chinese business investment is expanding Beijing's influence into a country that borders the Arabian Sea and offers overland access from there to China's western provinces.

The United States need not necessarily fear Chinese involvement in Pakistan. Washington may even seek to encourage it as a means to improve infrastructure, provide much-needed foreign investment, and help to stabilize Pakistan's ailing economy. Troubles will arise, however, if a weak and inward-looking Pakistan turns away from the United States and toward China as its primary benefactor. Because Beijing does not share America's belief in the stabilizing influence of democratic rule or the value of individual political freedoms, its prescription for stability in Pakistan is likely to be a harshly repressive authoritarianism. That model has never worked in Pakistan; success would almost certainly demand a great deal of bloodletting, as it did in Mao's China or Stalin's Russia. It is more likely to send Pakistan off a revolutionary cliff than to bring lasting stability.

In addition, the more Pakistan assumes a role similar to that of North Korea – as an insecure, nuclear-armed Chinese protégé – the more it is likely to represent another flashpoint for crisis between Washington and Beijing. Such a scenario may seem far-fetched, but it is not. As U.S.-Pakistan relations cratered in 2011 and 2012, Chinese diplomats repeatedly warned Pakistani leaders that they needed to patch things up, specifically because Beijing had no interest in finding itself embroiled in a dispute with Washington.

Because of the number of variables at play, America's future geopolitical interests in Pakistan are more difficult to pin down than U.S. concerns regarding terrorism and nuclear weapons. At present, Pakistan is playing its most challenging regional role in Afghanistan. In the future, Islamabad has the potential to play the part of the spoiler on a much grander stage, whether by undermining India's progress or exacerbating differences between Washington and Beijing. Looking beyond the Afghan arena, these regional concerns are thus far only emergent challenges, but they suggest the utility of thinking about U.S. interests in Pakistan within a broader regional framework. In particular, they point to the fact that a U.S. rupture with Pakistan over immediate concerns like the Afghan war would have long-lasting implications that extend well beyond Afghanistan itself.

WHAT IS ACHIEVABLE?

Given these immediate, vital, and emergent U.S. interests in Pakistan, the next question is what Washington might realistically expect to achieve in its relationship with Islamabad. There is no point in tilting at windmills.

Over the sweep of history since Pakistan's independence in 1947, senior American policymakers have experienced more frustrations than successes in dealing with Pakistan. This discouraging track record could easily lead to the conclusion that the United States has repeatedly set its sights too high in Pakistan. By this logic, the United States simply lacks sufficient policy tools, whether carrots (like military and civilian aid) or sticks (like diplomatic coercion or sanctions), to set Pakistan or the U.S.-Pakistan relationship onto a track that advances U.S. interests.

This particular critique is unwarranted. The historical record is full of disappointments, but rather than simply interpreting these episodes as evidence of an American pattern of over-ambition, it is smarter to read them as individual failures that occurred for a variety of reasons, some even because Washington lacked sufficient ambition to seize opportunities when they presented themselves.

As Chapter 4 describes, it was a narrow, focused U.S. ambition that characterized the period shortly after 9/11. The Bush administration confined its attention to the hunt for al-Qaeda rather than taking on a comprehensive approach to its dealings with Pakistan. This approach paid immediate dividends in terms of mopping up a number of senior al-Qaeda leaders like Khalid Sheikh Mohammed, but as Osama bin Laden's trail went cold and the war in Iraq eclipsed the war in Afghanistan, Washington found itself poorly positioned to grapple with the growing problem of Taliban safe havens on Pakistani soil and in even worse shape to respond to Musharraf's waning hold on power. Inattention and missed opportunities, not the attempt and failure to achieve overambitious ends, characterized this frustrating period in U.S. relations with Pakistan.

On assuming office, the new Obama administration expanded its agenda in Pakistan in a variety of important ways, each discussed in Chapter 5. The White House announced plans to seek what it called a "strategic" rather than "transactional" relationship with Islamabad, intensified diplomatic interaction across the board, and received from Congress a massive infusion of new funds to assist Pakistan's civilians. These efforts were met with initial enthusiasm on both sides, but the high-flying bubble burst within less than two years. A series of crises over the course of 2011 sent the relationship crashing to its lowest point since 9/11. The apparent failure of Washington's intensified diplomacy threw the entire enterprise into doubt. If any experience could prove that no amount of American effort would "fix" Pakistan or build a better working relationship between Washington and Islamabad, this looked to be it.

Yet, here too there was more to the story than initially meets the eye. American assistance programs were freighted with great fanfare and terrible follow-through. Washington's intention had been to demonstrate the value of U.S. partnership to a wide swathe of the Pakistani public, but the diplomatic rollout of new American aid was botched from the start. In addition, Washington's inadequate planning, the limitations of the U.S. Agency for International Development (USAID), and bureaucratic infighting delayed the delivery of most new aid dollars for over a year after they were announced. Long after that, well-informed Pakistanis complained that whatever U.S. funds were entering Pakistan were invisible to the public, perhaps even unknown to the beneficiaries themselves. In retrospect, it is possible to imagine that U.S. officials might have handled each of these challenges more effectively. Some of the missteps were even apparent without the benefit of hindsight. This suggests the strategy itself was not impossibly overambitious.

Any effort to improve America's relationship with Pakistan during this period would have faced stiff headwinds, some of Washington's own creation. Expanded U.S. efforts at diplomacy and development were taking place within the context of the Obama administration's intensified counterterror operations. As he had promised during his 2008 campaign, President Obama was determined to deliver a crushing blow to al-Qaeda, if necessary without Pakistan's cooperation or consent. U.S. armed drones toted up major new kills, and the raid on bin Laden's Abbottabad hideout was a spectacular demonstration of America's twenty-first-century fusion of military power and intelligence work. These were important victories.

That said, neither these counterterror victories nor Washington's military surge in Afghanistan were crafted in ways designed to contribute to a strategic breakthrough with Pakistan. In practice, what would that have meant? On the one hand, if the Obama administration had placed a greater value on Pakistani public sentiment, it might have taken a very different approach to the counterterror war. Washington could have stressed diplomacy and cooperative operations over drone strikes and unilateral Special Forces missions. On the other hand, if Washington had sought to back Pakistan's leadership into a corner and force it to take painful steps against terrorists based on Pakistani soil, the impressive demonstrations of U.S. power – like the military surge in Afghanistan or the bin Laden raid – might have been used as points of coercive leverage.

Instead, counterterror operations were pursued for the urgent yet narrow purpose of eliminating specific threats, above all, Osama bin Laden. This achievement should not be minimized. When viewed from the perspective of Pakistan's intransigent military leadership, however, even the most successful American counterterror missions like the raid on Abbottabad were humiliating irritants. They undermined trust without being quite threatening enough to coerce a constructive shift in Pakistan's outlook or behavior.

Once again, it is not clear that the American problem was an over-ambitious agenda in Pakistan. Faced with multiple continuous challenges, Washington focused on counterterrorism. Success in the fight against al-Qaeda's leadership was real, but it was achieved in a way that gave less priority to other goals.

Pragmatism, Not Fatalism

Although even the best-laid U.S. plans could well fail, Americans should not be too quick to run from realistic self-criticism into paralyzing self-doubt. Successes are possible, even with Pakistan. It is important to recall that throughout the 1990s, the working relationship between Washington and Islamabad was sharply constrained. Points of cooperation were few and far between, overshadowed by fundamental policy differences and stiff U.S. sanctions. Then, after 9/11, working under intense American pressure, Pakistan executed significant – if incomplete – changes in its foreign and defense policies. These changes opened the door to U.S. financial assistance and expanded cooperation on a range of counterterror and counterinsurgency missions.

   Pakistan's dramatic policy shift after 9/11 is best described as the product of a cold calculation by its top generals who control national policy. They reasoned that working with America on certain issues served their interests better than obstruction or inaction. Their motives may always have been more cynical than altruistic or sympathetic. But they were not, in the main, implacably hostile or irrational.

   This remains true; the primary purpose of the Pakistani military is to advance or defend its institutional interests. As Pakistan's dominant institution, these interests are often consistent with a broader national interest, but not always.[17] Recognizing that Pakistan's leaders tend to be tough negotiators with high thresholds for pain, Washington can cut new deals and level credible threats to achieve U.S. goals. This is not a friendly game, but out of it both sides can still benefit.

   At the same time, it bears noting that the United States has already made lasting contributions to Pakistan's economy, infrastructure, security, and quality of life, a fact that is too rarely appreciated by Pakistanis or Americans. Projects like Pakistan's colossal Tarbela Dam, for instance, have shown that the United States can assist Pakistan's economy, and – indirectly at least – address some of the country's underlying causes of instability and violence. Built in the 1960s and 1970s with heavy infusions of American cash, Tarbela now serves as an essential part of Pakistan's national water management system.[18] It provides roughly 30 percent of the nation's irrigation water in the dry season. Tarbela also generates over 3,000 megawatts of electricity to the national grid as it has for decades. In 2010, the United States began to refurbish and improve the dam as part of its expanded assistance programming in Pakistan.[19]

   This is not to suggest that U.S. assistance can solve all, or even most, of Pakistan's internal challenges. Pakistanis must do that job. Fortunately, every day millions of Pakistanis search for new ways to improve conditions for themselves and their countrymen. Some of their projects are paying remarkable dividends.

   One example of this reality is the Indus Hospital in Karachi. Opened in 2007, the hospital was the brainchild of a group of Pakistani graduates of the city's prestigious Dow Medical College. Their common bond was forged when they chose to work for Karachi Civil Hospital's Patients Welfare Association, a student group dedicated to helping indigent patients. As the hospital's bearded

---

[17] Indeed, it is even possible to argue that the military's institutional interest in maintaining its budgets and autonomy leads it to overstate the threat posed by India and, as a consequence, to work at cross purposes with the national interest.

[18] "$2-Billion Irrigation Project Will Tame the Indus," *New York Times*, January 19, 1968, search.proquest.com/docview/118371546/fulltextPDF/1381FD9F3D74626F4CF/1? accountid=37722.

[19] "Energy: Tarbela Dam Project," USAID, January 25, 2012, http://transition.usaid.gov/pk/db/sectors/energy/project_10.html.

and kind-eyed CEO, Dr. Abdul Bari Khan, explains, that volunteer experience convinced him of how much more work needed to be done. Together, he has joined forces with a dedicated team of clinicians motivated by a similar humanitarian and religious spirit.[20] They have built a world-class institution that routinely hosts volunteer surgeons and specialists from some of the best hospitals around the world. After two years, the hospital's doctors had already conducted over 10,000 surgeries. By the end of 2010, they had treated over 100,000 patients in the hospital's emergency room.

The Indus Hospital owes some of its success to smart, first-in-Pakistan innovations. The hospital is paperless; tens of thousands of patients and their procedures are tracked by a proprietary database that was conceived and coded at the hospital (and cost much less than off-the-shelf computer programs). Most important of all, every bit of the hospital's work is free to the patients, financed by charitable contributions.

The leaders of the hospital are far from ready to rest on their laurels. They have plans to enlarge the facility from 150 to 700 beds; to build Pakistan's first pediatric hospital; to expand a program to use inexpensive cell phones as a means to monitor outpatient care; and to open a nursing school to train more high-quality hospital staff. Their success has won national and international attention. The World Health Organization is eager to partner with the hospital to tackle Pakistan's many public health problems, like tuberculosis.

Perhaps more significant than its own individual success story, the Indus Hospital has established a model for care that its visionary leaders intend to replicate in other Pakistani cities. With outside help, including from the United States, other projects of this sort could be implemented. If Pakistan finds a way to tap the economic potential inherent in its geographic location, especially by opening its doors to greater trade and economic cooperation with India, even more significant breakthroughs await. By revising its own trade policies, America may be able to assist here too, and all the more so if Washington enjoys good relations with both New Delhi and Islamabad.

Above all, the United States must recognize that as dim as the present outlook may seem, Pakistan is not yet a lost cause. It is no North Korea, no Iran. Not yet. Nor is the U.S.-Pakistan relationship necessarily condemned to repeat the disappointing patterns of the past.

AMERICA'S OPTIONS

Painting with a broad brush, America has three options for dealing with Pakistan in the future: defensive insulation, military-first cooperation, and comprehensive cooperation. All three are explored at length in Chapter 7. To be

---

[20] Author conversations with Dr. Abdul Bari Khan, Dr. Muhammad Amin Chinoy, and Dr. Akhtar Aziz Khan, May 22, 2012.

clear, these options are in fact points along a spectrum of U.S. policy choices and they are not necessarily mutually exclusive.

In a defensive insulation strategy, Washington would devote the bulk of its efforts to protecting the United States from Pakistan-based threats. Assuming that mounting mutual frustrations stymie cooperation with Islamabad, U.S. policies would rely on coercion, deterrence, and closer military and intelligence cooperation with Afghanistan and India.

In a strategy of military-first cooperation, Washington would focus on cultivating a businesslike relationship with Pakistan's military, not unlike the one China enjoys. By taking its diplomacy out of the public eye, as the United States has long done with other important but difficult states, Washington would seek greater flexibility in its negotiations with Islamabad. Both carrots and sticks could be used to advance specific U.S. counterterrorism and nuclear goals.

Washington's third option of comprehensive cooperation would mean working with and providing support to Pakistan's military and civilian leadership as well as with its civil society. The goal would be to help tip the scales inside Pakistan in ways – such as improved governance, infrastructure, and educational opportunities – that would, over time, render its state and society more peaceful and less threatening to American interests.

Unfortunately, there is no perfect path for America to walk in its relations with Pakistan. As has been true in the past, Washington faces conflicting priorities, political pressures, and logistical hurdles. If the United States insulates itself from threats through coercion and deterrence, it increases the likelihood that Pakistan will respond with unremitting hostility. That pattern could take decades to break. If the United States puts all its eggs in the Pakistani military's basket, it commits the same error it did with Musharraf or as it has with other authoritarian allies like Mubarak's Egypt, the Shah's Iran, or Marcos's Philippines. A return to military rule in Pakistan would contribute to the country's unhealthy political culture and the hollowing out of its civilian government as well as the dangerous politicization of the military itself. That, in turn, would tee up the prospect of revolutionary change and instability in a nuclear-armed state. Finally, if the United States takes another shot at comprehensive cooperation, it would require new U.S. policies characterized by less hype, more tangible follow-through, and longer timelines. Any one of these would be a tall order.

Alone, each of these broad strategic options is therefore conceivable but flawed. The real question is how best to balance (and re-balance) between the three in order to advance American goals in the short and long run.

GET ON WITH IT

At the very end of Sartre's *No Exit*, his sinners finally accept their sorry circumstances and agree that they have no choice but to "get on with it." Sartre's tragic sense of the world – written at one of the darkest periods in human history – will always resonate with pessimists and pragmatists alike, but it is only one aspect of reality.

In the summer of 1944, just months after *Huis Clos* debuted in Paris, invading American and allied forces collapsed the German occupation of France and went on to destroy Hitler's Nazi menace. After terrible human sacrifice, the Second World War ended and brighter days returned. Progress is possible; the U.S.-Pakistan relationship is not necessarily trapped in a perpetual hell.

Yet progress of any sort will only be achieved through a patient, sustained effort, not by way of quick fixes or neglect. No U.S. policy or set of policies will solve the challenges posed by Pakistan all at once, or maybe ever. Managing and mitigating threats over time is a more realistic expectation, as hard as that may be to stomach for Americans, whose "can do" spirit often mobilizes crests of energy followed by troughs of impatience. We are better at waging total war or thriving in peace; the murky gray of uncertainty sits poorly with us. Compromise and trade-offs are unwelcome concepts for a superpower, especially in dealings with a country that is so relatively poor and weak. Yet we must face up to all of these challenges in Pakistan.

The first order of business is to better understand the nature of the various problems Pakistan poses (Chapter 2). The next step is to learn from our shared history, keeping a close eye on how Pakistanis have come to understand the United States (Chapter 3), and paying careful attention to how American officials have handled recent episodes in the relationship (Chapters 4 and 5). Finally, Washington needs to craft a vision of the future that places Pakistan into a much larger regional context (Chapter 6).

No single magic-bullet strategy is delivered from this process, but a set of broad guidelines, born from hard experience and leavened by a realistic hope for the future, emerges from the gloom (Chapter 7). By remaining focused on the long term even as it grapples with crises and by selectively implementing parts of defensive insulation as well as cooperative strategies, America can successfully "get on with it" in Pakistan. In practice, this boils down to preparing for the worst, aiming for the best, and avoiding the most dangerous mistakes of the past.

2

The Four Faces of Pakistan

Understanding Pakistan on its own terms is no mere academic pursuit. Too often over the past decade, America has stumbled in its dealings with Pakistan because U.S. policymakers made incorrect assumptions about how Pakistan works.

In Washington, views of Pakistan seem to swing like a pendulum between the extremes of ungrounded exuberance and overstated fear. Both have influenced U.S. policies for the worse. For instance, in 2008 and 2009, many in Washington dreamt that Islamabad's newly elected civilian leaders could implement a liberal agenda and finally rein in Pakistan's military after President (and former General) Pervez Musharraf left the scene. They failed to perceive how deeply entrenched was the army's power, and how limited was the liberal impulse and capacity of Pakistan's ruling politicians and their constituents. At other times, similarly faulty American assumptions led Washington's policymakers to perceive – and portray – Pakistan as if it stood just at the edge of violent Islamist revolution.

To think seriously about a U.S. strategy for Pakistan, we need to know how close (or far) it is to the abyss of failure, nuclear nightmare, or revolution; how to assess its potential for reform and growth; and how to anticipate the interests and ambitions of its people. Answering such questions first requires us to paint a realistic portrait of Pakistan's state and society.

The trouble with painting such a portrait is that Pakistan shows different faces to different audiences. To the uninitiated, any one of these faces could present itself as the defining image of Pakistan's reality. In fact, each one provides an important layer of truth, but a layer that must be combined with the others to achieve a full picture.[1]

---

[1] Stephen P. Cohen portrays the complexity of Pakistan's politics and strategic posture in his authoritative work *The Idea of Pakistan* (Washington: Brookings Institution Press, 2004).

From one perspective, Pakistan is an elite-dominated basket case of a country, mired in a repressive tradition that makes sure a tiny number of "haves" possess a great deal of power and wealth while the rest have not. From a second perspective, Pakistan is a garrison state. The military has grown to control not only its own budgets and authorities but also to dictate national politics and a big slice of the economy as well. From a third point of view, Pakistan is a terrorist incubator. The nation suffers from the cancerous growth of violent and extreme ideologies, now embedded too deeply and dispersed too widely to be removed by the political equivalent of minor surgery. And from a final vantage point, Pakistan is a youthful idealist, teeming with the energy and reform-minded ambition of its rapidly growing population.

BASKET CASE

Pakistan's caste system is not as overt as India's, but as in many traditional societies, it is difficult to escape the consequences of one's family name. Throughout much of the countryside, Pakistan's "feudals" hold millions of Pakistani peasants in their thrall as they have for centuries. The nation's half-hearted attempts at land reform flopped. By denying education and other basic opportunities to the people who work their fields, landlords maintain a grip on political and economic power. By and large, however, Pakistanis simply accept and play out their roles – whether peasant or landlord – because they know that to do otherwise would be deeply disruptive.[2] In much of the country, change – whether reform or revolution – remains a foreign concept.

Even in Pakistan's teeming cities, vast majorities also feel powerful ties to communities that pre-date Pakistan's existence as a state. Some bonds are to family and tribe, others to language or the practice of a particular strain of Islam. Pakistan is no melting pot; its ethnic groups may live side by side, but at home they speak different languages and hold fast to their particular customs.

Pakistan's people are distributed among five principal ethno-linguistic groups: Punjabis, Sindhis, Baloch, Pashtuns, and Mohajirs.[3] Punjabis, who have long maintained a dominant position in Pakistan's politics, military, and economy, comprise just under half of the total population and are clustered in the north and east, Pakistan's agricultural and industrial heartland. Sindhis (in the southeastern plains), Pashtuns (in the west along the Afghan border), and the Baloch (in the southwestern desert) together make up about 35 percent of the population but have historically had less access to the levers of Pakistani power. "Mohajirs," derived from the Arabic word for immigrants, are the descendants of those who moved from India to Pakistan at the time

---

[2] This is one of the essential findings in Stephen M. Lyon's doctoral thesis, *Power and Patronage in Pakistan*, University of Kent, Canterbury, 1993, p. 228.

[3] For a detailed look at Pakistan's ethnic groups, see Chapter 6 of Cohen, *Idea of Pakistan*, pp. 201–230.

of Partition. Although Mohajirs played a prominent role in Pakistan's early establishment, they have since been displaced.[4] Throughout Pakistan's history, ethnic tensions – and, at the extremes, Pashtun and Baloch separatist movements – have posed significant challenges to Pakistani unity.

Once, on a trip to Quetta, the capital of Pakistan's least-developed Baluchistan province, I was surprised to learn that even Pakistanis who had moved to the city with their families many decades earlier were still called the derogatory "settlers" by the ethnic Baloch and Pashtuns. In spite of the fact that Pakistan has seen its share of population movements over the centuries – whether from invasion, colonial rule, or partition – history runs deep. Identities are inculcated into each of Pakistan's rapidly expanding generations, reinforcing patterns of behavior and, to a greater extent than one might expect in this era of individualism and globalization, thought as well.

Reforming a traditional society like Pakistan's has proven beyond the means of even some of the country's most powerful men. Pakistanis readily recall that Chief of Army Staff Pervez Musharraf, upon seizing power in a 1999 coup against Prime Minister Nawaz Sharif's government, declared his intention to clean out the dirty, corrupt politicians and start fresh. "Never before so few have plundered so many," he said at his first news conference. "Accountability is the demand of everyone... And we want to do it quickly."[5] For several years, Musharraf enjoyed the broad support of Pakistanis exhausted by a decade of revolving door democracy that witnessed two of Benazir Bhutto's Pakistan Peoples Party (PPP) governments alternating with two led by Nawaz Sharif's Pakistan Muslim League (PML-N). By the public's reckoning, both parties had broken new records for corruption, mismanagement, and political gamesmanship.

Musharraf failed to capitalize on the opportunity for change. One simple measure of Musharraf's failure to transform, or even to reform, Pakistan's politics is the fact that when he was hounded out of office in 2008, the very same Bhutto and Sharif showed him to the door. By then, Musharraf and his own ramshackle political party (the Pakistan Muslim League (Quaid-e-Azam), or PML-Q) were the ones accused of corruption and dereliction of duty. The problem was that the PML-Q, populated by the nation's traditional political elite, never had any serious plan to deviate from the status quo. Musharraf cannot be absolved from blame for the many failures of his regime, but it is clear that one of the worst failures of all was to expect different results from the same, tired old politicians.

---

4 As Steve Inskeep points out, the self-conscious creation of "Mohajirs" as a politically active ethnic identity was the seminal work of Altaf Husain, leader of the MQM, which initially stood for "Mohaijir Qaumi Movement," *Instant City: Life and Death in Karachi* (New York: Penguin Press, 2011), pp. 174–175.

5 "Musharraf Forms Accountability Bureau," Associated Press, November 2, 1999, http://www .indianexpress.com/Storyold/130023/.

After Musharraf's collapse, the new civilian government benefited from the legitimacy of popular elections and the public euphoria of seeing the military sent back to the barracks. The benefits of civilian rule should not be underestimated. Most of the liberalizing reforms of the Musharraf era, from the media to political activity, were protected or even expanded during the five-year term of the democratically elected government led at the center by the PPP under Benazir Bhutto's widower, President Asif Ali Zardari. Beyond that, the parliament voted for a series of constitutional amendments and struck political accords that granted greater autonomy to Pakistan's provincial governments and returned power to the prime minister from the president. Pakistan's civilians passed an important milestone in democratic political development simply by serving out a full five-year term and conducting a second set of national elections in May 2013.[6]

Yet with respect to tangible accomplishments – economic growth, law and order, or administrative services – the vast majority of Pakistanis still found their elected leadership wanting. As one prominent Pakistani think tank observed, "Apart from some historic achievements during its five year term, the 13th National Assembly remained unsuccessful in providing workable recommendations on resolving Pakistan's key issues including terrorism, law and order situations in Balochistan, Karachi and FATA, and growing sectarianism. Regardless of the severity of these issues, the Assembly's response never moved beyond expressing sorrow." Moreover, "the performance of democracy, also known as governance, remained dismal in 5 years.... There have been palpable failures in the domain of economy, control of corruption, maintenance of peace and order in the society and provision of speedy justice to the citizens in which National Assembly remained unable to play an effective oversight role. There have been charges of corruption on cabinet members while the state of economy is worse than in 2008."[7]

Indeed, according to national surveys conducted in late 2012 and early 2013, 58 percent of Pakistanis felt the overall quality of democratic governance had deteriorated over the period from 2008 to 2013.[8] Nearly all (94 percent) of Pakistanis surveyed between the ages of eighteen and twenty-nine believed the country was heading in the wrong direction. Of that same age group, 77 percent viewed the army favorably, while the civilian government got favourable

---

[6] For a brief assessment of the accomplishments of the PPP government, see Shamila N. Chaudhary, "How Did They Do? Grading the PPP," afpak.foreignpolicy.com/posts/2013/03/28/how_did_they_do_grading_the_ppp.

[7] *Citizens Report, Five Years of the 13th National Assembly of Pakistan*, Pakistan Institute of Legislative Development and Transparency, Islamabad, Pakistan, March 2013, http://www .pildat.org/publications/publication/Democracy&LegStr/5Yearsof13thNationalAssemblyof Pakistan-CitizensReport.pdf.

[8] Thirty-one percent of Pakistanis felt the quality of governance had improved, while 15 percent felt the quality was unchanged. See *Public Verdict on Democracy 2008–2013*, Pakistan Institute of Legislative Development and Transparency, Islamabad, Pakistan, February 2013, http://www .pildat.org/Publications/publication/SDR/PublicVerdictonDemocracy_2008to2013.pdf.

reviews from only 14 percent. Most disconcerting of all, only 29 percent of those young Pakistanis saw democracy as the best form of government for Pakistan, whereas 38 percent preferred some sort of Islamic law, or Shariah, and 32 percent thought military rule would be best.[9]

Growth without Development

It is important to appreciate that despite decades of unfulfilled promises by Pakistan's leaders – both military and civilian – most Pakistanis are still better off, at least by basic economic measures, than their grandparents. Average wages increased fivefold for Pakistanis from 1947 to 2003. In 1947, the country could not feed its 30 million people, while in 2002 the country produced more than enough wheat, rice, sugar, and milk to meet the demands of its burgeoning population of 145 million. Over its history, Pakistan has dramatically expanded its network of roads, factories, power plants, dams, and canals. Moreover, in absolute terms, Pakistanis also have greater access to health services and education than their parents or grandparents did before them.[10]

Yet Pakistan might have done a lot better for itself if its government had invested greater resources in the health and education of its people. Pakistan is a model of what one prominent economist has called "growth without development."[11] Pakistan's history of economic growth has been respectable, but it "systematically underperforms on most social and political indicators– education, health, sanitation, fertility, gender equality, corruption, political instability and violence, and democracy – for its level of income."[12] In other words, the country has routinely done less with more.

A country's infant mortality rate – the number of children in 1,000 who die before reaching one year of age – is a good way to measure living standards across countries. As countries develop, the rate tends to go down. In some of the world's richest countries, like Japan, the number is very low (just over 2 per 1,000 in 2012). In Pakistan, over 60 out of 1,000 children die before the age of one, putting it right between Rwanda and Uganda in global rankings.[13]

[9] Alex Rodriguez, "Survey: Young Pakistanis Harbor Doubts about Future, Democracy," *Los Angeles Times*, April 3, 2013, http://www.latimes.com/news/world/worldnow/la-fg-wn-survey-young-pakistanis-democracy-20130403,0,2015291.story.

[10] All of these points are made in detail by Ishrat Husain, "The Economy of Pakistan: Past, Present and Future," in Robert Hathaway, Wilson Lee, and Ishrat Husain, eds., *Islamization and the Pakistani Economy* (Washington: Woodrow Wilson International Center for Scholars, 2004), pp. 11–35.

[11] William Easterly, "The Political Economy of Growth without Development: A Case Study of Pakistan," paper for the Analytical Narratives of Growth Project, Kennedy School of Government, Harvard University (June 2001), http://www.nyu.edu/fas/institute/dri/Easterly/File/Pakistan.pdf.

[12] Easterly, "The Political Economy of Growth without Development."

[13] "Country Comparison: Infant Mortality Rate," CIA World Factbook, www.cia.gov/library/publications/the-world-factbook/rankorder/2091rank.html.

Those miserable living standards, however, are not the worst part of the story. The real tragedy is that Pakistan's wealth should have translated into a better quality of life. As the years went by, Pakistanis earned more than their developing country peers, but especially during the 1980s and 1990s, Pakistan failed to improve infant mortality rates commensurate with its income level. Compared with average infant mortality rates among countries where people had similar incomes, out of every 1,000 infants, twenty-seven more Pakistanis died before age one.[14]

Nor is Pakistan very good at educating its infants who survive until school age. Today, 50 percent of Pakistani schoolchildren between the ages of six and sixteen cannot read a sentence.[15] In 2011, there were twenty-six countries in the world that sent a higher percentage of their children to primary school even though they were poorer than Pakistan.[16] According to the United Nations Children's Fund, roughly 60 percent of Pakistani kids finish primary school and only about a third attend secondary school.[17] These figures are appallingly low. Pakistan's historic rival, India, reported rates of 95 percent and over 50 percent, respectively.[18] Even Bangladesh, which declared its independence from Pakistan in 1971, fares better.[19]

And this is to say nothing of the abysmal quality of education in most Pakistani schools. Pakistan's public schools face a crisis of mismanagement, inadequate materials, and poorly trained teachers.[20] Thousands of state schools even go without teachers. In many case, instructors collect paychecks but never bother to show up to the classroom.[21]

In response, millions of Pakistani parents simply have given up on public schools. They send their kids – at considerable cost – to private institutions.[22] Starting in the early 1980s, tens of thousands of private schools opened their

[14] Easterly, "The Political Economy of Growth without Development."

[15] "Education Emergency Pakistan," Pakistan Education Task Force, p. 7, www.education-emergency.com.pk.

[16] "Education Emergency Pakistan," Pakistan Education Task Force, p. 7.

[17] "Pakistan," United Nations Children's Fund, http://www.unicef.org/infobycountry/pakistan_pakistan_statistics.html.

[18] "India," United Nations Children's Fund, http://www.unicef.org/infobycountry/india_statistics.html.

[19] "Bangladesh," United Nations Children's Fund, http://www.unicef.org/infobycountry/bangladesh_bangladesh_statistics.html.

[20] Shahid Javed Burki, "Educating the Pakistani Masses," in Robert Hathaway, ed., *Education Reform in Pakistan* (Washington: Woodrow Wilson International Center for Scholars, 2005), p. 16. On the poor facilities in Pakistan's schools, see also "Education Emergency Pakistan," Pakistan Education Task Force, p. 7, www.educationemergency.com.pk.

[21] Public school teachers are absent from the classroom an average of 15–20 percent of the time, "Education Emergency Pakistan," p. 7; see also "Pakistan: The Next Generation," British Council Pakistan (November 2009), p. 14, http://www.britishcouncil.pk/pakistan-Next-Generation-Report.pdf.

[22] In Pakistan, the average rural family spends 13 percent of its income on public schooling. See "Education Emergency Pakistan," pp. 7, 11.

doors. They now serve more than half of the students in many of Pakistan's cities.[23] Other children attend madrassas, or Islamic seminaries, where tuition is free.

A handful of Pakistan's madrassas are better known as terrorist training centers than founts of theological wisdom. In reality, however, the greatest danger posed by most Pakistani seminaries is that their narrow curriculum fails to prepare children for jobs outside the clergy after graduation. Unfortunately, Pakistan's public schools do not fare much better. A close look at Pakistan's public school curriculum reveals that its typical graduates do not just leave the classroom unprepared for work, but they are also indoctrinated in a harshly anti-Indian, anti-Semitic, and anti-Western view of the world.[24]

Across the board, the failure of Pakistan's public education system has made the country less productive and more dangerous. These are not, however, insurmountable challenges. The Pakistani government devotes less than 2 percent of the nation's gross domestic product (GDP) to education, which is half the level India spends and just over a third of the American figure.[25] Resources are not the whole of the story, but they are an important part. India's concerted focus on primary education since the mid-1980s has posted impressive gains in terms of getting more boys and girls into school and keeping them there.[26] India is moving ten times faster than Pakistan to reduce the number of young children out of school.[27]

Failing Infrastructure

Pakistan also faces other huge shortfalls when it comes to investing in the infrastructure required of a modern economy. The most obvious problem is electricity. It is now part of the daily routine for homes and businesses across Pakistan to experience power outages, or as the locals say, "load shedding." Part of the problem is that Pakistan's energy supply has not kept up with growing demand. Yet technical experts suggest that financial mismanagement, theft, and an antiquated distribution network are in fact the main barriers to a steady energy supply.[28] Pakistani consumers, including the government and military, routinely fail to pay electricity bills, starving energy suppliers and forcing them

[23] Hathaway, "Introduction," *Education Reform in Pakistan*, p. 3.
[24] C. Christine Fair, *Madrassah Challenge: Militancy and Religious Education in Pakistan* (Washington: United States Institute of Peace, 2008), pp. 94–101.
[25] "Education Emergency Pakistan," p. 8. See also "Education Spending (percent of GDP) (most recent) by Country," www.nationmaster.com/graph/edu_edu_spe-education-spending-of-gdp.
[26] "Pakistan: The Next Generation," British Council Pakistan (November 2009), pp. 23–4, http://www.britishcouncil.pk/pakistan-Next-Generation-Report.pdf.
[27] "Education Emergency Pakistan," p. 19.
[28] "Country Report Presentation: Pakistan Energy Crisis and Solution," presentation at JICA Training and Dialogue Program on Energy Policy by Muhammad Latif, chief, Energy Wing, Planning Commission of Pakistan, May 2011, http://eneken.ieej.or.jp/data/3843.pdf.

to cut production. Artificially low energy costs (set by the state to appeal to consumers) also reduce the incentive for investment in the power sector.

In a country with scorching summers, the loss of air conditioning can make modern buildings uninhabitable. Even for wealthy Pakistanis who have invested in generators for their homes, it usually takes a few minutes for the new power source to kick in. For an American visitor, having the lights go out abruptly in the middle of a conversation is unnerving, yet most Pakistanis are so accustomed to the inconvenience that they don't even miss a beat. If sitting in the pitch dark, they may simply flip on their cell phones and place them on the table as dim bluish torches.

Of course, as any Karachi businessman can explain, sitting in the dark over dinner is the least of his troubles. In 2011, a couple of successful Pakistani manufacturers generously hosted me for lunch at a fine French bistro in Karachi. Over chilled cucumber soup, they explained that Pakistanis pay an average of about twice what their Bangladeshi competitors pay for gas and electricity.[29] Worse, because they could not be sure of a steady power supply, their factories could not operate at full capacity and faced unexpected delays. Foreign buyers who needed guaranteed on-time deliveries had already moved on to more reliable manufacturers outside Pakistan. International investors were also scarce.

My lunch companions went on to explain that their Bangladeshi competitors squeeze over four times more export value out of a bale of cotton by turning it into finished goods ready for sale to rich Western consumers. Pakistan, on the other hand, exports a lot of unfinished goods – raw cotton, yarn, and cloth – because its factories are in such sorry shape. As a consequence, Pakistan also forgoes jobs and the profits that would come from turning cotton into designer jeans or high-end dress shirts. In an economy where textiles account for over 40 percent of urban jobs and about 60 percent of export earnings, such lost opportunities are costly.[30]

Even if Pakistan manages to address its electricity woes, it is still running out of water. Rain falls infrequently in Pakistan; seasonal snow melt from the Himalayan glaciers provides the freshwater that flows through Pakistan's rivers, and those rivers feed the world's single largest network of irrigation canals. This irrigated network accounts for one-fourth of Pakistan's GDP, two-thirds of its jobs, and 80 percent of its exports.[31] Canal construction

[29] Author conversation with Karachi businessmen, October 2011.
[30] "The Case for US Market Access for Pakistani Textiles," Punjab Board of Trade & Investment, Government of Punjab, December 4, 2009, p. 3, http://www.pbit.gop.pk/pbit/uploaded/projects/The%20Case%20for%20Market%20Access%20for%20Pakistani%20Textiles.pdf; Khurram Anis, "Pakistan Textile Exports May Be Hurt by Gas Shortage, Group Says," *Bloomberg*, December 9, 2011, http://www.bloomberg.com/news/2011-12-09/pakistan-textile-exports-may-be-hurt-by-gas-shortage-group-says.html.
[31] "Pakistan's Water Economy," World Bank Group, http://www.worldbank.org.pk/WBSITE/EXTERNAL/COUNTRIES/SOUTHASIAEXT/PAKISTANEXTN/0,,contentMDK:21102841~pagePK:141137~piPK:141127~theSitePK:293052,00.html.

was a revolutionary transformation of the national landscape that began under British colonial rule and was expanded and reinvigorated by World Bank – and heavy American – investments that began in the 1950s.[32] But the canals are falling apart after decades of inadequate repair; too many Pakistani farmers still rely on old-fashioned flooding techniques for irrigation, and Pakistani megacities demand many times more water than in generations past.

Scientists predict that climate change will cause glaciers to melt more rapidly than in the past. As a consequence, Pakistan will go through decades of unpredictable floods and droughts. Devastating inundations like those of 2010, which temporarily left one-fifth of the country under water, are likely to be a regular occurrence unless Pakistan builds new dams and modern water management systems.[33] Even today, however, Pakistan lives on less water per person than any other country in Asia. A third of all Pakistanis do not have access to safe drinking water. By some estimates, 30,000 residents of Karachi alone die from this problem each year.[34] The social and economic costs of Pakistan's water crisis are already staggering.

Why then, with education, energy, and water challenges so glaringly apparent, has Pakistan's government done so little to reform or invest? A big part of the answer to this question takes us back to the identity of Pakistan's leadership. Over the course of the nation's history, too many of them sent their children to private boarding schools while millions of other children never learned to read. Too many sipped cool cucumber soup even as their countrymen struggled to find safe drinking water.

Rather than contributing to revenues that could provide better public services, Pakistan's elites have also selfishly kept their tax burden at a minimum. So severe is the tax problem in Pakistan that only 1 percent of the country's citizens – and only a third of its legislators – paid taxes in 2011, helping to make Pakistan's tax-to-GDP ratio the lowest in South Asia.[35] Many of the country's rich may also be deliberately denying resources to the poor for fear that an

[32] Douglas J. Merrey and James M. Wolf, "Irrigation Management in Pakistan: Four Papers," IMI Research Paper No. 4, p. 14; International Irrigation Management Institute: Digana Village, Sri Lanka (1986), http://books.google.com/books?id=Xw1MoR6PxfoC&pg=PP4&dq=united+states+investment+pakistan+irrigation+1950s&source=gbs_selected_pages&cad=3#v=onepage&q=united%20states%20investment%20pakistan%20irrigation%201950s&f=false.

[33] "Construction of Dams Is the Only Solution to Prevent Floods: ICCI," *Pakistan Today*, September 7, 2011, http://www.pakistantoday.com.pk/2011/09/07/news/profit/construction-of-dams-is-the-only-solution-to-prevent-floods-icci.

[34] See Michael Kugelman, "Introduction," in Michael Kugelman and Robert M. Hathaway, eds., *Running on Empty: Pakistan's Water Crisis* (Washington: Woodrow Wilson International Center for Scholars, 2009), pp. 5–27.

[35] Farhan Bokhari and Serena Tarling, "Pakistan Seeks Access to Western Markets," *Financial Times*, March 21, 2010, http://www.ft.com/intl/cms/s/0/f669734e-3504-11df-9cfb-00144feabdco.html#axzz1rBpQ5lSR; Umar Cheema, "Representation without Taxation: An Analysis of MPs' Income Tax Returns for 2011," Center for Peace and Development Initiatives, 2012, http://www.cirp.pk/Electronic%20Copy.pdf.

educated, prosperous, and healthy public would challenge their monopoly on political power.[36] Pakistan's pattern of elite rule is thus deeply entrenched and self-reinforcing. When reform-minded leaders have gained power in Islamabad, they have always found it expedient to depend on established politicians with a vested interest in the status quo.

GARRISON STATE

Pakistan's infamous journalist and political analyst Dr. Shireen Mazari has been dubbed the "Lady Taliban" for her extreme views, not least her defense of the Taliban and diatribes against the United States. Yet her nickname doesn't quite do Mazari justice. In 2007, after a dinner conversation with Mazari and several others in Islamabad, a Pakistani friend observed that Mazari – who does not wear a headscarf, sometimes dyes her hair in bright, unnatural colors, and has a Ph.D. from Columbia University – would not last five minutes in a country ruled by the obscurantist Taliban. Indeed, Mazari is less of a Talib than the archetype of a hyper-nationalist. Unfortunately, her worldview is pervasive throughout the Pakistani military.

With access to army documents, she wrote Pakistan's official history of the 1999 Kargil conflict, a near-war with India that began when Pakistan infiltrated fighters across its de facto border with India.[37] Mazari's book, widely derided as a work of army propaganda, claims that India was responsible for escalating the conflict and that Pakistan's civilians have unfairly attempted to blame the army for the failed military campaign that ensued. Whatever its factual basis, there is little doubt that Mazari's book won her friends inside the army and cost her the respect of the academy.

When the Musharraf regime came crashing down in 2008, the new government quickly stripped Mazari of her job as the director of a government-funded think tank in Islamabad. Soon after, she also lost her regular column in one of Pakistan's English-language newspapers, *The News*, for writing unsubstantiated stories about an American aid contractor, naming him in print, and describing him as a U.S. spy. "Clearly," she wrote, "there is a threatening U.S. agenda seeking out our nuclear sites and assassinating people, thereby adding to our chaos and violence."[38]

Mazari angrily blamed the then-U.S. ambassador, Anne Patterson, for her ill fortune, but soon landed on her feet as the new editor of a staunchly nationalist paper, *The Nation*.[39] From that new perch, she lashed out again in late 2009

---

[36] See Easterly, "The Political Economy of Growth without Development," pp. 3–4, 21–2.

[37] Shireen Mazari, *The Kargil Conflict, 1999: Separating Fact from Fiction* (Islamabad: Institute of Strategic Studies, 2003).

[38] Quote is taken from Nicholas Schmidle, "Shireen Mazari: The Ann Coulter of Pakistan," *The New Republic*, January 8, 2010, http://www.tnr.com/article/world/slander.

[39] "Anne Patterson Blocks Shireen Mazari," *Pakistan Daily*, September 3, 2009, http://www.daily.pk/news-break-anne-patterson-blocks-shireen-mazari-10053/.

by running front-page stories that accused Matthew Rosenberg, a reporter from the *Wall Street Journal*, and Daniel Berehulak, a photographer with Getty Images, of being CIA spies. On November 5, *The Nation* warned its readers that "Agents of notorious spy agencies are using journalistic cover to engage themselves in intelligence activities" in Pakistan's northwest and tribal areas.[40] Considering that Daniel Pearl, the *Wall Street Journal* reporter beheaded by terrorists in Pakistan in 2002, was also declared a "CIA spy," the U.S. embassy in Pakistan feared these allegations were intended as an incitement to violence.[41]

Mazari's worldview begins with the conviction that the United States is untrustworthy, India is the enemy, and China is Pakistan's one true ally.[42] In this respect, she reflects a mind-set that runs throughout much of Pakistan's military, no matter that tens of billions of dollars in U.S. assistance and weaponry has flowed to Pakistan over the decades. As explained in the next chapter, distrust of the United States has roots in the way many Pakistanis think about U.S. policy over the course of the Cold War, especially Washington's "abandonments" in the 1970s and 1990s.

The India Threat

America bashing is Mazari's favorite sport today, but she – like all other members of Pakistan's defense establishment – was raised on a steady diet of anti-India vitriol that runs to the very core of her being. Popular animosity toward India flows from Pakistan's violent birthing process; from the country's national identity as a Muslim (read: not Hindu) state; from the Indo-Pakistani wars of 1947, 1965, and 1971; and from continuing territorial disputes, most notably over Kashmir. Pakistani officials have justified their nation's conventional armed forces, nuclear weapons, and even its investments in militant groups like Lashkar-e-Taiba (LeT) or the Afghan Taliban by citing the threat posed by Pakistan's much larger neighbor.

Pakistan's army of more than a half-million men serves as its primary defense against India's 1.3 million soldiers across the border. In addition, Pakistan maintains some 300,000 paramilitary soldiers and a reserve force of another half-million men.[43] This makes Pakistan's armed forces the sixth largest, by

---

[40] Kaswar Klasra, "Journalists as Spies in FATA?" *The Nation*, November 5, 2009, http://www.nation.com.pk/pakistan-news-newspaper-daily-english-online/politics/05-Nov-2009/Journalists-as-spies-in-FATA.

[41] Amanda Hodge, "CIA Slur Has Chilling Parallel with Daniel Pearl," *The Australian*, November 26, 2009, http://www.theaustralian.com.au/news/world/cia-slur-has-chilling-parallel-with-daniel-pearl/story-e6frg6so-1225803878082.

[42] Shireen Mazari, "America's Mala Fide Intent," *Express Tribune*, February 25, 2011, http://tribune.com.pk/story/123887/americas-mala-fide-intent/.

[43] *The Military Balance 2012*, International Institute of Strategic Studies (London: Routledge, 2012), pp. 272–3; "Pakistan Army," GlobalSecurity.org, http://www.globalsecurity.org/military/world/pakistan/army.htm.

personnel, in the world.[44] Even though Taliban-affiliated insurgents have plagued the nation's western frontier, the overwhelming bulk of Pakistan's military was trained, positioned, and equipped to fight India.

Pakistan has had a difficult relationship with Afghanistan from the time of independence, owing to unresolved border disputes and the lurking fear that Pakistani Pashtuns might align with their ethnic compatriots to form a "greater Afghanistan." These suspicions would be more than enough to raise hackles in Islamabad, but Pakistani officers also tend to see an Indian lurking behind every tree in Afghanistan; they worry that India might use its influence in Afghanistan to threaten Pakistan's western flank and set up a two-front war. Ever since 9/11, Pakistanis have complained to American officials that Indian spies have set up shop in as many as two-dozen "consulates" inside Afghanistan, from where they pay informants and undermine Pakistani interests. Pakistani military briefers have also tended to characterize the Afghan government of President Karzai as irredeemably pro-Indian.

This has been the principal Pakistani justification for retaining ties with Afghan Taliban leaders in spite of the fact that such leaders and their groups are anti-modern, hostile to the lifestyle choices of many top officers in the Pakistani military, and actively killing U.S., NATO, and Afghan troops. These are not new relationships; some date back to the anti-Soviet jihad of the 1980s, others to the formation of the Afghan Taliban movement in the mid-1990s. The ties persist in part because the Afghan fighters are tough, battle-hardened, and (in several important cases) capable of inflicting great pain on Pakistan if Islamabad actually decided to turn against them. The ties also persist because after decades of ruthless, bloody intervention in Afghanistan, Pakistan has no other Afghan allies, nor even very many potential allies, but remains committed to the goal of fighting Indian influence by any and all means. Pakistan's strategy in Afghanistan has been driven by a combination of fear, poor options, and a firm conviction that whatever Washington's promises of Afghan stability, eventually Pakistan will be left to fend for itself.

Worse still, some Pakistanis believe that India has been playing nasty tricks inside Pakistan itself. As Taliban violence spiked inside Pakistan after 2006, the popular explanation was that the "hidden Hindu hand" was responsible for the ghastly horrors of suicide attacks on Pakistan's markets and mosques. "No Muslim would possibly do such a thing to other Muslims," was a common refrain. Other Pakistanis, including some relatively senior army officers, have explained in euphemistic terms that they are "certain" that many of the fighters along the Afghan border are Hindus, noting that many of the men they have killed or captured are uncircumcised. But as a Pakistani reporter from South Waziristan explained during a visit to Pakistan in December 2008, some of

---

[44] *The Military Balance 2012*, pp. 467–73.

the tribes of that area – although Muslim – do not practice circumcision.[45] Moreover, the reporter explained, stories of Indian intervention were concocted by the military to justify unpopular operations in Pakistan's own tribal areas. In other words, Pakistani officers were almost certainly suffering from blowback of their own propaganda.

Even if there are reasons to doubt Pakistani claims about extensive Indian meddling in the Pashtun tribal areas along the Afghan border, it is undeniable that India has played sides in Afghanistan. During the 1990s, New Delhi (along with Moscow and Teheran) supported the anti-Taliban Afghan militias of the Northern Alliance. That support probably kept Ahmad Shah Massoud, the "Lion of the Panjshir" and leader of the anti-Taliban alliance, alive and fighting until al-Qaeda assassinated him just two days before 9/11. Some analysts also give greater credence to the idea that India has aided other insurgent movements in Pakistan, foremost among them the Baluch separatists, as a part of its tit-for-tat spy games with Islamabad. Yet those allegations overstate the level of support and the extent to which these groups depend upon India's largesse or are directed in any way by New Delhi.[46]

From an outsider's point of view, one puzzle is why Pakistan feels so threatened by India. A glance at the recent past shows that Indian governments – whether the right-wing Bharatiya Janata Party (BJP)-led coalition government that ruled from 1998 to 2004 or the Congress-led coalition that came after it – have recognized that diplomacy, not war, was the only way to manage relations with Pakistan. Indians in positions of power view neither military conquest nor the breakup of Pakistan as realistic or even desirable, despite having suffered from so many Pakistan-based terrorist attacks. Most Indian strategists see Pakistan as a huge mess, not one India would want to inherit even if it had the military tools to sweep across the border unobstructed. Indian strategists fear Pakistani instability more than its strength. They are increasingly fixated on China's strength and concerned about how it might constrain India's own rise to global power status.

These arguments hold little water in Pakistani military circles. First, Pakistani officers have clearly been schooled in Otto von Bismarck's theories of Realpolitik, for they never tire of explaining that a state must guard against its adversary's capabilities, not its intentions. From this perspective, India's

---

[45] See also Omer Farooq Khan, "Circumcision no Longer Acid Test to Identify Indian Spies," *Times of India*, April 11, 2009, http://articles.timesofindia.indiatimes.com/2009-04-11/india/28039644_1_circumcision-waziristan-acid-test.

[46] Saeed Shah, "In Remote Balochistan, Pakistan Fights a Shadowy War," *McClatchy Newspapers*, March 30, 2012, http://www.kansascity.com/2012/03/29/3522817/in-remote-baluchistan-pakistan.html; "No India Role in Balochistan," *Press Trust of India*, March 26, 2011, http://www.hindustantimes.com/world-news/Americas/Baloch-separatist-movement-not-fuelled-by-India-US/Article1-702136.aspx; "Holbrooke Rubbishes Pak's Baloch Allegations," *Economic Times*, July 31, 2009, http://articles.economictimes.indiatimes.com/2009-07-31/news/28447547_1_balochistan-joint-statement-afghanistan-richard-holbrooke.

arsenal is expanding and modernizing, so Pakistan must find a way to keep pace, no matter that New Delhi routinely characterizes its intentions as defensive and directed toward China more than Pakistan.

In addition, Pakistanis appear to be worried about something far more sinister than an Indian invasion. They wish to avoid the fate of the smaller states on India's periphery – from Nepal and Sri Lanka to Bangladesh – which, to hear Pakistanis tell it, routinely suffer the indignity of taking dictation from New Delhi. This is a point of national pride and it runs to the core of Pakistan's myth of itself as a homeland for South Asian Muslims. Pakistan's founders could not accept the prospect of Hindu political domination within a larger India; their successors have no greater intention of accepting subordination to New Delhi today.

Moreover, Pakistan is not content with the way the lines are drawn on South Asia's maps. In this respect, Pakistan does not fear Indian aggression so much as it fears the status quo. It has never recognized India's claim to Kashmir, that mountainous stretch of land due east from Pakistan's capital, known today for its recent violence and bloodshed, but once upon a time famous for its picturesque valley and romantic houseboats on Dal Lake that offered British colonials a refuge from India's hot, dusty summers.

At its core, the dissension about Kashmir is a political dispute over who should govern the majority-Muslim territory that was once ruled by a Hindu maharaja. India and Pakistan clearly disagree on the answer to that question, but there is also the complicated issue of what the Kashmiris – a diverse group – want for themselves.[47] Looming above and beyond these issues are Kashmir's remarkable geography and topography. Its glaciers feed the rivers that give life to India and Pakistan alike. As populations grow and glaciers melt, that water has become increasingly precious. And because Kashmir's sky-touching ranges stand at the intersection of India, Pakistan, and China, many unfortunate souls have been lost to the elements in vain attempts to secure the commanding heights, even though they offer little discernible military utility. At 18,000 feet, the Siachen glacier, claimed by India and Pakistan, is the world's highest battlefield.[48] Hundreds of men have died there in temperatures that routinely drop to fifty below. In the spring of 2012, an avalanche buried a Pakistani army camp near the glacier, killing 139 soldiers and civilians.

The first two of Pakistan's three major wars with India centered on Kashmir, as did the Kargil conflict of 1999 and multiple other crises. Pakistan's international diplomacy has at times been thoroughly consumed with the Kashmir agenda. And, particularly since the late 1980s, Pakistan has aided and abetted "freedom fighters" in Kashmir, better known to most Indians as terrorists, in

---

[47] Navnita Chadha Behera, *Demystifying Kashmir* (Washington: Brookings Institution Press, 2006).

[48] Barry Bearak, "The Coldest War: Frozen in Fury on the Roof of the World," *New York Times*, May 23, 1999, http://www.nytimes.com/1999/05/23/world/the-coldest-war-frozen-in-fury-on-the-roof-of-the-world.html?src=pm.

their violent struggle against the Indian state. None of these costly exercises has yielded tangible gains; India has shown itself able to absorb the butchery, deliver punishing blows of its own, and bear tremendous costs. Since 1947, tens of thousands of Kashmiris have died in the conflict, and despite several valiant efforts to achieve a diplomatic breakthrough, it remains a core Pakistani grievance.[49] Given India's greater size and military power, the conflict is unlikely ever to be resolved to Pakistan's full satisfaction.

In its effort to counter India, Pakistan's military owes a great deal to China. The very fact of China's military might is the greatest equalizer in Pakistan's stand against India. There is simply no way for Pakistan to keep up with India on its own, but with an even larger Chinese patron that is willing to share arms and technology and simultaneously demands the bulk of India's attention, Pakistani generals believe they have a fighting chance. Pakistan depends on Chinese military hardware. Its main battle tank (Al-Khalid), many of its new fighter jets (JF-17), some of its nuclear warhead blueprints, and several of its nuclear-capable missiles come from its cooperation with the Chinese.[50]

Although Pakistan's last major land war with India is beyond the recollection of most of its young population, the humiliating loss of 1971 still resonates with the army's top brass. The 1965 Indo-Pakistani war featured some of the largest tank battles since the Second World War.[51] Senior military officers on both sides of the border do not think about another war as a theoretical exercise or expect it to be a trifling affair. However, if war memories should ever start to fade, they have routinely been brought back into sharp relief by Indo-Pakistani crises in 1987, 1990, 1999, and 2001–2, not to mention the escalation of tension after the Mumbai terrorist attacks of 2008.[52] Each of these crises, to a greater or lesser extent, raised the realistic prospect of another full-blown war.[53]

The Nuclear Dimension

Fortunately, recent Indo-Pakistani crises have all cooled before they turned into anything truly horrific. Central to Cold War era theories of nuclear deterrence was "mutually assured destruction," the idea that when two hostile countries

---

[49] On the American effort to broker peace in Kashmir, see Howard B. Schaffer, *The Limits of Influence: America's Role in Kashmir* (Washington: Brookings Institution Press, 2009).

[50] SIPRI Arms Transfer Database, http://armstrade.sipri.org/armstrade/page/trade_register.php; also Paul K. Kerr and Mary Beth Nikitin, "Pakistan's Nuclear Weapons: Proliferation and Security Issues," Congressional Research Service, 7–5700, RL34248, May 10, 2012, p. 3, www.fas.org/sgp/crs/nuke/RL34248.pdf.

[51] Shuja Nawaz, *Crossed Swords: Pakistan, Its Army, and the Wars Within* (Oxford: Oxford University Press, 2008), p. 229.

[52] P. R. Chari, Pervaiz Iqbal Cheema, and Stephen P. Cohen, *Four Crises and a Peace Process: American Engagement in South Asia* (Washington: Brookings Institution Press, 2007).

[53] Polly Nayak and Michael Krepon, *The Unfinished Crisis: U.S. Crisis Management after the 2008 Mumbai Attacks* (Washington, DC: Henry L. Stimson Center), February 2012, p. 7.

are nuclear-armed – and therefore have the unquestioned ability to unleash hell against the other side – fear of the consequences will induce mutual restraint. Perhaps there is truth to this theory, but unless relations between India and Pakistan are altered in fundamental ways, a nuclear exchange will remain a legitimate fear. That fear is aggravated by the fact that both sides are taking steps to develop military options that make a war more likely.

For its part, Pakistan is expanding its nuclear arsenal. According to recent U.S. estimates, Pakistan has about 100 deployed nuclear warheads and enough fissile material to build 40 to 100 additional nuclear weapons.[54] To hear Pakistani strategists explain it, the South Asian nuclear arms race is being spurred by India in two ways. First, India's non-nuclear military advantage is growing, and Pakistan has no other way to address that asymmetry. Second, India unlocked the door to expanding its own nuclear program when it concluded a civilian nuclear agreement with the United States in 2005. Although that deal clearly excluded the part of India's nuclear program related to the military, Pakistanis – and even some American analysts who opposed the agreement – asserted that it would free up limited Indian stocks of fissile material and allow it to go on a bomb-making spree.[55] Pakistan's National Command Authority – its top leaders and nuclear decision makers – most likely decided to accelerate Pakistan's nuclear production at a meeting in early April 2006, after the Indo-U.S. civil nuclear deal and India's non-nuclear defense plans became clear to Islamabad.[56]

The size of Pakistan's nuclear arsenal makes a difference. More weapons also increase the chance that something will go wrong.[57] Historians of America's own nuclear program explain how on multiple occasions the United States came perilously close to launching World War III by accident; how in 1961 a B-52 bomber fell apart in flight near Goldsboro, North Carolina, sending

[54] David E. Sanger and Eric Schmitt, "Pakistani Nuclear Arms Pose Challenge to U.S. Policy," *New York Times*, January 31, 2011, http://www.nytimes.com/2011/02/01/world/asia/01policy.html?pagewanted=all.

[55] Among the American opponents of the deal, Michael Krepon has made this point repeatedly. See "Unwarranted Assessments," *Dawn*, July 23, 2012, http://dawn.com/2012/07/23/unwarranted-assessments/; and "Betting the Ranch on the U.S.-India Nuclear Deal," Stimson Briefing, June 5, 2005, http://www.stimson.org/essays/betting-the-ranch-on-the-us-india-nuclear-deal/. For more on India's nuclear weapons development and policies, see George Perkovich, *India's Nuclear Bomb: The Impact on Global Proliferation* (Berkeley: University of California Press, 2001); and Ashley Tellis, *India's Emerging Nuclear Posture: Between Recessed Deterrent and Ready Arsenal* (Washington: RAND, 2001).

[56] Peter R. Lavoy, "Pakistan's Nuclear Posture: Security and Survivability," paper for the Nonproliferation Policy Education Center, January 21, 2007, pp. 16–17, http://www.npolicy.org/article.php?aid=291&rid=6. Lavoy's assessment fits with the findings of Michael Krepon, *The False Promise of the Civil Nuclear Deal* (Washington, DC: Henry L. Stimson Center), July 14, 2011, http://www.stimson.org/spotlight/the-false-promise-of-the-civil-nuclear-deal/.

[57] Scott D. Sagan and Kenneth Waltz, "The Great Debate: Is Nuclear Zero the Best Option?" *The National Interest* (September/October 2010).

two nearly-activated hydrogen bombs crashing to earth; how in 1966 another B-52 crashed off the coast of Spain with four hydrogen bombs on board, two of which contaminated the nearby area with plutonium; or how in 2007 the U.S. Air Force lost track of two nuclear warheads and flew them from North Dakota to Louisiana without proper security.[58] In Pakistan, similar incidents are possible, even if Pakistani officials claim their safety and security are every bit as good as those of the United States.

Pakistan's plans for when and how to use nuclear weapons also make for disturbing reading. To be clear, it is not as if Pakistani strategists are crazy or irrational. In fact, there are similarities between Pakistan's nuclear doctrine and the doctrine used by the United States during the Cold War. Just as Washington tried to balance the overwhelming size of the Soviet ground forces in Europe by threatening to use nuclear weapons, Pakistan also rattles its nuclear saber to ward off India's more capable military.

In both cases, the problem facing the country threatening to use nuclear weapons has been how to convince its adversary that the nuclear threat – one that would likely carry devastating consequences for both sides – is not hollow. In Cold War Europe, one of Washington's answers to that problem was to develop and field very short range, or "tactical," nuclear weapons; a risky and unpopular move among many Europeans, but one that signaled to Moscow that a Soviet armored offensive into Germany would trigger a nuclear conflict.

Not surprisingly, Pakistan has also started down a similar path. Again, Pakistani officials point to India as provoking the move, observing that the Indian military has taken steps to improve its own ability to hit Pakistan harder and faster with a non-nuclear strike, as a means to punish Pakistan for any future terrorist strikes that might originate from its soil.[59] Pakistan, fearing that India might get its punches in before defenses are adequately prepared, is developing a tactical nuclear program featuring short-range missiles tipped with small plutonium-based warheads.[60]

There is little public information about how far Pakistan's program has progressed, but already a fair amount of hand-wringing is occurring in international arms control circles about what might happen if Pakistan fields tactical weapons after very limited testing in a region plagued by routine crises and miscommunication, where the two adversaries share a land border of nearly 2,000 miles.[61] Nor is it clear how Pakistan intends to address India's ever-widening

[58] Josh White, "Military Probes How Nukes Flew over U.S.," *Washington Post*, September 6, 2007, http://articles.chicagotribune.com/2007-09-06/news/0709051421_1_nuclear-warheads-nuclear-weapons-munitions.
[59] Walter C. Ladwig, "A Cold Start for Hot Wars? The Indian Army's New Limited War Doctrine," *International Security*, 32, no. 3 (Winter 2007/8), pp. 158–90.
[60] Inter Services Public Relations Press release, April 19, 2011, www.ispr.gov.pk/front/main.asp?o=t-press_release&id=1721.
[61] Michael Krepon, "Arms Crawl That Wasn't," *Dawn*, November 2, 2011, http://dawn.com/2011/11/02/arms-crawl-that-wasnt/.

advantage in non-nuclear arms. Pakistani generals might continue to build more tactical nuclear weapons to keep up, or they might decide that a minimal arsenal is enough. These and other related issues pose serious challenges to regional stability.

Oddly enough, when Indians and Pakistanis come together to talk about the nuclear issue, they tend to discount the potential for nuclear war. South Asian analysts and officials act as if Americans are entirely too alarmist and reject Cold War analogies as being inappropriate to the cultural norms of their own region. Yet there is one undeniable and dangerous consequence of nuclear weapons that has already taken place. Both sides have turned their efforts to finding ways short of nuclear war to punish each other.[62] At times, minor conflicts have come close to spiraling out of control and provoking precisely the sort of war that nuclear weapons are supposed to deter in the first place.

Afghanistan has been one such proxy battleground. In the summer of 2008, Pakistan-backed terrorists in the Haqqani network rammed a suicide car bomb into India's Kabul embassy, killing 58 and wounding over 130.[63] Yet to hear Indian and Pakistani officials tell it, their spy-versus-spy games extend throughout the region – including Bangladesh, Sri Lanka, and Nepal. Most frightening, Pakistan has nurtured militants and terrorist organizations that have pulled off spectacular attacks inside India, such as the suicidal raid on India's parliament building in December 2001 by five Pakistani gunmen. Fortunately, that attack failed in its mission to kill India's top political leaders, but it nearly provoked a war. As U.S. Secretary of Defense Robert Gates said in January 2010, "I think it is not unreasonable to assume that Indian patience would be limited were there to be further attacks."[64] Under such circumstances, it is hard to place great faith in the stabilizing attributes of nuclear weapons.

---

[62] Ashley J. Tellis identifies the various dangers posed by "subconventional violence" between India and Pakistan in *Stability in South Asia* (Santa Monica, CA: RAND Corporation, 1997), http://www.rand.org/pubs/documented_briefings/DB185. Much of the recent scholarly discussion of this topic centers on the concept of the "stability-instability paradox." See S. Paul Kapur, "India and Pakistan's Unstable Peace: Why Nuclear South Asia Is Not Like Cold War Europe," *International Security*, 30, no. 2 (Fall 2005), pp. 127–52; S. Paul Kapur, "Ten Years of Instability in a Nuclear South Asia," *International Security*, 33, no. 2 (Fall 2008), pp. 71–94; Michael Krepon, Rodney W. Jones, and Ziad Haider, eds., *Escalation Control and the Nuclear Option in South Asia* (Washington: Henry L. Stimson Center, 2004); Michael Krepon and Chris Gagne, eds. *The Stability-Instability Paradox: Nuclear Weapons and Brinksmanship in South Asia* (Washington: Henry L. Stimson Center, 2001).

[63] Declan Walsh, "Deadly Kabul Bomb Targets Indian Embassy," *The Guardian*, October 8, 2009, http://www.guardian.co.uk/world/2009/oct/08/kabul-bomb-indian-embassy.

[64] Julian E. Barnes and Mark Magnier, "Gates Increases Pressure on Pakistan," *Los Angeles Times*, January 21, 2010, http://articles.latimes.com/2010/jan/21/world/la-fg-gates-india-terror 21-2010jan21.

Military Inc.

Critics of the Pakistani military are quick to point out that the generals have always exaggerated the threat posed by India to serve their own purposes.[65] Even if much of the rest of the country has suffered, Pakistan's military has always done well for itself.[66]

For proof, one needs only to visit the Pakistani military's cantonments, where roads are well tended, schools are good, and high-quality hospitals treat servicemen and their families. Servicemen associations founded to care for retired veterans have come to hold substantial stakes in major sectors of the Pakistani economy, like cement, fertilizer, oil and gas, and various agricultural industries.[67] The Pakistani military has also rewarded its officers with massive land entitlements, with officers at the rank of major general or above each allocated fifty acres.[68] In land-starved Karachi, an entire oceanside peninsula roughly the size of Manhattan was doled out in this fashion.[69]

In part because the military commands a disproportionate share of Pakistan's resources, it has come closer than any other national institution at instilling professionalism, discipline, and esprit de corps throughout its ranks. It has also accomplished at least some of its own strategic purposes, above all, maintaining the nation's sovereign independence from India. In times of grave national crisis, such as 2010's epic floods, its personnel have performed heroically. And when the army has set its mind to taking the fight to domestic insurgents, it has been effective, if brutal. This was certainly true in the spring of 2009 when Pakistani Taliban were ousted from control over the Swat Valley. No militant group in the land can stand its ground in the face of a concerted army offensive, although just as the U.S. military has found in Afghanistan and Iraq, guerrilla operations and suicide terrorists make for extremely difficult adversaries.

The army has too often dominated Pakistani politics even when civilians were nominally in charge. The generals dictate their own budgets, jealously guard their autonomy, and – with minor historical exceptions – set the nation's foreign and defense policy. When they have felt threatened by civilian leaders, they have taken swift and effective countermeasures. For instance, General Musharraf's 1999 coup against Prime Minister Nawaz Sharif was prompted by Sharif's own plan to dismiss Musharraf. When the army has wanted to tip

---

[65] The title of this section borrows from Ayesha Siddiqa, *Military Inc.: Inside Pakistan's Military Economy* (Ann Arbor, MI: Pluto Press, 2008).

[66] The economic influence of Pakistan's military has been documented in a recent book by Ayesha Siddiqa and an earlier one by Ayesha Jalal. See Ayesha Siddiqa, *Military Inc.*, and Ayesha Jalal, *The State of Martial Rule: The Origins of Pakistan's Political Economy of Defence* (Cambridge: Cambridge University Press, 1990).

[67] Siddiqa, *Military Inc.*, pp. 145–150.

[68] Siddiqa, *Military Inc.*, p. 183.

[69] Inskeep, *Instant City*, p. 209.

the political balance in its favor – as it did for that same Nawaz Sharif in the early 1990s – the generals have done that too.

The Inter-Services Intelligence directorate, or ISI, has typically handled the army's political manipulations as but one of its many responsibilities. The record of such dealings is now public, thanks to court proceedings starting in the late 1990s that investigated whether the ISI funneled money to its favored political candidates. Although General Musharraf suspended the case following his 1999 coup, activist judges on Pakistan's Supreme Court decided to revive the case in early 2012. Lieutenant General Asad Durrani, who directed the ISI during the period in question, admitted in court that he followed instructions from the then-Pakistan army chief to distribute the equivalent of $1.6 million to right-wing candidates in 1990.[70]

This practice is no relic of the distant past. Pakistan's 2002 elections were thoroughly rigged by the Musharraf regime.[71] Worse, even though national polls in 2008 were relatively free and fair, the campaigns that preceded them were almost certainly coursing with ISI money. In one uncomfortable exchange during a May 2010 briefing with ISI officials in Islamabad, I asked how their organization had changed since the return of civilian-led government in Islamabad. An eager mid-level analyst jumped in to say, "One big shift is that we shut down the political wing." He might have expounded upon this issue but his boss, one of the ISI's most senior officers, cut him off quickly, stating, "Of course, you must understand, there never was a political wing of the ISI."[72] The former head of the ISI, Lieutenant General Asad Durrani, later contradicted both of these statements when he testified before Pakistan's Supreme Court in May 2012 and explained that the ISI's political cell was still operational.[73]

For all its political scheming and activities throughout Pakistan's neighborhood, the ISI has earned quite a bit of attention and even more notoriety. Pakistani journalists tend to write about the agency in euphemistic terms, citing it as a driving force in the "establishment" or the "deep state." It is easy to get the impression that the ISI controls practically everything that moves in Pakistan (or for that matter, in Afghanistan). The ISI is powerful, but that power also has limits. If Pakistan's spies were as omnipresent and all-seeing as the rumors suggest, the agency probably would have done a much better job at securing the country, or at least at securing its own personnel. In combating

[70] Saeed Shah, "Pakistani High Court Challenges Spy Agency over Payments," *McClatchy Newspapers*, March 9, 2012, http://www.mcclatchydc.com/2012/03/09/v-print/141344/pakistani-high-court-challenges.html.

[71] "Reforming Pakistan's Electoral System," International Crisis Group Asia Report No. 203, March 30, 2011, p. 6, http://www.crisisgroup.org/~/media/Files/asia/southasia/pakistan/203%20Reforming%20Pakistans%20Electoral%20System.ashx.

[72] Author's conversation, Islamabad, May 2010.

[73] Nasir Iqbal, "SC Asks Govt to Provide ISI Political Cell Notification," *Dawn*, May 17, 2012, http://dawn.com/2012/05/18/sc-asks-govt-to-provide-isi-political-cell-notification/.

the Pakistani Taliban, the ISI is said to have lost some seventy officers by the end of 2009.[74] One glance at the ISI's fortress-like compound in Islamabad suggests that even its own leaders doubt its omnipotence.

It is safe to conclude, however, that the ISI is one essential element in a larger military machine that remains far and away Pakistan's single most powerful institution. It is possible that over time Pakistan's civilian leaders will wrest power from the generals, or simply chip away at it, bit by bit. But as long as the military continues to hold a deciding influence, Pakistan's foreign and defense policies are more likely to be defined by continuity than by change.

TERRORIST INCUBATOR

Pakistan's founder, Muhammad Ali Jinnah, bequeathed his new nation a noble motto: "unity, faith and discipline." Jinnah's three words may ring a bell with anyone who has traveled to Islamabad from the airport, since they are mounted on a hilltop – sort of like the Hollywood sign above Los Angeles – under a huge illuminated profile of Jinnah himself. So it is noteworthy that Pakistan's army now fights under the Arabic banner: "Iman, Taqwa, Jihad fi Sabilillah," or "Faith, Piety, Struggle in the way of Allah," a pointedly Islamic formulation assumed in the late 1970s during the harsh military rule of General Zia-ul-Haq. A motto need not have grave significance, but in Pakistan's case it lays bare a central question of national identity: What is the role of Islam in the state?

Debates still rage in Pakistan over how Jinnah answered this question. Liberals argue that the nation's founder sought to protect the rights of all Pakistani citizens, regardless of religious creed. For instance, in 2011, *Dawn*, the English-language daily newspaper, ran a series of seven large advertisements proclaiming Jinnah's progressive views on women's and minority rights, good governance, and education.[75] *Dawn* cited Jinnah's speech of August 11, 1947, in which he told the Pakistani constituent assembly:

You are free; you are free to go to your temples, you are free to go to your mosques or to any other place or worship in this State of Pakistan. You may belong to any religion or caste or creed that has nothing to do with the business of the State.... Now I think...you will find that in course of time Hindus would cease to be Hindus and Muslims would cease to be Muslims, not in the religious sense, because that is the personal faith of each individual, but in the political sense as citizens of the State.[76]

---

74 Anatol Lieven, "Understanding Pakistan's Military," OpenDemocracy.Net, August 9, 2010, http://www.opendemocracy.net/anatol-lieven/understanding-pakistan%E2%80%99s-military.

75 See *Dawn's* half-page description of this ad campaign on May 23, 2012, p. 4.

76 "Mr. Jinnah's Presidential Address to the Constituent Assembly of Pakistan, August 11, 1947," *Dawn*, Independence Day Supplement, August 14, 1999, http://www.pakistani.org/pakistan/legislation/constituent_address_11aug1947.html.

On the other hand, Pakistan's Islamists point out that Jinnah founded the state in explicit opposition to the Hindu-dominated politics of India.[77] Under those circumstances, how could Pakistan *not* grant the primacy of Islamic law and practice? Of greater import than Jinnah's view is the fact that Pakistan has evolved over time. The nation's politics, rhetoric, and practices are more self-consciously "Islamic" than they were in Jinnah's day. The political and social consequences of this shift are by no means straightforward.

Islam under Attack

The topic of blasphemy – speaking or acting in ways that are believed to defame Islam – has stirred great passion in Pakistan. In May 2011, as I hopped out of the car to have a quick lunch with a Pakistani colleague at an upscale market in Islamabad, he turned to me and pointed to a spot just to our left: "That's where Salman Taseer was shot dead." And so it was. Taseer, the outspoken liberal governor of Punjab province, had been killed by one of his own bodyguards, Mumtaz Qadri, who after firing several rounds into the back of the man he was sworn to protect, dropped his weapon and surrendered. The assassin's motive? Salman Taseer had dared to question Pakistan's law against blasphemy, which was at the time being used to prosecute a Christian woman for her alleged use of the prophet's name in vain.

The Taseer murder troubled Pakistanis, but for a range of reasons. Among the high-living liberal elites, who commonly employ drivers, cooks, maids, and security guards, it sent a chilling message that their families were not safe. The political, social, or religious sympathies of their hired help could make them dangerous. For other moderates and minorities, especially Pakistan's Christians and Hindus, the killing was another reminder of the difficulties of living in an increasingly intolerant society.

Perhaps the most shocking aspect of the entire episode, however, was that mainstream religious leaders sat silently or openly blamed Taseer, the victim, for having questioned Pakistan's blasphemy law in the first place. This was true for leaders of Pakistan's Barelvi school of Islam, one followed by a majority of Pakistan's Sunni Muslims and widely viewed as more "moderate" in its teachings.[78] The Sunni Ittehad Council, a conglomerate of Barelvi groups, went so far as to call on Pakistan's president to pardon Taseer's assassin and declared it would celebrate January 4 as Mumtaz Qadri day.[79] Later, when

[77] For an excellent study of Pakistan's largest Islamist political party, see Syed Vali Reza Nasr, *The Vanguard of the Islamic Revolution: The Jama'at-i Islami of Pakistan* (Berkeley: University of California Press, 1994).

[78] Salman Siddiqui, "Hardline Stance: Religious Bloc Condones Murder," *Express Tribune*, January 5, 2011, http://tribune.com.pk/story/99313/hardline-stance-religious-bloc-condones-murder/.

[79] "SIC Demands Ban on Renamed Terrorist Groups," *Express Tribune*, December 15, 2011, http://tribune.com.pk/story/306716/barelvi-parties-conference-sic-demands-ban-on-renamed-terrorist-groups/.

Qadri showed up in court, a group of lawyers assembled in solidarity and showered him with rose petals.[80]

The blasphemy issue touches a special chord for millions of Pakistanis, many of whom believe that Islam is under attack and must be defended from abuses of all sorts. Hamid Gul, who served as the chief of the ISI from 1987 to 1989, is today one of Pakistan's most vocal champions of this mind-set. Like other retired senior officers, Gul lives in a comfortable home granted to him as part of his retirement package. He is surrounded by family, including his son Abdullah, who is following in his father's footsteps to launch a national youth movement with a revolutionary, anti-Western agenda.[81]

Gul was removed from his ISI job when civilians retook power in Islamabad from the military dictator Zia-ul-Haq who died in a mysterious plane crash. After leaving his office, the spy chief never fully abandoned the Taliban or the other violent extremists he had done so much to nurture. He has admitted to membership in a group that tried to share nuclear information with al-Qaeda prior to 9/11.[82] An unabashed critic of the United States, Gul called the 9/11 attacks "a bloody hoax" and "an inside job."[83] He claimed that Osama bin Laden "has sworn to me [Gul] on the Koran it was not him [responsible for the attacks] and he is truthful to a fault."[84]

What separates Gul from other garden-variety anti-Americans or Pakistani nationalists is that he sees Pakistan's Muslim identity as its defining feature. As Gul explained in a 2004 interview, he has long been "a proponent of the idea that all the Muslim countries, which are an endangered species, they must get together and sign a defense pact.... Forty-five percent of the world area can be described as Muslim land. So we have tremendous potential. But we have to understand that we are different in the definition of a nation than the other nations of the world. And this is called pan-Islamism. And people are afraid, the West is afraid of this spirit of pan-Islamism."[85] To another interviewer,

[80] "Lawyers Shower Roses for Governor's Killer," *Associated Press*, January 5, 2011, http://www.dawn.com/2011/01/05/lawyers-shower-roses-for-governors-killer.html.

[81] Author interview, Rawalpindi, May 16, 2012.

[82] The group, Ummah Tameer-e-Nau (UTN), is considered a terrorist organization by the U.S. government. UTN's nuclear plotting with al-Qaeda never appears to have gotten past a very preliminary discussion, but it did worry the U.S. intelligence community. For more, see Condoleezza Rice, *No Higher Honor: A Memoir of My Years in Washington* (New York: Crown, 2011), p. 125; David E. Sanger, *The Inheritance: The World Obama Confronts and the Challenges to American Power* (New York: Crown, 2011), pp. 206–212.

[83] Candace Rondeaux, "Former Pakistani Intelligence Official Denies Aiding Group Tied to Mumbai Seige," *Washington Post*, December 9, 2008, http://www.washingtonpost.com/wp-dyn/content/article/2008/12/08/AR2008120803612.html.

[84] Arnaud de Borchgrave, "Arnaud de Borchgrave's Exclusive September 2001 Interview with Hamid Gul," *Washington Times*, July 28, 2010, http://www.washingtontimes.com/news/2010/jul/28/deborchgrave-sept-2001-interview-hameed-gul/?page=all#pagebreak.

[85] "Voices from the Whirlwind: Assessing Musharraf's Predicament," *PBS Frontline*, March 2004, http://www.washingtontimes.com/news/2010/jul/28/deborchgrave-sept-2001-interview-hameed-gul/?page=all#pagebreak.

Gul argued, "The world needs a post-modern state system. . . . A global village under divine order, or we will have global bloodshed until good triumphs over evil." The Taliban in Afghanistan, he observed, represented "Islam in its purest form so far . . . they had perfect law and order with no formal police force, only traffic cops without sidearms."[86]

Armed with conspiracy theories and vitriol, Gul stands at Pakistan's nexus of the Taliban, Lashkar-e-Taiba, Islamist political parties, international terrorists, and the nation's most bloodthirsty sectarian outfits. In late 2011, they all joined forces to launch the Defence of Pakistan Council (Difa-e-Pakistan, or DPC). The group held rallies in each of Pakistan's major cities and published a polished website to proclaim its commitment to "defending Pakistan, the only ideological nation carved in the name of Islam with our wealth and lives."[87] Pakistan should begin, Gul believes, with a "soft revolution" that would "return" the country to its roots in Muslim law and do away with the current multiparty political system.[88] Gul and the DPC hope to trigger that revolution through nonviolent protests against the United States, to translate anti-American fervor into anti-government action.

As one brave Pakistani commentator put it, "Far from this [Defence of Pakistan] Council defending Pakistan, Pakistan needs to be defended in right earnest from this cast of characters."[89] One of the biggest draws for DPC events was Hafiz Saeed, the leader and principal ideologue of Jamaat-ud-Dawa (JuD), the charitable arm of LeT. If there is any single terrorist organization in Pakistan most likely to provoke an all-out war with India, it is LeT.[90]

Second to Saeed was Maulana Sami ul Haq, whose ties to the Afghan Taliban are legendary. His madrassa, the Darul Uloom Haqqania, is based along the Afghan border and trained many of the region's most notorious Taliban leaders. The patriarch of the Haqqani network that has so threatened the NATO mission in Afghanistan, commander Jalaluddin Haqqani derives his name from this seminary where he studied many decades ago. The media often calls the seminary the "university of jihad." Over decades, it has indoctrinated thousands of Pakistanis, Afghans, and – before it was made illegal – young men from all over the world in a violent, anti-Western view of the world.

In the decade after 9/11, Pakistan's Taliban brought insurgency, suicide terrorism, and a campaign of assassinations to Pakistani soil. The attacks exposed the vulnerabilities of Pakistan's security forces, both along the Afghan border

---

[86] de Borchgrave, "Arnaud de Borchgrave's Exclusive September 2001 Interview with Hamid Gul."

[87] Difa-e-Pakistan Homepage, http://www.difaepakistan.com/vision.html.

[88] Author interview, May 16, 2012.

[89] Ejaz Haider, "Is This a Joke?" *Express Tribune*, February 14, 2012, http://tribune.com.pk/story/336328/is-this-a-joke/.

[90] For an extended discussion of LeT, see Chapter 3.

and, at times, in the country's biggest cities. That said, Pakistan's Taliban insurgents have had little success in taking their violent conquests much beyond the frontier with Afghanistan. Pakistani Taliban (TTP) atrocities and the fact that the group is overwhelmingly Pashtun makes it foreign and deeply unappealing to the vast majority of Pakistan's people who hail from other ethnic groups. A June 2012 survey conducted by the Pew Research Center found that only 17 percent of Pakistanis supported the Pakistani Taliban while 52 percent of Pakistanis opposed them.[91]

The general unpopularity of the Pakistani Taliban is encouraging but hardly sufficient grounds for comfort. The city of Karachi, Pakistan's economic capital and trading hub, is now home to hundreds of thousands of recent migrants from the tribal areas bordering Afghanistan. Their arrival has created opportunities for the TTP to exploit the city's wealth and to expand the scope of their fight against the Pakistani state.[92]

Earlier, starting in the mid-2000s, a different movement of militants brought a spike in nationwide violence. Hundreds of "Punjabi Taliban" fighters moved from Pakistan's heartland into the remote tribal areas along the Afghan border, where they joined forces with the Pashtun insurgents. By some accounts, these new fighters were even more vicious and sophisticated than their tribal colleagues.[93] Perhaps because they originally hailed from more cosmopolitan parts of the country, they had grander ambitions for their war against Islamabad, not to mention their struggle against India and the West.

The Punjabi Taliban's linguistic and cultural ties to Pakistan's much more heavily populated heartland could open the door to a far more widespread Islamist movement in Pakistan. Swathes of Punjab are already sympathetic to these sorts of ideas. There, for instance, terrorist groups like Lashkar-e-Taiba and its humanitarian wing, Jamaat-ud-Dawa, have won sympathy and new recruits both for their hard-line ideology as well as their Hamas-like outreach efforts through schools and clinics.

Pakistan's New Extremists

Pakistanis typically point to the 1980s as the period when hard-line Islamist groups first gained traction in their country. As explained in the next

[91] Pew Global Attitudes Project, June 27, 2012, http://www.pewglobal.org/2012/06/27/pakistani-public-opinion-ever-more-critical-of-u-s/.

[92] Declan Walsh and Zia ur-Rehman, "Taliban Spread Terror in Karachi as the New Gang in Town," *New York Times*, March 28, 2013, http://www.nytimes.com/2013/03/29/world/asia/taliban-extending-reach-across-pakistan.html?pagewanted=all&_r=0.

[93] Author interview with Pakistani expert, Islamabad, May 2010. See also Katja Riikonen, "Punjabi Taliban and the Sectarian Groups in Pakistan," Pakistan Security Research Unit Brief Number 55, University of Bradford, February 12, 2010; Syed Saleem Shahzad, "The Gathering Strength of Taliban and Tribal Militants in Pakistan," Pakistan Security Research Unit Brief Number 24, University of Bradford, November 19, 2007.

chapter, the military rule of General Zia energized a variety of Islamist groups, including political parties such as the Jamaat-e-Islami, and granted them a privileged place in the Pakistani state. That pattern of mainstreaming more extreme ideologies did not die with Zia, but neither did it transform Pakistan into "Talibanistan" overnight. Pakistan's moderates (not to mention many American policymakers) have comforted themselves with the observation that even at their most successful moments, Pakistan's Islamist politicians have had trouble winning more than 10 percent of the national assembly. In addition, at least since Musharraf's decision to align with Washington after 9/11, Pakistan's senior officer corps has been carefully scrutinized for possible radical leanings.[94]

Even so, the trends in Pakistan are worrisome. Many close and longtime observers of Pakistan perceive a general shift away from traditional religious practices, including those rooted in a tolerant Sufi mysticism, and toward either a Taliban-style view of Islam (particularly in the Pashtun areas of the country), known as Deobandism, or a version of Sunni practice more in line with that of the Saudis, known as Salafism, Ahle Hadith, or the more derogatory term, "Wahhabi." All of these schools are actually rather modern phenomena, reactions to what their nineteenth-century founders considered heretical deviations from the original meaning and rites of Islam.[95]

It is in this context of social and political ferment that Pakistan has witnessed the rise of Al-Huda, a network of Islamist schools for women. Founded in Pakistan in 1994 by Farhat Hashmi, the daughter of an Islamist party (Jamaat-e-Islami) leader, the organization has over 200 "franchises" around Pakistan.[96] To the dismay of Pakistan's liberals and hard-line Islamists alike, Al-Huda is transforming the way many of Pakistan's most influential women, particularly well-educated ones from the middle and upper classes, relate to their faith.

Hashmi, who appears veiled in black with just a slit from her eyebrows to the bridge of her nose, was born in Pakistan in 1957 but did her doctoral work at the University of Glasgow. She has since relocated to Toronto where she directs her expanding global organization. Despite her globetrotting ways, Hashmi remains a household name in Pakistan, where radio stations broadcast her sermons and she can easily draw thousands for her live appearances.[97]

[94] Owais Tohid, "Pakistan Gradually Purges Army Extremists," *Christian Science Monitor*, September 11, 2003, http://www.csmonitor.com/2003/0911/p10s01-wosc.html. See also "Nuclear Black Markets: Pakistan, A. Q. Khan, and the Rise of Proliferation Networks," International Institute of Strategic Studies, May 2, 2007.
[95] Barbara Metcalf, *Islamic Revival in British India: Deoband, 1860–1900* (New York: Oxford University Press, 2004).
[96] Author interview with sociologist Faiza Mushtaq, Karachi, May 21, 2012; also Asma Khalid, "Religious Schools Court Wealthy Women in Pakistan," *National Public Radio*, April 5, 2010, http://www.npr.org/templates/story/story.php?storyId=125570048.
[97] Khalid, "Religious Schools Court Wealthy Women in Pakistan."

At its core, Al-Huda promotes practices one might associate with today's Arab Gulf states. Women are taught (but not forced) to veil themselves, to study Quranic texts rather than praying at Pakistan's traditional shrines, and to accept practices that more "moderate" Pakistanis consider outdated, including polygamy. The fact that thousands of privileged, upper-class women are choosing to study at Al-Huda schools poses a special threat to liberals, who expect that with greater education and opportunity will also come a more progressive outlook and less outward religiosity. Professor Pervez Hoodbhoy, a nuclear physicist and one of Pakistan's most iconoclastic voices on trends in education and social practices, laments that Al-Huda members are, "in comparison with students of earlier decades...less confident, less willing to ask questions in class, and most have become silent note-takers. To sing, dance, play sports or act in dramas is, of course, out of the question for these unfortunates."[98]

At the same time, Al-Huda is considered dangerous among Pakistan's traditional – and all-male – clergy. They see that Hashmi is breaking down gender barriers to Islamic scholarship and leadership. They question her academic credentials and preach against the idea that women should pray outside the home or lead their own prayers.[99] Al-Huda threatens their control over how religion is taught. It offers women a certain type of power – gained from greater comfort and understanding of religious texts – previously held almost exclusively by men.

From its far-flung organization to the fact that Hashmi's veiled figure can be seen preaching on the Internet seated behind a black laptop, Al-Huda is stunningly modern in the way it transmits its illiberal worldview. Its members are also sophisticated in their marketing and outreach efforts, consciously seeking new ways to build Al-Huda's "brand" in Pakistan and beyond. Al-Huda's hybrid identity is a testament to the fact that Pakistan, similar to many other Muslim countries, is in the middle of a national debate not readily characterized as liberal versus fundamentalist or modern versus traditional. New social movements like Al-Huda are picking up whatever works and running with it.

The Insider Threat

Another very different Islamist organization is also taking advantage of global networks to assert itself in Pakistan: Hizb ut-Tahrir (HuT). Like al-Qaeda and other radical Islamists, HuT's goal is to create a new "Khalifah state to be an

---

[98] Nahal Toosi, "In Pakistan, Islamic Schools for Women Thrive," *MSNBC*, June 27, 2010, http://www.msnbc.msn.com/id/37959628/ns/world_news-south_and_central_asia/t/pakistan-islamic-schools-women-thrive/.

[99] For some of the most extensive scholarship on Al-Huda to date, see Fazia Mushtaq, "A Controversial Role Model for Pakistani Women," *South Asia Multidisciplinary Academic Journal*, April 2010, http://samaj.revues.org/index3030.html.

example for the others and re-unify the Islamic world."[100] Unlike al-Qaeda, however, HuT claims not to engage in terrorism. Yet, HuT also distinguishes itself from Pakistan's other Islamist parties by refusing to participate in democratic politics. Instead, its plan is to cultivate a following among small groups of influential Pakistanis – especially army officers – who will overthrow the existing order when the time is right.

Banned in Pakistan for its revolutionary ideology, HuT maintains its headquarters in the United Kingdom. There it takes full advantage of British protections on free speech and religion as well as direct access to recruits from the country's burgeoning population of young Muslim immigrants, both men and women, many from South Asia. Like Al-Huda, HuT harnesses the global telecommunications network to organize and spread its message. HuT is made up of a secretive network of cells, rendering it difficult to know just how many members it actually has. At the lowest levels, HuT is broken into groups of five who receive anonymous calls to inform them of weekly meetings and may not even know the identities of other cell members.[101] Some claim that HuT's total size in Pakistan is in the low thousands, others suggest it may be far larger. Around the world, HuT may have as many as 1 million members.[102]

Shortly after America's 2011 bin Laden raid, the Pakistani army made a disturbing and high profile set of arrests. A serving officer, Brigadier Ali Khan, along with four junior officers, were charged with alleged HuT ties, sparking rumors that they had planned to stage a coup at a time when the army was feeling particularly vulnerable.[103] Later that summer, several others were arrested for their participation in HuT online activities.[104] Looking back, it appears that HuT was behind at least two other failed coup attempts as well as an unsuccessful 2010 plot to attack Pakistan's Shamsi airbase in Baluchistan,

---

[100] "Manifesto of Hizb-ut Tahrir for Pakistan," Hizb ut Tahrir Waliyah Pakistan, p. 3, http://www.hizb-pakistan.com/hizb/images/books/manifesto-english.pdf.

[101] Ed Husain, *The Islamist* (London: Penguin, 2008), p. 96.

[102] Simon Ross Valentine, "Fighting Kufr and the American Raj: Hizb-ut-Tahrir in Pakistan," Pakistan Security Research Unit Brief Number 56, University of Bradford, February 2, 2010, http://www.hizb-pakistan.com/hizb/images/books/manifesto-english.pdf.

[103] In retrospect, it is difficult to tell whether it was the Brigadier's HuT affiliation or his outspoken criticism of the army's cooperation with the United States that landed him in jail. See "Brigadier Ali Khan: Pakistan's Dissenting Army Officer," *BBC*, June 23, 2011, http://www.bbc.co.uk/news/world-south-asia-13873188; Kamran Yousaf, "Alleged HuT Links: 'Brigadier Ali Likely to Be Released Soon,'" *Express Tribune*, June 29, 2011, http://tribune.com.pk/story/198538/alleged-hut-links-brigadier-ali-likely-to-be-released-soon/. That said, rumors persist that the Brigadier told colleagues that he was actively planning to help turn Pakistan into a Caliphate and was in league with air force officers who would bomb a meeting of Pakistan's top officers and open the door to a coup. See "Brigadier Ali Wanted to Establish Caliphate: Witness," *Pakistan Today*, March 7, 2012, http://www.pakistantoday.com.pk/2012/03/07/news/national/brigadier-ali-wanted-to-establish-caliphate-witness/.

[104] Zia Khan, "Agencies Struggle to Dismantle Hizb ut-Tahrir Network," *Express Tribune*, August 8, 2011, http://tribune.com.pk/story/226503/agencies-struggle-to-dismantle-hizb-ut-tahrir-network/.

which at the time was thought to be the main Pakistani launch site for U.S. drones.

HuT is a modern and viciously intolerant organization. Founded in the early 1950s in East Jerusalem, it is also a foreign transplant into Pakistani soil. HuT's Palestinian founder broke with Egypt's famous Muslim Brotherhood because he considered the Brotherhood not militant enough.[105] HuT is active in many parts of the Muslim world. In late 2011, the government of Bangladesh claimed to have foiled a coup plot by over a dozen mid-ranking officers who were HuT members.[106] The group's focus on Pakistan is relatively recent and intensified only after the country's 1998 nuclear tests, when HuT sent ten senior members to Pakistan hoping to spark a revolution so that the new caliphate would be born as a nuclear power.[107] British HuT members also managed to recruit several Pakistani army officers during their training at Sandhurst military academy, but in 2003 the men were arrested by the Musharraf regime. In February 2013, as part of a wider campaign to win influence with Pakistan's rising generation, HuT activists showed up in force at a meeting of youth leaders hosted by Oxford University.[108]

Naveed Butt, HuT's Pakistan-based spokesman, graduated from the University of Illinois and worked for Motorola. He is no turbaned Talib. He is easy to find on the Internet, where he presents a modern and sophisticated image, sporting a short beard and Western-style suit as well as the dark spots on his forehead common to Muslims who prostrate themselves frequently. Butt's English is impeccable, and everything about him seems tailored specifically to reach a target audience within the Pakistani military. His January 2011 "Open Letter to Pakistan Armed Forces" begins with the exhortation: "Oh, officers of Pakistan's armed forces! You are leading the largest and the most capable Muslim armed forces in the world. . . . You must move now to uproot Pakistan's traitor rulers."[109] In May 2012, Butt was allegedly arrested by the ISI outside

---

[105] The single best available publication on HuT in Pakistan is Muhammad Amir Rana, "Hizbut Tahrir in Pakistan: Discourse and Impact," *Pakistan Institute for Peace Studies*, October 2010.

[106] "Army Foils Coup Plot aAgainst Hasina," BDNews24.com, January 19, 2012, http://bdnews 24.com/details.php?cid=2&id=216375&hb=top; "Former Bangladesh PM Accused of December 2011 Coup Attempt," *ANI Dhaka*, February 14, 2012, http://www.rediff.com/news/report/former-bangladesh-pm-accused-of-december-2011-coup-attempt/20120214.htm.

[107] Maajid Nawaz is a major source for information about HuT activities. Now reformed, Nawaz was once a member of the organization but has since founded the Quilliam Foundation, a counterterrorism think tank that receives significant support from the British government. One of his colleagues and co-founder is Ed Husain, now a senior fellow at the Council on Foreign Relations. As cited earlier, Ed wrote his own book detailing his experiences as an Islamist. See Ed Husain, *The Islamist*.

[108] Murtaza Ali Shah, "Hizb-ut-Tahrir Targets Pakistanis on Orders of Global Leaders," *The News*, February 28, 2013, http://www.thenews.com.pk/Todays-News-13-21279-Hizb-ut-Tahrir-targets-Pakistanis-on-orders-of-global-leaders.

[109] "Open Letter to Pakistan Armed Forces (English): Naveed Butt (HT. Pak. Media rep.)," January 30, 2011, http://www.youtube.com/watch?v=lHoTte3yFtQ.

his home in Lahore, and it appears that other HuT operations in Pakistan have so far been foiled.[110] Still, the group holds appeal – and may have built a wider network of secret members – within Pakistan's most sensitive and powerful security institutions, possibly even its nuclear program.[111]

In short, Pakistan is now a country where individuals like Navid Butt can call for a revolution on the Internet, where a thirty-three-year veteran of the army like Brigadier Ali Khan was arrested for treason, where conspiracy theorists and terrorists like Hamid Gul and Hafiz Saeed rant before public rallies, and where groups like Al-Huda are redefining mainstream religious practice. Under such circumstances, new sorts of revolutionary Islamist movements – somewhere between Al-Huda and HuT – seem ever more likely to gain political traction where the country's tired old Islamist parties and the Pashtun insurgents of the wild western border regions have thus far failed.

YOUTHFUL IDEALIST

In 1992, Imran Khan captained an underdog Pakistani national team to the World Cup championship, beating favorites New Zealand and England along the way. When the lime-green uniformed Khan finally hoisted the globe-shaped trophy over his head in triumph, it was a victory of mind over matter. The thirty-nine-year-old Khan was well past his prime and had been coaxed out of retirement for the series. Despite a severe shoulder injury, the fiercely competitive superstar – Pakistan's nearest equivalent to Michael Jordan – managed to keep his teammates inspired after they lost four of the tournament's first five matches. For tens of millions of his cricket-obsessed countrymen, the feat won Khan everlasting glory and placed him among a tiny pantheon of national heroes.[112]

Almost twenty years later, on October 30, 2011, Khan's underdog political party, the Pakistan Tehreek-e-Insaf (Movement for Justice, or PTI), which had won only a single seat in Pakistan's 2002 national elections and had skipped the 2008 election altogether, drew huge crowds to a rally in the center of Lahore, the capital of Pakistan's largest Punjab province. Commentators noted

[110] On Butt's alleged arrest, see www.freenaveedbutt.com.
[111] For more on HuT, see Michael Kugelman, "Another Threat in Pakistan, in Sheep's Clothing," *New York Times*, August 3, 2012, http://www.nytimes.com/2012/08/04/opinion/hizb-ut-tahrir-threatens-pakistan-from-within.html.
[112] There have been several recent profiles of Khan that discuss his life, personality, and place in Pakistani politics. See Madiha R. Tahir, "I'll Be Your Mirror," *The Caravan*, January 1, 2012, http://www.caravanmagazine.in/reportage/i%E2%80%99ll-be-your-mirror; Steve Coll, "Sporting Chance," *The New Yorker*, August 13, 2012, http://www.newyorker.com/reporting/2012/08/13/120813fa_fact_coll; Pankaj Mishra, "Imran Khan Must Be Doing Something Right," *New York Times Magazine*, August 16, 2012, http://www.nytimes.com/2012/08/19/magazine/pakistans-imran-khan-must-be-doing-something-right.html.

that Pakistan had not seen such a large rally for decades. It looked like a major turning point in Khan's post-cricket career as a national politician.

Most political rallies in Pakistan are staged events managed by party hacks and thugs. The politicians pay to bus peasants in from the surrounding countryside to create the illusion of popular support. Khan's rally in Lahore was different. It felt more like a giant picnic, with pop singers on hand to warm up the crowd before Khan and other PTI leaders took the stage. Pakistanis streamed into the city from all over the country. The assembled masses included rich and poor, men, women, and children. Hundreds of green, red, and white PTI flags waved above the sea of humanity, framed by mammoth campaign posters and a towering stage for the party leadership and performers.

People who had never before attended political events came out in droves, especially students, eager to show their dissatisfaction with the ruling government and the other major parties that have dominated Pakistani politics for decades. Eventually, their chants and cheers gave way to rousing renditions of Pakistan's national anthem. When he stepped to the podium, Khan described the PTI's success as a "tsunami" and warned, "Anyone up against it will be swept away."[113]

Many of Imran Khan's supporters that day were young urbanites, a population that has grown rapidly over the past several decades. One impressive young graduate of the Lahore University of Management Sciences, among Pakistan's very best institutions of higher education, explained later that she supported Imran Khan because he represented something entirely different from the other failed and corrupt politicians. When asked whether her parents felt the same way, she quickly replied that they did not, and that it was not a topic she could even broach with them.[114] The generational divide over Imran Khan is severe.[115]

Teens and twenty-somethings mobbed Khan's rally. They organized on high school and university campuses, delighting in their newfound engagement in politics. In Lahore, one eighteen-year-old Pakistani student sported a badge labeled "hope" under a picture of Khan. She changed her Facebook profile to show support for PTI and might have fit right in with the crowds of young, idealistic Americans who helped Barack Obama win in 2008. Others, like a young Pakistani entrepreneur who flew from Britain to Lahore for the rally and explained, "I am doing this for the love of my country and for change," might

---

[113] Salman Masood, "Political Shift Seen in Rally in Pakistan," *New York Times*, October 30, 2011, http://www.nytimes.com/2011/10/31/world/asia/ex-cricket-star-imran-khan-leads-anti government-protest-in-pakistan.html?_r=2&ref=asia.

[114] Author interview, Lahore, May 2012.

[115] For a smart take on how Pakistan's younger generation is starting to mobilize politically, see Arsla Jawaid, "Game Changer," *World Policy Journal*, Winter 2012/2013, http://www .worldpolicy.org/journal/winter2012/game-changer.

have found themselves at home in one of the "Arab Spring" uprisings earlier the same year.[116]

Young Pakistanis cheered for Khan, but also for the popular musicians who participated in his Lahore rally and at another enormous gathering in Karachi at the end of December. Two prominent musicians to take the stage were Salman Ahmad and Abrar Ul-Haq. Both are artists who, like U2's Bono, have devoted their talents to larger humanitarian causes. These musicians were not merely looking to sell a few million more albums or promote their latest releases; they were associating their own heartfelt idealism with Khan's party.

In Salman Ahmad's case, he was lending the credibility of his own struggle to promote greater tolerance within the Muslim world and between people of different faiths. The United Nations Goodwill Ambassador was calling upon the well of support he built by raising money for countrymen in need, as in 2010 when he released the single "Open Your Eyes" with Peter Gabriel to help Pakistan's millions of flood victims.

Abrar ul Haq took his PTI affiliation even further. He officially joined Khan's party and was later nominated head of its youth wing. In ways that echo and complement Khan's own life story, ul Haq's career began as a teacher at the same Aitchison College that Khan had attended. He went on to become a huge Pakistani pop star, and later a philanthropist who built a general hospital in his hometown near Lahore. Like Khan and so many of the young men and women who came out in support of PTI, Haq was not born into politics.[117] In a country of so many political dynasties, where parliamentary seats are often bequeathed from fathers to sons, this was in itself a meaningful distinction. At Khan's Karachi rally, Haq spoke movingly of the need for a government of the "common man, of the youth, not that of the VIPs," and declared that "a revolution is just waiting to happen."[118]

A Reform Agenda

These passionate endorsements and the palpable energy of Khan's fans over-whelmed some of the cynicism of Pakistani politics, at least temporarily. Khan's party claimed it would back its idealism with action. Unlike the other major parties, the PTI would require its candidates to submit tax records and run in internal primary elections to win the right to fight in national polls. Khan announced that if elected his government would cut corruption by half in

[116] Taha Siddiqui, "Youth Sees Imran as Agent of Change, Hope," *Express Tribune*, October 30, 2011, http://tribune.com.pk/story/284806/youth-sees-imran-as-agent-of-change-hope/.

[117] Waqar Gillani, "Abrar's Hospital All Set to Serve Humanity," *Daily Times*, July 26, 2003, http://www.dailytimes.com.pk/default.asp?page=story_26-7-2003_pg7_15.

[118] Saba Imtiaz, "Imran's Dream Team Wows Karachi," *Express Tribune*, December 25, 2011, http://tribune.com.pk/story/311748/pakistan-tehreek-i-insaf-rally-in-karachi-live-updates/.

its first ninety days.[119] After making examples of some of the nation's most thoroughly corrupt leaders, Khan argued, others would quickly fall into line. They would begin paying their taxes, creating a new stream of revenue that would allow Pakistan to improve government salaries and education funding, and would make Islamabad less dependent on outside donors or international loans. That, in turn, would give Pakistan greater leverage in its relationship with the United States, something that Khan also believed would require a thorough overhaul.[120]

Khan's many critics, and even some of his friends, worried that he erred in overstating just how quick and easy tax reform, anti-corruption, and renegotiating relations with Washington would be. They were right; there is a big difference between igniting a popular movement and governing a nation, as so many revolutionaries have learned throughout history.

Even Khan's efforts to build a new style of party for the 2013 elections, one less rife with corruption and more responsive to constituents, ran headlong into the persistent realities of Pakistani patronage politics. Bowing to the local vote-getting power of entrenched politicians, the PTI only partially implemented internal partly elections even as it took on board a number of seasoned, high profile candidates. These defectors from other political parties, such as Javed Hashmi (from PML-N) and Shah Mahmood Qureshi (from PPP), were not credible standard-bearers for a new style of reformed politics.

Nor, ultimately, did the tsunami of youthful energy and idealism launch Khan into the prime minister's office in May 2013. Instead, in a triumph of traditional machine politics, that job went to Nawaz Sharif, an old-style politician who had already served two terms as prime minister in the 1990s.

PTI's 2013 electoral setbacks do not necessarily diminish the potential benefits of political and economic reform. If Pakistan were to undertake serious reforms in education and the economy, some of the nation's liabilities could turn into assets. Properly employed, Pakistan's bulging youth population could spark massive economic growth as it has in neighboring countries like China and India.

Maleeha Lodhi, Pakistan's former ambassador to the United States and now one of the country's best-known political commentators, believes an agenda of "bold reform" is conceivable despite Pakistan's huge challenges. She argues that Pakistan is already witnessing the rise of an urban middle class that is better able to engage in organized politics. By her logic, the "Mehran men" – lower-middle-class owners of Mehrans, cheap Pakistani-made Suzuki hatchbacks that

[119] Ahmad Hassan, "Imran Announces Intra-Party Polls," *Dawn*, March 26, 2012, http://www.dawn.com/2012/03/26/imran-announces-intra-party-polls.html.
[120] Author interview, May 15, 2012; also Alex Rodriguez, "Pakistan Cricket Legend Imran Khan's Political Cachet Grows," *Los Angeles Times*, March 1, 2012, http://articles.latimes.com/2012/mar/01/world/la-fg-pakistan-khan-20120302/2.

clog many city streets – will be more likely to determine the fate of their nation than the country's Islamist insurgents or feudal lords.[121] Pakistan already has the highest share of population living in urban centers among all South Asian countries. By 2030, half of the country's entire population will live in cities.[122]

The full political mobilization of Pakistan's growing urban middle class would represent a culmination of many different trends in Pakistani society. Chief among these would be the dramatic changes experienced by Pakistan's news media over the past decade.

Media Matters

Pakistan's media culture changed radically after Musharraf opened the airwaves to private competition in 2002. To be sure, "the country has a long tradition of oppositional journalism," as one of Pakistan's top national security reporters explained to me over coffee during his visit to Washington in late 2011. For decades, Pakistan's most intrepid journalists expected that they would land in jail as the inescapable consequence of speaking truth to power. Until the Musharraf regime came in, overt and often heavy-handed censorship was Pakistan's standard practice. This was true even under Pakistan's civilian leaders. For instance, Najam Sethi, one of the country's most decorated and outspoken journalists, was first detained in 1978 by the Zulfikar Ali Bhutto government, then in 1984 by the Zia-ul-Haq regime, and again in 1999 during the rule of Nawaz Sharif. Each time, the detentions were politically motivated.

Pakistan's journalists still work under threat from the state and, increasingly, from terrorists. In addition to his bouts in prison, Sethi has received written death threats from al-Qaeda and the Pakistani Taliban. Several young journalists have been forced to leave their homes in Pakistan and resettle in the United States because their stories had so upset the authorities. In May 2011, the body of Syed Saleem Shahzad, a reporter who routinely wrote about the seamy underbelly of relations between various terrorist groups and the ISI, was fished out of a canal 100 miles from Islamabad. Days before, Shahzad had published a story about secret negotiations between the Pakistani military and al-Qaeda. U.S. officials, including then-chairman of the Joint Chiefs of Staff, Admiral Michael Mullen, claimed that senior Pakistani officials sanctioned the murder.[123]

Pakistan has a very long way to go before its media is remotely free or fair. But these problems cannot negate the huge changes that have already taken

---

[121] Maleeha Lodhi, ed. *Beyond the Crisis State* (New York: Columbia University Press, 2011), p. 74.

[122] G. M. Arif and Shahnaz Hamid, "Urbanization, City Growth, and Quality of Life in Pakistan," *European Journal of Social Sciences*, 10, no. 2 (2009), http://www.eurojournals.com/ejss_10_2_04.pdf.

[123] "Pakistan 'Approved Saleem Shahzad Murder' Says Mullen," *BBC*, July 8, 2011, http://www.bbc.co.uk/news/world-south-asia-14074814.

placc. Where in 1999 the country had two television channels, in 2009 it had seventy-one.[124]

In late 2007, I. A. Rehman, once a major newspaper editor and now a highly respected member of Pakistan's Human Rights Commission, shared his mixed feelings about that incredible expansion.[125] He observed that Pakistan's media outlets provided an enormous megaphone to a new crop of untrained, often irresponsible, reporters and pundits. This new wave swamped an old guard of editors and reporters with its no-holds-barred style. It broke taboos by showing graphic images and broadcasting confrontational debates, quite similar to the way Al Jazeera revolutionized news programming in the Arab world. At the time, the trend was more likely to raise an unpredictable ruckus than to inspire reasoned debate, but if the media started to take its role more seriously, the future might look brighter.

Later in his tenure, Musharraf himself lamented that a media that owed its relatively greater freedom to him had turned so harshly critical of his government. The real turning point came as his regime faltered and he tried to turn off the media as a means to silence his critics. On March 16, 2007, Musharraf attempted to shut down broadcasts by GeoTV – Pakistan's most popular Urdu-language broadcaster – by ordering local police to fire teargas into its Islamabad studio. The move failed. Geo defied the government and was soon back on the air. As the political crisis escalated, the regime and private broadcasters played a game of cat and mouse; each time the government ordered new limits on broadcasts, the news networks attempted to flout or circumvent them. When Pakistani cable networks were turned off, GeoTV and another independent network broadcast by satellite. When satellite dish sales were banned, the networks streamed programming on the Internet.[126]

Eventually, for several weeks in November 2007, it looked as if the authoritarian power of the military-led state would win out. The Musharraf regime finally prevailed upon the United Arab Emirates to shutter the last two broadcasters that had until then escaped Islamabad's reach. At that point, e-mail lists, blogs, YouTube videos, Flickr photos, Facebook groups, and text messages filled the vacuum, spreading news to anyone within earshot of a computer account or cell phone (which is to say nearly everyone in the entire country, since over 40 percent of Pakistanis owned cell phones by 2006).[127]

With the help of new communications technologies and the ingenuity of Pakistani protesters, the news media could no longer be completely fettered, even by a very determined military regime. That moment was a historic breakthrough

---

[124] Muhammad Atif Khan, "The Mediatization of Politics in Pakistan: A Structural Analysis," *Pakistaniaat: A Journal of Pakistan Studies*, 1, no. 1 (2009), p. 33.

[125] Author conversation with I. A. Rehman, September 17, 2007, Washington, DC.

[126] Huma Yusuf, "Old and New Media: Converging during the Pakistan Emergency (March 2007–February 2008)," MIT Center for Civic Media, p. 9.

[127] Yusuf, "Old and New Media," p. 13.

for Pakistan; the media became a power to be reckoned with, not silenced. Musharraf did not immediately appreciate this, nor did his civilian successor, Asif Ali Zardari, who also attempted to shutter GeoTV early in his presidency and later temporarily banned, multiple times, Facebook and YouTube.[128] Yet the reality is that Pakistan's media environment now favors a new breed of politicians whose goal is to exploit the power of the media, not to control it. In today's Pakistan, the news will probably get out, one way or another. This is not to say that Pakistan's government or security services won't ever try to crack down again, but only that they will have to be very committed and willing to pay a high cost, both in terms of public outrage and economic disruption, to silence the media for very long.

The power of the media may one day enable Khan – or another similarly savvy politician – to beat the entrenched patronage networks that have dominated national elections for so long. After that, the question is whether Pakistan's media might also help reformers implement their idealistic agendas. Can the media improve the quality of political debate, or will it remain the raucous and irresponsible force that I. A. Rehman observed in 2007, more prone to destructive sensationalism than anything else? Unfortunately, many journalists in Pakistan today are still part of the problem. They lament that the industry is thoroughly corrupt and that some prominent news editors expect reporters to earn their livings through extortion or trading in privileged information.[129]

Such stories are disillusioning, but there is at least some reason for hope. Members of the media and some citizen groups have attempted to start various forms of nongovernmental regulation. In early 2012, the group Citizens for Free and Responsible Media launched an Internet and letter campaign against a morning show that purported to film raids on Pakistani parks, where young men and women were socializing against the wishes of their conservative families. The protest forced the network to cancel the show, fire its host, and admit that the raids were faked in the first place.[130] The quality of Pakistani journalism may also improve over time, since "there has been an explosion of journalism programs at university level, meaning more qualified workers will be entering the industry."[131] That training has been supplemented by various exchange programs meant to introduce Pakistani journalists to American and other international counterparts.[132]

[128] Michael Kugelman, "Pakistan's Pugnacious Press," *Foreign Policy*, March 22, 2012, http://af pak.foreignpolicy.com/posts/2012/03/22/pakistans_pugnacious_press.

[129] Author conversation with Pakistani journalists, Islamabad, May 16, 2012.

[130] Malik Siraj Akbar, "Sensational Shows Imperil the Future of Pakistan's Fledgling Broadcast Media," *Huffington Post*, March 14, 2012, http://www.huffingtonpost.com/malik-siraj-akbar/sensational-shows-imperil_b_1336819.html?view=print&comm_ref=false.

[131] Huma Yusuf quoted in Akbar, "Sensational Shows Imperil the Future of Pakistan's Fledgling Broadcast Media."

[132] On exchange programs, see http://www.eastwestcenter.org/seminars-and-journalism-fellow ships/journalism-fellowships/pakistan-us-journalists-exchange.

The media has relished its role as a government watchdog, if perhaps too gleefully and indiscriminately for the taste of the last ruling coalition in Islamabad. Although the civilian politicians have suffered the worst abuses at the hands of pundits and columnists, even the military came under fire from the media in 2011 after the U.S. raid on bin Laden's compound. As journalists explained in Islamabad just one week after the raid, the shock and humiliation – first that bin Laden was discovered so deep inside Pakistani territory, second that he was killed by American SEALs, and both without the apparent knowledge of Pakistan's armed forces – was too much for even some of the most "pro-military" television journalists to bear. They vented, publicly, in ways that once would have been impossible. One such Pakistani television anchor, Kamran Khan, told his viewers, "We had the belief that our defense was impenetrable, but look what has happened. Such a massive intrusion and it went undetected."[133]

Unfortunately, even though the media's criticism of government has given its politicians fits, it has yet to make them discernibly better at running the country. For its part, the military has responded to the media with a combination of genuine outreach, some shrewd propaganda, and a heavy dose of intimidation. The latter, along with the threat of violence posed by militants, helps to explain why in 2013 the group Reporters without Borders ranked Pakistan 159th out of 179 nations in press freedom.[134]

Stepping back, it is clear that change is afoot in Pakistan, but it still has a long way to go. The positive potential of Pakistan's youth, its urbanizing middle class, and the media may turn out to be huge. Still, it may be no match for Pakistan's terribly powerful web of entrenched interests, all heavily invested in defending the status quo. Even inside Imran Khan's PTI, an organization energized by the theme of reform and change, it would be hard to bet on the idealistic youth wing beating out the likes of Hamid Gul or Shireen Mazari, both of whom have also enjoyed long-standing ties to the cricket star and his party.

Debating Pakistan's Prospects

Pakistan's future portrait is likely to be a composite sketch with features drawn from each of its four faces. But which features will be most prominent? Pakistan has an abundance of dynamic forces that have already rendered parts of its landscape unrecognizable to its founding generation. The single greatest challenge to contemplating Pakistan's future is that the country is pregnant with possibilities. Twenty years from now Pakistan will have 85 million more people than it does today. In other words, to its nearly 200 million citizens

---

[133] Jane Perlez, "Pakistani Army, Shaken by Raid, Faces New Scrutiny," *New York Times*, May 4, 2011, http://www.nytimes.com/2011/05/05/world/asia/05pakistan.html.

[134] *Press Freedom Index 2013*, Reporters without Borders, Paris, France, http://fr.rsf.org/IMG/pdf/classement_2013_gb-bd.pdf.

Pakistan will add a population equivalent to the size of today's Iran. By mid-century, Pakistan is likely to be home to over 300 million people. That would be over ten times its number at independence in 1947. Those figures alone should offer some perspective about the nature and scale of the changes Pakistan could experience.

Yet there are also important enduring features in Pakistani society that Jinnah and his contemporaries would find familiar, if not necessarily attractive. The core question is how these forces stack up against one another, and how their interplay will shape Pakistan's future. The current scholarly debate over this question breaks down into four camps. Some argue that Pakistan's status quo forces – the feudals and the army – will continue to dominate, producing relative stability for years to come. A second camp, however, sees those same status quo forces as fundamentally destabilizing because they block necessary reforms. A third camp is similarly convinced of potential for social and political instability, but instead of blaming the weakness of the status quo it focuses on the strength of rising challengers, especially Pakistan's violent extremists. And a final camp suggests that change is brewing, but it will be more reformist than revolutionary.[135]

The preeminent example of the first perspective is found in Anatol Lieven's magisterial review of Pakistan's state and society. Lieven writes that the "highly conservative, archaic, even sometimes quite inert and somnolent" Pakistan is most likely to shrug off the competing forces of modernization and change and then "roll over and go back to sleep."[136]

Lieven cautions that Pakistan is a "hard country," immunized to most threats of revolution because the basic building blocks of its society – those immensely powerful kinship networks that bind individuals to their families and communities – "so far have changed with glacial slowness." Pakistan is less susceptible to change, for the better or the worse, than we think.

In the second camp in the debate is John Schmidt, who served as the U.S. political counselor in Islamabad from 1998 to 2001. Schmidt turns Lieven's argument on its head. He argues that the roots of Pakistan's present instability are to be found in its "feudal political establishment."[137] Far from seeing the status quo as a source of stability, as Lieven would have it, Schmidt stresses that the ineptitude, warped outlook, and corruption inherent in Pakistan's

[135] There is growing literature on Pakistan's possible futures. In particular, see Stephen P. Cohen, *The Future of Pakistan* (Washington: Brookings Institution Press, 2011); Michael F. Oppenheimer and Rorry Daniels, "Pakistan 2020," *CGA Scenarios No. 7*, NYU Center for Global Affairs (Fall 2011), http://www.scps.nyu.edu/export/sites/scps/pdf/global-affairs/pakistan-2020-scenarios.pdf; and Jonathan Paris, "Prospects for Pakistan," Legatum Institute (January 2010), http://www.li.com/attachments/ProspectsForPakistan.pdf.
[136] Anatol Lieven, *Pakistan: A Hard Country* (New York: Public Affairs, 2011), pp. 29, 16.
[137] John R. Schmidt, "The Unravelling of Pakistan," *Survival*, 51, no. 3 (June/July 2009), p. 29. See also John R. Schmidt, *The Unraveling: Pakistan in the Age of Jihad* (New York: Farrar, Straus and Giroux, 2011).

traditional political culture props open the door to the extremists. "Resistant to change, disposed to muddle through, inclined to blame others for their problems and single-mindedly determined to preserve their narrow class interests even as their world is collapsing around them, [Pakistan's elites] are leading their country along a short road to chaos," he warns darkly.[138]

Fearing that Pakistan is playing with fire as it faces "a dangerous and fluid moment" in its history, veteran *Washington Post* reporter Pamela Constable takes up the third position in the debate.[139] Unlike Schmidt and Lieven, who focus on Pakistan's repressive continuity, Constable is more concerned about the forces of change. Her reporting from the region over more than a decade is marked by a focus on the everyday lives of Pakistanis. It leads her to observe that some recent trends in Pakistani society – such as the "new phenomenon of grassroots leaders and women becoming involved in politics" – are beneficial.[140] Yet on balance she worries that positive reforms are being swamped by "the growing violent threat and the popular appeal of radical Islam."[141] Unless Pakistan's political and military leaders more effectively grapple with the profound changes sweeping Pakistani society, Constable concludes that "they may be condemning a new generation of Pakistanis to make bricks, mop floors, or put on suicide vests."[142]

Finally, Maleeha Lodhi, the former Pakistani ambassador to the United States, takes up the case for a less pessimistic outlook. Lodhi argues that constructive – rather than destructive – change is quite possible in Pakistan. She admits that the country faces significant obstacles, but it "may yet escape its difficult first sixty-three years, resolve its problems, and re-imagine its future."[143] Pakistan's urban, barely bourgeois classes could redirect the energies of an existing political party or coalesce behind an entirely new organization. Either way, Lodhi concludes that it would be a mistake to minimize their power or overlook their potential to improve the quality of Pakistan's government and pave the way to a brighter future.

Clearly, even for people who know it well, Pakistan can look as if it is standing still or heading in opposite directions, with radically different implications for its people and the rest of the world. Each of these perspectives actually captures an important truth about Pakistan's present as well as clues to foreseeing its deeply uncertain future.

Lieven is right that Pakistan changes slowly, that important aspects of the society look remarkably like they did decades or even centuries ago. This is an important corrective to the hyperventilating newspaper headlines and

[138] Schmidt, "The Unravelling," p. 51.
[139] Pamela Constable, *Playing with Fire* (New York: Random House, 2011), p. xii.
[140] Constable, *Playing with Fire*, p. xx.
[141] Constable, *Playing with Fire*, p. xii.
[142] Constable, *Playing with Fire*, p. xx.
[143] Lodhi, *Beyond the Crisis State*, p. 2.

magazine articles that have too often predicted Pakistan's imminent collapse. Yet in his search for continuity, Lieven underestimates the ways in which the inherent corruption of Pakistan's establishment makes it vulnerable. That is Schmidt's essential contribution; Pakistan's traditional powerbrokers have been weakened by time, not strengthened. More troubling, as Constable describes, they now face challengers who are at once more popular and more violent than in the past. However, all is not lost. Lodhi's call to arms suggests that if Pakistani reformers are effectively mobilized, they still have a chance to alter Pakistan's unsettling trends.

These important insights help to frame the following three conclusions about Pakistan's trajectory.

(1) Revolution and state failure are unlikely in Pakistan . . . at least for now.

One of the most frequent questions Americans ask about Pakistan is whether it might suffer an Iran-style revolution or surrender to a Somalia-like collapse. This is not especially surprising, since if you look at any of the lists of "fragile" or "failing" states, Pakistan usually shows up near the top in bright red.[144]

As this chapter shows, all of the standard warning signs are there. Pakistan suffers from ethnic and sectarian conflicts, state corruption, internal insurgency, a history of turbulent politics, and a troubled economy.[145] Its ruling governments are usually ineffective when it comes to meeting the basic needs of the country's people. Even when civilian politicians are nominally in charge, their popular legitimacy is weakened because their parties are run like corrupt family dynasties, not democracies.[146] In Islamabad, governments come and go, but nearly all are what scholars of international development might call "limited access orders," where the rich and powerful use the state mainly to make sure that they stay rich and powerful, and everyone else suffers.[147]

However, even though Pakistan is vulnerable to failure and revolution, we have not seen it . . . yet. The reason is twofold. First, Pakistan's ruling elites and its army are still strong enough to resist revolutionary change or a dramatic collapse. They still have a finger in every pie, even those, like Imran Khan's PTI, that claim to be dedicated to change.

Second, even though Pakistan's media is growing more outspoken and its activists successfully took to the streets to bring down the Musharraf regime,

---

[144] "The Failed States Index 2011," *Foreign Policy*, http://www.foreignpolicy.com/articles/2011/06/17/2011_failed_states_index_interactive_map_and_rankings.

[145] These are very close to Jack Goldstone's five "pathways to state failure" in Jack A. Goldstone, "Pathways to State Failure," *Conflict Management and Peace Science*, 25 (2008), p. 288.

[146] Jack Goldstone, one of the world's foremost experts on revolution and state failure, argues that effectiveness and legitimacy (or the perception of justice) are the two factors that make a state prone to revolution. See Jack A. Goldstone, "Toward a Fourth Generation of Revolutionary Theory," *Annual Review of Political Science*, 4 (2001), p. 148.

[147] On "limited access orders," see Daron Acemoglu and James Robinson, *Why Nations Fail: The Origins of Power, Prosperity, and Poverty* (New York: Crown, 2012).

the country still lacks a "transmission belt" to channel the grievances felt by many of its people into effective political action. The best example of this came in 2010, when epic floods inundated a fifth of the country and displaced tens of millions of Pakistanis from their homes. Many foreign observers worried that this might be a turning point in Pakistan's history; that the already rickety institutions of the state and society would finally come undone by the stress. In fact, nothing of the sort happened. Part of the explanation has to be that the Pakistanis who suffered most from the floods were also disproportionately poor and incapable of turning their desperate needs into political action. As has been the case for decades, they suffered in silence, with little effect on the country's politics.

As long as Pakistan's status quo has its staunch defenders and most everyone else lacks the ability to rise up in opposition, Pakistan will muddle along as it has for decades. Slowly but surely, however, both of these conditions appear to be changing. Traditional elites face a welter of new challenges and threats. Opposition forces are finding new resources and tools to help them mobilize. One day, perhaps even within the next few years, Pakistan's balance could tip unexpectedly, as it did in Tunisia when in late December 2010 a young fruit seller set himself on fire in protest against the government and sparked a successful revolution. If that happens, many of the other prerequisites for revolutionary change, or even for state collapse, will be found in abundance. One revealing indicator of this is that many of Pakistan's wealthiest citizens have prepared quick exit plans. They have purchased homes and secured citizenship abroad, from Dubai and Malaysia to the United Kingdom and Canada. If and when they rush to the exits, Washington should brace for the ugly consequences.

(2) Pakistan is already vulnerable to nightmarish scenarios, even if they are not likely to result in revolution or state collapse.
Pakistan is a country of crises. Even if it finds a way to pull out of its gradual downward slide, it will remain vulnerable to horrible acts of terrorism and violence. Pakistan's terrorists could once again provoke deadly confrontations with India, or even with the United States. Historic ties between Pakistan's security services and groups like LeT, the "insider threat" posed by outfits like HuT, and the continual growth of its nuclear arsenal mean that every day without a new crisis is a fortunate one for Pakistan.

Three weeks after the U.S. raid on bin Laden's compound, a very different sort of raid took place in Karachi. A small group of terrorist commandos attacked the Mehran naval base. They held out for over fifteen hours, killed thirteen personnel, and destroyed two of Pakistan's U.S.-supplied P-3 Orion patrol planes. The attack bore all the hallmarks of an inside job. Numerous eyewitnesses said the raiders appeared to know the compound and may have been wearing navy uniforms. Subsequent investigations linked the raid to al-Qaeda and the Pakistani Taliban. A former Navy commando, terminated from service in 2003, was arrested for providing support to the raiding party.

The point of this story is not, as some would have it, that Pakistan's nuclear installations are easy targets for the terrorists. By all accounts, those installations are far better protected than Mehran was. Moreover, it is a far easier thing to destroy a couple of planes than to make off with a nuclear weapon.

The point is that the terrorist cancer has clearly taken root in parts of Pakistan's military. If it is permitted to spread, then the chances of a far more dangerous outcome, like the gradual theft of small amounts of fissile material or the successful assassination of Pakistan's top political and military leadership, become immeasurably higher. When characters like Hafiz Saeed, Hamid Gul, and Sami ul Haq appear together at public rallies, they appear to enjoy at least the tacit support of the state. Such developments offer too little confidence in Pakistan's ability to ward off the entire range of insider threats it faces.[148]

(3) To achieve their goals, reformers need to think beyond Pakistan's borders. Looking to the potential for constructive change, it is clear that any successful reform of Pakistan will require a great deal of hard work by Pakistanis themselves. The country is too vast and complicated to be "fixed" from the outside in. However, even well-intentioned Pakistani reformers will face enormous obstacles and could use a helping hand. Their countrymen with the deepest pockets – the ones most capable of paying for improvements in education or the nation's physical infrastructure – are also the most heavily invested in perpetuating business as usual. And the nation's most powerful institutions – the military and intelligence services – also prefer to maintain the status quo and to protect their privileges and autonomy.

To break the logjam, reformers will need allies from beyond their borders, at least at the outset. In time, they may be able to extract a greater share of resources from inside Pakistan, if only because collecting taxes from an expanding economic base should be easier than squeezing revenues from an economy in crisis.

This is not to say that Pakistan should continue to depend upon foreign assistance and loans. That may be a necessary stopgap, but the better way to think about Pakistan's economic opportunity is to more effectively realize its geographic potential. Situated between India, China, and the energy-rich lands of the Persian Gulf and Central Asia, Pakistan is naturally positioned to benefit from freer trade and investments in corridors that would improve, for instance, the flow of fossil fuels across Asia from west and north to east and south. China is the easiest regional target for securing greater investments in the Pakistani economy, but India offers the greatest untapped potential for trade and business collaboration.

---

[148] For a catalogue of many "insider threats" over the past two decades, see Imtiaz Gul, "Jihadis in the Ranks," *Newsline*, September 28, 2012, http://www.newslinemagazine.com/2012/09/cover-story-jihadis-in-the-ranks/.

For reform-minded Pakistanis, the goal in any of these ventures would be to structure new economic relationships in ways that provide jobs and expand tax revenues so that even if Pakistan's rich and powerful continue to take a healthy cut, there is more left over for everyone else. These are not easy tasks, but they at least hint at how Pakistan's reformers might team up with foreign allies – possibly even with the United States – to achieve a better future for Pakistan.

Unfortunately, that potential remains a long way off. Today's advocates of reform, including politicians like Imran Khan, often sound decidedly parochial, sometimes even xenophobic, when they discuss solutions to Pakistan's problems. For its part, Washington often finds itself in bed with many of Pakistan's least reform-minded leaders, from the feudal elites to the military. This reflects a reasonable American fear of change and instability inside Pakistan. But to the extent that the United States influences Pakistan's future, that prophecy could be a self-fulfilling one. In other words, if the United States keeps picking the sides it has chosen for the past sixty years, it will do little to help potential reformers and far more to support the kind of repression that fuels a revolutionary backlash.

3

Why Do They Hate Us?

Since Pakistan's founding in 1947, its relationship with the United States has gone through extreme highs and lows. Pakistanis often talk of American swings from alliance to abandonment.[1] If the post-9/11 period of cooperation runs its course and ends in estrangement or conflict, it would only reinforce that long-standing pattern and lend credence to the idea that Washington and Islamabad are incapable of building a lasting foundation for any sort of mutually beneficial relationship.

Part of the problem between the United States and Pakistan throughout the first five decades of their interaction was that both sides failed to value the relationship on its own terms.[2] In its cooperation with many other states, the United States often sees inherent value in trade, cultural affinities, or a shared worldview. In cooperation with Pakistan, on the other hand, Washington tended to focus on external goals, such as containing communism, opening secret talks with Beijing, or arming the Afghan mujahedeen. American leaders saw Pakistan as but a pawn in the broader geopolitical chess match.

Over its entire history, Pakistan kept its eyes trained on India. Pakistan always valued Washington's assistance as an external balancer in the regional competition against its larger neighbor, with which it had split in the violent Partition of 1947 after years of political infighting among the top leaders of the movement that ejected British rule from the subcontinent. Whenever the

[1] Long time South Asia hands Teresita and Howard Schaffer use the evocative metaphor of marriages and divorces in describing the ups and downs of the relationship. See Howard B. Schaffer and Teresita C. Schaffer, *How Pakistan Negotiates with the United States: Riding the Roller Coaster* (Washington: United States Institute of Peace, 2011).

[2] See especially Dennis Kux, *The United States and Pakistan, 1947–2000: Disenchanted Allies* (Baltimore: Johns Hopkins University Press, 2001) and Robert J. McMahon, *The Cold War on the Periphery* (New York: Columbia University Press, 1996), both of which serve as essential sources for this chapter.

United States was unhelpful in this respect, Pakistan sought other – often much riskier – solutions, such as arming and training militant groups and expanding its nuclear arsenal.

The upshot of this unhappy history is that for each side, disagreements have been layered one upon the next. In Pakistan, the experience of dealing with the United States has bred alienation, anger, and in some cases, hatred. All threaten prospects for a constructive relationship. Whether military or civilian, ruling regimes in Islamabad now face a public that doubts the benefit of cooperation with Washington. American officials stationed in Pakistan face debilitating security threats, and they also confront the more mundane challenge of living and working in a society that tends to view the United States with hostility. Stunning majorities – usually over 75 percent – of Pakistanis have unfavorable views of the United States.[3]

PAKISTAN'S THREE STRANDS OF ANTI-AMERICANISM

Three types of anti-Americanism define Pakistani perspectives today.[4] The first, what might be called a "liberal anti-Americanism," is primarily a reaction to Washington's all-too-cozy relations with Pakistan's military. Now a minority view, the perspective remains rooted in the left of Pakistan's political spectrum. Its origins date to the earliest phase of cooperation between the United States and Pakistan's army-dominated state. This perspective was again on prominent display during the waning days of the Musharraf regime, when Pakistani civilian politicians and liberal activists accused the United States of serially coddling military dictators.

The second strand of "nationalist anti-Americanism" comes from the center-right, and reflects a sense that partnership with the United States has never lived up to its strategic promise. It has cost Pakistan dearly but delivered little. The origins of this perspective can be traced to America's "abandonments" of Pakistan in 1965 and again at the close of the Cold War. Pakistani nationalists have developed an entire narrative of relations with the United States centered upon America as a fair-weather friend.

Finally, the 1980s – and especially Washington's support to the Afghan mujahedeen – fueled the rise of the most violent anti-Americanism of the jihadists. This strand is founded upon a rejection not merely of U.S. policies and strategies but of American principles and ideals. Pakistan's Islamist extremists are not unified; fortunately their internal divisions keep them at war

---

[3] According to a 2012 survey, 80 percent of Pakistanis hold an unfavorable view of the United States, and 74 percent of Pakistanis viewed the United States as an enemy. Pew Global Attitudes Project, June 27, 2012, http://www.pewglobal.org/2012/06/27/pakistani-public-opinion-ever-more-critical-of-u-s/.

[4] Professor Mohammad Waseem of the Lahore University of Management Sciences provides an outstanding scholarly treatment of similar issues in his symposium paper, "Perceptions about America in Pakistan," *Aziya Kenkyu*, 50, no. 2 (April 2004).

with one another in ways that undermine their prospects for seizing power over the state. They are dangerous nonetheless, and their ideas find sympathy, or stoke fears, among a much larger segment of the society.

Together, the history of these strands of anti-Americanism offers a window into the overall history of the relationship between the United States and Pakistan. Unfortunately, the post-9/11 decade has added new layers of frustration, grievances, and complications.

THE ANTI-AMERICANISM OF PAKISTAN'S LEFTISTS AND LIBERALS

In January 1955, John Foster Dulles was named *Time*'s Man of the Year. The magazine's editors lauded President Eisenhower's secretary of state for his energetic diplomacy, noting that Dulles spent 1954 in a "ceaseless round of travel, logging 101,521 miles." True to his reputation as one of America's foremost cold warriors, Dulles's primary mission in foreign capitals was "to develop the cohesion and strength that would make Communist aggression less likely."[5]

Eisenhower came into office committed to reducing U.S. military expenditures without opening vulnerabilities to Moscow.[6] To achieve this goal on the military front, he adopted the controversial strategy of "massive retaliation," which Dulles unveiled in a famously provocative speech to the Council on Foreign Relations on January 12, 1954.[7] By threatening a devastating nuclear response, the administration believed it could deter Moscow from aggression even though the Soviet Union was believed to have a stronger conventional military than the United States.

In the diplomatic arena, Dulles set to work building a web of new formal and informal alliances to extend U.S. influence worldwide without having to pay for, or deploy, U.S. troops at every point of possible communist expansion. The Korean War had convinced the administration of the extreme costs of the alternative. Because "massive atomic and thermonuclear retaliation is not the kind of power which could most usefully be evoked under all circumstances," he wrote in *Foreign Affairs*, "security for the free world depends... upon the development of collective security and community power rather than upon purely national potentials."[8] Dulles fit Pakistan – and a good many other states – into his sweeping vision of the Cold War conflict, even though

---

[5] "Man of the Year," *Time*, January 3, 1955.

[6] On Eisenhower's "New Look" strategy, see John Lewis Gaddis, *Strategies of Containment*, (Oxford: Oxford University, 1982), pp. 127–197; also Richard H. Immerman, *John Foster Dulles: Piety, Pragmatism, and Power in U.S. Foreign Policy* (Wilmington: SR Books, 1999), p. 50.

[7] Samuel F. Wells, "The Origins of Massive Retaliation," *Political Science Quarterly*, 96, no. 1 (Spring 1981), p. 34.

[8] John Foster Dulles, "Policy for Security and Peace," *Foreign Affairs*, 32, no. 3 (April 1954).

there were good reasons from the start to fear that the fit was not a good one.[9]

Dulles believed that Pakistan, along with other states of the "Northern tier" – Turkey, Iran, and Iraq – could be pulled together to defend a fraying Middle East and its essential oil fields from Soviet invasion. He thought that the Northern Tier, if properly trained and equipped, could blunt a Soviet move against the Persian Gulf long enough for the United States to muster a counterstrike. After its own assessments, the Pentagon endorsed Dulles's plan for Pakistan, based on a similar logic of regional defense.

In retrospect, the strategy behind the U.S. military alliance with Pakistan looks, as historian Robert J. McMahon puts it, "curiously imprecise and inchoate."[10] McMahon and others have raised doubts about whether Pakistan could ever have provided a defensive platform for the Middle East anything like what Dulles had in mind, at any realistic price. They also observe that building up a relatively weak Pakistani ally soured relations with much larger India. Indeed, New Delhi's prickly Jawaharlal Nehru railed against U.S. plans to assist Pakistan's military. He contended, correctly, that whatever Pakistan's anti-communist rhetoric might be, U.S. assistance to Pakistan would more likely be directed against India than against a Soviet invasion.

Dulles, for his part, was confident in his approach and angered by Nehru's argument, being deeply skeptical that neutralist India would help the United States in its Cold War struggle under any circumstances. Dulles's view prevailed. Eight months after Dulles's trip to Karachi, President Eisenhower agreed to provide Pakistan with military aid. In May 1954, the United States and Pakistan formally signed a mutual assistance agreement.

The scale of the assistance package would be a source of contentious negotiations over the next two years. Washington's initial aid proposals of roughly $30 million shocked Pakistan's leaders; they had expected a more generous offer.[11] When General Ayub Khan, Pakistan's top military officer and later its first military autocrat, heard Washington's proposal he complained to the U.S. consul general in Lahore, "I've stuck my neck out for the Americans. But now I can't go on doing it, because you've gone back on your word."[12] Ayub's frustration was not confined to closed-door diplomacy. Through multiple channels,

---

[9] On the general Cold War strategy of establishing regional groupings to resist Soviet aggression and Pakistan's place in that approach, see James Spain, "Military Assistance for Pakistan," *American Political Science Review*, 48, no. 3 (September 1954), p. 749. Dulles's predecessors in the Truman administration had also appreciated that logic, but not to the extent of seeking a formal alliance with Pakistan. George Lerski argues this point in "The Pakistan-American Alliance: A Reevaluation of the Past Decade," *Asian Survey*, 8, no. 5 (May 1968), p. 402.

[10] McMahon, *The Cold War on the Periphery*, p. 274.

[11] See the conversation with Pakistan's prime minister as recounted by U.S. State Department officials in *Foreign Relations of the United States*, 1952–1954, Vol. 11, pp. 1868–9, http://images.library.wisc.edu/FRUS/EFacs2/1952-54v11p2/reference/frus.frus195254v11p2.i0007.pdf.

[12] McMahon, *The Cold War on the Periphery*, pp. 200–205, esp. p. 204.

including timely leaks to the media, Pakistan skillfully lobbied Washington. Eventually the Eisenhower administration agreed to arm and equip five-and-a-half Pakistani army divisions at a huge total cost of over \$500 million from 1956 through December 1959.[13] Sustaining the force in subsequent years was projected to cost billions more. Pakistan's own weak economy meant that Washington would foot the bill with no end in sight.

After the fact, Eisenhower harbored grave doubts about the decision to assist Pakistan. The president had always been concerned that by arming Pakistan Washington was also alienating India. He became increasingly worried about the spiraling costs to Washington of building a Pakistani military that was well beyond the means of Pakistan's own developing economy. At a meeting of the National Security Council on January 3, 1957, he lamented the "terrible error" of committing to military investments in such a weak ally. But at that stage the president concluded there was no easy way out of the mess, since Washington had made a commitment and breaking it "might have severe repercussions on our relations with Pakistan, and might even destroy the Baghdad Pact."[14]

On the Pakistani side, cracks in public support for partnership with the United States appeared almost as soon as the two countries signed their 1954 mutual assistance agreement. The main problem was the instability of Pakistan's own political system. Pakistan's weak and increasingly undemocratic governing institutions could not manage the country's rolling political and economic crises. The more fragile Pakistan's ruling clique felt, the more it turned to Washington for support. And Washington, fearing the downfall of its Pakistani partners, especially those in the military, grudgingly stuck with them even when they lacked popular legitimacy. The United States watched throughout the 1950s as its partners in Pakistan's military and civilian bureaucracy gradually edged out the vestiges of parliamentary democracy. U.S. officials never took firm action to defend electoral democracy in Pakistan, even if they did fear the consequences of its failure.[15] Pakistan's first attempt at elected government ended in 1958 when General Ayub Khan placed the country under army rule. This, in turn, reinforced popular resentment toward the United States.[16]

The perceptive Pakistani professor of political science, Mohammad Waseem, observes that the protest movement that ousted Ayub in 1969 dubbed him and his colleagues "American stooges."[17] Pakistani opponents of military rule

[13] The assistance figures are in 1950s dollars. See McMahon, *The Cold War on the Periphery*, p. 206.
[14] U.S. Department of State, *Foreign Relations of the United States, 1955–1957: South Asia*, p. 27.
[15] Kux recounts that the U.S. embassy in Pakistan was under instruction to counsel Pakistani leaders against the anti-democratic 1958 coup, but that advice went unheeded, perhaps because there was nothing backing it up. See Kux, *The United States and Pakistan, 1947–2000*, p. 99 where he cites "State Department telegram to Embassy Karachi," October 6, 1958, *Foreign Relations of the United States, 1968–60*, Vol. 15, pp. 666–7.
[16] See McMahon, *The Cold War on the Periphery*, pp. 209–10.
[17] Waseem, "Perceptions about America in Pakistan," p. 36.

reprised similar themes – that military dictators were in power only by the grace of the United States – during the Zia (1977–88) and Musharraf (1999–2008) eras. But it was Zulfikar Ali Bhutto who most effectively combined his anti-Americanism with his political agenda. Bhutto's populist leadership in the early 1970s "cultivated a mass perception that American intervention had worked against democracy in favor of the military establishment."[18]

Zulfikar Ali Bhutto

Bhutto was born to an elite landowning family in Pakistan's Sindh province. His hometown was not far from the ruined city of Mohenjo-daro, constructed well over 4,000 years ago as part of a majestic Indus valley civilization that reached its heights during the time of Egypt's Old Kingdom.[19] For millennia, Bhutto's home region of Larkhana was extremely fertile, unlike much of the rest of the province. That fertility translated into vast wealth for the Bhuttos, who ruled over huge tracts of farmland in a style that can only be described as feudal. Sadly, much of Sindh is ruled in a similar manner to this day.[20]

Zulfikar Ali Bhutto enjoyed the privileges of that wealth and the unusual opportunities it offered. His undergraduate years at the University of California at Berkeley exposed him to political science, history, and a heavy dose of the American "high life" that was easily afforded by the well-heeled playboy. It also proved that greater familiarity with America does not always inspire greater affection.[21]

Upon his return to Pakistan, Bhutto's family connections and political acumen earned the young politician a spot in Ayub's cabinet practically overnight. By the 1960s, Bhutto's anti-Western diatribes and his pro-Beijing attitude irritated Washington, which at the time considered Mao's communist China a dangerous, revolutionary state.[22] Bhutto was perfectly happy to be the Pakistani government's most outspoken "Yankee hater," a role he played most prominently when he served as Ayub's foreign minister from 1963 to 1966.[23]

[18] Waseem, "Perceptions about America in Pakistan," p. 36.
[19] For more on Mohenjo-daro, see Alice Albinia, *Empires of the Indus: The Story of a River* (New York: W.W. Norton, 2010).
[20] On the present state of Sindh's feudals, see William Dalrymple, "A New Deal in Pakistan," *New York Review of Books*, April 3, 2008, http://www.nybooks.com/articles/archives/2008/apr/03/a-new-deal-in-pakistan; also Lieven, *Pakistan: A Hard Country* (New York: Public Affairs, 2011), pp. 329–38.
[21] The wellsprings of Bhutto's own anti-Americanism are not entirely clear. Later in his career, he identified American imperialism in South Asia and, in particular, Washington's hypocritical and imbalanced dealings with India and Pakistan, as the source of his disillusionment, and it is possible that this was his perspective even during his days as a student in California. See Zulfikar Ali Bhutto, *The Myth of Independence* (London: Oxford University Press, 1969).
[22] For a revealing exchange between Bhutto and President Lyndon Johnson, see Kux, *The United States and Pakistan, 1947–2000*, pp. 147–8.
[23] Bhutto used these words himself when he met with President Nixon in 1971. See Kux, *The United States and Pakistan, 1947–2000*, p. 204.

At various points in his political career, Bhutto moderated his anti-Western rhetoric, but he never surrendered his basic suspicions of the United States.

Ayub broke with Bhutto in 1966. By some accounts, Ayub finally acceded to Washington's demand that Bhutto be ditched in the aftermath of the 1965 war with India.[24] The Pakistanis started that war in an attempt to seize the contested territory of Kashmir. Failing at that mission and facing a costly stalemate or worse, Ayub grudgingly accepted a settlement brokered by the Soviets in Tashkent that delivered a cease-fire but no Indian concessions on Kashmir. Because the Ayub regime had so stoked anti-Indian war hysteria at home and raised expectations of imminent territorial conquest, Tashkent was politically radioactive. Bhutto, Ayub's foreign minister at the time, later claimed that he opposed Tashkent and offered his resignation over it several times but was at first refused by Ayub.[25] Whatever the case, Bhutto was out of a job and thoroughly alienated from Ayub.

In the political wilderness, Bhutto founded the Pakistan Peoples Party (PPP), "an anti-Ayub political movement that espoused populist economic policies and a pro-China, anti-U.S., and anti-India foreign policy."[26] Bhutto appealed to the masses like none other, promising "roti, kapra, makaan," or food, clothing, and shelter for all. From 1966 to 1970, he built the PPP from scratch, assiduously cultivating a range of constituencies. He honed his skills at mass politics, something that had not been part of his repertoire in the Ayub government. On the campaign trail, he never missed an opportunity to blast the Ayub regime for its ignominious acceptance of Tashkent.[27] When this charge was lashed to Bhutto's fiery rhetoric about American imperialism, it was quite clear that the charismatic politician had found a devastatingly effective way to tar Ayub and Washington with the same brush.

With speed that surprised even the extraordinarily ambitious Bhutto, the PPP grew into a mass movement and catapulted him to victory in West Pakistan's 1970 elections, even though the PPP had no appeal in East Pakistan. After Pakistan's agonizing loss to India in the 1971 war, in which East Pakistan declared its independence as Bangladesh, Bhutto assumed power over the rump state in the west. The defeated military lay in shambles. Almost 80,000 of its troops were held by India as prisoners of war. Pakistan's top general had resigned, handing uncontested power to Bhutto.[28]

---

[24] See George J. Lerski, "The Pakistan-American Alliance: A Reevaluation of the Past Decade," *Asian Survey*, 8, no. 5 (May 1968), p. 414.

[25] See J. Henry Korson, "Contemporary Problems of Pakistan," *International Studies in Sociology and Social Anthropology*, 15 (1974), p. 58; Salmaan Taseer, *Bhutto: A Political Biography* (1980) reproduced by Sani Hussain Panhwar, pp. 69–73, www.bhutto.org.

[26] Kux, *The United States and Pakistan*, 1947–2000, p. 171.

[27] Taseer, *Bhutto: A Political Biography*, p. 67, www.bhutto.org.

[28] The long list of senior officers forced out after the war by Bhutto demonstrated his supremacy. See Hasan-Askari Rizvi, *Military, State and Society in Pakistan* (Lahore: Sang-e-Meel, 2003), p. 144.

Bhutto's total dominance over his traumatized nation is still viewed by many Pakistanis as the apotheosis of civilian control over the military. In liberal circles there is a nostalgic sense that he might have used that authority to cement the primacy of civilian rule and representative democracy once and for all. Bhutto instead attempted to rebuild the military, believing he could control it and use it to suppress opposition in the provinces of Baluchistan and the northwest frontier. Similarly, Bhutto's socialist-tinged economic schemes, including his selective nationalization of companies held by some of Pakistan's wealthiest families, paid no real dividends.[29]

Moreover, Bhutto's credentials as a democrat must be scrutinized closely. Bhutto's creation of the PPP as a party in civilian opposition to the military is only one piece of the story. Often less well remembered is that his ascent to power was enabled, or at least accelerated, by the breakup of East and West Pakistan in 1971. Bhutto's intransigence in negotiations with the Awami League (AL) – the majority party of East Pakistan, later Bangladesh – contributed to the breakup of the state.[30]

Of course, the pairing of East and West Pakistan in a single political unit separated by a hostile India was an odd one from the start. Underlying differences between the Punjabi-dominated west and the Bengali-dominated east were only exacerbated in the decades after independence. At the core of the AL's 1970 appeal to East Pakistanis was the sense that West Pakistan treated them more like a colony than an equal part of the nation. The AL campaigned for greater autonomy from Islamabad. When the AL swept the balloting in East Pakistan to score a surprising majority in the parliamentary elections of 1970, it presented West Pakistanis with the uncomfortable specter of Bengali rule.

Had Pakistan remained united, Bhutto's PPP would have had to play second fiddle to the AL. This did not sit well with the ambitious Bhutto, who argued repeatedly during the post-election period that "a majority alone doesn't count in national politics," thus revealing at least some discomfort with one of democracy's core principles.[31] Bhutto's intransigence on this point – coupled, of course, with the army's genocidal mishandling of opposition in East Pakistan, the AL's own political aspirations, and India's intervention in the civil war that ensued – ultimately cut Pakistan in two and created an independent Bangladesh.

Bhutto's discomfort with the principles of democratic majority rule did not dissipate after the war. For him, the purpose of the PPP was to serve as a

---

[29] This is the conclusion reached by historian Ian Talbot in his excellent review of Bhutto's legacy in *Pakistan: A Modern History* (New York: Palgrave Macmillan, 2005), pp. 215–44.

[30] For an even-handed historical review of the 1970 elections and Bhutto's involvement in the events that led to Bangladeshi independence, see Talbot, *Pakistan: A Modern History*, pp. 194–213.

[31] Bhutto's broader point was that the PPP's special place as a voice of opposition to the military warranted it a special role in any future government, but of course the AL's leader, Sheikh Mujib, argued that his party was entitled to rule as it had won a majority of Pakistan's national assembly seats. See Talbot, *Pakistan: A Modern History*, p. 205.

vehicle to advance his own power. Bhutto ran the PPP like the Sindhi feudal he was, with no regard for building an institution that was internally democratic. That the party has become a dynastic inheritance, passed from Bhutto to his daughter Benazir, then to her husband Asif Ali Zardari, and almost certainly to their son, Bilawal, after that, bears testament to its compromised democratic foundations.

Bhutto's Legacy

In spite of all the weaknesses of the PPP, the aspiration of civilian democratic rule that Bhutto symbolized in the early 1970s also left an imprint that persists to this day. In the first week of May 2011, the shocking revelation that the United States had found and killed bin Laden right under the army's nose raised a chorus of Pakistani criticism about the army's ineptitude. For at least a few days after the Abbottabad raid, there was a lively debate over whether Pakistan might again have reached a "1971 moment" in which the civilian government could firmly impose its will over the army. It was quickly apparent that Pakistan had not. Had there been a politician of Bhutto's ambition and caliber poised to seize power, perhaps the situation would have been different.[32]

There is a sad irony to the fact that Bhutto eventually met his end at the hands of the army, an institution he had failed to cut down to size when he had the chance. Army Chief Zia-ul-Haq unseated him in 1977 and had him hanged in 1979. The proximate cause of Bhutto's downfall was the PPP's heavy-handed rigging of national elections in 1977. The manipulation was so blatant that opposition groups came out to protest en masse, and Bhutto could only restore order by calling the army into the streets. In the midst of the crisis, Bhutto's anti-Americanism was on display once more. On the floor of the National Assembly, he charged, without any serious basis, that the United States was financing a "vast, colossal, huge international conspiracy" against him. He sought to do so in an effort to rally his own supporters and deflect attention from the domestic crisis of his own making.[33] Bhutto's desperate ploy failed.

Bhutto's political legacy, inherited by a range of influential intellectuals and politicians, informs a leftist and liberal anti-Americanism that is today a tiny minority view. It is important, however, because it deprives the United States of vocal, articulate friends in elite Pakistani circles. In April 2008, at a high-end hotel restaurant in Islamabad, I sat down to lunch with one such individual,

---

[32] Some Pakistanis have argued that members of the Zardari government actually attempted a similar sort of power play in the days after the Abbottabad raid, ultimately leading to the "memogate" scandal in fall 2011. For more on this highly contested episode, see "Memo Offered to Revamp Pakistan's Security Policy," *Dawn*, November 18, 2011, http://dawn.com/2011/11/19/memo-offered-to-revamp-pakistans-security-policy/; Mansoor Ijaz, "An Insider Analysis of Pakistan's 'Memogate'" *The Daily Beast*, December 5, 2011, http://www.thedailybeast.com/newsweek/2011/12/04/an-insider-analysis-of-pakistan-s-memogate.html.

[33] For the backstory to these allegations, see Kux, *The United States and Pakistan, 1947–2000*, p. 230. See also, Rizvi, *Military, State and Society in Pakistan*, p. 164.

Aitzaz Ahsan. The trim, graying sixty-three-year-old president of Pakistan's Supreme Court Bar Association offered me a nod and then, gazing somewhere over my right shoulder, stated in a matter-of-fact tone, "I hope you realize the extreme discomfort I feel dining with an American these days." Ahsan, born just two years before Pakistan's birth, is the quintessential Pakistani liberal anti-American.

Ahsan's testy mood at our lunch meeting was not a surprise. A gifted politician and activist, he was stopped on the way to our table by several other well-heeled patrons hoping to shake his hand and offer thanks to the man who had stood at the center of the latest bout of Pakistan's national civil-military drama. The previous year, Ahsan had won fame for being the driving force of the epic lawyers' movement that had defied Musharraf and forced him to reinstate Supreme Court Chief Justice Iftikhar Muhammad Chaudhry. Ahsan was the chief justice's attorney and, at times, his "chauffeur." The two cruised at a snail's pace in Ahsan's Mitsubishi SUV as they led massive street protests through a number of Pakistan's largest cities, surrounded by boisterous, black-suited lawyers and their rose-petal throwing supporters. The chief justice episode presaged the downfall of Musharraf's army-led regime. Given that Pakistan's history is littered with cases of the courts caving to the military and political powers that be, Aitzaz Ahsan's feat was entirely unexpected. For a country that so craved some semblance of blind justice and had grown weary of army rule, Ahsan was a hero.

The chief justice episode was but the latest chapter in Ahsan's long career. A member of Bhutto's PPP, Ahsan has been elected to the Punjab Provincial Assembly and the National Assembly. In 1988, he served in Prime Minister Benazir Bhutto's cabinet in the first civilian government after General Zia's death. As an attorney, Ahsan is distinguished in having represented two prime ministers from his own party (Benazir Bhutto and Yousuf Raza Gilani) and their chief political opponent and former prime minister, Nawaz Sharif. And as an activist, he has lent his articulate voice and fiery passion to a wide range of progressive causes.

It is not hard to see that Ahsan's opposition to American "imperialism" and to Washington's support for Musharraf's military rule has drawn inspiration from Zulfikar Ali Bhutto's example. The anthem of the lawyers' movement, "Kal Aaj Aur Kal" ("Yesterday, Today, and Tomorrow") is an Urdu poem that Ahsan penned himself. He chanted the poem to fervent protestors in a defiant call-and-response style at their rallies. In its historical allusions to anti-imperialist heroes of the Cold War, it reveals Ahsan's leftist roots in ways that would have been familiar to Bhutto:

> And then when Che [Guevara] leapt forward
> We all marched with him
> And when Cho [En Lai] raised his voice
> Hand in hand we followed

Subsequently, the poem wheels on Musharraf and fires a barrage at the general's American patrons:

> Just for the ego of a dictator [Musharraf]
> Justice has been trampled
> It seems that one force straddles the earth [the United States]
> Roaming the entire world
> It seems like every power falls at its feet
> Its bombardment has resulted in rivers of blood
> It has made religion extreme, and suicide bombers have grown[34]

The message Ahsan delivered from 2004 to 2008 was always the same: the United States was on the wrong side of history in Pakistan. By backing President Musharraf, Washington was committing the same error that it had during the period of army rule by Generals Ayub and Zia. When Musharraf came crashing down, so too would the U.S.-Pakistan relationship. Better to back a new horse before that final crisis, or at least to deftly pull back from Musharraf before it was too late. I will never forget his belligerent mood on the eve of the lawyer's historic twenty-four-hour march from Islamabad to Lahore in early May 2007, when he harangued the United States up and down during a long, late dinner at the home of a mutual friend.[35] Even in the car on my ride home my ears rang with Ahsan's message that time was up for Washington and its army puppet.

Ahsan had a point. As described in the next chapter, the Bush administration did not manage the twilight of the Musharraf era in ways that best served U.S. or Pakistani interests. But the problem with Ahsan, and with other like-minded Pakistani critics, is that they can only offer risky, uncertain alternatives to U.S. partnership with Pakistan's military. Ahsan and other Pakistani liberals have correctly diagnosed one problem: by bolstering the army, the United States contributes to Pakistan's dysfunction.[36] They have failed, however, to appreciate the second problem: the United States has been forced by circumstances to deal with whatever government it finds in power. Moreover, Pakistan's civilian political class has not – from the 1950s to the present – offered compelling evidence of its ability or desire to stabilize Pakistan itself, let alone meet America's needs. The promise of Pakistan's civilian politicians, and its democracy as a whole, is more aspiration than reality.

---

[34] "Yesterday, Today, and Tomorrow," *MR Zine*, Monthly Review Foundation, November 11, 2008, http://mrzine.monthlyreview.org/2008/ahsan111108.html.

[35] On the march, see Salman Masood, "Throngs Attend Speech by Pakistan's Suspended Justice," *New York Times*, May 7, 2007, http://www.nytimes.com/2007/05/07/world/asia/07pakistan.html. Thanks go to Dr. Abdullah Riar for playing host that memorable night in Islamabad.

[36] For a similar American argument, see George Perkovich, "Stop Enabling Pakistan's Dangerous Dysfunction," Carnegie Endowment for International Peace, Washington, DC, September 6, 2011.

Be that as it may, American support to the army has cost it the admiration of natural partners in Pakistan. In many ways Aitzaz Ahsan represents the American liberal ideal. He was awarded the American Bar Association Rule of Law Award in 2008. And yet at his acceptance reception, he observed:

> The U.S. administration takes pride in advancing the cause of democracy in Pakistan. We do not accept this claim. It is well known that before the lawyers began to march, there was no challenge to General Musharraf. Before the Chief Justice refused to resign on demand, no one had said no to the General. A dictator, weakened by the Denial and the Lawyers' Movement, turned to Washington. That is when the US did some stitch-work and pitched in with the demand for elections. But in the process its ally had destroyed the judicial edifice.[37]

In Pakistan, as in many other states around the world, liberal ideals that are so thoroughly embedded in American society have been trumped by U.S. interests, above all the need to deal with immediate security threats. That Pakistanis like Aitzaz Ahsan would quarrel with Washington's priorities, if not necessarily with the American people or way of life, is unsurprising. These quarrels are likely to resurface until U.S. officials gain confidence that Pakistan's civilian democrats are not merely more popularly legitimate than (or morally superior to) their military counterparts, but that they are also better at running the country and managing relations with Washington. Only then can America's democratic principles and security interests achieve an easy harmony.

THE ANTI-AMERICANISM OF PAKISTAN'S NATIONALISTS

Returning to the depths of the Cold War, Eisenhower's successors in the Kennedy and Johnson administrations had even less patience for Pakistan. Their perspectives had everything to do with the evolution of the Cold War and their strategies for waging it.

On January 6, 1961, Soviet Premier Nikita Khrushchev delivered a secret speech to a closed-door meeting of some of the principal organizations for the formulation and dissemination of official Soviet ideology.[38] In a summary text released by the Kremlin just two days before Kennedy's inauguration, Khrushchev declared ominously, "We will beat the United States with small wars of liberation. We will nibble them to exhaustion all over the globe, in South America, Africa, and Southeast Asia."[39]

---

[37] Aitzaz Ahsan speech to the American Bar Association, New York, August 9, 2008, http://apps .americanbar.org/rol/luncheon_08/aitzaz_ahsan_speech_8-9-2008.pdf.

[38] "Hearing before the Subcommittee to Investigate the Administration of the Internal Security Act and Internal Security Laws," Committee on the Judiciary, U.S. Senate, June 16, 1961," http://www.foia.cia.gov/BerlinWall/1961-Spring/1961-06-16.pdf.

[39] Frederick Kempe, *Berlin 1961: Kennedy, Khrushchev, and the Most Dangerous Place on Earth* (New York: G. P. Putnam's Sons, 2011), p. 78.

The speech caught the eye of young President Kennedy. The new president probably should have given greater weight, in ways Eisenhower did, to the fact that Khrushchev was prone to rhetorical bluster of this sort. In fact, Khrushchev had taken a number of steps to reach out to the incoming President Kennedy, hoping that he might be a more cooperative partner than his Republican predecessor.[40] Kennedy should also have been advised that Khrushchev's words were primarily directed not at the United States but at the Chinese in a vain attempt to manage their revolutionary appeal within the communist world.

Instead, Kennedy read a great deal into the speech. He told his advisers, "You've got to understand it, and so does everybody else around here. This is our clue to the Soviet Union."[41] He believed Khrushchev was launching a new "campaign to seize control of anti-colonial and other revolutionary movements in the Third World."[42] Already inclined to worry that the Soviets were on the march and that the Eisenhower administration had been too lax in its response, Kennedy determined that Khrushchev's speech demanded an immediate response.

Kennedy's first State of the Union speech, in January 1961, provided that opportunity. He called on the Pentagon to "reappraise our entire defense strategy," and warned darkly that "Each day, the crises multiply. Each day, their solution grows more difficult. Each day, we draw nearer the hour of maximum danger, as weapons spread and hostile forces grow stronger."[43] In transforming this rhetoric into action, President Kennedy – and after his assassination President Johnson – expanded civilian and military assistance to a wide range of states in Asia, Africa, and Latin America. Prominent among these states was India, a country Kennedy considered a major battleground in the anti-communist struggle. In the spring of 1961, Kennedy requested $500 million in economic assistance for New Delhi and only $400 million for the rest of the world.[44] This was three times what the Eisenhower administration had requested for India just the year before.[45]

Another major strategic shift also took place in the 1960s. After the harrowing Cuban Missile Crisis in October 1962 passed without degenerating into nuclear war, senior U.S. officials started to view the Soviet Union as relatively less radical in intent than communist, nuclear-armed China. By mid-decade, Beijing and Moscow had parted ways; they no longer posed the monolithic communist threat perceived by Eisenhower and Dulles. So concerned were

[40] Kempe, *Berlin 1961*, pp. 73–5.
[41] Michael R. Beschloss, *The Crisis Years* (New York: Harper Collins, 1991), p. 61.
[42] Gaddis, *Strategies of Containment*, p. 208.
[43] Beschloss, *The Crisis Years*, p. 63.
[44] McMahon, *Cold War in the Periphery*, p. 277.
[45] Dennis Kux, *India and the United States: Estranged Democracies, 1941–1991* (Washington: National Defense University Press, 1992), p. 186.

U.S. officials about the Chinese that in 1964 the Johnson administration seriously considered – but in the end did not endorse – a policy of cooperation with Moscow to counter China. Washington even debated the wisdom of "preventive military action" against Beijing's nuclear facilities.[46]

For U.S. policy in South Asia, context was everything. Whereas Dulles had placed Pakistan in the context of his "Northern Tier" defense strategy for the oil fields of the Persian Gulf, Kennedy and Johnson saw Pakistan and India within the context of the global threat posed by the appeal of Soviet-style development and revolutionary China. Unlike Dulles, who saw Nehru's India as irresponsible and hypocritical, the subsequent two administrations saw in India a potential Asian bulwark against communist expansion. Unlike Dulles, who viewed Pakistan as a steadfast ally, Kennedy viewed Pakistan as irresponsible and prone to adventurism, while Johnson became increasingly frustrated by Zulfikar Ali Bhutto's anti-imperialist rhetoric, particularly as the United States sank into the morass of Vietnam.

Washington's response to two wars in the region clarified its new stance and sent shockwaves through Pakistan. In the autumn of 1962, India badly miscalculated its military balance with China. A long-standing border dispute spiraled out of New Delhi's control when Chinese forces overwhelmed Indian positions in the country's north and east. By November, India's leaders feared that China might strike Calcutta and could even seize control over much of eastern India. The Kennedy administration, confronting Soviet adventurism in the Cuban Missile Crisis at almost the same time, saw an opportunity to confront another face of communist aggression. The White House quickly agreed to send emergency military aid to India, which was now embroiled in a full-scale war, and followed up by moving the USS *Enterprise* aircraft carrier task force to the Bay of Bengal in a show of support. Eventually, however, it was Beijing's own restraint that ended the war. In mid-November, China declared a unilateral cease-fire. Chinese troops then pulled back from eastern India but retained control over the areas that Beijing had from the start claimed as its own.[47]

Not surprisingly, Pakistan was enraged by America's assistance to India. Washington had come to the aid of Pakistan's worst enemy. As General Ayub pointed out to anyone who would listen, it had done so in spite of the fact that, quite unlike Pakistan, India had done nothing to cast its lot with the anti-communist world.[48] Eventually, Ayub argued, India would use its American-supplied military equipment against Pakistan. Moreover, the Sino-Indian war had taken place at the same time that Pakistan was drawing closer to China,

---

[46] Gaddis, *Strategies of Containment*, p. 210.
[47] For more on the war, see Kux, *India and the United States: Estranged Democracies*, pp. 201–8.
[48] Mohammed Ayub Khan, "The Pakistan-American Alliance: Stresses and Strains," *Foreign Affairs*, 42, no. 2 (January 1964), pp. 195–209.

normalizing relations in the hope that the relationship would provide another means to balance against India.[49]

For all of these reasons, Washington's standing with Pakistan suffered after 1962. But it was U.S. policy during Pakistan's 1965 war with India that knocked the relationship to a new low. Resolved to neutrality in a war that had no potential benefit to the United States whatever its outcome, Washington suspended military aid to both India and Pakistan. Washington felt no need to come to Pakistan's defense since it viewed Pakistan as the aggressor, not a hapless victim. As a further slap in Pakistan's face, the Johnson administration left the management of postwar negotiations to Moscow, which Pakistan assumed would be biased in India's favor. The final straw came later that year, when President Johnson explained to General Ayub that the alliance, at least in anything resembling its earlier form, was over.[50]

In Pakistani eyes, the U.S. abandonment was complete; not only was Washington content to walk away when Pakistan's partnership was less prized, but the Americans were even willing to abandon their ally to India's depredations without remorse. Bhutto, who had by then emerged as a chief critic of the American alliance, saw America's "betrayal" as a confirmation of his long-standing distrust.[51] But 1965 was a bitter pill to swallow for many other Pakistanis who had perceived their alliance with the United States primarily as a means to secure their nation against India. Most chose to cast blame on Washington rather than to accept responsibility for their own leaders' disastrous decision to start another war over Kashmir. Pakistani leaders ignored the fact that the United States had promised only to defend against unprovoked aggressors, not to provide assistance if Pakistan picked a fight with India.[52]

That said, Pakistanis were correct to conclude that U.S. policy toward Pakistan had been dictated by broader Cold War calculations and not by any specific American interest in Pakistan per se. This remained the case throughout the Nixon administration. Henry Kissinger, Nixon's national security advisor at the time of the next major Indo-Pakistani war in 1971, explains that Washington's decision to tilt in Pakistan's favor during that war was entirely a consequence of Washington's plan to approach China and to peel it away from the Soviet camp.[53] "Pakistan was our only channel to China," Kissinger writes. "We had no other means of communication with Peking. A major American initiative of fundamental importance to the global balance of power could not

[49] McMahon, *Cold War on the Periphery*, p. 285.
[50] McMahon, *Cold War on the Periphery*, p. 335.
[51] Kux, *The United States and Pakistan, 1947–2000*, p. 225.
[52] Kux notes two important conversations prior to 1965 that suggest the United States might well have come to Pakistan's defense had it been the target of unprovoked Indian aggression, an event Kennedy considered very unlikely. See Kux, *The United States and Pakistan, 1947–2000*, p. 145.
[53] "The Tilt: The U.S. and the South Asian Crisis of 1971," National Security Archive, December 16, 2002, http://www.gwu.edu/~nsarchiv/NSAEBB/NSAEBB79/.

have survived" if Pakistan had been left to India's mercy.[54] That choice cast America as the villain in Indian eyes for decades to come.

Nixon's pro-Pakistan tilt won Americans relatively little credit in Pakistani eyes. U.S. policies had not saved Pakistan from dismemberment or humiliation. Washington had clearly taken the minimum steps necessary to maintain its connection with Beijing, and once the dramatic opening to China had been achieved, Pakistan lost even the utility perceived by Nixon and Kissinger. The subsequent Carter administration found even fewer reasons to invest in partnership with Pakistan.

Dr. A. Q. Khan

Pakistan did not ride this roller-coaster comfortably; no self-respecting state appreciates being treated as a pawn in another's game. And yet as the U.S.-Pakistan relationship wore on, it was Pakistan's own behavior, especially its decision to develop a nuclear arsenal over American objections, which created the deepest rifts with the United States.

Zulfikar Ali Bhutto, that towering figure of Pakistani politics, played a central role in the early stages of Pakistan's nuclear drama. Driven by a deep nationalism and an over-arching fear of India, he kick-started Pakistan's nuclear quest in the early 1970s. He declared in 1965, "If India builds the bomb, we will eat grass or leaves, even go hungry, but we will get one of our own. We have no other choice."[55] In the process, Bhutto was joined by a range of other Pakistani nationalists, among them the now-infamous Dr. Abdul Qadeer Khan, who shared Bhutto's fear of India and skepticism about the United States, not his leftist ideology.

A. Q. Khan was born in present-day India and only made his way to Pakistan in 1952, five years after independence. Khan appears never to have forgotten the trauma of Partition. In order to pursue his scientific studies, he moved to Europe in the early 1960s. Nothing about this early period of his life suggested any particular ideological or religious commitment. By 1972, Khan had married a Dutch-speaking, British-South African dual national named Henny. The couple had two young girls and seemed destined for a comfortable and productive life in the Netherlands. Khan's Dutch colleagues considered him an affable and generous character. That changed years later when they learned what he had done right under their noses.

Khan's work at a highly classified (but poorly secured) facility devoted to uranium enrichment exposed him to technologies essential to producing the

54 Henry Kissinger, *White House Years* (Boston: Little, Brown, 1979), p. 913.
55 Gordon Corera, *Shopping for Bombs: Nuclear Proliferation, Global Insecurity, and the Rise and Fall of the A.Q. Khan Network* (New York: Oxford University Press, 2006), p. 9. A new, comprehensive history of the Pakistani nuclear program takes this quote for its title: Feroz Hassan Khan, *Eating Grass: The Making of the Pakistani Bomb* (Stanford: Stanford University Press, 2012).

type of fuel required for a nuclear bomb. On his own initiative, Khan started stealing plans and equipment for Pakistan's own fledgling nuclear program in 1974. In 1976, before the Dutch could arrest him, Khan fled to Pakistan with his family. Once there, Prime Minister Bhutto put him in charge of his own program to build Pakistan's nuclear capabilities. That program was eventually named the Khan Research Laboratory (KRL) in his honor. Khan's successes in this endeavor – in addition to his tireless self-promotion – earned him the sobriquet "father of Pakistan's atomic bomb."[56]

In later years, Khan would become the world's most notorious proliferator of nuclear technology. By way of an illicit global supply network, he sold nuclear secrets to Iran, North Korea, and Libya.[57] More than his scientific know-how, his genius was his ability to circumvent international controls on restricted technologies and to stay one step ahead of foreign intelligence agencies. U.S. pressure finally forced President Musharraf to remove Khan from KRL's management in 2001, and in 2004 overwhelming evidence of his proliferation activities became public.[58] In a choreographed deal with Musharraf, Khan confessed his role and was immediately pardoned. By silencing Khan and shutting down his activities, Musharraf managed to deflect American pressure for a more comprehensive investigation or interrogation by U.S. officials and to keep a firm lid on public opinion.

Until then, Khan enjoyed unquestioned backing from Pakistan's leaders, in part because his program successfully imported illicit materials for the state's uranium enrichment, warhead, and missile programs. It is less clear precisely what Pakistan's military and civilian leaders knew about all of his many export activities. General Jehangir Karamat, who had been Pakistan's army chief in the 1990s when Khan's proliferation ring was riding high, shared the official army line on the very day that Musharraf pardoned Khan in February 2004. Over tea in Karamat's well-appointed sitting room, he explained that by the mid-1990s Khan had become a larger-than-life figure. Not only did Khan enjoy nearly unquestioned authority over a range of state assets, but he had also armed himself with a team of propagandists who would make short work of anyone who got in his way. Karamat, who was prematurely bounced from office by Prime Minister Nawaz Sharif in 1998, indicated that a fight with A. Q. Khan was not one he thought he could win.

[56] Although Khan proudly takes credit for Pakistan's nuclear bomb, other Pakistani researchers and laboratories, especially Munir Ahmed Khan and the Pakistan Atomic Energy Commission, were at least as responsible. See William Langewiesche, "The Wrath of Khan," *Atlantic* (November 2005), http://www.theatlantic.com/magazine/print/2005/11/the-wrath-of-khan/4333/.
[57] Khan also attempted deals with South Africa and Iraq. One highly speculative article suggests that Khan's nuclear technology may have even ended up in Indian hands. See Joshua Pollack, "The Secret Treachery of A.Q. Khan," *Playboy* (January/February 2012).
[58] David Rohde and Talat Hussain, "Delicate Dance for Musharraf In Nuclear Case," *New York Times*, February 8, 2004, http://www.nytimes.com/2004/02/08/world/delicate-dance-for-musharraf-in-nuclear-case.html?pagewanted=print&src=pm.

When A. Q. Khan was freed from house arrest in 2009, he alleged that Karamat, among others, had known – and profited – from his deals. Karamat dismissed these allegations out of hand, but the debate over who knew what and when is far from resolved. Most outside observers suggest that at the very least Pakistan's military was grotesquely negligent in its failure to oversee Khan's activities, and there is evidence to suggest that its complicity, and even the complicity of Pakistan's civilian leaders, went much further than that.[59]

There are many theories about why Khan shared nuclear secrets with other countries. Some focus on personal motivations, like ego or wealth. Khan clearly bought into his own greatness, and judging from his boastful tone in recent newspaper columns, he still does. It is also true that Khan's transactions made him rich. By the time of his house arrest, he owned all sorts of real estate, made generous contributions to charities, and lived well beyond the means of any normal government employee. Other theories tend to emphasize ideological and strategic commitments. Khan is said to have built an "Islamic bomb" and to have supported anti-Western Pakistani military strategies.[60]

On the other hand, it is clear what motivated Khan to steal classified information from the Europeans in the early 1970s. Khan was an ardent nationalist. Like many Pakistanis, he believed that the 1971 war exposed the nation's profound vulnerability to Indian conquest. Looking back, Khan calls it the "darkest day in Pakistan's history" and remembers, "It was a very, very sad day. I cried a lot that night. I didn't eat for many days.... The mental scar remained forever, and the pain of that wound could never subside." In his words, after India's own "peaceful nuclear explosion" in May 1974 "the world was shaken. Pakistan was all the more shaken because we had not even recovered from the tragedy of 1971."[61] These two events convinced Khan that only a nuclear bomb could guarantee Pakistan against new predations by its neighbor.

Khan took the initiative and contacted the Bhutto government multiple times in 1974. Overcoming initial skepticism, Khan managed to convince Bhutto's advisers that his access and expertise would be invaluable. Khan had no qualms about exploiting the trust and confidence of his fellow employees in the Netherlands, breaking security rules, or violating provisions of international law as he worked feverishly to transfer nuclear know-how to his homeland. In those early days, there was no financial reward either; Khan took a pay cut to return home to Pakistan. Yet he believed he was serving a higher purpose,

---

[59] For more on official Pakistani complicity, including the involvement of Musharraf and Benazir Bhutto in transfers to North Korea, see Matthew Kroenig, *Exporting the Bomb: Technology Transfer and the Spread of Nuclear Weapons* (Ithaca: Cornell University Press, 2010), pp. 135–9.

[60] For more on these debates, see Matthew Kroenig, *Exporting the Bomb*, pp. 134–47.

[61] Translated from Urdu interview with ARY television, http://notesfromsaudiarabia.blogspot.com/2010/08/dr-abdul-qadeer-khan-narrates-history.html.

and more important, that the rules he was breaking to protect his country were inherently discriminatory. In a letter to the editor of a German magazine in 1979, he revealed his disdain:

I want to question the bloody holier-than-thou attitudes of the Americans and the British. Are these bastards God-appointed guardians of the world to stockpile hundreds of thousands of nuclear warheads and have they God-given authority to carry out explosions every month? If we start a modest programme, we are the satans, the devils.[62]

There can be no doubting that Khan saw himself as a Pakistani patriot. In subsequent decades, his language would become increasingly peppered with religious overtones and references from the Qur'an. His secret dealings would make him wealthy and powerful. But his initial drive to bring home the bomb and the popularity that his project won him in Pakistan were based on his ability to channel a nationalistic resentment that had become increasingly common in the 1960s and 1970s.

The diplomatic consequence of Pakistan's nuclear program was that it drove a deep wedge between Washington and Islamabad. The Ford administration was the first to recognize what Bhutto and his nuclear scientists, including Khan, were up to. Kissinger, then Ford's secretary of state, attempted to convince Pakistan that Washington could provide military assistance to meet Islamabad's needs without having to go down the costly nuclear path. The U.S. Congress had also drafted legislation intended to deter Pakistan's program by threatening what remained of U.S. civilian aid. None of this had any effect on Bhutto or other top Pakistani officials, who were hell-bent on developing the bomb.[63]

Jimmy Carter's national security team, deeply committed to the nuclear nonproliferation agenda, was desperate to keep Pakistan's program in check. By then General Zia had ousted Bhutto, but Pakistan's new dictator was no more inclined to walk away from the nuclear program. Nuclear differences sparked a short-lived rupture in the relationship; Washington suspended civilian aid to Pakistan. In 1979, the U.S. embassy in Islamabad was nearly overrun by radical student protesters while the Zia regime stood idly by. The grounds were torched and two Americans were killed; more than 100 others took shelter inside the embassy's communications vault and barely escaped the violence.[64] The U.S.-Pakistan relationship had reached an all-time low. If not for the Soviet invasion of Afghanistan in 1980 and the Reagan administration's rekindled cooperation with Islamabad to arm the Afghan insurgency, disagreements over the nuclear issue would have sent the U.S.-Pakistan relationship completely over the cliff.

---

[62] Khan's letter is cited in Langewiesche, "The Wrath of Khan."
[63] See Kux, *The United States and Pakistan, 1947–2000*, pp. 221–4.
[64] On the embassy attack, see Coll, *Ghost Wars*, pp. 22–37.

Pressler, Abandonment, and National Honor

Pakistan's nuclear program came back to haunt the relationship again in the late 1980s. When Soviet forces pulled out of Afghanistan, the George H. W. Bush administration found it impossible to overlook Pakistan's nuclear transgressions. In 1985, the U.S. Congress passed legislation requiring a yearly White House certification that Pakistan did not possess a nuclear device. Senator John Glenn introduced the original legislation, but because Senator Larry Pressler amended it, the mechanism came to be known in Pakistan as the Pressler Amendment.[65] By 1990, the U.S. intelligence community found conclusive evidence that Pakistan had crossed the nuclear line.

When they hit, U.S. sanctions were painful. Over half a billion dollars in annual military and civilian assistance was eventually frozen. Twenty-eight F-16s on order for delivery to Pakistan were instead put in storage in Arizona. It was not until 1998 that the Clinton administration agreed to a plan that allowed Pakistan to recoup its financial losses in the deal. Pakistani officials acted stung, as if they had thought Washington would never actually follow through on its threats.

From the perspective of U.S. diplomats, however, no one in Islamabad should have been the least surprised. Ambassador Robert Oakley had pointedly warned Pakistan's president, prime minister, and army chief. Washington had simply followed through on the threats it had leveled for years.

No matter; like A. Q. Khan, most Pakistanis and their leaders chose not to face up to their own responsibility. Instead, they tended to see America's nuclear policy as blatantly hypocritical. They rejected the idea that Washington's 1990 aid cutoff was a predictable consequence of Pakistan's own decision to violate clear U.S. conditions. Neither India nor Israel had suffered a similar fate, they observed. They were skeptical of claims that Washington's intelligence only picked up clear evidence of Pakistan having a nuclear bomb after the Soviets had been defeated in Afghanistan. After all, somehow the Reagan and Carter administrations had been willing to put off sanctions when they needed Pakistan to counter the Soviets in Afghanistan. If those exceptions were possible, why hadn't Bush done the same? The typical conclusion was that Washington was a "fickle friend" who had used Pakistan then discarded it "like a piece of used Kleenex."[66]

By 9/11, the Pressler episode had assumed almost legendary proportions for Pakistanis, who considered it to be America's ultimate abandonment. Not only did America leave the region in turmoil, the narrative went, but it was punishing Pakistan for arming itself with nuclear weapons just as its foe, India, was doing the same.

---

[65] Vilified in Pakistan, the Pressler amendment was in fact an attempt to water down the nuclear restrictions imposed by Senator Glenn.

[66] Kux, *The United States and Pakistan, 1947–2000*, p. 310.

Both the Bush and Obama administrations tried, without success, to overcome Pakistan's powerful abandonment narrative. Unfortunately, it has become a central part of the nationalist worldview. As the previous chapter describes, extreme nationalism has a prominent place in the Pakistani military, amplified by vocal advocates like Shireen Mazari who have a disproportionate influence on the public policy debate. This school of thought had gotten so strong that Pakistan's media even gave it a name: the "Ghairat [honor] Brigade."[67]

Having been freed from the muzzle imposed during the Musharraf years, today, A. Q. Khan routinely writes about the need to defend Pakistan's ghairat from American predations. In one 2011 essay, he catalogues the litany of U.S. betrayals in 1965, 1971, and 1989 and observes that "now after 50 years we are still slaves to the US."[68] Again and again, his language is that of the archetypal nationalist, obsessed with honor and shame, pride and cowardice.

In 2011, a free-spirited Pakistani pop band satirically named itself the Beygairat Brigade (a brigade without honor) and released a single "Aalu Anday" ("Potatoes and Eggs"). In the band's video, the three young musicians are dressed as rebellious schoolboys who start by complaining about the lunches packed by their mothers – potato and egg curry – but quickly turn their ire to more controversial subjects. With thinly veiled references to a wide cast of Pakistani xenophobes, religious extremists, and conspiracy theorists, the lyrics lampoon many of the notions associated with defending Pakistan's national pride.[69]

Released straight to YouTube to avoid any sort of censorship, the song was a sensation with urban Pakistani youth. Its success says good things about the potential for a different Pakistani future. For the time being, however, the nationalistic strand of anti-Americanism, symbolized by the likes of A. Q. Khan and Shireen Mazari, holds the high ground.

THE ANTI-AMERICANISM OF PAKISTAN'S JIHADISTS

After the Soviet invasion of Afghanistan in 1979, Pakistan became more strategically important to the United States than ever before. Without Pakistan as a conduit for the weapons and money that flowed to Afghan insurgents, the anti-Soviet resistance there would have been crushed.

One of the most stunning features of the partnership between Washington and Islamabad during the Afghan war was the extent to which Pakistan insisted

---

[67] Salman Masood, "Satirical Song, a YouTube Hit, Challenges Extremism in Pakistan," *New York Times*, November 6, 2011, http://www.nytimes.com/2011/11/07/world/asia/beygairat-brigades-youtube-hit-song-challenges-extremism-in-pakistan.html.

[68] Dr. A. Q. Khan, "God Save the Country from Bad Governance," *The News*, August 15, 2011, http://www.thenews.com.pk/TodaysPrintDetail.aspx?ID=62911&Cat=9&dt=8/15/2011.

[69] Masood, "Satirical Song, a YouTube Hit, Challenges Extremism in Pakistan," *New York Times*, November 6, 2011.

that U.S. funds and supplies had to be managed by Pakistan's military and Inter-Services Intelligence directorate, with meager American oversight or control. In the early years of the program, it was managed in Pakistan by a CIA station of only a half-dozen officers.[70] American trainers and other technical experts would come to Pakistan, but only for short stints.[71] Due to the small footprint of the covert program, Islamabad and Washington could plausibly deny the existence of their joint venture. Such an arrangement made it far less likely that the Soviets would expand their war into Pakistan, a contingency that both Islamabad and Washington feared from the start.

Years later, the arrangement came out of the shadows. Washington had expanded its annual funding to over $600 million and armed Afghan forces with the shoulder-launched Stinger missile that was deadly accurate against Russian attack helicopters. By then, however, the tide had turned against the Soviets. Washington had effectively turned Afghanistan into a Vietnam-style quagmire from which all Moscow could hope to do was withdraw. It was a stunning blow to Soviet prestige at the worst possible time for Moscow.

Throughout the 1980s, the U.S.-Pakistan partnership offered Islamabad the autonomy to support its chosen Afghan groups and, for the most part, to manage the Afghan fight as it saw fit. Not surprisingly, Pakistan aided Afghan fighters who took direction from Islamabad. In practice, this meant chan-neling money and supplies to the most extreme Islamists of the bunch, like Jalaluddin Haqqani and Gulbuddin Hekmatyar.[72] These same groups retained Islamabad's favor after the Soviet withdrawal and throughout the 1990s when Afghanistan fell into a bloody civil war. Even 9/11 and the start of America's new war in Afghanistan did not sever the ties between these seasoned fighters and their Pakistani handlers. Pakistan's aid to Afghan militants, now drenched in American blood, is today one of the deepest causes of friction between Washington and Islamabad.

The tiny U.S. footprint in Pakistan throughout the 1980s meant that some of the most significant American action in Afghanistan's fight against the Red Army took place back home in Washington, DC. The scandal-prone Texas congressman, Charlie Wilson, waged the battle on Capitol Hill to secure fund-ing for the mujahedeen. George Crile's 2003 bestseller and the Hollywood adaptation of *Charlie Wilson's War* delivered this most unlikely chapter of American history to bookshops and multiplexes around the world.[73] Suffice it to say, Wilson's Hugh Hefner tendencies were mixed up with a rabid anti-communism that, in time, resulted in a deep attachment to the Afghan cause. His unorthodox working relationship with Gust Avrakotos, the cranky CIA officer who fought off agency bureaucrats and kept the whole secret operation alive, broke a lot of rules along the way to victory. As Crile records in his

[70] Coll, *Ghost Wars*, p. 57.
[71] Kux, *The United States and Pakistan, 1947–2000*, p. 263.
[72] On Haqqani, see Coll, *Ghost Wars*, p. 131. On Hekmatyar, see Coll, *Ghost Wars*, p. 67.
[73] George Crile, *Charlie Wilson's War* (New York: Grove Press, 2003).

jaunty history, when Pakistan's President Zia was asked to explain the defeat of the Russians in Afghanistan, he uttered but three words: "Charlie did it."[74]

Of course, that was only a part of the story. The stage for Congressman Wilson's bravura performance was not set by itself. A trickle of U.S. support for the Afghan insurgents was already flowing through Pakistan before he came on the scene. Immediately after the 1979 Soviet invasion, the Carter administration slammed the door on détente with Moscow and announced that "any attempt by any outside force to gain control of the Persian Gulf region will be regarded as an assault on the vital interests of the United States of America, and such an assault will be repelled by any means necessary, including military force."[75] The White House cut off wheat and technology sales to Russia, pulled the plug on a nuclear arms treaty, started a new round of draft registrations, and boycotted the 1980 Moscow Olympics in protest.

Rhetoric aside, the Carter and Reagan administrations cared rather little about Afghanistan per se. What drove them to oppose the Soviet intervention was the concern that Afghanistan might be little more than a first step in Moscow's march to the Arabian Sea. To American cold warriors, it required no imagination to perceive another chapter in Russia's long historic quest for a warm water port.[76] After Afghanistan, the Soviets would strike Pakistan or Iran. That would put vital oilfields and shipping routes within Moscow's reach, precisely as John Foster Dulles had feared during the early days of the Cold War.

President Carter had arrived in office without any expectation that he would turn up the heat on Moscow. By the end of his term, however, he bequeathed to the Reagan administration the makings of a global American military expansion and a firm commitment to oppose Soviet aggression in and around the Persian Gulf. Carter's national security advisor, Zbigniew Brzezinski, a Polish-born émigré whose greatest cunning was reserved for fighting Russians, charted out the first steps for American aid to the Afghan resistance. Within twenty-four hours of the initial Soviet invasion, he concluded that Washington would need a new relationship with Pakistan to channel assistance to Afghan insurgents. For Brzezinski, circumstances required the United States to set aside concerns about Pakistan's nuclear program, at least temporarily.[77]

This about-face by the Carter team was not enough to get back into General Zia's good graces. Zia preferred to wait until the new Reagan team took office.

[74] Crile, *Charlie Wilson's War*, p. 4.
[75] From Carter's January 23, 1980, State of the Union address, cited in Gaddis, *Strategies of Containment*, p. 345.
[76] It is worth noting, however, that contrary to Washington's apprehensions, Moscow may have been sucked into Afghanistan by "mission creep" rather than a considered strategic offensive to conquer warm water ports. See "Soviet Invasion of Afghanistan a Case of Mission Creep, According to New Book and Original Soviet Documents," National Security Archive, October 13, 2012, http://www.gwu.edu/~nsarchiv/NSAEBB/NSAEBB396/.
[77] Coll, *Ghost Wars*, p. 51.

For Zia, hawkish Republicans were more committed to the fight against communism and more likely to put aside issues that had plagued his relationship with Carter, such as Pakistan's nuclear program and his dictatorship's human rights violations. Zia was correct. Pakistan drove a hard bargain, winning a U.S. assistance package of $3.2 billion over six years and a fast-tracked deal for forty F-16 fighter jets.[78] For Islamabad, such assistance would go a long way toward rebalancing its military competition with India. Even more, Zia got what he took to be a wink and a nod on the contentious nuclear issue and a promise that Washington would not meddle in Pakistan's internal affairs.

The Reagan administration also framed the strategy for expanding the Afghan conflict well beyond anything Brzezinski had earlier considered. Charlie Wilson and his CIA friends deserve credit for realizing that, if properly armed, the mujahedeen might actually manage to beat the Soviet empire. They deserve even more credit for pulling out all the stops to bring that goal to fruition. Yet the scheme to use Moscow's own aggression – its involvement in brushfire wars across the globe – against it, to bleed the Soviet empire by way of a thousand cuts, was neither their work alone nor Afghanistan-specific. Eventually it would come to be known as the "Reagan Doctrine," and it was most vigorously applied in Nicaragua and Angola along with Afghanistan. From the Reagan White House came authorization for dramatic expansions of the Afghan war, first with improved weapons and satellite intelligence, later with the Stingers.[79]

In hindsight, critics of the Reagan administration argue that the Cold War victory in Afghanistan was purchased at the cost of causing 9/11. There can be no doubt that the jihadist seeds planted in that war eventually grew into the hopelessly crooked trees of al-Qaeda, the Afghan Taliban, and other terrorist groups. Even in the 1980s, questions were raised within and outside government about the wisdom of supporting Afghan and Arab fighters with decidedly anti-Western worldviews.[80] That said, to draw a straight line from Charlie Wilson to Osama bin Laden skips too many steps. Washington may have planted the seeds of jihad, but they were well tended in Pakistan's fertile soil.[81]

---

[78] In contrast, the Carter administration had offered an initial deal of $400 million. "Peanuts," Zia scoffed. See Kux, *The United States and Pakistan, 1947–2000*, p. 249. In addition to U.S. funds, Pakistan also profited from the support of the Saudis, equally engaged on the side of the Afghan anti-Soviet mujahedeen.

[79] Coll, *Ghost Wars*, p. 127, pp. 149–51; Crile, *Charlie Wilson's War*, pp. 403–21.

[80] Dennis Kux attributes State Department intelligence analyst Eliza Van Hollen with some foresight on this point, but she was overruled by the CIA. See *The United States and Pakistan, 1947–2000*, p. 275.

[81] For a broader discussion on the evolution of extremism in Pakistan, see Ayesha Jalal, *Partisans of Allah: Jihad in South Asia* (Cambridge, MA: Harvard University Press, 2008); Hassan Abbas, *Pakistan's Drift into Extremism: Allah, the Army, and America's War on Terror* (Armonk, NY: M.E. Sharpe, 2005); and Zahid Hussain, *The Scorpion's Tail: The Relentless Rise of Islamic Militants in Pakistan – And How It Threatens America* (New York: Free Press, 2010).

Zia's Islamization

Initial responsibility for Pakistan's enthusiastic embrace of the most radical Afghan fighters and their associates falls in the lap of the man who hanged Zulfikar Ali Bhutto: General Muhammad Zia-ul-Haq. Bhutto misjudged Zia when he hand-picked him as army chief in 1976, thinking that the quiet general with slicked-back hair and an obsequious manner would never challenge the politician's authority. But Zia was made of sterner, or at least more ruthless, stuff. Not only did he dispatch Bhutto in 1977 in the face of wide international condemnation, but he also stayed on to rule Pakistan until 1988, when he finally met his end in a mysterious plane crash along with the American ambassador and several other top Pakistani officials.[82]

Some biographers view Zia's political successes as a consequence of his background and family upbringing. Born in 1924, his family hailed from Jallundur, a town in the eastern part of Punjab that ended up on the Indian side of the border after Partition. His father, a junior civil servant, was from the Arain caste, stereotyped by the British colonials as hardworking, frugal farmers, not soldiers. In this sense, Zia was the classic striver from humble beginnings. He lacked the pedigree of the men who routinely rose to the most senior ranks of the army. All of these traits made him look less threatening when Bhutto promoted him to army chief of staff.[83] But those same characteristics probably also prepared him for the rigors of leadership. Zia, after all, exceeded expectations and overcame his adversaries at multiple points throughout his career.

Other biographers stress that whatever Zia's background, he was politically gifted, coldly calculating, and more than a little lucky.[84] Either way, Zia could hardly have been more different from Bhutto. One of the most politically relevant distinctions between them was the way they observed their Muslim faith. Bhutto's practices, common in much of Pakistan but especially his home in rural Sindh province, were marked by a syncretic tradition that draws from many sources for spiritual inspiration and teaching. The emphasis on scholars, saints, and shrines has some similarities with the Shia sect of Islam, although the vast majority of Pakistanis who follow such practices are in fact Sunnis.[85]

Zia, on the other hand, was raised in an austere tradition that rejected medieval interpretations of Islamic law and held that the only two sources of Islamic law were the Qur'an and hadith (the sayings of the Prophet

---

[82] Nawaz, *Crossed Swords*, pp. 393–6.

[83] See Shahid Javed Burki, "Pakistan under Zia, 1977–1988," *Asian Survey*, 28, no. 10 (October 1988), pp. 1082–100.

[84] Talbot, *Pakistan*, pp. 245–6.

[85] Surprisingly, Bhutto's own sectarian identity is contested. According to his family, he was a Sunni. According to many others, he was a Shia who may have hidden his sectarian identity for political or other reasons. See Benazir Bhutto, *Daughter of the East: An Autobiography* (London: Hamish Hamilton, 1988), p. 32; Vali Nasr, *The Shia Revival: How Conflicts within Islam Will Shape the Future* (New York: W. W. Norton, 2006), p. 88.

Muhammad). He came much closer to the Sunni extremes revived at the end of the nineteenth century by movements such as the Deobandis – from which today's Taliban draw inspiration – and the Salafis – from which al-Qaeda and Lashkar-e-Taiba derive their views.[86]

Zia was more pious than radical in his own religious observance, and his deep attachment to the army made it inconceivable that he would have subscribed to the sorts of anti-state views held by al-Qaeda. He did, however, pursue a policy of "Islamization" during his rule, which provided political cover and funneled resources to some of Pakistan's most extreme Islamist groups. Islamization also had an especially durable and poisonous effect on Pakistan's educational system. Public schools were weakened, their textbooks and curriculum infused with jihadist ideology, rhetoric, and historical revision.[87] The decay of public schools also contributed to the rise of private ones. The best of these were priced beyond the reach of most Pakistani families. As a consequence, religious seminaries (known as madaris or madrassahs) became an increasingly common option.[88] In many instances, such seminaries were unprepared to teach children the sorts of knowledge or skills required for jobs outside the mosque. In a small but influential number of cases, seminaries were simply dressed up militant training camps that prepared students only to serve as cannon fodder in Afghanistan or Pakistan's other enduring insurgency, Kashmir.

Zia's campaign was also a scheme to construct a unifying national identity and legitimize his own undemocratic authority. Once Bangladesh had broken away from Pakistan in 1971, Pakistan had even less reason to claim to be *the* Muslim homeland for South Asia. Even in the half of Pakistan that remained, significant ethnic and linguistic diversity ruled out cultural appeals to unity. Zia mistakenly believed that "Islam" offered a solution.[89] The problem was that Islam meant different things to different Pakistanis. Religious cleavages ran through Pakistan just as they distinguished Zia from Bhutto. Rather than pulling the country together, Zia's Islamization strengthened divisions in

[86] For a detailed discussion of the Deobandi tradition in historical context, see Barbara Daly Metcalf, *Islamic Revival in British India: Deoband, 1860–1900* (Oxford: Oxford University Press, 2005).

[87] For recent examples of this curriculum, see Pamela Constable, *Playing with Fire* (New York: Random House, 2011), p. 139; Fair, *The Madrassah Challenge: Militancy and Religious Education in Pakistan*, pp. 16–28; Zubeida Mustafa, "The Continuing Biases in Our Textbooks," *Policy Brief*, Jinnah Institute, April 30, 2012, http://jinnah-institute.org/programs/governance/429-the-continuing-biases-in-our-textbooks.

[88] According to official figures, 1,000 new madrasas were opened in the years from 1982 to 1988. See "Pakistan: Madrasas, Extremism and the Military," July 29, 2002, International Crisis Group Asia Report No. 36, p. 9.

[89] For more on Zia's belief that Islam would provide the unifying principle for Pakistan, see Husain Haqqani, *Pakistan: Between Mosque and Military* (Washington, DC: Carnegie Endowment for International Peace, 2005), pp. 131–7.

increasingly violent ways.[90] Sectarian and theological debates fed spasms of communal bloodletting.[91]

U.S. dollars undoubtedly contributed to radicalizing trends in Afghanistan and Pakistan, and America's departure from the scene in the 1990s left a dangerous, festering sore. Yet for those who might place all responsibility at Washington's feet, it is important to note that Zia's Islamization campaign pre-dated the Soviet invasion of Afghanistan and the windfall of American aid to Pakistan.

Moreover, Washington's use of radical Islamists for military purposes, or for that matter, Zia's appeal to religion for political ends, would never have been possible if not for other contemporaneous changes taking place in the Muslim world. The 1979 Iranian revolution that swept out the U.S.-backed Shah and catapulted the fire-breathing Ayatollah Ruhollah Khomeini to power was the most recent and dramatic of these. For many Pakistanis, even those with no sympathy for Teheran's new Shia regime, the revolution revealed that a Muslim nation could stand up to any country on earth, including the American superpower. Iran's clerical revolution also raised contentious issues about the appropriate relationship between the mosque and the state. These issues were never resolved; they resonate down to the present day in the context of the "Arab spring" of 2011.

As is true today, oil-rich Saudi Arabia had an important role to play throughout the 1980s. The Saudis bankrolled the Afghan mujahedeen through the Pakistani conduit, matching U.S. contributions dollar for dollar. And because the Saudis saw themselves in a political and sectarian competition with revolutionary Iran, they shoveled cash into Sunni projects throughout the Muslim world. In Pakistan, this included high-profile gifts like the cavernous Faisal mosque in Islamabad, named after the Saudi king who financed it. More influential was the Saudi money that sponsored a vast array of other Pakistani mosques, schools, and organizations, especially those that hewed to Salafism, the official Saudi creed.[92]

All told, Zia's Islamization, Charlie Wilson's war, and the Sunni-Shia competition engulfed Pakistan in weapons, money, and radical ideas. Each of these helped to beat the Soviets in Afghanistan, and by extension, to win the Cold War. In turn, that victory cultivated a taste for jihad in a small, hardened group

---

[90] For more on the various aspects of Islamization, from its exacerbation of Sunni-Shia tensions to judicial reform, the Islamic Penal Code, economic activity, education, and impact on women and minorities, see Talbot, *Pakistan*, pp. 270–83.

[91] For an excellent study of the rise of sectarianism in Pakistan, see Muhammad Qasim Zaman, "Sectarianism in Pakistan: The Radicalization of Shi'i and Sunni Identities," *Modern Asian Studies*, 32, no. 3 (1998), pp. 689–716. Importantly, Zaman observes that radical sectarian identities are "imports" into rural Pakistani communities, have modern, urban origins, and hold the potential to revolutionize religious practice, especially in parts of Punjab.

[92] For more on the Saudi role, see "Pakistan: Madrasas, Extremism and the Military," International Crisis Group Asia Report No. 36, pp. 9–13.

of Pakistanis, Afghans, and foreign fighters. It also reinforced ties between the Pakistani state and Islamist militants. By way of officially sanctioned indoctrination in public and private schools, jihadist ideals sank roots throughout the country, even in places far from the Pashtun mountain villages and sanctuaries that were directly touched by Afghanistan's war. These groups remain united in hatred for India and America, even if doctrinal, political, and other differences mean they cannot agree on much else.

Hafiz Saeed

Osama bin Laden was the most notorious, globally recognized face to have been produced, if indirectly, by the era of Afghan jihad. Mullah Mohammed Omar's Afghan Taliban and his Pakistani counterparts like the late leader of the Pakistani Taliban, Baitullah Mehsud (allegedly responsible for, among other attacks inside Pakistan, the killing of Benazir Bhutto, Zulfikar's daughter and leader of the PPP), are the most important Pashtun faces. However, because both al-Qaeda and the Pakistani Taliban have taken up arms against the Pakistani state, and because their ethnic and regional backgrounds (Arab or tribal Pashtun) set them apart, their appeal throughout most of the country is limited.

In the heartland of Pakistan's dominant province, Punjab, is found another face of jihad, also born from the cauldron of the 1980s. That is the face of Hafiz Muhammad Saeed. One day, if Islamists win control over Pakistan, they are likely to have more in common with Saeed than either bin Laden or Baitullah Mehsud.

Born in 1950, Saeed is now heavy-set, his face framed by large glasses, a long scraggly beard, and the dark forehead spot common to Muslims who prostrate themselves routinely. He is the founder of Lashkar-e-Taiba (LeT), Pakistan's most powerful and sophisticated terrorist organization and the one that enjoys the closest relationship with Pakistan's military.

In 2002, Saeed sidestepped an official ban on LeT by taking up a new title as the leader of LeT's humanitarian and charitable wing, Jamaat-ud-Dawa (JuD). Yet there can be no doubt that Saeed, like a mafia godfather, still runs LeT even as he denies its very existence.[93] In any event, JuD is now listed as a terrorist organization by the United Nations and the United States. Saeed is its chief ideologue and most outspoken voice. Among his many bloody deeds, Saeed is said to have blessed personally the Mumbai terrorist operation over Thanksgiving weekend in 2008 that ended 166 innocent lives.[94]

Saeed is a "hafiz" because he learned to recite from memory all 114 chapters of the Qur'an, a feat he accomplished by the age of twelve. His family members

---

[93] Declan Walsh, "Pakistani Militant, Price on Head, Lives in Open," *New York Times*, February 6, 2013, http://www.nytimes.com/2013/02/07/world/asia/lashkar-e-taiba-founder-takes-less-militant-tone-in-pakistan.html.

[94] Stephen Tankel, *Storming the World Stage* (New York: Columbia/Hurst Press, 2011), p. 222. On this point, Tankel cites testimony from American LeT operative David Headley.

were Ahle Hadith Muslims with conservative views very similar to those of the Salafis of Saudi Arabia. At the time, this made them unusual. Most Pakistanis practice other variants of Islam and perceive Salafism as a dangerous, imported creed that threatens to rid Islam of a rich tradition of centuries-long practice.

Over the years, massive injections of Saudi money and persistent efforts of leaders like Saeed have attracted an influential and growing contingent of followers to Salafism in Pakistan. Gulf oil money has enabled LeT to maintain a sprawling 200-acre campus for training and conventions at Muridke, near Lahore. Most important, LeT's humanitarian outreach efforts – from hospitals and schools to rapid disaster response teams in the wake of earthquakes and floods – have won over converts as well as sympathizers who may not share Saeed's particular brand of religion. Annual conferences at Muridke attracted as many as 1 million attendees by the late 1990s.[95]

After studying Islam and Arabic at the University of Punjab, Saeed moved to Riyadh in the mid-1970s, where he expanded his connections with a range of renowned Salafist scholars. In the early 1980s, Saeed returned to Pakistan to take up an Islamic Studies professorship in Lahore. That position offered him the ideal platform from which to translate his scholarship into practice. In 1986, Saeed joined with sixteen others to found an organization devoted to proselytizing the Ahle Hadith creed through preaching and social services (dawa) and war (jihad).[96] With the war raging in Afghanistan, Saudi support flowing freely to Salafis throughout the region, and Zia's Islamization campaign in full swing, Saeed and his compatriots – including Osama bin Laden's early co-conspirator, Abdullah Azzam – could not have asked for a more auspicious time to start.

As it happened, things would get even better for Saeed's fledgling organization that formally gave birth to LeT in 1990. As the Afghan war wound down in the late 1980s, the insurgency in Kashmir was on the rise. Because Saeed and a number of his colleagues were Punjabis scarred by Partition in ways that made them rabidly anti-Indian, their organization was well suited to waging jihad in Kashmir. And since the Pakistani military and ISI were eager to find militant proxies that would push India to the breaking point, LeT found itself a powerful ally and protector.

From 1993 until 2000, LeT was first and foremost an anti-Indian organization with intimate ISI connections, in spite of the fact that it was initially formed in the anti-Soviet Afghan campaign. LeT quickly grew into the most dangerous insurgent force in Kashmir. Safely ensconced in Pakistani training camps, where LeT militants worked alongside army and intelligence officers, LeT learned how to take its suicidal commando (fedayeen) raids to new levels of sophistication.[97]

---

[95] Tankel, *Storming the World Stage*, p. 81.
[96] On the early history of LeT, see Tankel, *Storming the World Stage*, pp. 2–4.
[97] Tankel, *Storming the World Stage*, pp. 60–1.

In December 2000, LeT crossed a new threshold by sending attackers into New Delhi's Red Fort garrison, far from the disputed Kashmiri territory. Over the course of 2001, Indian officials credited LeT with responsibility for a majority of the twenty-nine suicide attacks on their military personnel and installations.[98]

The next step came in Mumbai. LeT's spectacular 2008 attack dominated television news across the world. LeT gunmen went out of their way to target a city far from Kashmir – and not claimed by Pakistan – and then murdered people, like Israeli Jews and Americans, who had nothing to do with that disputed territory. Symbolically, at least, LeT had gone global. And LeT's worldwide aspirations also had other, less visible, effects. For years, the group had established and maintained a network for recruitment and fundraising that included members in Asia and Europe.[99] After 2008, it was painfully clear that LeT's global network even extended into the United States. An American, David Coleman Headley (born Daood Sayed Gilani), was the primary source for LeT surveillance on targets in Mumbai prior to the attacks.[100]

Judging by Saeed's own rhetoric, none of these developments should be particularly surprising. For instance, shortly after the United States invaded Iraq in 2003, he argued in an interview that "Jihad is prescribed in the Quran. Muslims are required to take up arms against the oppressor. The powerful western world is terrorizing the Muslims. We are being invaded, humiliated, manipulated, and looted. How else can we respond but through jihad?" He went on to add, "Suicide missions are in accordance with Islam. In fact, a suicide attack is the best form of jihad."[101] In May 2008, Saeed reiterated that "the Crusaders, the Jews, and the Hindus – all have united against the Muslims, and launched the 'war on terror' which is in fact a pretext to impose a horrible war to further the nefarious goals of the enemies of Islam."[102]

After bin Laden's death, Saeed called the al-Qaeda leader "a great man" and unloaded on the United States, calling on Muslims around the world to "stand up against America," and declaring that "now is the start of a battle

[98] Tankel, *Storming the World Stage*, p. 65.
[99] On LeT's global ambitions and networks, see Mark Mazzetti, "A Shooting in Pakistan Reveals Fraying Alliance," *New York Times*, March 12, 2011; Tankel, *Storming the World Stage*, pp. 88–102, 150–71.
[100] "Chicago Resident David Coleman Headley Pleads Guilty to Role in India and Denmark Terrorism Conspiracies," U.S. Department of Justice, Office of Public Affairs, March 18, 2010, http://www.justice.gov/opa/pr/2010/March/10-ag-277.html. CNN's expert on al-Qaeda, Peter Bergen, notes that since 2001 at least eight Americans have been caught after they received training from LeT. See Peter Bergen, *The Longest War: The Enduring Conflict between America and Al-Qaeda* (New York: Simon & Schuster, 2011), p. 237.
[101] Mohammad Shehzad, "Suicide Bombing Is the Best Form of Jihad," *Friday Times*, April 17, 2003, http://forum.pakistanidefence.com/index.php?showtopic=10243.
[102] Praveen Swami, "Pakistan and the Lashkar's Jihad in India," *Hindu*, December 9, 2008, http://www.hindu.com/2008/12/09/stories/2008120955670800.htm.

between Islam and infidels."[103] In 2012, Saeed was a prominent member of the Pakistan Defense Council, along with the former ISI chief Hamid Gul. He appeared before LeT flag-waving crowds to taunt the United States, even after Washington declared it would offer $10 million for "information leading to his arrest or conviction."

The question now is whether LeT really intends to take its fight all the way to American territory: whether it will launch attacks on U.S. soil. The answer is complicated by LeT's unusually close connections with Pakistan's military and intelligence services. In the 1990s Hafiz Saeed's organization enjoyed carte blanche to rail against all enemies of Islam, safe in the assumption that LeT enjoyed full state protection.

After President Musharraf joined Washington against al-Qaeda, LeT had to play a more sophisticated game. As scholar Stephen Tankel argues in his extensive study of LeT, *Storming the World Stage*, in the years following 9/11 Saeed navigated his organization between the seams of the U.S.-Pakistan relationship. Given that LeT continued to benefit from its sanctuary in Pakistan, its leaders preferred to avoid an open break with the Pakistani military. But because LeT's ideological compulsions also did not permit a soft line in its struggle against India or the United States, it chafed at attempts by Islamabad to rein in the jihad. Moreover, LeT could not afford to be outflanked by harder line organizations.

To complicate matters further, LeT-trained fighters routinely work with other radical groups focused on the Afghan front and beyond. Many of these groups are completely untethered, even opposed, to the Pakistani state. For instance, the al-Qaeda-linked perpetrators of the July 2005 London bombings trained in LeT camps before carrying out their attacks.[104] David Headley's LeT handlers also shared him with al-Qaeda, who sent him to conduct surveillance in Denmark against the newspaper that had published what al-Qaeda considered blasphemous cartoons in preparation for a planned attack in 2009.[105] These facts belie the notion too often voiced by Pakistanis that Washington's concerns about LeT are overblown or driven merely by an eagerness to cultivate better relations with India.

Whether or not LeT, Hafiz Saeed, and the Ahle Hadith creed enjoy continued success is less important than the fact that they have already provided a model for how violent Islamist movements can gain steam in Pakistan. Vicious attacks against external enemies, humanitarian service at home, and favor from Islamabad could permit LeT or a successor organization to take jihadist

---

[103] "JuD Holds Prayers for Osama in Lahore, Karachi," *The News*, May 4, 2011; Patrick Quinn, "Kerry: US-Pakistan Alliance at 'Critical Moment,'" Associated Press, May 15, 2011, http://cnsnews.com/news/article/kerry-us-pakistan-alliance-critical-moment.

[104] Tankel, *Storming the World Stage*, pp. 162–3.

[105] See Bruce Riedel, *Deadly Embrace: Pakistan, America, and the Future of Global Jihad* (Washington: Brookings Institution Press, 2011), p. 101.

anti-Americanism to new heights. And that would take U.S.-Pakistan relations to new lows.

LESSONS OF HISTORY

Even before the George W. Bush administration threw its weight behind President Musharraf's undemocratic regime or launched its war in Afghanistan, before President Obama accelerated the use of drones in Pakistan's Federally Administered Tribal Areas or sent Navy SEALs to kill Osama bin Laden, the Pakistani public had deep misgivings about the United States. Pakistani anti-Americanism in the post-9/11 period has its roots in the tortured history of U.S.-Pakistan relations from the early stages of the Cold War.

As new Pakistani grievances against the United States pile up, they tend to look like variations on existing themes. Different segments of the Pakistani public have had different misgivings about the United States. Some liberal Pakistanis, like Aitzaz Ahsan, saw the American tendency to back military dictators as its greatest flaw. Others, rabid nationalists like A. Q. Khan, felt that Pakistan could not trust America when the chips were down, particularly when it came to dealing with arch-nemesis India. And still others, jihadists like Hafiz Saeed, have been indoctrinated in a worldview that places hostility toward the United States, India, and Israel at its core. Together, these three strands of anti-Americanism define the vast majority of Pakistani public opinion.

History also shows the essential continuity in American and Pakistani strategies over time. Pakistan has, through thick and thin, perceived its relationship with Washington as a means to deal with India. After 9/11, this was again the case. As President Musharraf explains in his 2006 memoir, Pakistan chose to partner with America out of fear that Washington and New Delhi might unite against Pakistan, not because Islamabad felt a genuine compulsion to assist after the 9/11 tragedies or a sense of shared interest in confronting Islamist terrorism.[106] For its part, Washington has also held true to its historical pattern of using Pakistan to serve other regional and international goals. If not for 9/11, it is a safe bet that U.S.-Pakistan relations would have continued along the downward spiral of the late 1990s.

America can learn from its history with Pakistan. Future U.S. policies would be improved if they take seriously the problems, so well appreciated by Pakistan's liberals, of Pakistan's civil-military imbalance. If not, Washington will again find itself tipping the political scales in the army's favor. Similarly, knowing that Pakistan's nationalists anticipate another American "abandonment," Washington would do well to consider how its relations with Pakistan fit with – or contradict – U.S. plans for Afghanistan and for the wider Asia-Pacific region, especially with India. Finally, U.S. policy would be more enlightened if it

---

[106] Pervez Musharraf, *In the Line of Fire* (New York: Free Press, 2006), p. 202.

includes a realistic plan that begins to address the socioeconomic and especially the political trends that have given strength to Pakistan's jihadists.[107] Otherwise, Pakistan's terrorists will silence the liberals and co-opt the nationalists.

Let there be no mistake, however, Pakistanis do not hate America simply because the United States has sinned against them. Anti-Americanism in Pakistan is a by-product of the interaction between U.S. policy and Pakistan's own national decisions and internal dynamics. Each nation has pursued its interests, as it perceived them at the time. Washington is guilty of placing other goals, from anti-communism and nonproliferation to counterterrorism, over its commitment to Pakistan per se. For its part, Islamabad is guilty of misrepresenting its commitment to American goals in order to extract the material benefits of partnership with a superpower.

[107] On the complicated interaction between politics, socioeconomic status, and education as drivers for Pakistani support of Islamist militancy, see Jacob N. Shapiro and C. Christine Fair, "Understanding Support for Islamist Militancy in Pakistan," *International Security*, 34, no. 3 (Winter 2009/2010), pp. 79–118.

4

U-Turn to Drift

U.S.-Pakistan Relations during the Musharraf Era

Almost exactly ten years after the 9/11 attacks, Admiral Michael Mullen, chairman of the Joint Chiefs of Staff, testified before the U.S. Congress that the Haqqani network – a branch of the Afghan Taliban based in Pakistan's tribal areas – operated as a "veritable arm" of the Pakistani state.[1] The chairman's claim came in the aftermath of several high-profile Haqqani-orchestrated attacks inside Afghanistan, including one in which armed gunmen briefly managed to fire into the U.S. Embassy grounds from a nearby Kabul construction site.[2]

None of these attacks threatened to dislodge NATO's International Security Assistance Force (ISAF) from Afghanistan in a military sense. Even so, such violence in the heart of heavily fortified Kabul cast new doubts about whether the United States had any serious prospect of winning the war. Public skepticism was already on the rise. By late October 2011, 63 percent of Americans opposed the U.S. war in Afghanistan.[3]

By his testimony, Mullen essentially accused Pakistan of being a state sponsor of terrorism. Given its ties to the Haqqanis, Pakistan's Inter-Services Intelligence directorate (ISI) had American blood on its hands. The senior-most U.S. military officer spoke before Congress sitting shoulder-to-shoulder with the secretary of defense, Leon Panetta. Although Mullen had made similar remarks to the Pakistani media months earlier, the formal Capitol Hill testimony carried

---

[1] Thanks to K. Alan Kronstadt at the Congressional Research Service for sharing detailed chronologies of the period covered in this chapter and the next.

[2] Alissa J. Rubin, Ray Rivera, and Jack Healy, "U.S. Embassy and NATO Headquarters Attacked in Kabul," *New York Times*, September 13, 2011, http://www.nytimes.com/2011/09/14/world/asia/14afghanistan.html?_r=1.

[3] "CNN Poll: Support for Afghanistan War at All Time Low," *CNN*, October 28, 2011, http://politicalticker.blogs.cnn.com/2011/10/28/cnn-poll-support-for-afghanistan-war-at-all-time-low/.

greater political weight in Washington and Islamabad.[4] In both instances, his damning conclusion came as a shock to many Pakistanis who had considered Mullen a "pro-Pakistani" voice among Obama's top officials. Mullen earned this distinction from spending long hours cultivating ties with Pakistan's army chief, General Ashfaq Kayani. Like many officers, Mullen placed a great deal of stock in the notion that personal connections with foreign officers build more effective state-to-state relationships. If Pakistan's generals had a friend in Washington, he was it.[5]

The normally mild-mannered admiral's blunt characterization of ISI-Haqqani links also surprised many outside observers. Other American officials had made similar accusations, but Mullen's tone, setting, and timing suggested the potential for a deeper policy shift within the administration. For several days, it was difficult to determine just what Mullen's testimony really meant. Even inside the U.S. State Department and parts of the National Security Council, officials scrambled to figure out how Mullen's statement – which apparently had not been blessed in detail by a full interagency consensus – would affect U.S. policy.[6] In the end, the White House and State Department tried to sweep the entire incident under the carpet. They downplayed the direct connections between the ISI and attacks on U.S. troops in Afghanistan.[7] But Mullen's remarks were a part of the indelible historical record, and on Capitol Hill they carried more weight than the disclaimers that followed.

Whatever the logic of Mullen's outburst, Pakistanis were quick to grasp that if the admiral had soured on them, Washington's sympathy was pretty well exhausted. Such a public rebuke by a senior official was rare. In Pakistan a few weeks after his testimony, I found widespread concern that Mullen's statement might be a precursor to war with America. Hard-line Pakistani pundits and politicians stoked these fears on television. They announced that Pakistan would resist American pressure and that the nation was prepared to go to war if necessary. In a conversation with a small group of young Pakistani professionals in Karachi, I observed that I could not rule out a deeper rupture in relations between Pakistan and the United States. In response, one earnest young man

---

[4] Baqir Sajjad Syed, "Mullen Launches Diatribe against ISI," *Dawn*, April 21, 2011, http://dawn .com/2011/04/21/pakistans-isi-links-with-haqqani-militants-us/.

[5] It is widely rumored that Mullen took a lead role in advocating a three-year extension for Kayani at the army's helm. Without it, Kayani would have retired in mid-2010. See Riedel, *Deadly Embrace* (Washington, DC: Brookings, 2011), p. 121. For his part, Mullen denies the rumors. See "Mullen Denies Involvement in General Kayani's Extension," *Canadian Asian News*, February 2012, http://www.canadianasiannews.com/images/e-issues/Canadian%20Asian%20News%20 (%20Febuary%2015–28%202012).pdf.

[6] Author conversations with State Department and National Security Council staff, September 2011.

[7] Greg Miller and Karen DeYoung, "Adm. Mullen's Words on Pakistan Come under Scrutiny," *Washington Post*, September 27, 2011, http://www.washingtonpost.com/world/national-securi ty/adm-mullens-words-on-pakistan-come-under-scrutiny/2011/09/27/gIQAHPJB3K_story.html.

ruefully commented, "you must understand, your words have made all our hearts pound faster – we are frightened of what the future might hold."

Over the fall, tensions ebbed slightly, but on November 26, 2011, NATO forces killed twenty-four Pakistani soldiers along the Afghan border, believing them to be insurgents. The news briefly made headlines in the United States but garnered nonstop media coverage in Pakistan. Some of the details of the case, including who fired first, remain disputed. There is no doubt, however, that one of the worst blunders of the incident came when NATO misinformed a Pakistani liaison officer about the location of a ground attack. The coordinates he shared were wrong by nine miles.

No matter the specifics of the incident, the toxicity of the U.S.-Pakistan relationship made it impossible to resolve matters quickly or easily. Even if Pakistan's army had wanted to absolve Washington of blame – which it clearly did not – Islamabad as a whole saw far greater political advantage in venting its anger. Politicians, including members of the left-leaning Pakistan People's Party (PPP) government, followed the army's lead. The PPP was already under intense pressure owing to an ongoing scandal (dubbed "memogate" by the hyperbolic media) that painted its leaders as pro-American, anti-army stooges. In an attempt not to be outdone by howling Islamists and nationalists, Pakistan's prime minister accused Washington of having launched a premeditated strike on Pakistani forces.

As compared to the past, when smaller friendly fire incidents had also claimed Pakistani lives along the Afghan border, Islamabad was no longer willing to seek a quiet accommodation with Washington or to chalk the latest deaths up to the tragedy of war. Pakistani officials demanded a full and public apology from Washington. The White House refused.[8] The U.S. embassy in Islamabad and the Pentagon shared their condolences, but that did rather little to assuage Pakistani anger.

Islamabad closed its border crossings to Afghanistan, stemming the flow of NATO war supplies. Those crossings were not reopened until July 3, 2012.[9] Under Pakistani pressure, Washington also agreed to shut down its "secret" Shamsi airbase located in a barren valley of Pakistan's Baluchistan province. Pakistan had originally leased the facility to the United Arab Emirates so that its royals could go on traditional hunting expeditions for bustards, the species of large birds that nest in the region.[10] After 9/11, Shamsi's airstrips were upgraded and subleased to the United States for emergency landings and a very

[8] Adam Entous, Siobhan Gorman, and Julian E. Barnes, "U.S. Agonizes over Apology to Pakistan," *Wall Street Journal*, May 17, 2012, http://online.wsj.com/article/SB1000142405270230 3505504577406151609731364.html.

[9] Eric Schmitt, "Clinton's 'Sorry' to Pakistan Ends Barrier to NATO," *New York Times*, July 3, 2012, http://www.nytimes.com/2012/07/04/world/asia/pakistan-opens-afghan-routes-to-nato-after-us-apology.html?pagewanted=all.

[10] "UAE mounts pressure to get airbase decision reversed," *Dawn*, November 29, 2011, http://www.dawn.com/2011/11/29/uae-mounts-pressure-to-get-airbase-decision-reversed.html.

different sort of hunting. Armed U.S. drones took off from Shamsi to fly over Pakistan's nearby tribal areas, their missiles loaded by contractors, presumably to reduce the official U.S. footprint there. Within weeks, the facility was emptied and returned to Pakistani authority.[11] Pakistan's leaders declared that they planned to reevaluate all remaining forms of cooperation with the United States.

Both the Mullen and Salala incidents demonstrated the significance of public, as compared to private, diplomacy between Washington and Islamabad. Mullen's testimony set off political explosions in Pakistan in ways that tough messages delivered in private never had. Similarly, the White House's initial refusal to apologize for Salala carried outsized political repercussions. In some ways, this was an unfamiliar dynamic; in a new era of intense Pakistani media scrutiny, the U.S.-Pakistan relationship was becoming more politicized and less amenable to behind-the-scenes management.

At the same time, past American policymakers had often appreciated that criticism delivered in public would be hard for their Pakistani counterparts to swallow, and should therefore be used sparingly and with purpose.[12] Unfortunately, neither the Mullen testimony nor the Salala non-apology were put to constructive ends. Washington's unwillingness to harness Mullen's verbal firepower as coercive leverage turned his parting shots into nothing more than disruptive irritants. Likewise, if the White House had made timely use of the "s-word" (sorry) after Salala, it is possible that months might have been shaved off the time taken to reopen NATO supply routes to Afghanistan.

AMERICA'S MISSED OPPORTUNITIES

All told, ten years after 9/11, relations between Washington and Islamabad looked at least as bad as they did before Musharraf was drafted into Bush's war on terror. Fresh wounds were inflicted atop the deep bruises of the past. The United States had fought a prolonged battle against al-Qaeda in ways that succeeded in killing most of its top leaders, but it never brought Americans and Pakistanis together in a common understanding of the terrorist threat. In the Afghan war, Washington suffered from distraction, setbacks, and stalemate, all the while failing to resolve fundamental differences with Islamabad over how to fight the war or how to end it. And despite extensive diplomacy, public outreach, and tens of billions of dollars in aid, the United States never managed to forge friendly, constructive relationships with Pakistan's people, government, or military.

---

[11] "US Equipment Vacated from Shamsi Air Base," *Geo News*, December 9, 2011, http://www.geo.tv/GeoDetail.aspx?ID=28257.

[12] President Clinton's televised critique of Pakistan's trajectory during his visit to Islamabad provides a good example of public criticism, recounted in Chapter 6.

It is possible that some, maybe many, of these failings were unavoidable. Both the Bush and Obama administrations have routinely identified Pakistan as one of the most difficult foreign policy challenges in the world. At times, these U.S. administrations acted in ways they knew would expose them to harsh criticism but preferred that outcome to other even less pleasant alternatives. More often than not, U.S. policies amounted to picking the "least bad" option from an unappetizing menu. That is the policymaker's tragic responsibility; it is what separates him from the idealist or the pundit.

That said, there were also times that Washington simply made bad choices. There are lessons to be learned from these mistakes and what they say about America's ability to act with purpose in the world. Those lessons may help us better manage future relations with Pakistan and, perhaps, with other countries as well.

Just One Damned Thing after Another

The fact that relations between the United States and Pakistan came full circle in the post-9/11 decade suggests a grand, tragic narrative. But for many of those who lived the history, it usually felt more like a series of barely manageable crises separated by brief periods of deceptive calm. As former Secretary of State Condoleezza Rice describes in her memoir of the Bush administration, "I once described [Pakistan] as taking care of a critically ill patient; you got up every day and dealt with the symptom of the moment, hoping over time to cure the underlying disease of extremism."[13] A few U.S. officials acted upon that hope, especially during the exhilarating period of political transition in 2008 and 2009, when leadership changed in both Islamabad and Washington. Most U.S. officials, however, tended to find that emergency triage was more than enough of a challenge to keep them occupied, particularly when other troubles, like Iraq, loomed large.

Some members of the early Bush administration simply held out less hope than Rice that history would ever amount to more than one damned thing after another. In other words, success in dealing with the challenges of the day was about the best you could expect to do. This perspective dominated the thinking of Secretary of State Colin Powell and his deputy, Richard Armitage. There is something deeply realistic, even humble, about such a worldview. At the time it represented a stark contrast to the more ambitious perspectives of other administration officials who believed that the United States had the power to change the world in fundamental ways, and the responsibility to act in order to realize those changes.

For Powell and Armitage, major changes in the world were possible yet difficult to engineer and, more often than not, unpredictable. Some have described

---

[13] Rice, *No Higher Honor* (New York: Crown, 2011), p. 128.

their differences with other members of the Bush administration in academic jargon, drawing contrasts between the "neoconservatives" and the "realists." And it is true that Powell and Armitage (along with Powell's Director of Policy Planning, Richard Haass) defined U.S. national interests narrowly. The famous "Powell Doctrine," for instance, sets firm limits on when and how the United States should go to war.

Powell and Armitage also seemed to share a very different temperament from that of most other members of the administration's national security team. Powell's memoir describes his passion for fixing beat-up old Volvos.[14] He would drag dead ones home on a rope, then toil away until they were up and running. Here was a man who took pleasure in putting things in their proper place, not someone who craved building something new from scratch. At the State Department, where Powell and Armitage worked so closely with one another that they could "mind meld," both tended to be fixers more than conceptualizers. Among Bush's national security team, they were arguably better than anyone at actually getting things done in the world, but less persuasive when it came to determining what ought to be done in the first place. Their inability to steer the president away from the Iraq war is the most widely cited example of that fact, but it was hardly the only one.

Securing Pakistan's Partial U-Turn

All of this mattered a great deal to relations between the United States and Pakistan because President George W. Bush entrusted Powell and Armitage to manage South Asia policy at critical junctures in the early post-9/11 period. From 2001 to 2005, they took the lead in shifting that relationship from estrangement to partially effective, if narrowly defined, cooperation. They established a pattern of interaction with Pakistani President Musharraf and the Pakistani military that persisted for nearly three years after they had retired from public office. In the process they helped to avert at least one major war between India and Pakistan.

These were no mean feats. Yet they were not transformative. Washington got the relationship with Pakistan up and running again like one of Powell's old Volvos. There was no expectation that it would end up looking or driving like a Porsche. The question is whether they could have aimed higher.

Born in 1945, Richard Armitage is no longer the fearless young man who volunteered to stalk the jungles of Vietnam as an "ambush adviser" to a South Vietnamese unit, or who led a convoy of ships loaded with over 20,000 South Vietnamese to safety in the Philippines in 1975.[15] Even so, this hard-charging

---

[14] Colin Powell, *My American Journey* (New York: Random House, 1995), pp. 212, 293–4, 392.
[15] Armitage claims he was not a part of the CIA's Phoenix program, despite claims by close friends and associates from the period. For more on his service in Vietnam, see James Mann, *Rise of the Vulcans* (New York: Penguin, 2004), pp. 37–8, 44–52.

power-lifter is by far the most intimidating presence I have met in government service. Bald and seemingly as wide and deep as he is tall, Armitage uses his heft to political advantage. His gravelly voice and direct manner can be terrifying. If he decides, as one of his State Department staffers used to say, to "wirebrush" you, you won't forget it. Yet because he fills a room so easily, his graciousness and extreme capacity for politeness in diplomatic settings can also be shockingly disarming. Armitage is also an inveterate gossip who has had brushes with political scandal, most recently in the case of outed Central Intelligence Agency (CIA) officer Valerie Plame. Above all, however, he is a gifted leader. He commands remarkable loyalty from a network of foreign policy professionals in Washington and throughout the world.

During a visit to Pakistan with Armitage in February 2010 as part of a Council on Foreign Relations project, I watched as Pakistanis of all stripes treated him like returning royalty. But equally he was nearly always asked whether in the days after 9/11 he had really told Pakistani officials – as reported in Musharraf's memoirs – that America would bomb Pakistan "back to the Stone Age" if Washington did not get full and immediate cooperation in the fight against al-Qaeda. Armitage vehemently rejects Musharraf's version of that history and claims he "never said anything about bombing or the Stone Age." The trouble is, when he tells you that, in all his massive, gruff intensity, you feel like he might just bomb *you* back to the Stone Age. So it is very easy to imagine Pakistanis hearing – or believing they heard – the same thing, under the circumstances.[16]

And what circumstances they were. The United States had been hit hard, and immediately sought to prepare a major military counterpunch against bin Laden and his Taliban hosts in remote, landlocked Afghanistan. That required ground and air access for U.S. planes and troops, preferably through Pakistan's ports, roads, and airspace. It also meant an about-face in Pakistan's supportive relations with the Taliban regime in Kabul as well as the need for intensive cooperation between the CIA and ISI in rounding up al-Qaeda operatives on Pakistani soil. As President Bush writes in his memoir, "Pakistan was the most pivotal nation" recruited to Washington's side in the post-9/11 fight.[17] In short order, stemming from Armitage's blunt request to the Pakistani ambassador, Maleeha Lodhi, and the head of the ISI, General Mahmoud Ahmad, Washington had a promise from Musharraf's government for all that it had requested.[18]

---

[16] In the official U.S. account of this conversation, Armitage suggests that "Pakistan faces a stark choice: either it is with us or it is not; this was a black-and-white choice, with no grey." See U.S. Department of State, Cable, "Deputy Secretary Armitage's Meeting with Pakistan Intel Chief Mahmud: You're Either With Us or You're Not," September 13, 2001, Secret, 9 pp. [Excised], *National Security Archive*, http://www.gwu.edu/~nsarchiv/NSAEBB/NSAEBB358a/doc03-1.pdf.

[17] George W. Bush, *Decision Points* (New York: Crown, 2010), p. 187.

[18] Armitage made seven specific requests to Mahmoud in their September 13 meeting, all of which were quickly accepted by Musharraf. See U.S. Department of State, Cable, "Deputy Secretary

America's demands were urgent, yet in a sense they were also defined quite narrowly. "History starts today," stated Armitage, meaning that Pakistan had to make up its mind whether it would stand with or against the United States. But it also meant that the Bush administration was willing to brush aside previous U.S. concerns that had defined relations between Islamabad and Washington for the better part of a decade, such as Pakistan's nuclear program or its undemocratic regime. U.S. sanctions that had been imposed for Musharraf's coup and Pakistan's 1998 nuclear tests were waived, and the Bush administration worked hard to craft a package of assistance that would rival the one President Reagan had offered General Zia in the 1980s.

The underlying assumption on the part of Washington's senior leadership was that in order to get Musharraf on its side, America would have to buy him some operating space with his army and his people who were not predisposed to support cooperation with the United States. As Powell explained in a November 5, 2001, memo to President Bush, "Musharraf's decision to fully cooperate with the US in the wake of 9/11, at considerable political risk, abruptly turned our stalled relationship around."[19] Powell clearly believed that to push Musharraf too hard or too fast might send him over the edge.

Critics at the time, and since, have wondered whether Musharraf was quite so fragile, and whether the deal could have been conditioned from the outset in ways that would have offered Washington persistent sources of leverage in the relationship. That these critics did not win the day in the traumatic period shortly after al-Qaeda's attacks makes sense. The Bush administration was playing a catch-up game in Afghanistan and hardly looking for more trouble with Pakistan. Yet the post-9/11 deal with Islamabad established a pattern of U.S. generosity that would prove difficult to escape even as its faults became more apparent.

Washington quickly cancelled $1 billion in Pakistani debts to the United States, deferred the payment of billions more, and directed international financial institutions to support Pakistan in other ways as well.[20] In June 2003, President Bush met with President Musharraf at Camp David and pledged a five-year aid package of $3 billion, split evenly between military and civilian

---

Armitage's Meeting with General Mahmud: Actions and Support Expected of Pakistan in Fight against Terrorism," September 14, 2001, Secret, 5 pp. [Excised], http://www.gwu.edu/~nsarchiv/NSAEBB/NSAEBB358a/doc05.pdf; U.S. Embassy (Islamabad), Cable, "Musharraf Accepts the Seven Points" September 14, 2001, Secret, 4 pp. [Excised], http://www.gwu.edu/~nsarchiv/NSAEBB/NSAEBB358a/doc05.pdf.

19 U.S. Department of State, Memorandum, From Secretary of State Colin Powell to U.S. President George W. Bush, "Your Meeting with Pakistani President Musharraf," November 5, 2001, Secret, 2 pp. [Excised], http://www.gwu.edu/~nsarchiv/NSAEBB/NSAEBB358a/doc21.pdf.

20 "US Formally Forgives $1B in Pakistani Loans," *Voice of America*, April 5, 2003, http://www.voanews.com/english/news/a-13-a-2003-04-05-1-US-66849252.html; "Economy on the Mend?" *Dawn*, August 26, 2002, http://archives.dawn.com/2002/08/26/ed.htm.

pots.[21] By the end of fiscal year 2004, Washington had provided Pakistan with $4 billion in assistance.[22]

By later that summer, the terms of that new arrangement were set and shielded from additional review even though there were already reasons to wonder whether the arrangement might be recalibrated to better serve U.S. interests. Senior administration officials considered the package more like a reward for wartime services Pakistan had already rendered than as a point of leverage for new negotiations. The administration chose to focus on what Pakistan had provided – from high level arrests of al-Qaeda operatives to logistical support for the U.S. invasion of Afghanistan – and not on what Pakistan had failed to do, like taking a decisive stance against the Taliban fighters who fled from Afghan battlefields.

Along with the aid deal, Washington also agreed to reimburse Pakistan for military expenditures related to the war in Afghanistan. Those "coalition support funds" sent a billion dollars per year into Pakistani coffers. They were only loosely based on verifiable Pakistani costs. Even more sensitive types of aid were provided without public fanfare. To help secure Pakistan's nuclear arsenal, Washington granted the Pakistani military's Strategic Plans Division at least $100 million, along with technical information and training.[23] Although there is no publicly available record, it is widely accepted that the United States also provided hundreds of millions of dollars or more to the ISI to encourage its cooperation and improve its ability to help find and kill terrorists. It is rumored that the new ISI headquarters in Islamabad was built with American funds.[24]

At the center of this arrangement was a quiet gentleman's agreement by President Bush not to take steps that might politically undermine his Pakistani counterpart. A month after the al-Qaeda attacks, Bush met with Musharraf in New York City and, in response to a question about whether the United States might again "abandon" Pakistan as it had at the end of the Cold War, Bush replied, "You tell your people that the President looked you in the eye and told you that he would stick with you."[25]

[21] David E. Sanger, "Bush Offers Pakistan Aid, but No F-16s," *New York Times*, June 25, 2003, http://www.nytimes.com/2003/06/25/world/bush-offers-pakistan-aid-but-no-f-16-s.html? pagewanted=all&src=pm.

[22] Susan B. Epstein and K. Alan Kronstadt, "Pakistan: U.S. Foreign Assistance," *Congressional Research Service*, CRS Report 7-5700, June 7, 2011, http://fpc.state.gov/documents/organization/166839.pdf.

[23] For more on this program, see David E. Sanger, *The Inheritance* (New York: Harmony Books, 2009), pp. 215–20.

[24] Greg Miller, "CIA Pays for Support in Pakistan," *Los Angeles Times*, November 15, 2009, http://articles.latimes.com/2009/nov/15/world/fg-cia-pakistan15.

[25] Quoted in Rashid, *Descent into Chaos*, p. 86, from James Carney and John F. Dickerson, "Inside the War Room," *Time*, December 31, 2001, http://www.time.com/time/magazine/article/0,9171,1001573,00.html.

Later, at the end of 2007 when Musharraf's grip on power was slipping, Bush appears to have recalled that initial pledge. "I don't want anyone pulling the rug out from under him. The United States isn't going to be in a position of trying to bring him down," he told his secretary of state, in full recognition that remaining true to Musharraf would cost Washington dearly with the Pakistani public who had long since soured on their undemocratic leader.[26]

The deal with Musharraf was essential for the opening phase of America's response to al-Qaeda. Pakistan's ports and airstrips made it far easier for the United States to launch an invasion of Afghanistan. Very soon, the fight against al-Qaeda inside Pakistan became equally significant. Musharraf purged Taliban and al-Qaeda sympathizers from official roles in the army's leadership. At Washington's forceful urging, he also helped to shut down and investigate nascent links between a small group of Pakistani nuclear scientists and al-Qaeda.[27] Overall, cooperation between the CIA and ISI led to the arrest of hundreds of al-Qaeda members, including the mastermind of 9/11, Khalid Sheikh Mohammed, in March 2003. Over those first few years after 9/11, CIA counterterror operations in Pakistani cities grew sufficiently sophisticated that remaining al-Qaeda operatives began to flee the cities for the remote tribal areas along the Afghan border.[28] In short, Musharraf took some very important steps in return for America's largesse and in response to American pressure.

Early Frustrations

But Musharraf's game with the United States was a lot more complicated than that. He worked overtime to minimize stresses on himself, his army, and his state (in roughly that order) while maximizing the flow of assistance and reimbursements from Washington. He and his top generals drew distinctions between different types of militants and terrorists, fighting some, such as al-Qaeda and various Pakistani sectarian extremist groups, while aiding and abetting others, such as anti-Indian terrorist organizations like Lashkar-e-Taiba and the fleeing Afghan Taliban leadership.[29] U.S. officials were reluctant to criticize Musharraf publicly, lest they jeopardize what help Pakistan was already providing. But despite this public American embrace, there was never any doubt in Washington that Musharraf was a less-than-ideal partner and Pakistan a difficult ally. Over time, American frustrations mounted.

One of the most significant problems with Pakistan became apparent mere months after 9/11, when on December 13, 2001, Pakistani terrorists launched

---

[26] Rice, *No Higher Honor*, p. 610.

[27] George Tenet, *At the Center of the Storm* (New York: HarperCollins, 2007), pp. 261–8.

[28] Bergen, *The Longest War* (New York: Free Press, 2011), p. 254.

[29] Ashley Tellis discusses the distinctions Pakistan drew in its relationships with extremist and terrorist groups in *Pakistan and the War on Terror* (Washington, DC: Carnegie Endowment for International Peace, 2008), http://www.carnegieendowment.org/files/tellis_pakistan_final .pdf.

an audacious raid on India's parliament in New Delhi. Fortunately, the attackers failed in their primary goal of killing India's top politicians, but they nearly succeeded in sparking a war between India and Pakistan. Both countries mobilized hundreds of thousands of troops along their shared border until late 2002.[30]

Analysts call this period the "Twin Peaks crisis" because there were two high points of Indo-Pakistani tension, the first after the parliament attack and the second in May 2002 when Pakistani terrorists massacred several dozen Indians, including women and children, at an army camp in Kashmir. With troops at the ready and patience near the breaking point, it looked like nuclear-armed India and Pakistan would go to war. In early June 2002, Armitage flew into action with a diplomatic mission to avert that disastrous outcome. In Islamabad, he elicited a quiet promise from Musharraf to end the movement of terrorists across the Kashmir divide. Armitage then shuttled to India where he publicly revealed Musharraf's pledge. By playing the intermediary role, Armitage effectively made the United States a guarantor of that pledge.

As a short-term fix, the gambit worked. But the affair exposed the reality that Musharraf's promises to crack down on all Pakistani-based militants could not be taken seriously. During his meeting with the Pakistani president in Islamabad, Armitage had shared evidence of terrorist training camps on the Pakistani side of the border. Musharraf became red-faced with surprise, either because he had been caught in the act or because his orders to disband the camps had not been followed. Neither Americans nor Indians honestly believed that Musharraf's pledge would end terrorist infiltration once and for all, but Armitage's intervention was welcomed as a politically expedient means to defuse a war.

American diplomacy did little, however, to address the persistent threat posed by terrorist safe havens on Pakistani soil.[31] This was equally true on Pakistan's western front, where Pakistanis, including members of the ISI, were welcoming fleeing Afghan fighters back into the same places that many of them had called home during the civil wars of the 1990s and the anti-Soviet campaigns of the 1980s.

In time, Pakistan's safe haven enabled a ragtag band of defeated refugees to regroup into an Afghan insurgency that challenges NATO and the Kabul government to this day. America's own failure to close the Afghan border and bottle up al-Qaeda in the mountain redoubt of Tora Bora in December 2001 was immediately recognized as a blunder.[32] But it was not until at least 2005 or 2006 that American officials in Washington fully appreciated the

---

[30] For a thorough study of this episode, see Polly Nayak and Michael Krepon, *U.S. Crisis Management in South Asia's Twin Peaks Crisis* (Washington: Stimson Center, 2006), http://www.stimson.org/books-reports/us-crisis-management-in-south-asias-twin-peaks-crisis/.

[31] This is one of the many insightful observations in Nayak and Krepon, *U.S. Crisis Management.*

[32] Gary Berntsen and Ralph Pezzullo, *Jawbreaker* (New York: Crown, 2005).

ramifications of the Taliban safe haven in Pakistan for what was by then a stalemated war in Afghanistan.

American mistakes in Afghanistan and Washington's distraction by the Iraq war had by then convinced Islamabad that the United States was not seriously interested in ridding Afghanistan of Taliban influence. From a Pakistani perspective, Washington was either unaware of or resigned to the fact that the Taliban were gradually reasserting their influence in Afghanistan. As a consequence, Pakistanis – many already sympathetic to the Afghan Taliban cause – chose to maintain and even to enhance their ties with the militants and to see them as political allies for that inevitable day when the Americans would pack up and leave Afghanistan once again.

Washington's tightly constrained definition of its post-9/11 mission in Pakistan was also made clear along a very different front. In 1999, Musharraf had grabbed power by toppling the civilian government of Nawaz Sharif. During his first couple of years he faced U.S. criticism, but riding high on American post-9/11 support, he believed the time was ripe to cement his political authority. To accomplish this, the army and ISI cynically rigged a 2002 national referendum and parliamentary elections. These moves sidelined Musharraf's political opponents and installed a pliant "king's party" in Islamabad. The entire exercise provided only the thinnest democratic veneer to Musharraf's regime, and the ham-handed manipulation of the polls really only undercut his claims of popularity and legitimacy.[33] His determination to invoke a constitutionally derived authority for his rule also set the tone for future conflicts with political opponents.

Musharraf's political shenanigans stirred no public rebuke from the Bush administration. The Pakistani general's anti-democratic practices were thoroughly at odds with what would later, especially after President Bush's second inaugural speech, be called the "freedom agenda."[34] Underpinning that agenda was the notion that the repressive politics of undemocratic regimes in the Muslim world were at least partially to blame for the Islamist terrorism of the early twenty-first century. Musharraf's version of authoritarianism in Pakistan looked rather tame next to that of Egypt or Saudi Arabia, but the essential logic of the freedom agenda could be applied just as readily.

America's hypocritical policy in Pakistan was, however, entirely consistent with the defining features of Washington's post-9/11 relationship with Musharraf. The first of these was Bush's pledge not to pressure him in ways that were politically uncomfortable. The pledge was buttressed by a view in other corners of the administration, including the State Department, that it was simply unrealistic to demand very much from Pakistan. America was having a hard enough time with al-Qaeda, the Taliban, and near-war between India and Pakistan. Could it simultaneously demand democratic reform by a country that

---

[33] For more on this episode, see Rashid, *Descent into Chaos*, pp. 149–51, 156–61.
[34] Rice, *No Higher Honor*, pp. 324–9.

had seen too little capable leadership – civilian or military – over the course of its independent history, and which lacked some of the basic building blocks for effective democratic rule? No; Powell and Armitage judged it was wiser to curb American ambitions and focus on the immediate problems at hand. Better to recognize that Pakistan would remain, at least for the foreseeable future, a rusty old Volvo.

DRIFT AND DISTRACTION

By crafting a narrow deal with Musharraf after 9/11, the Bush administration got what it needed to launch its opening salvo in the campaign to punish al-Qaeda and its allies. That was a big deal. But when that salvo failed to find and finish al-Qaeda in short order, Washington found itself with too little leverage in its relationship with Islamabad. The United States needed to renegotiate terms with Pakistan, but that would have to wait until both Presidents Bush and Musharraf left the scene.

From about 2003 until 2007, the relationship stayed stuck in first gear, routinely buffeted by crises and, after 2003, increasingly a victim of the massive distractions caused by the U.S. war in Iraq. In American policy debates, it is now commonplace to argue that if not for Iraq, Washington might have kept its focus on Afghanistan and finished the job it started after 9/11.[35] This critique is fair. It is equally applicable to U.S. policy in Pakistan.

The Iraq war reconfigured U.S. priorities globally, including in South Asia. For instance, on joining the policy planning staff at the State Department in 2003, I was tasked to determine whether South Asian countries might contribute troops for the war in Iraq. Today, it seems more than a little quixotic that Washington could have cajoled Pakistan, Bangladesh, or India (among other states) into sending their soldiers into the quicksand of Iraq. But in June 2003, undoubtedly out of a desire to curry favor with the United States, Musharraf had in fact accepted "in principle" a U.S. request to contribute peacekeepers to an anticipated Iraqi stabilization force.[36] There were similarly lukewarm responses from other potential contributing nations.

The fact that global troop solicitations occupied a good part of America's diplomatic agenda provides an accurate reflection of Washington's priorities during that period. The war in Iraq redirected American money, troops, weapons, intelligence assets, and the attention of senior administration officials away from South Asia. Afghanistan turned into an "economy of force"

---

[35] This point won easy and bipartisan support among the members of the Council on Foreign Relations Task Force I directed in 2010. See *Independent Task Force on U.S. Strategy for Pakistan and Afghanistan*, Task Force Report No. 65, Council on Foreign Relations (November 2010), http://www.cfr.org/pakistan/us-strategy-pakistan-afghanistan/p23253?co=C007305.

[36] See K. Alan Kronstadt, "Pakistan: Chronology of Events," *Congressional Research Service*, August 4, 2003, http://www.iwar.org.uk/news-archive/crs/23387.pdf.

operation.[37] According to David D. McKiernan, the U.S. general in charge of the mission in Afghanistan from 2008 to 2009, "There was a saying when I got there: If you're in Iraq and you need something, you ask for it. If you're in Afghanistan and you need it, you figure out how to do without it."[38] In short, U.S. troops in Afghanistan were too few and lacked too much of what they needed to do their jobs.

Pakistan was also an afterthought. Even setting aside everything other than the fight against al-Qaeda, the initial burst of post-9/11 counterterror successes gradually slowed to a trickle. By 2007, it was clear that Washington's counterterror effort in Pakistan was failing. Such was the frightening judgment of a U.S. National Intelligence Estimate released that summer, in which the U.S. intelligence community concluded that al-Qaeda "has protected or regenerated key elements of its Homeland attack capability, including: a safe haven in the Pakistan Federally Administered Tribal Areas (FATA), operational lieutenants, and its top leadership."[39]

A Musharraf-Centric Strategy

Washington might have been captivated by Iraq, but there were regular reminders of how dangerous the situation in Pakistan could be. For a time, it felt like just keeping Musharraf alive was a major accomplishment. Over a two-week period at the end of 2003, the general-turned-president narrowly escaped being blown up in two separate attacks. In both cases, extremist sympathizers within the Pakistani military tipped off the terrorists about Musharraf's travel plans.

Musharraf opens his 2006 memoir with a description of the gruesome scene during one of those attacks.[40] It is horrifying for what it says about the levels of violence in Pakistan. Most striking to U.S. officials at the time was the sense that Musharraf faced enemies within his own military who were in league with the terrorists and who might, with a lucky bomb or bullet, send Pakistan into even deeper turmoil than it already faced.

The assassination attempts undoubtedly reinforced a sense among senior U.S. officials that Musharraf's life was on the line because he had cast his lot on America's side in the war against the terrorists. This was only partially true. Musharraf's alliance was in fact grudging and incomplete. Persistent differences of interest remained between Washington and Islamabad. Nevertheless, the

---

[37] News Transcript, "DoD News Briefing with Adm. Mullen at the Pentagon," July 2, 2008, http://www.defense.gov/transcripts/transcript.aspx?transcriptid=4256.

[38] Rajiv Chandrasekaran, "Pentagon Worries Led to Command Change," *Washington Post*, August 17, 2009, http://www.washingtonpost.com/wp-dyn/content/article/2009/08/16/AR200 9081602304_pf.html.

[39] "The Terrorist Threat to the U.S. Homeland," *National Intelligence Estimate* (July 2007), www.c-span.org/pdf/nie_071707.pdf.

[40] Pervez Musharraf, *In the Line of Fire: A Memoir* (New York: Free Press, 2006), p. 1.

assassination attempts encouraged the prevailing American aversion to policies that might put Musharraf at greater risk.

That aversion manifested itself in a range of ways. Washington's muted public response to Musharraf's handling of the A. Q. Khan affair in early 2004 was one of them. Khan's forced confession, official pardon, and house arrest all came just weeks after the attempts on Musharraf's life. The Khan denouement followed a string of public reports that Pakistan had been the source of nuclear technologies and know-how to Iran, Libya, and North Korea.[41]

Musharraf had assured top American officials, including Colin Powell, that Pakistan was not involved in such nuclear smuggling activity. Yet when the truth came out, he was let off the hook. Publicly, Washington accepted his cooperation in shutting down and investigating Khan's activities as a sign of good faith. Nuclear nonproliferation activists around the world howled.[42] As a practical matter, Bush administration officials saw greater utility in focusing on pressing threats – like the possibility that al-Qaeda had made contact with Khan's network – than in turning up the heat on Musharraf to unravel the nature of the historical relationship between Khan and the Pakistani military.

All of this might have been entirely different if Washington had not invested so heavily in the Pakistani president. The unhealthy personalization of the U.S.-Pakistan relationship was widely derided at the time by Pakistanis and American critics alike. As many observers pointed out, Musharraf was hardly a lonely defender of Pakistani stability. Even if Musharraf disappeared, the Pakistani "establishment" – the army and its political allies – would end up following a path similar to the one Musharraf had taken, driven by a powerful instinct for self-preservation.[43]

By this logic, the alternative to Musharraf was not a bunch of wild-eyed jihadists but a look-alike from the all-powerful Pakistani army. Therefore, it did not make sense to worry too much about Musharraf per se. Then again, it also did not make much sense to seek change, since Musharraf's replacement was not likely to be a major improvement and might even be slightly worse. Moreover, any political shift in Islamabad risked an undesirable, if temporary, disruption to patterns of interaction that had emerged since 9/11.

A harsher critique, and one that got louder the longer Musharraf remained in office, held that he and his army were the primary obstacles to Pakistan's

---

[41] For the former CIA director's version of this episode, see Tenet, *At the Center of the Storm*, pp. 281–7.

[42] "Security Check: Confronting Today's Global Threats," Stanley Foundation, May 2005, pp. 10–11, http://www.stanleyfoundation.org/radiopdf/securitycheck.pdf.

[43] For contemporary arguments along these lines, see Pervez Hoodbhoy, "Can Pakistan Work? A Country in Search of Itself," *Foreign Affairs* (November/December 2004), http://www.foreig naffairs.com/articles/60285/pervez-hoodbhoy/can-pakistan-work-a-country-in-search-of-itself; Sharon Otterman, "Pakistan: Threats to Musharraf's Rule," CFR.org Backgrounder, Council on Foreign Relations, January 16, 2004, http://www.cfr.org/pakistan/pakistan-threats-musha rrafs-rule/p7743#p4.

stability. One version of this argument came from Musharraf's political opponents in Pakistan. They saw his decision to align the country with America after 9/11 as the chief cause of violence inside Pakistan. They blamed Musharraf for permitting "America's war" to take place on Pakistani soil. This line of reasoning did not hold much water in Washington. It smacked of a willful Pakistani ignorance about the genuine threats posed by the violent extremists in their midst.

On the other hand, the combination of Musharraf's undemocratic practices and inadequate performance in the fight against regional and international terrorists was harder and harder for Americans to ignore. Pakistan's opposition politicians, particularly from Benazir Bhutto's PPP, chastised Americans for failing to appreciate Musharraf's shortcomings. In February 2004, Bhutto herself proclaimed to an audience in Washington:

At this time of political crisis in Pakistan, with a military dictatorship strangling our Constitution, America should stand for its values and principles, and reject tyranny. General Musharraf uses Pakistan's importance to the United States in Afghanistan to further his own dictatorship. This is at the cost of the human and democratic rights of the people of Pakistan. He says he will contain terrorists and militants but they keep regrouping under different names.[44]

Over the same period, Husain Haqqani, the politician-turned-scholar who would later return to politics as Pakistan's ambassador in 2008, warned about the dangerous, long-standing nexus between Pakistan's military and its mullahs.[45] He advised that only a civilian-led democracy would really want to stamp out extremism or be able to mobilize public support to its cause.

By 2005, arguments like these began to resonate, if faintly, in Washington. They had the benefit of some truth. The Pakistani army did have historical ties to the terrorists, and in important cases, like Lashkar-e-Taiba and the Afghan Taliban, those ties were still active. Moreover, with his second electoral win, Bush promoted his national security advisor, Condoleezza Rice, to the position of secretary of state and displaced Powell and Armitage. Not only were the "realists" with their decidedly low expectations for a Pakistani democratic transition out of power, but the close working relationship between the Powell/Armitage team and President Musharraf was lost. No longer could the secretary of state speak "general-to-general" with the Pakistani, either to provide frank counsel or a boost of confidence. As Pakistani advisers to Musharraf explained at the time, he felt cut adrift by the personnel change.

The Bush administration's "freedom agenda" was also kicking into a higher gear. Rice's June 2005 speech at the American University in Cairo showed that she was firmly onboard with a diplomatic agenda that would prioritize

[44] Benazir Bhutto, "Address at Woodrow Wilson Centre," speech given at the Woodrow Wilson International Center for Scholars, Washington, DC, February 9, 2004, http://benazir.bhutto.org/speeches/speech-54.htm.
[45] See Husain Haqqani, *Pakistan: Between Mosque and Military* (Washington: Carnegie Endowment for International Peace, 2005).

elections and democracy, even in states of the Muslim world, like Egypt, where pro-American strongmen ruled. "Liberty is the universal longing of every soul," she concluded, "and democracy is the ideal path for every nation."[46]

More important than ideological developments in Washington, Pakistan was itself starting to stir against Musharraf. His political strategy had inherent contradictions. On the one hand, he reserved the authority to behave as a dictator, shunting aside opponents with the backing of the army and the courts. On the other hand, he claimed to be placing Pakistan on the path to what he called "enlightened moderation" and "sustainable democracy" by enabling a profusion of private media outlets and holding national elections.

Had Musharraf been either a ruthlessly effective dictator or a genuinely popular democrat, it is conceivable that he might have found a way to steer Pakistan in his preferred direction. He was neither. He repeatedly sought the trappings of democratic legitimacy to validate the political power that plainly flowed from his position as the army chief. Since even his rigged 2002 elections had failed to produce a malleable and dominant parliamentary coalition, Musharraf struggled throughout 2003 to pass a constitutional amendment that granted him sweeping authorities as president. Then, over the course of 2004, he fought to stave off opposition demands that he honor an earlier promise to hold only one office – either president or army chief – but not both.

These struggles reached a climax at the end of 2004, when in a televised speech on December 30, 2004, he declared to the nation, "I have decided to retain both offices. In my view, any change in internal and external policies can be extremely dangerous for Pakistan."[47] Musharraf's decision to keep wearing his army uniform as president was not, by that point, a big surprise to Washington. The consensus view within the U.S. government was that if he surrendered his uniform, his political power would be diminished, rendering him even less able to respond to American demands. At the same time, there was no doubt that Musharraf's move was a step away from the democratic transition that he had promised. On the whole, the Bush administration viewed the episode as regrettable, but not one that should force a serious reconsideration of Washington's Musharraf-centric strategy.

Musharraf did not appear to have a viable political road map for the future. His cobbled-together party, known as the Pakistan Muslim League (Quaid-e-Azam), was neither internally democratic nor a strong voice for policies that would reduce extremism, improve relations with the United States, or contribute to economic development. His plan to hold local elections in 2005 between candidates who were not supposed to hold partisan affiliations, and his formation of a National Security Council that solidified the army's dominant

---

[46] Condoleezza Rice, "Remarks at the American University in Cairo" (speech, Cairo, Egypt, June 20, 2005), U.S. Department of State Archive, http://2001-2009.state.gov/secretary/rm/2005/48328.htm.

[47] "Text of Gen. Pervez Musharraf's Address to the Nation on December 30, 2004," http://www.satp.org/satporgtp/countries/pakistan/document/papers/mussaraf_30Dec04.htm.

role in Pakistan's foreign and defense policy both suggested that his goal was to circumvent or escape from the messiness inherent in democratic political competition.

Musharraf's political allies stood to gain from these moves, but at root they exposed a deep political naiveté on Musharraf's part. He seemed to believe that he was cleaning up Pakistani politics even though his partners in the project were some of Pakistan's most unprincipled politicians, the army, and ISI.

On a trip to Islamabad in June 2005 with Stephen Krasner, then Secretary Rice's director of policy planning, my suspicions of Musharraf's weak political instincts were strengthened. Krasner seemed genuinely curious to hear Musharraf's thoughts on democracy in Pakistan but cautious not to ruffle any feathers. Gingerly, and reflecting his own academic background, he asked how the president understood the role of "checks and balances," a core principle enshrined in the U.S. Constitution, in the Pakistani context. Musharraf took the question as a cue to launch into a lengthy monologue about Pakistan's new, military-dominated National Security Council. Apparently, when he heard "checks and balances," it triggered in his mind the need for the military to check and balance the destabilizing impulses of civilian politicians, not the idea – as in the American example – that executive, legislative, and judicial branches of government should have the capacity to block excesses by the others.

Musharraf was trying to erect a bulwark against political instability in the only way he thought viable – by granting the military a permanent veto. Given Pakistan's history of civil-military discord, Musharraf's desire to maintain the military's dominant role in national security policy making is comprehensible. It was also entirely out of line with American democratic sensibilities. Words like "sustainable democracy" or "checks and balances" clearly had different meanings in the two different capitals. The episode foreshadowed the disagreements and disappointments that would emerge when Musharraf's regime started to crumble in 2007.

Bright Spots in U.S.-Pakistan Relations

There is a strong tendency to read subsequent troubles in U.S.-Pakistan relations back through the entire history since 9/11. In reality, there were several noteworthy successes and reasons to hope that the future would be brighter than it has turned out to be.

One of these bright spots in relations between Washington and Islamabad was unanticipated and came at a time of terrible Pakistani suffering. In October 2005, an earthquake measuring 7.6 on the Richter scale hit Pakistan's side of the contested Kashmir region, near the city of Muzaffarabad. It claimed over 86,000 Pakistani lives, flattened tens of thousands of buildings, triggered landslides, and left 4 million without homes.[48]

---

[48] Earthquake data retrieved from "Magnitude 7.6 – Pakistan," United States Geological Survey, http://earthquake.usgs.gov/earthquakes/eqinthenews/2005/usdyae/#summary.

Swinging into action without delay, the U.S. military and its Chinook helicopters based in Afghanistan played a vital role in humanitarian operations, delivering food and medical supplies to stranded survivors. In those Chinooks, Pakistanis witnessed the tangible benefits of cooperation with the United States. They probably made a more positive dent in public perceptions than the billions of dollars Washington had granted the Pakistani state for debt relief and other assistance programs. Public goodwill toward America was reflected, if temporarily, in Pakistani opinion polls.[49]

During this period there were other developments that also suggested the potential for a brighter future between the United States and Pakistan. In March 2005, the Bush administration announced that it would resume sales of F-16 aircraft to Pakistan.[50] No matter what Pakistani and American officials said at the time or since, the planes were valuable to Islamabad mainly in the context of its regional rivalry with India, not as a tool for fighting insurgents along the Afghan border. U.S. policymakers knew this, but they also believed that the Indo-Pakistani military balance would remain firmly in India's favor with or without the F-16 delivery.[51] By opening the door to these sales, Washington was trying to send a political signal to Pakistanis of its commitment to long-term cooperation. Those F-16s were especially symbolic. The U.S. refusal in the early 1990s to deliver planes that Pakistan had purchased was, fifteen years later, still considered a lingering diplomatic headache.

The F-16 deal came about in the context of a new American effort to remove historical irritants in its relationship with India as well. Just as the Bush administration unveiled its decision to sell F-16s, it also explained its intention "to help India become a major world power in the twenty-first century."[52] As a practical matter, this would mean accelerated and intensified diplomacy, military cooperation and sales, and most important, a breakthrough deal between Washington and New Delhi on civilian nuclear technology. These were big changes,

---

[49] "A Dramatic Change of Public Opinion in the Muslim World," Terror Free Tomorrow (2005), http://www.terrorfreetomorrow.org/upimagestft/Pakistan%20Poll%20Report-updated.pdf. See also Tahir Andrabi and Jishnu Das, "In Aid We Trust: Hearts and Minds and the Pakistan Earthquake of 2005," Working Paper (September 2010), www.cgdev.org/doc/events/9.14 .10/InAidWeTrust.pdf; and Testimony of Andrew Wilder, "Hearing on U.S. Aid to Pakistan: Planning and Accountability," U.S. House of Representatives Committee on Oversight and Governmental Reform, Subcommittee on National Security and Foreign Affairs, December 9, 2009, http://www.hks.harvard.edu/cchrp/sbhrap/news/Wilder_PakistanAidTestimony_ 12_9_09.pdf.

[50] On the F-16 announcement as well as the Bush administration's new South Asia strategy, see "Background Briefing by Administration Officials on U.S.-South Asia Relations," Press Conference, Washington, D.C., March 25, 2005, www.fas.org/terrorism/at/docs/2005/ StatePressConfer25maro5.htm.

[51] See S. Arun Mohan, "Behind the Pakistan F-16 Deal, a Tale of Many Wheels," *Hindu*, May 30, 2011.

[52] "Background Briefing by Administration Officials on U.S.-South Asia Relations," March 25, 2005, www.fas.org/terrorism/at/docs/2005/StatePressConfer25maro5.htm.

spearheaded by a small group of officials who surrounded Condoleezza Rice when she arrived at the State Department.[53]

By combining its announcements of progress in relations with India and Pakistan, the Bush team walked a fine line. On the one hand, it demonstrated that Washington sought to improve relations with both New Delhi and Islamabad at the same time. On the other hand, the announcement also looked as though Washington was doling out gifts to both sides as a means to quell inevitable Indian and Pakistani resentment.

In the end, the tactic worked, at least when compared to prior diplomatic travails. Almost exactly a year earlier, for instance, Secretary Powell had conferred "Major Non NATO Ally" status on Pakistan just forty-eight hours after departing New Delhi. During his meetings in India, he had given no hint of this plan. The resulting Indian furor over Powell's diplomatic "stab in the back" was intense.[54] But the bad feelings blew over in time and Washington's careful management of the March 2005 announcements, including a preview of American plans by Secretary Rice in New Delhi, showed that U.S. officials had learned a valuable lesson about how to manage relationships in the region.

Other reasons for cautious American optimism came in the form of steadily mellowing relations between New Delhi and Islamabad themselves. In the spring of 2003, Indian Prime Minister Atal Bihari Vajpayee took the first step back from the hostilities of 2001–2 and extended a "hand of friendship" to Pakistan. Even though Vajpayee's government lost the 2004 elections, his initiative survived into the next Indian government. Over the next several years, Indo-Pakistani negotiations took two forms, one public – the "composite dialogue" between the foreign ministries – and the other a secret backchannel, managed by Pakistan's national security adviser, Tariq Aziz, together with a succession of several Indian envoys. Aziz and his Indian counterparts met about two dozen times from 2004 to 2007 in various hotel rooms from Southeast Asia to London, hammering away at the text of an agreement on Kashmir and other outstanding disputes between India and Pakistan.[55]

All along the way, the policy challenge for the United States was to support, and if possible to accelerate, progress between India and Pakistan without interfering in ways that might end up being counterproductive. The American impulse to dive into the dispute and try to sort out a grand bargain was strong. As one jaded U.S. State Department official explained in early 2005, "pretty much every new secretary of state comes in thinking that solving Kashmir will be an easy ticket to a Nobel Prize. So they each demand a policy review. But

[53] Ashley Tellis, "South Asian Seesaw: A New U.S. Policy on the Subcontinent," *Policy Brief No. 38*, Carnegie Endowment for International Peace, May 2006, http://www.carnegieendowment.org/files/PB38.pdf.
[54] V. Sudarshan, "Uncle Sam's Sly Sally," *Outlook India*, April 5, 2004, http://www.outlookindia.com/printarticle.aspx?223514.
[55] Steve Coll, "The Back Channel," *The New Yorker*, March 2, 2009, pp. 38–51.

pretty soon they realize just how complicated Kashmir really is. Then they lose interest and go back to making peace in the Middle East."[56]

This time, what really convinced U.S. officials not to interfere in Indo-Pakistani diplomacy was the widely held belief that both President Musharraf and Prime Minister Manmohan Singh were as serious about making a deal as anyone could ever expect leaders from these often hostile neighbors to be. Neither man could, however, afford to have his peacemaking efforts look like a weak capitulation to American pressure. By accepting that reality, the Bush administration also accepted that its public role in the process would be limited to friendly cheerleading.[57] New Delhi and Islamabad would set the pace and terms of their negotiations. Up until 2007, however, when Musharraf's world came tumbling down, the trends looked encouraging. To many outside observers, it appeared that India and Pakistan were closer to a breakthrough on Kashmir than ever before.

The Resurgent Threat

Unfortunately, Pakistan's active diplomacy was not limited to its pathbreaking negotiations with India. Starting in 2004, Musharraf's team was also cutting deals of a very different sort on its western front. Former senior Bush administration officials now blame several of these accords, struck between the Pakistani army and militants in Pakistan's Federally Administered Tribal Areas (FATA), for the return of the Taliban insurgency in Afghanistan. As Condoleezza Rice argues in her memoir, Musharraf's deals led "to a new safe haven for the Taliban and a downward spiral in Afghanistan, one that we were unable to halt before the end of our term."[58]

By 2006, Washington was beginning to see Pakistan's peace negotiations as a real problem. That year, Governor (and retired Lieutenant General) Ali Muhammad Jan Aurakzai helped to strike a deal with tribesmen in North Waziristan. Aurakzai is an intense military man with a closely cropped mustache and piercing blue-gray eyes. His taut manner evokes the Prussian high command more than the tribal badlands of Pakistan's frontier. But at the time of his peace dealings, Aurakzai claimed, by dint of his Pashtun ancestry, to understand the "mind-set" of the tribesmen.[59]

One afternoon in April 2007, Aurakzai held forth over a formal lunch at the head of an enormous banquet table set for himself, me, and one other colleague. Between courses served by stiff, uniformed waiters, he lectured on the history of the region and described how he had cleverly appealed to the

[56] Author conversation, Washington, DC, March 2005.
[57] Coll, "The Back Channel," p. 50.
[58] Rice, *No Higher Honor*, pp. 345, 443–5; see also Cheney, *In My Time* (New York: Simon & Schuster, 2011), p. 498; Bush, *Decision Points*, p. 216.
[59] Author conversation with Governor Aurakzai, Peshawar, April 30, 2007.

tribal need for due respect when he forged his peace deal. Subsequently, other Pakistanis would argue that Aurakzai had actually failed to understand the tribal mentality because his displays of "due respect" were interpreted as signs of weakness. In either case, skepticism is warranted; generalizations about the Pashtun "mentality" are often little more than cultural stereotypes fashioned in the service of dubious policy choices.

Aurakzai's deal was a disaster. Rather than stemming the flow of Taliban fighters into Afghanistan – as the Pakistanis first promised Washington – it only magnified the problem. Karl Eikenberry, then the commander of U.S. forces in Afghanistan and later the Obama administration's controversial ambassador in Kabul, reported at the time that the deal led to a tripling of Taliban attacks from Pakistan's side of the border.[60]

It is nonetheless a misleading exaggeration to blame Pakistan's 2006 deal for the deteriorating situation in Afghanistan. Blaming Pakistan's peace deals for the downward spiral in Afghanistan deflects too much attention from Washington's own inattention to the many problems it faced in Afghanistan. U.S. missteps set the stage for Pakistan's bad policy choices and magnified their consequences.

Central to Pakistani calculations about Afghanistan was the reality that U.S. forces would eventually depart. Pakistan would have to be ready for whatever followed. A number of Washington's policy choices fed Pakistani suspicions that a U.S. departure would come sooner rather than later. For instance, Islamabad perceived a series of U.S. decisions to reduce its direct command authority over operations inside Afghanistan, culminating in 2006 when all security responsibility fell under the NATO flag, as evidence that Washington was looking for a way to exit the war.[61]

Pakistanis were not wrong to see drift and inattention in Washington's Afghan war policy. Inside Afghanistan, Kabul's barely-there government and weak economy opened the door to insecurity as the new democratic state struggled to get off the ground. Courts, police, and other authorities were impossibly corrupt or missing in action. Reflecting and contributing to these problems, Afghanistan's opium production shot through the roof, increasing 34 percent in 2007 over the previous year's levels.[62] Afghanistan's Helmand

[60] Ann Scott Tyson, "Generals Warn of Perils in Afghanistan," *Washington Post*, February 14, 2007, http://www.washingtonpost.com/wp-dyn/content/article/2007/02/13/AR2007021301259.html.
[61] The early part of the Afghan war was prosecuted through a "lead nation" approach, in which the United States and its allies each took primary responsibility for specific regional/functional tasks. This strategy did not produce convincing results, and as such NATO gradually took on a more prominent leadership role. By 2006 NATO had assumed operational control of the war. For a detailed account of this transition, see Seth Jones, *In the Graveyard of Empires* (New York: W. W. Norton, 2009), pp. 239–48.
[62] "Afghanistan Opium Survey 2007: Executive Summary," United Nations Office of Drugs and Crime (August 2007), http://www.unodc.org/documents/crop-monitoring/AFG07_ExSum_web.pdf.

province, which borders Pakistan, was a bigger source of illicit drugs than either Colombia or Myanmar.

American officials in the field, including Ronald Neumann, who served as the U.S. ambassador in Kabul from 2005 to 2007, recognized that Washington had invested too few resources to achieve stability in war-torn Afghanistan, especially with its rapidly growing cities, remote villages, difficult terrain, and nearly 30 million people. In a February 6, 2006, plea to Secretary Rice for additional resources, Neumann concluded, "We have dared so greatly, and spent so much in blood and money that to try to skimp on what is needed for victory seems to me to be too risky."[63] Unfortunately, the ambassador's calls for more resources made little headway.[64] Officials back in Washington obligated available funds, manpower, and focus to Iraq.

Also undercutting the argument that Pakistan's peace deals in the FATA were the root cause of trouble in Afghanistan, many of the most important Taliban leaders, like Mullah Omar and his top lieutenants, were believed to enjoy sanctuary in and around Quetta, in Pakistan's Baluchistan province, not the FATA. Afghan leaders in Kabul, from Hamid Karzai down, routinely complained about the machinations of the "Quetta Shura" to anyone who would listen. And Afghan-born Zalmay Khalilzad, the U.S. ambassador in Kabul from 2003 to 2005, practically screamed himself hoarse about those Taliban sanctuaries.[65]

Such warnings did little to change U.S. policy toward Pakistan. Looking back, Ambassador Eikenberry observes that "until at least 2005, the Bush administration simply did not prioritize the Taliban's Quetta sanctuary in its discussions with Pakistani officials. Al-Qaeda dominated U.S. attention. Pakistanis saw this as a green light to keep doing what they were doing with the Taliban. Afghans saw it as evidence that America was only a temporary, fickle ally."[66]

Nor was Pakistan's infamous 2006 peace accord the first (or last) of its kind. The Pakistani army cut its first major peace deal, known as the Shakai Agreement, in 2004. The circumstances of that deal revealed another problem

[63] U.S. Embassy (Kabul), Cable, "Afghan Supplemental" February 6, 2006, Secret, 3 pp. [Excised], http://www.gwu.edu/~nsarchiv/NSAEBB/NSAEBB358a/doc25.pdf.

[64] Neumann, emphasizing the relationship between investments in infrastructure and gaining the trust of the Afghan people, explained in a February 6, 2006, cable to Secretary Rice that "The lack of some USD 400 million will not lose the war. But it will make the narcotics problem worse by next year. It will make it slower to build the Afghan government outside Kabul. It will make the margin of our victory tighter and the Taliban's role easier." Six months later, Neumann reiterated that "because we have not adjusted resources to the pace of the increased Taliban offensive and loss of internal Afghan support we face escalating risks today." His bottom line: "The stakes in Afghanistan deserve a bigger margin for victory." See U.S. Embassy (Kabul), Cable, "Afghanistan: Where We Stand and What We Need" August 29, 2006, Secret, 8 pp. [Excised], http://www.gwu.edu/~nsarchiv/NSAEBB/NSAEBB358a/doc26.pdf.

[65] David Rohde and David E. Sanger, "How a Good War in Afghanistan Went Bad," *New York Times*, August 12, 2007.

[66] Author interview with Ambassador Karl Eikenberry, January 24, 2012.

128No Exit from Pakistan

that persisted over the course of the Bush administration. Despite having signed on to a counterterror alliance with Washington, Musharraf and his generals remained allergic to any acknowledged U.S. fighting presence on Pakistani soil. They claimed they would not survive the backlash from their own people, including from the rank and file of the military.

At first, this was not such a problem. Americans kept a low profile in joint counterterror operations. But as these gained steam in Pakistan's major cities, al-Qaeda took greater advantage of its refuge in the FATA. There the tribesmen of the region had always governed themselves, with Islamabad acting through neo-colonial liaison officers still known as "political agents" in a method very similar to that used by the British.

Facing American pressure to go after al-Qaeda, and believing these traditional administrative methods would never uproot the well-armed, well-heeled international terrorists, Musharraf sent his army into the FATA, starting in 2002 and more extensively in 2004. These were the first major army operations in the semi-autonomous region in Pakistan's independent history. Unfortunately, they were met with ferocious counterattacks. Pakistan's troops, trained to fight India, were poorly prepared for guerrilla warfare. Bloodied and demoralized, their energies were quickly exhausted.[67]

The peace deals, intended to save face for the army and quell the violence, only reinforced troubles on the ground. By coming to terms with the militants – young hotheads with little traditional standing in their tribes – the army granted its enemies legitimacy and preserved their safe havens. Nor did the army have any ability to enforce provisions in the accords that prohibited harboring international terrorists or sending fighters into Afghanistan. Taliban assassination campaigns killed dozens of prominent tribal elders who attempted to live up to deals with the army or otherwise block the rising power of the militants.

All told, foreign influences – the jihadist ideology of al-Qaeda and the Taliban, along with the heavy-handed presence of the Pakistani army – were destroying what remained of the region's traditional political and social hierarchy. Islamabad had no good answer to these problems. The fact that Pakistani leaders continued to draw distinctions between different militant groups – favoring some and attacking others – muddled the picture even more.

The sad truth was that Pakistan lacked a sustainable counterinsurgency option. With effort, its troops could clear and occupy territory, but holding the land against a resilient enemy and then turning authority over to civilian administrators was beyond their means. Pakistani generals were not lying when

---

[67] On Pakistan's peace deals and military operations in the FATA, see Hassan Abbas, "Militancy in Pakistan's Borderlands: Implications for the Nation and for Afghan Policy," Century Foundation, 2010, http://tcf.org/publications/2010/10/militancy-in-pakistan2019s-borderlands-implications-for-the-nation-and-for-afghan-policy/pdf; C. Christine Fair and Seth G. Jones, "Counterinsurgency in Pakistan," RAND Corporation (2009), http://www.rand.org/pubs/monographs/2010/RAND_MG982.pdf.

they explained the stresses the tribal insurgency placed on their forces. This does not absolve Islamabad for its failure to tackle some of the worst Afghan Taliban groups, like the Haqqanis, but it does place Pakistan's tribal dilemma in context. Islamabad's ill-fated peace deals resemble Neville Chamberlain's appeasement of Germany prior to the Second World War: tactically appealing but strategically unwise.

Negotiated in weakness and desperation, Islamabad's peace deals were sold to the outside world in disingenuous terms. Washington also took its eye off the ball, investing its military and intelligence resources in Iraq rather than Afghanistan or Pakistan. As a consequence, America blinded itself to the resurgent Taliban threat and sent mixed signals to the region. The Bush administration failed to come to terms with the Musharraf government on a workable plan to deal with terrorist sanctuaries along the Afghan border.

We cannot be certain whether earlier attention from Washington and a heavy injection of U.S. resources could have transformed a post-Taliban Afghanistan into a more stable, effective nation-state. Perhaps no realistic American investment would ever have been sufficient. What we do know is that a serious debate on the subject was delayed by several years, during which time the threat posed by the Taliban and their terrorist allies grew. By 2007, militants of various stripes had consolidated power in many parts of Pakistan's tribal belt and established new footholds in Pakistan's major cities. In the years that followed, Afghanistan, Pakistan, and the United States all paid a heavy price.[68]

Exit Musharraf

Washington had always known that Musharraf's regime could not last forever. Even so, the drama of its collapse sent shockwaves throughout the world. The timeline for Pakistan's transition was set, in part, by Pakistan's electoral cycle, inasmuch as Musharraf's five-year presidential term was up in October 2007. But the real question was whether he would once again attempt to retain his job as army chief, stepping away from earlier pledges as he had done at the end of 2004. In late 2006, even early 2007, that script looked very likely to play out again. Washington – and perhaps Musharraf himself – had little idea of the trouble just over the horizon.

Months after he left office, Musharraf spoke at a luncheon in Washington, DC. When asked about the lessons he had learned from the tumultuous end to his hold on power, his meandering, inconclusive reflections showed that he had not come to terms with his own failings as a politician.[69] In the end, Musharraf was a victim of contradictions inherent in his rule; he was a liberal autocrat who thought he could reform politics on his own terms and timetable. He seemed

---

[68] On the militant threat in Pakistan's tribal areas, see Imtiaz Gul, *The Most Dangerous Place: Pakistan's Lawless Frontier* (New York: Viking Press, 2010).

[69] Author's conversation, Washington, DC, January 29, 2009.

deeply troubled when his people did not love him for the enlightened aspects
of his rule that he so generously bestowed, like allowing a relatively free media
or not personally stealing from the national till. His military mind was closed
to the practice of genuine political competition. He understood the concept of
"unity of command" far better. Instead of building a new, competitive party
with grassroots appeal, he bought off established politicians who were willing
to bolt from Pakistan's main opposition parties. His only real constituency was
the one that usually mattered most: the army. In the end, that was not enough.

Under normal conditions, Musharraf's control over the military probably
would have been sufficient. But Pakistan in early 2007 was not living under
normal conditions. The country was rocked by two different, unanticipated
crises almost at the same time. Both were of Musharraf's own making.

First was Musharraf's confrontation with the chief justice of Pakistan's
Supreme Court, Iftikhar Muhammad Chaudhry. The conflict started with
Musharraf's ill-considered decision to sack the judge in early March. Musharraf
expected that the judiciary, long a pliant institution manipulated by successive
Pakistani regimes, would bend to his will. Instead, the move triggered the pas-
sion and vigor of the black-suited lawyers' movement, expertly organized by
Aitzaz Ahsan (described in the previous chapter) and his associates.

At once, the lawyers' protest gained steam across the nation. Its ranks swelled
not only due to its principled defense of the judiciary but also because it
served as a powerful unifying vehicle for all of Pakistan's opposition forces.
Opportunistic critics of Musharraf jumped at the chance to exploit this chink
in his armor. Over the period since he seized power in 1999, Musharraf had
gradually alienated various constituencies. Liberals who had hoped for a brief
military interregnum had lost patience. Hawks who favored a tough anti-
Indian, anti-Western stance were troubled by Musharraf's overtures to New
Delhi and appalled by his cooperation with Washington. Businessmen feared
that the best days of the market were behind them. The relatively free, still
immature media trained its vicious gaze on the president. The commander-in-
chief started to look vulnerable. His opponents were energized.

The second crisis was equally unexpected. It began with the 2007 uprising
at the Red Mosque, or Lal Masjid, in the center of normally staid Islamabad.
The radical clerics of the mosque had for years collected money and recruits
for Pakistan's various jihadist causes. But in the spring of 2007 their students
launched a new movement, perhaps touched off by an escalating land dispute with the city government.[70] Whatever its proximate cause, the radicals
began a mini-Talibanization campaign in nearby neighborhoods. They ter-
rorized city residents who violated harsh interpretations of Islamic practice,
including owners of local DVD shops, and even "liberated" a number of Chinese women who they claimed to be prostitutes.

---

[70] Asad Munir, "Lal Masjid Siege – Four Years On," *Express Tribune*, July 2, 2011, http://tribune
.com.pk/story/201068/lal-masjid-siege-four-years-on/.

Islamabad's initially tepid response to this strange disruption reflected its own contradictory impulses. Aligned with Washington's war on terror, Musharraf's political party, the PML-Q, had also cut numerous political deals with hard-line Islamist parties. The principal civilian faces of the party leadership – the Chaudhry family of Punjab – were unwilling to take a firm, public stance against extremists. They always preferred concessions to confrontation and distanced themselves from the alliance with Washington.

Prevarication by the government and the army allowed the Red Mosque movement to grow. By mid-summer some 1,100 extremists had packed the grounds. Many of them were well armed.[71] At the time, one of the most stunning aspects of the situation was that no one in Islamabad seemed to know what was really going on. As always, rumors and conspiracy theories abounded. How, Pakistanis asked during the early days of the crisis, could the uprising not have the support of the army and the ISI, considering that it was taking shape almost literally under their noses?[72]

Only in July, when Musharraf sent army commandos to crush the uprising by force, would it be clear which side the regime was on. Even then, rumors persisted that some military units had refused to participate in the raid and that Musharraf had acted contrary to the wishes of his civilian political allies. Televised images from the mosque, where at least sixty jihadists, and possibly many more, were killed, did little to unite the country behind its president.[73]

To the contrary, the affair inspired Pakistan's Islamist militants to turn their fire against the state in a sustained rash of suicide attacks and other violence that engulfed the country. Supporters of Abdul Rashid Ghazi, who was killed at the Red Mosque by Pakistani forces and was the brother of the mosque's head cleric, even formed their own shadowy terrorist organization, the so-called Ghazi Force. Over the next two years, terrorists killed over 4,600 Pakistanis, nearly six times the number killed in the two years preceding the mosque crisis.[74] Other Pakistanis, even those with little sympathy for the extremists' cause, still found fault with what they considered a heavy-handed use of force by Musharraf. If the lawyers' movement united Pakistan's progressives and centrists against the regime, the Red Mosque crisis angered most other parts of the political spectrum.

As each of these crises unfolded, Musharraf was frantically seeking a way to extend his grip on power. Washington was mostly eager to avoid a risky, disruptive transition in Islamabad, one that would jeopardize American counterterror operations or the war in Afghanistan. Together, these impulses led the

[71] Somini Sengupta and Salman Masood, "Battle at Pakistani Mosque Ends," *New York Times*, July 11, 2007, http://www.nytimes.com/2007/07/11/world/asia/11cnd-pakistan.html.

[72] Author conversations, Islamabad, April 2007.

[73] Salman Masood, "Musharraf Defends Raid that Ends Red Mosque Siege," *New York Times*, July 13, 2007, http://www.nytimes.com/2007/07/11/world/asia/11cnd-pakistan.html.

[74] Worldwide Incidents Tracking System, National Counter-Terrorism Center, http://wits.nctc.gov on January 30, 2012.

Bush administration to cooperate in a bit of high-stakes matchmaking between Musharraf and Benazir Bhutto, daughter of Zulfikar and self-exiled leader of what remained Pakistan's largest opposition party, the PPP. On the back of a Washington-brokered deal with Musharraf, Bhutto made her way to Pakistan in October 2007. Nawaz Sharif, exiled leader of the other large opposition party, the PML-N, followed her the next month. The Saudis sponsored his return.

The secret deal making between Musharraf and Benazir was originally conceived as an effort to mate Musharraf, the moderate army chief who lacked a legitimate electoral base, with Bhutto, a popular and progressive politician, to enable a gradual transition away from military rule. The oddness of the couple was lampooned in Pakistani circles, where one political cartoon – an impressive photo-shopped image – put Bhutto and Musharraf in the traditional pose of a bride and groom. Proudly flanking the newlyweds were their "parents," a beaming President Bush and Secretary Rice.

The pairing was odd, but it was not Washington's brainchild. For years, Pakistanis from both Musharraf's and Benazir's camps had floated similar proposals. The United Kingdom also played an extensive role in these conversations.[75] In the early lead-up to elections in 2007, the deal held particular appeal in Washington since the most realistic alternative – at least until the dual crises of the Supreme Court and the Red Mosque shook Musharraf's hold on power – looked like a repetition of 2002, when Musharraf had blatantly manipulated elections and reasserted his dictatorial authority. In her account of Musharraf's final days, Condoleezza Rice argues that a negotiated power-sharing arrangement looked like the best way to assure a smooth path for Pakistani elections.[76]

The deal unraveled as Musharraf's regime faced blistering attacks from all sides. Over the summer and autumn, Musharraf's desperation mounted. He maneuvered himself into another presidential term through a constitutionally suspect game, holding an indirect election before taking off his army uniform. He then clamped down on opposition and the media by imposing a state of emergency. These moves destroyed what little trust he had cultivated with Bhutto and made Musharraf so politically radioactive that Bhutto – and every other opposition politician – had to keep a distance.

Bhutto traveled to Washington, DC, in late September 2007, a couple of weeks before she returned to Pakistan. Her visit made it clear that she viewed the Americans as an important political constituency, one she wanted to cultivate as part of her plan to retake power in Islamabad. During a limo ride across town, shuttling between a think tank discussion and an interview at CNN, she explained that she was not at all convinced she would be able to strike a deal with Musharraf. There were many sticking points. She needed a deal that would protect her (and other members of her party, including her husband)

[75] Ahmed Rashid, *Descent into Chaos* (New York: Viking, 2008), p. 376.
[76] Rice, *No Higher Honor*, pp. 605–12, esp. p. 608.

from outstanding legal cases that might otherwise tie them in knots on their return to Pakistan. She also needed more confidence in Musharraf's willingness to surrender his uniform and open the way for her to contest elections on an even playing field.

Finally, the intensely charismatic Bhutto was worried about her personal security. She had every reason to fear; there were many extremists in Pakistan who hated everything she represented and wanted her dead. Bhutto's return to Pakistan was driven by cold political calculations. She knew it was a make-or-break opportunity for her and her party. It was also undeniably courageous, given the degree of political violence that plagued Pakistan at the time.

In the end, everyone lost. On December 27, 2007, terrorists murdered Benazir Bhutto on the campaign trail at a rally in Rawalpindi.[77] Her death deprived Pakistan of its only politician with a large, relatively progressive, and truly national following. Musharraf, whose political allies suffered massive losses at the polls in early 2008, was forced to resign from the presidency in August 2008. Asif Ali Zardari, Benazir Bhutto's widower and inheritor of the dynastic PPP, quickly replaced Musharraf, who then left the country for several years of self-imposed exile in London.

Nearly every Pakistani blamed the Bush administration for something. Most felt Washington had propped up a dictator far too long, demonstrating its self-serving, hypocritical disregard for democracy. Others believed Bush had betrayed his friend and ally, proving untrustworthy when the chips were down.

Americans drew a variety of lessons from Musharraf's downfall. It pointed to the dangers of personalizing a relationship between states, of becoming too dependent upon an autocrat, no matter how accommodating – or relatively enlightened – he might appear. It showed that managing democratic transitions is an exceedingly difficult, perhaps even impossible, business.

Five years later, as Pakistan prepared for its next round of national elections, U.S. Secretary of State John Kerry postponed travel to Pakistan with the hope of avoiding any impression that Washington would interfere in the democratic process. As one Obama administration official explained, "Given the kind of historic nature of where Pakistan is right now, we wanted to be holier than the Pope on this one on staying away ... while the electoral process unfolded."[78] The move turned out to be a smart one; at just about the same time Kerry was considering his visit to Islamabad, Musharraf decided to fly home and re-launch his own political campaign. Musharraf's return was ill-considered; he quickly ran afoul of Pakistan's courts and spent the 2013 election under

---

[77] Responsibility for the attack is still a matter of some dispute, but at the time officials in Islamabad blamed the Pakistani Taliban. See Waqar Gillani, "Pakistan Indicts 7 in Bhutto Assassination," *New York Times*, November 5, 2011, http://www.nytimes.com/2011/11/06/world/asia/7-pakistanis-are-indicted-in-benazir-bhuttos-killing.html?_r=0.

[78] Julian Pecquet, "Kerry Warned Off Trip to Pakistan Ahead of Elections," *The Hill*, March 25, 2013, http://thehill.com/blogs/global-affairs/asia-pacific/290141-kerry-warned-off-trip-to-pakistan-ahead-of-elections.

house arrest. That Washington managed to avoid further entanglements with Musharraf was probably the only silver lining of the episode.

But it must be understood that the temptation to get involved in Pakistani politics in 2007–8 was more of a well-intentioned response to Pakistani overtures than a unilateral American interference. Similar temptations, with similar risks, will undoubtedly surface again. It would hardly be surprising if American officials choose to back a friendly Pakistani face, whether autocrat or democrat, in order to ride out a threatening political storm. When the stakes are as high as they are in Pakistan, even temporary stability can be very appealing. It may even be the least-bad policy option available. Of course, such a doctrine of convenience always comes at a cost. Over time, America will be better off if it advocates universal principles and supports stronger democratic institutions in Pakistan rather than specific individuals.

Unfortunately, the American experience to date suggests that U.S. officials are likely to be presented with less-than-ideal options when it comes to Pakistani politics. Winning strategies will be rare, and the more realistic goal may be to mitigate the downside risks inherent in any choice that Washington makes.

LIVING IN LIMBO

The 9/11 attacks forced an abrupt about-face in U.S. policy toward Pakistan. A welter of important decisions had to be made quickly, all under the shadow of an al-Qaeda menace that had already shown itself capable of pure evil. Unknown in those early days was how long it might take to bring Osama bin Laden and his organization to justice. Few would have guessed that the world's most notorious terrorist could elude the United States for nearly a decade, or that the United States would find itself mired in the war in Afghanistan even longer than that. Few imagined that Iraq would demand the lion's share of America's attention even as al-Qaeda and the Taliban regrouped in Afghanistan and Pakistan.

After the dramatic changes of 2001 and early 2002, Washington's policies in Afghanistan and Pakistan entered what might best be described as a state of limbo. Iraq was to blame for much of the drift, but not all. The Bush administration failed to resolve fundamental contradictions in its strategy for Afghanistan and Pakistan. This was easily pardoned in the shell-shocked months after the twin towers fell. Yet as months passed, then years, Washington's initial post-9/11 deal with Musharraf's Pakistan became an increasingly rickety foundation upon which to build America's regional strategy. The terms of Pakistan's counterterror cooperation were too narrowly defined. Pakistan's ambiguous stance on regional terrorist groups and Musharraf's clumsy steps along the path to democratic transition threatened American interests. Lurching from crisis to crisis, Washington lacked a vision for its relationship with Islamabad broader than the desire to keep Pakistan and Afghanistan on the rails long enough to see bin Laden dead and buried.

By the summer of 2008, however, Musharraf was out, a fresh army chief installed, and a new civilian government elected. For its part, Washington was busy rethinking and revising its own strategies and tactics in Pakistan. The United States was also on the way to electing a very different sort of president, one who pledged to put Afghanistan and Pakistan at the top of his national security strategy. Change was very much in the air.

5

Great Expectations to Greater Frustrations

U.S.-Pakistan Relations after Musharraf

In the mid-afternoon of January 27, 2011, a burly thirty-six-year-old Virginia native named Raymond Davis killed two Pakistanis. The shots from his pistol rang out on a busy street in the middle of Lahore, the capital of Pakistan's largest province. Accounts from Pakistani bystanders differ, but Davis may have pumped as many as five rounds into each of his victims. He then calmly stepped out of his car to take photos of the corpses with his cell phone camera. According to a Pakistani report, Davis got back into his car and attempted to escape, only to be arrested minutes later by Pakistani police officers at a traffic roundabout.[1] When interrogated, Davis claimed that he acted in self-defense, and that the two men had approached him waving guns. For a man described by one of his former high school classmates as "friends with everyone, just a salt of the earth person," Davis had ended up in an unusually tight spot.

The situation quickly went from bad to worse. Minutes after the shootings, a Toyota Land Cruiser sped to the scene. In its desperate effort to reach Davis in the crowded city, the unlicensed American vehicle drove up the wrong side of a busy street, slammed into an oncoming Pakistani motorcyclist, and left him dead. By that point, Davis was nowhere in sight, so the Land Cruiser raced to the U.S. consulate. In its haste, the vehicle somehow dumped an odd array of incriminating items: 100 bullets, a black mask, and a piece of cloth with an American flag. As an exasperated senior military officer at the U.S. embassy in Islamabad once told me, referring not to Davis but to the general state of affairs in the U.S.-Pakistan relationship, "You can't make this kind of shit up."

---

[1] For the best overview of the Raymond Davis episode, see Mark Mazzetti, Ashley Parker, Jane Perlez and Eric Schmitt, "American Held in Pakistan Worked with C.I.A.," *New York Times*, February 21, 2011, http://www.nytimes.com/2011/02/22/world/asia/22pakistan.html?pagewanted=all.

The Raymond Davis affair made news in the United States, but nothing like the way it dominated headlines and airwaves in Pakistan. Having been stopped by Lahore traffic police, Davis was detained, and after a few days of American fumbling – including a claim by the U.S. State Department spokesman Philip J. Crowley that the media actually had Davis's name wrong – Washington clarified that Davis was a member of the "administrative and technical staff of the U.S. embassy," and declared that he should be granted diplomatic immunity.

Pakistani officials disputed Davis's diplomatic status, refused to grant immunity, and charged Davis with two counts of murder. For weeks, Davis sat behind bars in a Pakistani prison, a dangerous spot for any American. Reports indicated that he had starved himself for fear of being poisoned by his guards. Meanwhile, the Pakistani media feverishly recounted new details of the case. At the time of his arrest, Davis was said to be carrying multiple illegal handguns, GPS equipment, a telescope, identity cards with different names, and theatrical makeup commonly used for disguises. A video of his initial police interrogation made its way to the Internet, in which Davis claimed to work as a consultant for the "RAO," or Regional Affairs Office, at the U.S. consulate in Lahore.[2] To complicate matters further, the anguished wife of one of the Pakistani victims poisoned herself to death.

The crisis dragged on, and on February 14, Senator John Kerry, chairman of the Senate Foreign Relations Committee, flew to Islamabad to seek Davis's release. A day later, President Obama took the unusual step of describing Davis as "our diplomat in Pakistan," suggesting that Davis was protected from prosecution by the terms of the Vienna Convention on Diplomatic Relations. Despite American diplomatic escalation, however, hopes for a backroom deal to get Davis out of the country went nowhere fast. Pakistani politicians quailed at the prospect of taking the heat that would surely come from bowing to Washington's pressure tactics.

In time, the Obama administration confirmed the rumors that Davis was a former U.S. Special Forces officer working as a contractor for the CIA. His duties are likely to have included helping a larger U.S. intelligence team track the movements of various militant groups, in particular Lashkar-e-Taiba (LeT). Because LeT is widely believed to enjoy close ties to Pakistan's military and intelligence services, Washington had to operate without Islamabad's consent. Contractors like Davis provided a way to expand Washington's presence in Pakistan without tipping its hand to the Inter-Services Intelligence directorate (ISI).

For Pakistani intelligence officials, Davis's clandestine activities – and what they said about a wider network of American spies operating on Pakistani soil – were a lot more important than whether he had acted in self-defense or what his legal diplomatic status might be. Pakistani officials used Davis as a bargaining chip and insisted that Washington must end its spy games. Several hundred

[2] The video can be accessed on YouTube at http://www.youtube.com/watch?v=iJN9fpylrkA.

Americans, including contractors, CIA officers, and U.S. military, were told to leave the country.[3]

The ISI must have believed it was making progress, because on March 16, Davis's release was brokered and the U.S. embassy immediately flew him home to America. In line with Islamic practice, the families of the victims accepted "blood money" payments of over $2 million in return for pardoning Davis. The details of that deal remain murky. Months later, in a final bit of absurdity, Davis made news again. Home in Colorado, he allegedly assaulted a fellow shopper in an Einstein Bros. Bagels parking lot for stealing his spot.[4]

Davis may have been freed from Pakistani captivity, but U.S.-Pakistan relations did not rebound. The day after his brokered release, a U.S. unmanned drone shot four missiles into a gathering of tribal leaders in North Waziristan agency – the hotbed of terrorist activity along the Afghan border. The Pakistani army chief screamed bloody murder, saying that "peaceful citizens" were "carelessly and callously targeted with complete disregard for human life."[5] Pakistani officials and local villagers claim that while there were a handful of Afghan Taliban at the gathering, thirty-eight civilians were killed. U.S. officials dispute the claim and argue that the group was heavily armed and "acted in a manner consistent with al-Qaeda-linked militants."[6]

Either way, the fact that the strike came immediately on the heels of the Davis deal infuriated Islamabad. It looked like a blunt reminder that the CIA would have its way in Pakistan with or without Islamabad's permission. In all, the affair demonstrated the enormous chasm that had opened between Washington and Islamabad. Nominal allies since 2001, nearly a decade later they could not even agree on who the terrorists were.

THE END OF THE AFFAIR

What made the Raymond Davis affair especially tragic was that it heralded the end of an era of great expectations for the U.S.-Pakistan relationship. That era, from 2008 to early 2011, was filled with extreme highs and lows, often over the course of the same week. Hardly a day passed when Pakistan fell from the pages of American newspapers. In Washington, Pakistan received more attention from more senior policymakers than ever before. Big plans were hatched, big money spent, big egos clashed.

---

[3] Jane Perlez and Ismail Khan, "Pakistan Tells U.S. It Must Sharply Cut C.I.A. Activities," *New York Times*, April 11, 2011, http://www.nytimes.com/2011/04/12/world/asia/12pakistan.html?pagewanted=all.

[4] Sara Burnett, "Former CIA Contractor Charged with Felony in Parking Fight," *Denver Post*, October 3, 2011, http://www.denverpost.com/breakingnews/ci_19029853.

[5] Salman Masood and Pir Zubair Shah, "C.I.A. Drones Kill Civilians in Pakistan," *New York Times*, March 17, 2011, http://www.nytimes.com/2011/03/18/world/asia/18pakistan.html.

[6] Sebastian Abbot, "New Light on Drone War's Death Toll," *Associated Press*, February 26, 2012.

Out of it all, Obama achieved a huge counterterror victory by killing Osama bin Laden and decimating al-Qaeda in Pakistan. The victory came at a cost in America's relations with Pakistan, but there were other reasons for the downward slide as well.

First and foremost, abiding differences of interest and perception continued to drive a wedge between decision makers in Islamabad and their U.S. counterparts. The discovery of bin Laden in Abbottabad crystallized these differences. For the world's most notorious terrorist to live practically under the Pakistani military's nose revealed complete incompetence, gross negligence, or outright complicity. U.S. officials tended to harbor dark suspicions, based in part on evidence of ISI support to a range of other Pakistani militant groups, some of which were also quite sympathetic to al-Qaeda. At the very least, Pakistan hardly looked like a satisfactory partner worthy of billions of dollars in American assistance. Pakistan's subsequent arrest and trial of Dr. Shakil Afridi, the doctor who ran a fake polio vaccination campaign in an effort to help the United States ascertain bin Laden's identity, only added insult to injury.

There should be no mistaking that Pakistan's failure to meet U.S. expectations in the fight against terrorism represented the core stumbling block in the relationship. To explain the remainder of the yawning chasm between aspirations of a transformed U.S.-Pakistan relationship in 2008 and the sad reality of 2011, however, the comic strip Pogo's famous line, "We have met the enemy, and he is us," captures an important part of the story. Recent episodes, including the Raymond Davis affair, suggest that the sole remaining superpower is better at hunting and killing terrorists than winning friends or influencing people.

A Tumultuous Transition

Stepping back to 2007–8, the final years of the Bush administration, both Pakistan itself and relations between Washington and Islamabad were in turmoil. Violence inside Pakistan spiked in the aftermath of the July 2007 Red Mosque raid. Not only did more of Pakistan's militants turn against the state in the tribal areas but they also extended their reach into nearby settled parts of the country and unleashed suicide bombers on its cities. In September 2008, when a massive truck bomb turned the Islamabad Marriott into a smoldering crater and killed more than fifty people, regular international visitors to Pakistan shuddered. "That could have been me," was the collective refrain. In November, when Lashkar-e-Taiba terrorists from Pakistan killed Indians, Americans, Israelis, and other international visitors in their commando-style raid on Mumbai, similar fears resurfaced.

Pakistanis, of course, routinely experienced violence beyond the oases of five-star hotels. Attacks escalated in the tribal areas as well as in the nation's urban centers. From January 2007 through December 2009, the number of Pakistanis killed or wounded by terrorism exceeded 2,300 in Peshawar, 1,300 in Lahore, and 800 in Karachi. In the previous three years, total violence was far lower; terrorists killed or wounded 90 Pakistanis in Peshawar and Lahore and about 500 Pakistanis in Karachi.[7] Major cities imposed draconian security measures in their effort to clamp down on the violence, but ending the threat posed by suicide bombers and gunmen was an impossibly difficult task.

In 2009, the army finally launched a major offensive in the Swat Valley of Pakistan's northwestern Khyber Pakhtunkhwa province, where the Pakistani Taliban had seized territory and reneged on a peace deal with the provincial government. Army operations that year forced 2 million people to flee their homes. Despite its huge human costs, the Pakistani public backed the campaign. A video clip circulated on the Internet and broadcast on Pakistani television of the Taliban mercilessly flogging a seventeen-year-old girl fueled public outrage against them.[8] Over a similar period, the army also expanded and intensified its fight in the tribal agencies of South Waziristan and Bajaur along the Afghan border, where anti-state militants were uprooted only at great cost, and then held at bay only by persistent army occupation.[9]

A Bright New Democratic Future?

Yet in the midst of this bloodshed, there was also an undeniable euphoria in Pakistan about the political change that had forced Musharraf to step down and returned civilian leaders to power. Hopes ran high, as the famous veteran diplomat Richard Holbrooke reported from Pakistan during a March 2008 trip. He argued that Washington should send a "clear and consistent" message to Pakistan: "democracy, reconciliation, the military out of politics, a new policy for the tribal areas – and more democracy."[10] That was nine months before president-elect Obama and his new secretary of state, Hillary Clinton, offered him the job of special representative for Afghanistan and Pakistan.

Once in office, Holbrooke set about putting his money where his mouth was. Washington's primary policy tool for helping Pakistan's civilian government was to be a vast infusion of cash. Such a plan had already been kicking around for a couple of years on Capitol Hill and inside the State Department. When

---

[7] Worldwide Incidents Tracking System, National Counterterrorism Center, http://www.wits.nctc.gov on February 1, 2012.
[8] Abubaker Siddique, "Pakistani Flogging Video Leads to Outrage against Increasing Taliban Influence," *Radio Free Europe / Radio Liberty*, April 7, 2009, http://www.rferl.org/content/Pakistani_Flogging_Video_Leads_to_Outrage_Against_Taliban/1604077.html.
[9] For a great deal more detail on the Pakistani military campaigns against the Pakistani Taliban (TTP) during this period, see Jerry Meyerle, *Unconventional Warfare and Counterinsurgency in Pakistan*, CNA Strategic Studies, November 2012, http://www.cna.org/sites/default/files/research/Pakistan.pdf.
[10] Richard Holbrooke, "Hope in Pakistan," *Washington Post*, March 21, 2008, http://www.washingtonpost.com/wp-dyn/content/article/2008/03/20/AR2008032003016.html.

one of its early sponsors, Senator Joe Biden, became vice president, the idea was nearly ready for prime time.

The legislative effort was driven by three U.S. politicians: the co-chairs of the Senate Foreign Relations Committee, John Kerry and Richard Lugar, and Representative Howard Berman, chair of the House Committee on Foreign Affairs. Together, they sponsored the authorizing legislation colloquially known as "Kerry-Lugar-Berman," "Kerry-Lugar," or "KLB" for short.[11] KLB tripled U.S. assistance for nonmilitary projects, raising it to roughly $1.5 billion per year for a five-year period. It also had provisions that in order for military aid to be sent to Pakistan, the secretary of state was required to certify that the Pakistani government was "continuing to cooperate" with the United States in dismantling nuclear supply networks, that it had "demonstrated a sustained commitment to and [was] making significant efforts towards combating terrorist groups," and that the Pakistani military was "not materially and substantially subverting the political and judicial processes of Pakistan." In addition to these certifications, the law required the secretary of state to submit reports to Congress on, among many other issues, the degree to which Pakistan's civilian leaders exercised effective control of the military.

The Obama South Asia team, with Holbrooke leading the charge, championed the bill as a means to trumpet America's sympathy for Pakistan's democrats. The bill was notable in comparison to the Bush administration's aid package, which had offered equal parts civilian and military assistance and later sent billions of dollars more to the Pakistani military. With this new package, Obama officials sought to signal to ordinary Pakistanis that the United States was committed to a long-term relationship with their people and not just their military.

Unfortunately, KLB stumbled right out of the gate. Over a year later, it still had not managed to find its footing. KLB became a tragic symbol of American diplomatic missteps in Pakistan and the yawning gap between Washington's rhetoric and its capacity for follow-through.

The political storm over KLB broke over Pakistan as soon as Congress passed it in early October 2009. For several drama-filled days, Pakistan's opposition politicians took to the floor of the National Assembly in Islamabad to decry KLB's "insulting" language that violated Pakistan's sovereignty and imposed unreasonable "conditions" on the aid.[12] They asked why the U.S. Congress had used the public language in an assistance authorization bill to raise questions about sensitive issues like Pakistan's nuclear program and counterterror policies.

---

[11] For the full text of the Enhanced Partnership with Pakistan Act, see http://www.gpo.gov/fdsys/pkg/BILLS-111s1707enr/pdf/BILLS-111s1707enr.pdf.

[12] Jane Perlez and Ismail Khan, "Aid Package from U.S. Jolts Army in Pakistan," *New York Times*, October 7, 2009, www.nytimes.com/2009/10/08/world/asia/08pstan.html?scp=7&sq=kerry%20lugar%20pakistan&st=cse.

The army and its civilian mouthpieces were especially upset over the KLB requirement that the state department report on civilian control over the military's "chain of command" and "the process of promotion for senior military leaders."[13] Given the history of tussles between the army and civilian leaders, this language was considered especially intrusive. During Pakistan's parliamentary debate, one prominent politician called the bill a historic defeat.[14] Another called it a "triumph for India."[15]

Instead of energizing a new relationship between Pakistan and the United States, skeptics of that relationship saw it as proof-positive of Washington's malign intent. Pakistan's ruling party was forced to defend its dealings with Washington in the face of angry statements from the army and indignation from across the political spectrum.[16]

The idea that American aid could be greeted with such hostility shocked many American policymakers and legislators in Washington. KLB was not a reincarnation of the infamous Pressler amendment.[17] Its "conditions" did not apply to civilian aid, and the certifications that were required from the secretary of state were carefully worded so as to provide flexibility on military aid as well. Contrary to the suspicions Pakistanis harbored, the American champions of the bill were genuinely interested in fostering a long-term, broad-based relationship between the United States and the people of Pakistan in ways that reflected Pakistan's own priorities.[18]

If that was the case, why did KLB use language that was certain to ruffle Pakistani feathers? Pakistani conspiracy theorists – including some national political leaders – saw the "evil hand" of Indian lobbyists at work on Capitol Hill.[19] The truth was more mundane.

A side-by-side comparison of the Kerry-Lugar (Senate) bill and the Berman (House) bill shows that the most inflammatory language in the final version of KLB came from the House.[20] Why the difference? Like Kerry and Lugar, Berman supported aid to Pakistan's civilian government and wanted to see

---

[13] The language on civilian control over the military is found in Section 302(a)(15) of the Enhanced Partnership with Pakistan Act.

[14] "Hashmi Terms Govt's Stance on KLB as a Historic Defeat," *Daily Regional Times*, October 17, 2009; "Kerry Lugar Bill Worth 'Peanuts': PML-N," *Asian News International*, September 29, 2009, http://www.newstrackindia.com/newsdetails/125375.

[15] "Kerry-Lugar Bill a 'Triumph for India': Shujaat Hussain," *Asian News International*, October 8, 2009, http://newstrackindia.com/newsdetails/127056.

[16] Iftikhar A. Khan, "Corps Commanders Express Concern over Kerry-Lugar," *Dawn*, October 8, 2009, http://archives.dawn.com/archives/41612.

[17] The 1985 Pressler amendment, which forced the cutoff in U.S. assistance to Pakistan, is discussed in Chapter 3.

[18] "Chairman Kerry and Chairman Berman Release Joint Explanatory Statement to Accompany Enhanced Partnership with Pakistan Act of 2009," Office of Senator John Kerry, October 14, 2009, http://kerry.senate.gov/press/release/?id=34cf9b3a-2791-4dec-bc23-8611417466ed.

[19] Author conversations with Pakistani officials and commentators, Islamabad, Pakistan, October 2009.

[20] For the text of H.R. 1886, the final bill passed by the House on June 11, 2009, see http://www.gpo.gov/fdsys/pkg/BILLS-111hr1886rh/pdf/BILLS-111hr1886rh.pdf. For the text of S. 962,

relations with Pakistan improve. However, he also believed that his legislation was a smarter, more comprehensive reflection of U.S. interests in Pakistan than the Senate version.[21] It covered more territory, authorizing military as well as civilian aid. It touched upon nearly all facets of the relationship.

Berman also faced more acute political pressures than his colleagues in the Senate. He needed to win over skeptical House members and explain why sending billions of dollars to Islamabad would make a direct, material contribution to American interests. He needed to show that the Pakistanis would be held accountable for the money they received. He was determined not to give Islamabad the sort of "blank check" President Bush had offered Musharraf. He was also determined not to give the Obama administration the latitude that he thought had been abused by the Bush administration.[22] By requiring the State Department to submit routine reports on its programs and on developments inside Pakistan, he and his staff believed his bill imposed greater accountability without creating inflexible conditions.

Finally, Berman also felt that the House Foreign Affairs Committee needed to demonstrate its relevance to the foreign policy-making process. If it did not, the administration, congressional appropriators, and other committees would violate its turf. That had been the story for years before Berman assumed the committee chairmanship, particularly with respect to military assistance.[23] The idea that these sorts of congressional turf battles might set the tone for a major piece of foreign policy legislation would not surprise anyone familiar with Capitol Hill. Yet these "inside the Beltway" explanations received little notice in Pakistan. In this respect, the episode reveals both the extent to which Congress "matters" in the U.S. policy process and, at the same time, the limited appreciation of this fact outside Washington.

The legislative process that yielded KLB was an unusually messy one, reflecting clear differences between Berman's vision and that of the bill's Senate sponsors. In June 2009, Kerry publicly criticized the House version of the bill for sending the wrong message to the Pakistani public. He said it threatened to paint Pakistan's government as "an American puppet," and suggested this ran "counter to some of the things that we're trying to do."[24] Senate staffers and

---

the final bill passed by the Senate on June 24, 2009, see: http://frwebgate.access.gpo.gov/cgi-bin/getdoc.cgi?dbname=111_cong_bills&docid=f:s962es.txt.pdf.

[21] Author conversations with House and Senate staffers, January 19–20, 2012.

[22] Many congressional observers perceived the Bush administration's use of Coalition Support Funds as a particularly cynical "blank check" exercise. See, for instance, the exchange between Senator Robert Menendez and Assistant Secretary of State Richard Boucher in "U.S. Foreign Assistance to Pakistan," Hearing before the Subcommittee on International Development and Foreign Assistance, Economic Affairs, and International Environmental Protection of the Committee on Foreign Relations, United States Senate, 110th Congress, First Session (Washington, DC: U.S. GPO), December 6, 2007, pp. 20–22, http://www.gpo.gov/fdsys/pkg/CHRG-110shrg45127/pdf/CHRG-110shrg45127.pdf.

[23] Author conversations with House and Senate staffers, January 19–20, 2012.

[24] Adam Graham-Silverman, "House to Consider Revised Pakistan Aid Measure," *Congressional Quarterly Today*, June 10, 2009.

administration officials tried to remove parts of the Berman bill they thought would most upset relations with Pakistan (and most tie Washington's own hands). Along the way, they were stunned by the intransigence of Berman's staff.[25]

Later, when Pakistanis cried foul over the final version of KLB, Berman rejected their complaints out of hand: "This is a created crisis, by people who either haven't read the bill or don't want to describe it accurately, and whose goal is either to destabilize the government or challenge some of the Pakistani military's priorities."[26] Since both Berman and Kerry had personally briefed General Kayani and other Pakistani officials on the legislation, he may have been correct to believe that, as Pakistani journalist Ahmed Rashid put it, "there had clearly been ample opportunities for the army to voice any objections to the bill months before."[27]

Berman may have had principled, political, and institutional reasons to write the bill the way he did. Pakistan's generals may have manipulated the crisis to gain maximum political benefit against the new civilian government. Even so, there is no discounting the fact that the KLB rollout was a diplomatic disaster that hurt the U.S. effort to build ties with Pakistan. It went off like a grenade in the midst of Pakistan's already tense civil-military standoff.

The crisis should have been avoided. Back in early May 2009, Ambassador Holbrooke testified before Berman's committee. In his written remarks, he suggested that Congress should not exacerbate "the 'trust deficit' that plagues our bilateral relationship.... Any legislation should engender the greatest level of cooperation by winning the trust of our civilian and military partners in Pakistan."[28]

"Whether the Pakistani uproar was warranted or manufactured, it was foreseeable," explains Jonah Blank, who at the time of the KLB episode was South Asia policy director for the Senate Foreign Relations Committee and intimately familiar with the KLB process. "In fact, it was foreseen. At the staff level, we warned many administration officials that they needed to manage the politics and diplomacy of the bill much better. Most, if not all, of the blowback could have been avoided with more concerted effort ahead of time."[29]

For the Obama administration, KLB was worse than irritating; it was unnecessary. The White House would have done better without the hassle of shepherding a major new congressional authorization bill. Ever since 1985,

---

[25] Author conversations with House and Senate staffers, January 19–20, 2012.

[26] Jane Perlez, "Pakistan Aid Places U.S. in the Midst of a Divide," *New York Times*, October 12, 2009, http://www.nytimes.com/2009/10/13/world/asia/13islambad.html?scp=13 &sq=pakistan&st=nyt.

[27] Ahmed Rashid, "Pakistan Civilian-Military Ties Hit New Low," *BBC*, October 16, 2009, http://news.bbc.co.uk/2/hi/8309532.stm.

[28] Statement by Richard C. Holbrooke, "From Strategy to Implementation: The Future of the U.S.-Pakistan Relationship," U.S. House of Representatives Committee on Foreign Affairs, May 5, 2009, http://foreignaffairs.house.gov/111/49547.pdf, p. 12.

[29] Author interview with Jonah Blank, April 18, 2012.

when the U.S. Congress passed its last annual Foreign Assistance Authorization Act, directives and earmarks for new U.S. foreign aid have usually been contained in yearly foreign operations appropriations acts without separate authorization acts.[30] In other words, the Obama administration might have skipped the KLB process altogether and secured funding directly – and with far less fanfare – from congressional appropriation committees. Senior administration officials could also have blocked legislation if they had determined it would be as counterproductive as it turned out to be. Or they could have taken a more active role in anticipating the difficult diplomacy that would ensue after the legislation was passed.

Instead, once the administration was convinced that the language in the bill was all bark and no bite – that is, the bill made it relatively simple for the administration to waive any of its paper thin "certifications" – Holbrooke and company focused on the bottom line. For them, getting the money was all-important. The assumption was that the specific language in the bill would amount to only a minor distraction.[31] That was a serious miscalculation.

A Flood of Cash

Much maligned at the outset, KLB nevertheless offered an important opportunity. The Obama administration now had a flood of cash to help grow Pakistan's economy, support its democratically elected government, and show millions of its people that America could be a trusted and helpful partner in the civilian as well as the military realm.

Turning cash into progress on any of these fronts would be the next challenge. Washington needed to answer two basic questions. First, precisely what sorts of projects should the United States fund given its sweeping goals in Pakistan? The answer was not immediately evident in a country where vast needs could easily outstrip the most generous American financial contributions. In a country of nearly 200 million people, even KLB's authorized $1.5 billion per year would amount to only about $7.50 per person. Clearly, Washington would need to prioritize its goals, to decide which sorts of projects were likely to offer the most bang for the buck.

The second basic question had to do with the mechanisms for spending U.S. money and implementing projects once they were selected. Who would do the work and how would they do it? Here too, the United States had many options. Washington could provide financial support to Pakistani government programs, hire private contractors, partner with nongovernment organizations, or even hire and deploy its own technical experts. While $1.5 billion would not be nearly enough to meet every Pakistani need, it was still vastly more money

30 For the history of the Foreign Assistance Authorization Act and efforts to reform the process, see Susan B. Epstein and Matthew C. Weed, "Foreign Aid Reform: Studies and Recommendations," Congressional Research Service, July 28, 2009, http://www.fas.org/sgp/crs/row/R40102.pdf.

31 Author conversation with former State Department staffer, January 19, 2012.

than U.S. officials had been spending to date. Such a sea change would require new personnel and new procedures.

To help answer these questions, the Obama administration appointed Ambassador Robin Raphel as the "coordinator for non-military assistance in Pakistan," a job that had not existed before her. A thirty-year veteran of the Foreign Service, Raphel is a confident, articulate woman with an almost aristocratic bearing. As befitting someone who has worked in Pakistan as well as India, she often drapes bright South Asian shawls over her well-tailored Western suits. In the Clinton administration, she served a contentious term as the assistant secretary of state for the department's newly minted Bureau of South Asian Affairs. Raphel landed in hot water with Indians for her blunt comments about Kashmir and with Afghans for her interaction with the Taliban leaders.[32]

After retiring from the State Department in 2005, Raphel's professional relationships with Pakistanis remained strong. In 2007, she was hired by the lobbying firm Cassidy & Associates to lead a contract to represent the government of Pakistan in Washington. She also enjoyed close, long-standing ties with the Clinton family. So, when Obama asked the former First Lady to take the helm of the State Department, it was hardly surprising that Raphel might be called back to work the Pakistan aid beat.

In September 2009, as Raphel was preparing to depart for Islamabad, she met with a small group of Pakistan watchers at the Middle East Institute in Washington. While each of the participants wished her the best of luck in her new assignment, there was a strong consensus that she had embarked upon an impossible mission. For her part, Raphel was careful to temper her ambition.

In late 2011, after having returned from a two-year stint in Islamabad, Raphel concluded that "it was unrealistic to think we could spend such a large amount of money so quickly." She added, "perhaps it would have been smarter to spread the same amount of money over a longer period because neither the Americans nor the Pakistanis were prepared to handle it."[33] Raphel is hardly alone in her basic conclusion.

Sadly, the KLB aid figure of $1.5 billion per year was not grounded in an assessment of specific Pakistani development needs or America's ability to meet them. The figure was a grand, symbolic gesture but laden with the heavy responsibility of considerable resources to manage. When it came down to the practical business of delivering aid to real people and projects, the U.S. Agency for International Development (USAID) was ill-prepared to design and implement a program of such magnitude.

After decades of debilitating staffing and budget cuts, USAID lacked the sorts of technical experts who in the 1960s and 1970s had managed such high

---

[32] See Coll, *Ghost Wars* (New York: Penguin, 2004), pp. 328–30; Ashish Kumar Sen, "Old Pak Hand Robin Raphel Returns," *Tribune India*, August 8, 2009, http://www.tribuneindia.com/2009/20090808/world.htm#1.

[33] Author conversation with Ambassador Robin Raphel, Washington, DC, October 4, 2011.

profile, big ticket infrastructure projects as dams or power plants that could offer tangible displays of U.S. partnership. Instead, USAID's focus had shifted to service delivery (health and education) and various training programs. Even in those areas, USAID officials were rewarded for soliciting and reviewing proposals and granting awards to a select group of outside contractors. As a consequence, they were far less skilled at getting out into the field to implement projects themselves.

From the start of KLB, there was a cultural, even a philosophical, difference between the State Department and USAID. State officials, including Holbrooke and Raphel, tended to emphasize the political and diplomatic utility of KLB funds. They wanted to help the Pakistani people, but also to do so in ways that would make the government more credible with its public and thus more able to cooperate with the United States on immediate issues like fighting terrorism. Most USAID officials, on the other hand, viewed development work in humanitarian, broadly apolitical terms. Properly crafted aid projects, from the traditional USAID point of view, would bear fruit in terms of alleviating poverty and stabilizing the society over the long term. They did not even need to wear an American label in order to serve Washington's core interests.

Holbrooke, in particular, had no patience for this USAID approach in Pakistan. He was in a hurry to shake things up, convinced that the prior administration had wasted billions of dollars in projects that had failed to help the government or improve Pakistani perceptions of the United States. Like many Pakistanis (and more than a few Americans), he railed against USAID's dependence on expensive private contractors. He vowed to funnel a far greater percentage of aid dollars into Pakistan's own government and local businesses rather than lining the pockets of Washington's "Beltway bandits." Holbrooke and Raphel also sought to focus U.S. spending on several critical needs, like Pakistan's infrastructure, in the belief that otherwise the money would be spread too thin to make a meaningful difference or to attract the attention of the Pakistani public.

USAID reacted defensively but lacked a political champion of Holbrooke's stature or energy.[34] Nevertheless, USAID personnel waged a rearguard campaign against him, citing the disruptive nature of his demands. One USAID economist in Islamabad cabled back to Washington that even if Holbrooke's "worthy goals" could all be achieved over time, without a reasonable transition period the desire to spend such huge sums quickly, smartly, and through all-Pakistani channels would end up representing "contradictory objectives."[35]

---

[34] USAID did not even have an administrator in the Obama administration until December 31, 2009.

[35] "Dissent Channel: Contradictory Objectives for the USAID/Pakistan Program," letter from C. Stuart Callison to Anne-Marie Slaughter, October 2, 2009, http://i.usatoday.net/news/pdf/Dissent%20on%20Holbrooke%20FATA%20actions.pdf.

Holbrooke dismissed the excuses offered by sluggish bureaucrats. "He thought everything we were doing was a failure," recalled one U.S. aid official.[36] Befitting his Balkans-era nickname, "the bulldozer" rolled over any lesser mortal who stood in the way. To ram home his disdain for business-as-usual in U.S. assistance programs in Pakistan, he inserted himself in the review process for ongoing projects and threatened to cancel some contracts.

After his untimely death on December 13, 2010, Holbrooke's admirers portrayed him as a tough, terrifically effective political operator.[37] Yet as one of Holbrooke's close friends, the former *New York Times* correspondent and president emeritus of the Council on Foreign Relations, Les Gelb, put it, "Only a novel could render his mythic contradictions – his stunning ability to see into the hearts and minds of others, but his blindness to how they saw him; his unrivaled gift for knocking down doors and walking smack into them."[38] Gelb's assessment rings true for Holbrooke's behavior in Pakistan.

Holbrooke was right to see grave failings in USAID's Pakistan mission. He zeroed in on problems that plagued American aid efforts there and elsewhere around the world. But the fact remained that neither the Pakistani government nor local contractors and NGOs were prepared to manage new flows of American money or implement big programs overnight. They did not know how to work with USAID – or vice versa. By picking fights and belittling staff in Islamabad's USAID mission and throughout the embassy, Holbrooke made enemies of the people who were on the ground to implement new programs. There was dissent, turmoil, and more than the usual turnover of personnel. Delays ensued. Given Washington's grand promises of assistance and the Pakistani skepticism that already prevailed about U.S. intentions, such delays were costly.

Holbrooke's bureaucratic wrangling and USAID's lack of experience in working through governments and other local institutions were not the only reasons for KLB's slow start. In late summer 2010, Pakistan suffered its worst floods since 1929.[39] One-fifth of the country – a piece of land the size of Italy – was inundated, and some 20 million Pakistanis were affected. Many new plans for American-funded projects were also washed away. Instead, the United

[36] Tom Wright, "Setbacks Plague U.S. Aid to Pakistan," *Wall Street Journal*, January 21, 2011, http://online.wsj.com/article/SB10001424052748703583404576080113980804354.html.
[37] Holbrooke died after emergency surgery failed to repair a torn aorta. See Daniel Dombey, "Holbrooke Dies after Heart Surgery," *Financial Times*, December 14, 2010, http://www.cbsnews.com/8301-504763_162-20025578-10391704.html.
[38] Leslie H. Gelb, "The Richard Holbrooke I Knew," *Daily Beast*, January 2, 2011, http://www.thedailybeast.com/articles/2011/01/02/leslie-h-gelb-on-the-late-richard-holbrookes-contributions-to-foreign-policy.html.
[39] "American Red Cross Supports Pakistan's Response to Worst Flooding in 80 Years," American Red Cross, August 4, 2010, http://www.redcross.org/portal/site/en/menuitem.1a019a978f421296e81ec89e43181aao/?vgnextoid=c02a25d459d3a210VgnVCM10000089f0870aRCRD.

States focused on diverting more than $500 million in previously unspent aid (pre-KLB funds) to pay for urgent relief and recovery operations.[40]

Pakistan's own messy politics and bureaucracy also got in the way of speedy aid delivery. With good reason, Pakistani officials were more enthusiastic about U.S. funds than about the cumbersome planning, auditing, and accounting procedures that came with them. In addition, a long-anticipated constitutional amendment by the new government in Islamabad placed greater administrative authority in the hands of provincial governments. This shift complicated certain types of cooperation with Washington. For instance, U.S. officials working on health issues lacked appropriate Pakistani counterparts for nearly eight months after the closure of the federal health ministry and before provincial governments picked up their duties.[41] Provincial governments, which now had jurisdiction over water and sanitation, had to finalize their own regulations before entering into agreements with USAID.[42]

Politics aside, Pakistan was also a dangerous, difficult place for Americans to deliver aid. Without a U.S. military presence in Pakistan, U.S. officials were constrained by limited numbers of armored cars and security officers, and contractors in Pakistan had to provide their own security or depend upon local law enforcement. The threat of attacks, harassment, and kidnappings was quite real. Al-Qaeda's 2011 kidnapping of sixty-three-year-old Warren Weinstein, an American aid contractor who had worked in Lahore for four years, showed that even experienced veterans were at risk.[43] Pakistani suspicions of American motivations also slowed the process of obtaining visas for U.S. aid officials and contractors. For many Pakistanis, the Raymond Davis affair only strengthened earlier suspicions that American aid officials in Pakistan might in fact be spies.

All told, KLB's first year was a difficult one. USAID disbursed only $179.5 million out of the first $1.5 billion authorized by the KLB legislation. To be fair, in late September 2010, USAID signed an agreement with the Pakistani government that would eventually support an additional $831 million in civilian programs.[44] But that would take more time, and to most

[40] Jane Perlez, "U.S. Aid Plan for Pakistan Is Foundering," *New York Times*, May 1, 2011, http://www.nytimes.com/2011/05/02/world/asia/02pakistan.html.

[41] "Quarterly Progress and Oversight Report on the Civilian Assistance Program in Pakistan as of December 31, 2010," U.S. Agency for International Development, February 7, 2011, http://www.usaid.gov/press/releases/2011/pr110207.html.

[42] The 18th amendment to the Constitution of Pakistan was signed into law on April 19, 2010. See I. A. Rehman, "What the Provinces Gain," *Dawn*, April 15, 2010, http://www.dawn.com/wps/wcm/connect/dawn-content-library/dawn/the-newspaper/columnists/i-e-rehman-what-the-provinces-gain-540.

[43] Ben Arnoldy, "Al Qaeda Claims Kidnapping of American Warren Weinstein," *Christian Science Monitor*, December 1, 2011, http://www.csmonitor.com/World/Asia-South-Central/2011/1201/Al-Qaeda-claims-kidnapping-of-American-Warren-Weinstein.

[44] USAID reports that it disbursed a total of $676 million in Pakistan for fiscal year 2010. Only $179.5 million of that total was from KLB authorized appropriations. The remainder of the $676 million was money left over from prior year U.S. commitments. Of the rest of the KLB

Pakistani ears it sounded like Washington's delivery had fallen well short of its promise.

Normally, it is a mistake to judge an aid program on the basis of how much money is spent and how quickly. It is far better to focus on outcomes than inputs. Yet in nearly every discussion with Pakistanis from 2010 to 2012, talk of KLB invariably turned to America's unmet pledges. By over-promising and at least appearing to under-deliver, Washington compounded the public relations nightmare of KLB's initial rollout.

In early 2011, just as efforts to spend KLB money (largely by funding Pakistani government programs) started to pick up steam, the U.S.-Pakistan relationship took a nosedive for completely unrelated reasons, starting with the Raymond Davis affair. The grandiose ambition of the early Obama administration to transform relations with Pakistan's civilians appeared to have died with its most active proponent, Richard Holbrooke.[45]

Holbrooke had positioned himself within the administration as a proponent of intensified diplomacy and cooperation with Pakistan. The loss of such a political heavyweight would have been difficult under any circumstances; it was doubly so in a situation beset by crises and increasingly hostage to U.S. policies that gave little weight to trying to build cooperation between Washington and Islamabad. More and more, rather than asking how U.S.-Pakistan relations might be made more effective, the bottom line question in Washington became "How can we keep relations with the Pakistanis on track long enough to avoid ruining our counter-terror agenda and our plans for Afghanistan?"

Even Pakistani supporters of cooperation with the United States had trouble explaining the specific benefits of KLB assistance. In February 2012, during her first public speech on the job as Pakistan's newly appointed ambassador to the United States, Sherry Rehman reflected a persistent confusion in Pakistan about what had and had not been delivered in the way of U.S. assistance to that country. As she explained, "there are divergent views on what's come through to Pakistan and what's been sent out from here [Washington]." She concluded, "So the question is asked [by Pakistanis]: what is our biggest ally doing for us while we stand on the frontlines? Ouch."[46]

money appropriated for FY 2010, the vast majority was not obligated until late September 2010, when the GAO reports that "USAID signed a bilateral assistance agreement with the government of Pakistan for up to $831 million." The remaining $171.2 million was neither obligated nor disbursed by the time the GAO report was released. See "Pakistan Assistance Strategy," GAO-11-310R, Government Accountability Office, February 17, 2011, p. 6, http://www.gao.gov/new.items/d11310r.pdf.

45 These ambitious plans were articulated soon after Obama took office. See "Remarks by the President on a New Strategy for Afghanistan and Pakistan," White House, Office of the Press Secretary, March 27, 2009, http://www.whitehouse.gov/the_press_office/Remarks-by-the-President-on-a-New-Strategy-for-Afghanistan-and-Pakistan/.

46 Event Transcript, "A Conversation with the New Ambassador of the Islamic Republic of Pakistan, Ambassador Sherry Rehman," United States Institute of Peace, Washington, DC, February 16, 2012.

DRONE WARS

In many ways, the Obama White House never appears to have cared much about the aid program for Pakistan, per se.[47] If aid provided a useful political tool to manage relations with Islamabad, fine; but the real action was in fighting terrorism, in preventing another major attack on the United States. President Obama held fast to the goal he outlined in March 2009 after his first review of U.S. strategy in Afghanistan and Pakistan: "to disrupt, dismantle and defeat al-Qaeda in Pakistan and Afghanistan, and to prevent their return to either country in the future."[48] For this job, as then-CIA Director Leon Panetta put it in May 2009, unmanned aerial vehicles, or drones, were "the only game in town."[49]

In the spring of 2001, I visited Palmdale, California, near Edwards Air Force Base. On my tour was the famous "Skunk Works" facility that gave birth to the U-2 spy plane. Those high-flying surveillance aircraft flew Cold War missions across Soviet territory. Even in 2012, thirty-two U-2s armed with a suite of technological upgrades remained in active use by the U.S. military.[50] On another tour stop, a retired Air Force pilot led us through the nearby Northrop Grumman facility. He offered an enthusiastic presentation about the company's contributions to the future of American airpower, but things got a little tense when someone asked about a white, awkwardly shaped, windowless plane on display. Our guide explained that it was a Global Hawk drone, capable of flying at high altitude over vast distances and taking high-resolution images very much like the U-2. He then went on an extended tirade about how these unmanned aircraft would never be as good as "real" planes.

What a difference a decade made. Just before September 11, 2001, the entire U.S. military had fewer than 200 drones. By the end of 2011, that number had grown to 7,000, accounting for over 30 percent of all Defense Department aircraft.[51] Only a very tiny percentage of those are the large, ungainly sort I first saw in Palmdale. Most are much smaller. They have several major advantages over piloted aircraft, including an ability to hover for many hours without fatigue and to crash without risking human death or capture. Newer models can now do much more than watch from above; they now hunt to kill. Controlled from even thousands of miles away, the Predator

---

[47] Author conversation with former White House official, January 19, 2012.

[48] "Remarks by the President on a New Strategy for Afghanistan and Pakistan," Office of the Press Secretary, White House, March 27, 2009, http://www.whitehouse.gov/the_press_office/Remarks-by-the-President-on-a-New-Strategy-for-Afghanistan-and-Pakistan/.

[49] Mary Louise Kelly, "Officials: Bin Laden Running Out of Space to Hide," *National Public Radio*, June 5, 2009, http://www.npr.org/templates/story/story.php?storyId=104938490.

[50] "U-2 High-Altitude Reconnaissance Aircraft, United States of America," http://www.airforce-technology.com/projects/u2/.

[51] Peter Finn, "The Do-It-Yourself Origins of the Drone," *Washington Post*, December 24, 2011, pp. A1, A9; Jeremiah Gertler, "U.S. Unmanned Aerial Systems," Congressional Research Service, January 3, 2012, p. 9.

and its newer cousin, the Reaper, can rain Hellfire precision-guided missiles down on their targets.[52] From 2004, when the first armed Predators flew over Pakistan's tribal areas, until late 2011, they have attacked hundreds of targets and are estimated to have killed roughly 2,000 militants.[53] In some parts of the FATA, tribesmen grew accustomed to the unnerving buzz of drones flying overhead.[54]

Drones are evolving quickly. Fifty years after the U-2, the Skunk Works facility introduced the Sentinel drone. Like the U-2, the Sentinel is built to spy over enemy territory. The Sentinel is stealthy, meaning that its shape and materials make it exceedingly difficult to detect by air defense systems. Sentinels are believed to have flown undetected over the Pakistani compound of Osama bin Laden both before and during the May 2011 raid. In the famous photograph that depicts President Obama and his team in the White House situation room staring in rapt attention, they may have been watching a Sentinel's live video feed.[55]

Earlier eras had their revolutionary military innovations, often tied to new technologies like gunpowder, the rifle, tanks, or aircraft carriers.[56] Now, drones and other robotic technologies are altering the conduct of war in fundamental ways.[57] They pose new strategic, legal, and ethical dilemmas.[58] The drone has already transformed America's counterterror campaign. It has allowed American forces to track and kill terrorists in some of the most remote, hostile corners of the earth at financial and human costs that pale in comparison to full-scale military invasions or bombing campaigns. Not surprisingly, Washington is growing its drone arsenal quickly. In 2011, the Congressional Budget Office estimated that the U.S. military plans to spend over $36 billion through 2020

[52] For a behind-the-scenes depiction of the drone pilots, see Tara McKelvey, "Inside the Killing Machine," *Newsweek*, February 13, 2011.

[53] "The Year of the Drone," New America Foundation, http://counterterrorism.newamerica.net/drones.

[54] Ron Moreau and Sami Yousafzai, "Killings Spark CIA Fears in Pakistan," *Daily Beast*, February 17, 2011, http://www.thedailybeast.com/articles/2011/02/17/afghanistan-the-mystery-of-the-drone-attacks.html.

[55] Greg Miller, "CIA Flew Stealth Drones into Pakistan to Monitor Bin Laden House," *Washington Post*, May 17, 2011, http://www.washingtonpost.com/world/national-security/cia-flew-stealth-drones-into-pakistan-to-monitor-bin-laden-house/2011/05/13/AF5dW55G_story.html.

[56] On revolutions in military affairs, see Stephen Peter Rosen, *Winning the Next War: Innovation and the Modern Military* (Ithaca: Cornell University Press, 1994).

[57] See P. W. Singer, *Wired for War: The Robotics Revolution and Conflict in the 21st Century* (New York: Penguin Press, 2009).

[58] On the various dilemmas raised by drones, see Micah Zenko, "Reforming U.S. Drone Strike Policies," *Council on Foreign Relations Special Report No. 65*, January 2013; Jane Mayer, "The Predator War," *The New Yorker*, October 26, 2009; Scott Wilson, "Drones Cast a Pall of Fear," *Washington Post*, December 4, 2011, pp. A1, A22–3; Peter Finn, "A Possible Future for Drones: Automated Killings," *Washington Post*, September 19, 2011, pp. A1, A10.

to buy over 700 new medium and large drones.[59] This does not include plans for thousands of mini-drones or anything that the CIA might have in the works.

From Oddity to Commonplace

Washington's use of drones in Pakistan from 2004 to 2012 reflected the broader shift of unmanned platforms in the American arsenal from oddity to commonplace. Only weeks before 9/11, the CIA rejected a proposal that it should deploy armed Predator drones against bin Laden in Afghanistan.[60] That position was hastily reversed when President Bush ordered far more aggressive counterterror operations in the aftermath of 9/11.[61] Over the next ten years, the drone became the single most effective counterterror weapon in Washington's arsenal. In 2010, drones pounded Pakistan's Federally Administered Tribal Areas (FATA) at a rate of one strike every three days.[62] From 9/11 to early 2010, drones had killed more than half of the twenty most-wanted al-Qaeda suspects.[63] By 2012, drones were an open secret; President Obama even discussed using them in Pakistan's FATA during an online "town hall" meeting sponsored by YouTube and Google. The president defended the use of drones, arguing that they have not caused "a huge number of civilian casualties," and that "for the most part, they have been very precise precision strikes against al-Qaeda and their affiliates."[64]

In addition to the president's comments, the White House counterterror chief, John Brennan, offered a more comprehensive defense of drones almost exactly a year after bin Laden's death.[65] Brennan's argument was based on legal, ethical, and strategic grounds. He argued that a range of considerations influenced U.S. targeting decisions, including the "broader strategic

---

[59] "Policy Options for Unmanned Aircraft Systems," Congressional Budget Office, June 2011, p. vii.

[60] Daniel Benjamin and Steven Simon, *The Age of Sacred Terror* (New York: Random House, 2002), pp. 344–6.

[61] Brian Glyn Williams, "The CIA's Covert Predator Drone War in Pakistan, 2004–2010: The History of an Assassination Campaign," *Studies in Conflict & Terrorism*, 33 (2010), p. 873. For an insider account of the challenges to developing the CIA's Predator program prior to 9/11, see Henry A. Crumpton, *The Art of Intelligence* (New York: Penguin, 2012), pp. 148–60.

[62] "The Year of the Drone," New America Foundation, http://counterterrorism.newamerica.net/drones/2010.

[63] "The Drone Wars," *Wall Street Journal*, January 9, 2010.

[64] Christi Parsons and Michael A. Memoli, "Obama Opens Up about Drone Strikes in Pakistan," *Los Angeles Times*, January 31, 2012, http://articles.latimes.com/2012/jan/31/nation/la-na-obama-drones-20120131.

[65] "The Ethics and Efficacy of the President's Counterterrorism Strategy," Transcript of Remarks by John O. Brennan, Assistant to the President for Homeland Security and Counterterrorism, Woodrow Wilson Center for International Scholars, April 30, 2012, http://www.wilsoncenter.org/event/the-efficacy-and-ethics-us-counterterrorism-strategy.

implications" such as "what effect, if any, an action might have on our relationships with other countries."

Brennan's 2012 speech was an important contribution to the American policy debate. It reflected years of experience. Indeed, central to the history of the drone campaign inside Pakistan was its evolution over time. At the outset, neither Islamabad nor Washington could have anticipated where the use of drones would lead.[66] Both struggled to manage the public face of the program.

The first U.S. drone attack in Pakistan killed Taliban leader and al-Qaeda affiliate Nek Muhammed in 2004. President Musharraf authorized it.[67] Publicly, Pakistan's military took responsibility for the missile strike, calling it a rocket attack even though eyewitnesses saw a drone overhead.[68] Washington stood by silently. Had drones remained a rarity, Pakistan's official claims might have been just plausible enough to get by. They would have offered the Americans latitude to kill important terrorist leaders while maintaining the convenient political fiction that Pakistan exercised full control over its sovereign territory.

In December 2005, however, a Pakistani journalist, Hayat Ullah Khan, published photos of Hellfire missile fragments at the North Waziristan site of a successful attack on a senior member of al-Qaeda.[69] Other media accounts also suggested that the U.S. drones were flying from Pakistani airbases – Jacobabad and Shamsi.[70] The cat was out of the bag. A month later, a drone strike in Bajaur agency near the Afghan border sparked anti-U.S. protests by thousands of tribesmen.

In October 2006, another drone killed some eighty people inside a Bajaur madrasah. The Pakistani military tried to take credit for the attack, but the intensity of the local and national backlash was impossible to contain. Tribesmen dismissed out of hand the army's claim that its own helicopters had

[66] According to one of the top CIA officers charged with developing the Predator program, "By 2011 some pundits, in a vigorous defense of President Obama's employment of armed Predators, noted that drone attacks have become a centerpiece of national security policy. Some experts would proclaim the armed Predator the most accurate weapon in the history of war. In 2001 we had no idea that would be the case. We just wanted verification of our HUMINT, a war to employ our intelligence and to eliminate UBL." See Crumpton, *The Art of Intelligence*, p. 158. Also, for an excellent firsthand perspective from a reporter covering the drone war in Pakistan's tribal areas, see Pir Zubair Shah, "My Drone War," *Foreign Policy* (March/April 2012), http://www.foreignpolicy.com/articles/2012/02/27/my_drone_war?page=full.
[67] Author conversation with Pakistani official, Islamabad, May 2012. That conversation was confirmed by Musharraf's subsequent statement to the press. See Nic Robertson and Greg Botelho, "Ex-Pakistani President Musharraf Admits Secret Deal with U.S. on Drone Strikes," CNN, April 12, 2013, http://edition.cnn.com/2013/04/11/world/asia/pakistan-musharraf-drones/.
[68] Ismail Khan and Dilawar Khan Wazir, "Night Raid Kills Nek, Four Other Militants: Wana Operation," *Dawn*, June 19, 2004, http://archives.dawn.com/2004/06/19/top1.htm.
[69] There are reasons to suspect that Hayat Ullah Khan may have paid for this story with his life. See "A Journalist in the Tribal Areas," *Front Line*, http://www.pbs.org/wgbh/pages/frontline/taliban/tribal/hayatullah.html.
[70] Williams, "The CIA's Covert Predator Drone War in Pakistan," pp. 874, 882.

fired the missiles. Too many people had heard the drones circling overhead. National Islamist politicians picked up the story and castigated the American drone strike as "an alien attack . . . tantamount to a declaration of war on Pakistan."[71] Finally, and most painfully for the Pakistani army, a suicide bomber retaliated for the Bajaur strike. He blew himself up and took forty soldiers with him in the deadliest terror attack on the army to that point.

As a consequence, the Musharraf regime altered its public stance on drones, but it did not tell the truth publicly about its tacit cooperation with Washington.[72] As new drone strikes took place, Pakistani leaders stayed mum or bowed to public opinion and issued empty denunciations of U.S. incursions on Pakistani territory. Without tangible signs that Islamabad was serious about curtailing drone strikes, however, U.S. officials could only interpret Pakistan's stance as a wink and a nod.

By 2008, the threat posed by al-Qaeda and its affiliates in the FATA had gotten out of hand. President Bush and members of his national security team resolved to expand America's counterterror campaign in the waning months of his term. In a momentous July decision, the president authorized Special Forces raids against terrorist compounds inside the FATA without prior consent from the Pakistani government or army.[73] This reflected concerns within the U.S. government that providing advance warning to the Pakistanis would too often translate into tipoffs to the terrorist targets. Those concerns could only have been reinforced by the Haqqani network's attack on the Indian embassy in Kabul that summer, which U.S. officials publicly linked to the ISI.[74] Nevertheless, given the relatively accommodating attitude that top leaders in Islamabad had so far demonstrated about drone attacks, Washington assumed there would be a similar response to its new escalation.[75]

That assumption was wrong. In September 2008, U.S. Special Forces in Afghanistan launched a raid on a compound in Angoor Ada, South Waziristan. American helicopters flew the commandos across the border from Afghanistan and the mission was supported by an AC-130 gunship circling overhead.

---

[71] Anwarullah Khan, "Pakistan Army kills Up to 80 at Qaeda-linked School," *Reuters*, October 31, 2006, http://www.nzherald.co.nz/world/news/article.cfm?c_id=2&objectid=10408444.

[72] On the beginning of this Pakistani re-think, see Christina Lamb, "U.S. Carried out Madrasah Bombing," *Sunday Times*, November 26, 2006.

[73] On the Bush policy shift in July 2008, see Eric Schmitt and Thom Shanker, *Counterstrike: The Untold Story of America's Secret Campaign against Al-Qaeda* (New York: Henry Holt, 2011), pp. 99–103.

[74] Mark Mazzetti and Eric Schmitt, "Pakistanis Aided Attack in Kabul, U.S. Officials Say," *New York Times*, August 1, 2008, http://www.nytimes.com/2008/08/01/world/asia/01pstan.html?_r=1.

[75] On the U.S. miscalculation, see Sean D. Naylor, "Spec Ops Raids into Pakistan Halted," *Army Times*, September 26, 2008, http://www.armytimes.com/news/2008/09/Army_border_ops_092608w/; also Schmitt and Shanker, *Counterstrike*, p. 123.

Two dozen militants were reported dead, none of them high-level terrorists.[76] Musharraf's successor as army chief, the chain-smoking, normally inscrutable General Kayani, went through the roof. "No external force is allowed to conduct operations inside Pakistan," Kayani declared, warning that Pakistan's sovereignty would be defended "at all costs."[77] The military's spokesman, Major General Athar Abbas, said the new orders to Pakistani forces were clear: "In case it happens again in this form, that there is a very significant detection, which is very definite, no ambiguity, across the border, on ground or in the air: open fire."[78] Pakistan's parliament echoed these calls and threatened to shut down U.S. supply routes into Afghanistan.[79]

In effect, Kayani was drawing a bright red line: U.S. commando raids were unacceptable. Not only were they a more blatant violation of Pakistan's territory, but they were more likely to be directed against Afghan Taliban groups like the Haqqanis with which Pakistani generals did not want to pick a fight. The Bush administration took the message and shelved plans for more cross-border raids.

Drones, on the other hand, were another story. Between 2004 and 2007, Washington launched nine drone attacks. In 2008 alone, it launched thirty-three, and all but five of these took place after President Bush's July policy shift.[80] President Obama accelerated the trend. If KLB was the new administration's carrot to dangle before the eyes of the Pakistani people, drones were its biggest stick for hitting Pakistan-based terrorists. In this case, the stick was much more effective than the carrot. The Obama team killed most of al-Qaeda's top leadership. The rest were forced to run for cover from the drones.

Groups like al-Qaeda are never defeated all at once. Terrorists can always regenerate their ranks if given the time and space. But there should be no question that by 2012 Washington had achieved major counterterror victories in Pakistan. As White House counterterror chief John Brennan put it a year after bin Laden's death, "for the first time since this fight began, we can look ahead and envision a world in which the al-Qaida core is simply no longer relevant."[81] The drone was the breakthrough tool that made such a vision possible.

[76] Eric Schmitt and Mark Mazzetti, "Bush Said to Give Orders Allowing Raids in Pakistan," *New York Times*, September 11, 2008, http://www.nytimes.com/2008/09/11/washington/11policy .html?pagewanted=all&_r=0.

[77] Jane Perlez, "Pakistan's Military Chief Criticizes U.S. over a Raid," *New York Times*, September 10, 2008, http://www.nytimes.com/2008/09/11/world/asia/11pstan.html.

[78] Mark Tran, "Pakistan Orders Troops to Fire on US Cross-Border Raids," *Guardian*, September 16, 2008, http://www.guardian.co.uk/world/2008/sep/16/pakistan.afghanistan.

[79] Raja Asghar, "Outraged Parliament Wants Border Raids Repulsed," *Dawn*, September 5, 2008, http://archives.dawn.com/2008/09/05/top1.htm.

[80] "The Year of the Drone," New America Foundation, http://counterterrorism.newamerica.net/ drones/2007.

[81] "The Ethics and Efficacy of the President's Counterterrorism Strategy," Wilson Center, April 30, 2012, http://www.wilsoncenter.org/event/the-efficacy-and-ethics-us-counterterrorism-strategy.

Pakistan's Drone Debate

As the drone attacks increased in the waning days of the Bush administration, Pakistan's official indignation over the obvious "violations" of its sovereignty remained muted. Over time, however, Pakistan's domestic debate over drones grew more complicated.

Inside Pakistan's tribal areas, U.S. drones became increasingly discerning about their targets, reducing civilian casualties and decimating the leadership ranks of al-Qaeda and the Taliban. In response, the terrorists took out their aggressions on local tribesmen who they accused of spying for the Americans. Their punishments were brutal. Beheaded corpses with "American spy" placards were strung up in the street for all to see. Squeezed between terrorists and drones, many locals started to see drones as the lesser evil.[82]

Islamabad continued to issue pro forma statements against the drones, but its position was transparently absurd. Behind closed doors, Pakistan's civilian leaders endorsed the American strategy.[83] For their part, Pakistani military officials negotiated with Americans about where armed drones were welcome and where they were not, narrowing attacks to specific regions, or "boxes," inside the FATA.[84]

On a summer night in 2009, a drone-launched Hellfire missile decapitated Baitullah Mehsud, the Pakistani Taliban leader responsible for the murder of Benazir Bhutto, among many other atrocities. The CIA shared its video of the attack with Pakistani officials who not only cheered the killing but also shared their amazement about the feat with journalists.[85] Some top Pakistani officials (including the retired Musharraf) stopped complaining about the drones per se and shifted their attention to the question of how Pakistan's military could get its own hands on armed drones.[86]

Even so, opposition leaders, including the increasingly popular cricket star-turned-politician Imran Khan, drew large crowds to anti-drone protests. They inveighed against America's humiliating violation of Pakistani sovereignty. However much drones might be appreciated in Washington, in Islamabad's highest offices, or even in the humble homes of many long-suffering tribesmen, they came at some political cost with the rest of the Pakistani public. To drone

---

[82] Mosharraf Zaidi, "The Consensus about Drones – Part I," *The News*, May 11, 2010, http://www.mosharrafzaidi.com/2010/05/11/the-consensus-about-drones-part-i/.

[83] Peter Bergen and Katherine Tiedemann, "Washington's Phantom War," *Foreign Affairs* (July/August 2011), p. 16.

[84] Eric Schmitt, "U.S. Prepares for a Curtailed Relationship with Pakistan," *New York Times*, December 25, 2011, http://www.nytimes.com/2011/12/26/world/asia/us-preparing-for-pakistan-to-restrict-support-for-afghan-war.html?pagewanted=all; Zia Khan, "CIA likely to resume drone strikes," *The Express Tribune*, January 9, 2012, http://tribune.com.pk/story/318690/cia-likely-to-resume-drone-strikes/.

[85] Mayer, "The Predator War."

[86] On these requests and Pakistan's own effort to field drones, see Williams, "The CIA's Covert Predator Drone War," p. 886.

opponents, U.S. officials viewed Pakistan as little more than its battleground, its leaders as stooges, and its people as pawns, or worse, as "collateral damage." In different ways, these arguments fit into many of Pakistan's preexisting anti-American narratives and rendered them all the more potent.

The Pakistani military was sensitive to these political costs. Even if the generals had tried to shift the national debate away from the sovereignty issue, they would have had trouble making the case effectively. The army's claim to being the sole defender of the nation and the fact that many rank-and-file soldiers felt deep misgivings about U.S. counterterror policies would pose real obstacles. Like Musharraf, Kayani was willing to push the bounds of his cooperation with Washington in narrow ways where he felt the politics could be managed and when the targets were not Pakistan's proxies.[87] Drone attacks were acceptable as long as they were targeted against groups that had declared war on the Pakistani state, like al-Qaeda and the Pakistani Taliban (TTP). Even then, strikes were better if they remained relatively infrequent and inside specified territorial limits so as to limit the public perception that Pakistan's sovereignty (and the army's honor) was being violated.

But the Obama administration chose to push each of these limits. Kayani and other senior officers grew more and more incensed by Washington's cavalier disregard of their concerns. They especially resented strikes – like the one on March 17, 2011, just a day after CIA contractor Raymond Davis was freed from jail in Lahore – that exposed their own very limited control over U.S. operations.[88] In May 2011, Kayani was further stung by public reports that unmasked his tacit consent on America's use of drones. Based on Wikileaks' online release of thousands of classified U.S. government documents, the news stories were hardly the product of a considered policy decision in Washington. Nevertheless, they complicated Pakistani drone politics and further soured relations between the Pakistani military and Washington.[89]

America's Drone Debate

This is not to say that Washington was in complete denial about the political and diplomatic downsides to the drones. The U.S. ambassador to Pakistan, an affable career diplomat named Cameron Munter, was plunged into the deep end of the pool when he showed up to Pakistan in October 2010, just months before the Raymond Davis affair broke. But by March 17, he had enough of a sense about Pakistan's military to understand that the CIA's planned drone

---

[87] For instance, Kayani was willing to accept U.S. training for Special Operations forces, as long as it was done quietly. See Jane Perlez, "Soldier Deaths Draw Focus to U.S. in Pakistan," *New York Times*, February 3, 2010, http://www.nytimes.com/2010/02/04/world/asia/04pstan.html.

[88] "Timing of US Drone Strike Questioned by Munter," *Associated Press*, August 2, 2011, http://www.dawn.com/2011/08/02/timing-of-us-drone-strike-questioned-by-munter.html.

[89] For one such story, see "Wikileaks: Kayani Wanted More Drone Strikes in Pakistan," *Express Tribune*, May 20, 2011, http://tribune.com.pk/story/172531/wikileaks-kayani-wanted-more-drone-strikes/.

strike would set back the relationship just as it was coming out of a crisis. Munter protested to no avail. Then-CIA Director Leon Panetta overruled him, either because the target was too important or he wished to send a firm message to Islamabad, or both.

The Pakistani army's explosive response to the March 17 strike convinced the Obama White House to review its drone policies.[90] That internal debate had evolved over time. Early on, the main question was how far to expand the program. In the first months of his presidency, President Obama considered sending armed drones beyond the FATA, including into Pakistan's Baluchistan province where senior Afghan Taliban leaders were believed to live.[91] This would have marked a significant shift in the drone campaign. Not only did Pakistan's military view the Afghan Taliban as unthreatening, but most of Pakistan also perceived a difference between the remote "tribal areas" where strikes had so far taken place and the "settled areas" where new strikes were being contemplated. The distinction was as much psychological as geographic or political. Nevertheless, some administration officials feared a major Pakistani public backlash would be sparked by an expanded drone campaign. The president decided against it.[92]

Instead of widening its scope, the United States intensified its drone campaign in the FATA. From 2008 to 2011, the CIA expanded its use of "signature strikes."[93] This meant the agency had the authority to launch strikes against people who acted like terrorists – for example, people who moved about in armed convoys or visited known terrorist camps – even if it was not entirely clear to the drone pilots who they were. Without that expanded authority, it would have been impossible to ramp up the drone program. Yet these less discriminating strikes were more likely to hit militant foot soldiers (or even innocent bystanders) than top terrorist leaders.

As U.S.-Pakistan relations frayed in 2011, American officials like Munter raised questions about whether killing no-name militants was worth the high diplomatic price with Islamabad.[94] That summer, the White House instituted minor changes in its drone policy intended to give the U.S. ambassador (and his boss, the secretary of state) more input. In some cases, Pakistani officials would also be informed of impending strikes. Still, final responsibility remained with the CIA director.

[90] Adam Entous, Siobhan Gorman, and Matthew Rosenberg, "Drone Attacks Split U.S. Officials," *Wall Street Journal*, June 4, 2011; Adam Entous, Siobhan Gorman, and Julian E. Barnes, "U.S. Tightens Drone Rules," *Wall Street Journal*, November 4, 2011.
[91] David E. Sanger, and Eric Schmitt, "U.S. Weighs Taliban Strike into Pakistan," *New York Times*, March 17, 2009, http://www.nytimes.com/2009/03/18/world/asia/18terror.html?hp.
[92] Mark Hosenball, "The Drone Dilemma," *Newsweek*, December 11, 2009, http://www.thedailybeast.com/newsweek/2009/12/12/the-drone-dilemma.html.
[93] Greg Miller reports that the chief of the CIA Counterterrorism Center was the chief advocate for the use of signature strikes. See "The CIA's Enigmatic al-Qaeda Hunter," *Washington Post*, March 25, 2012, pp. A1, A16.
[94] See Entous, Gorman, and Barnes, "U.S. Tightens Drone Rules."

The Power of (Classified) Information

The Obama administration's internal drone debate was accompanied by greater public scrutiny and discussion. Most of that debate centered on the question of whether Washington has overreached in its use of drones; whether the political costs in Pakistan outweigh the counterterror benefits. The problem with the debate has always been that the public has no realistic way to judge the significance of killing any terrorist or small group of militants. Arguments that stress the futility of targeted assassination campaigns and their negative effects on local populations, however compelling, are still hard to square with apparent reality that al-Qaeda has been dealt a devastating blow.[95]

The Munter-versus-Panetta dispute over specific drone strikes suggests that perhaps the CIA is poorly suited to making the cost-benefit calculations associated with any particular targeting decision. This tactical issue misses the larger point. Weighing the potential political repercussions of a strike is a routine part of the targeting process. Numerous terrorists have escaped missile strikes because they traveled with women or children or because they found refuge inside a mosque and the trigger-pullers decided to hold off.[96] Only members of the intelligence community, armed with a keen appreciation for the value of killing a specific target as well as relevant political input from someone like the U.S. ambassador in Islamabad, could possibly attempt such a tactical calculation. They will not always decide wisely, but it is hard to imagine anyone else who could do better.

The fundamental decision about the use of drones takes place well before any specific targets are selected. This decision is about how to prioritize U.S. counterterror objectives against other political and diplomatic goals. President Obama clearly put counterterrorism first. He dealt a strong hand to members of the administration who argued for more aggressive tactics, including the expanded use of drones in Pakistan.

In general, access to privileged, highly classified information will always give the CIA (or any other agency conducting covert activities) an upper hand in a policy debate with officials from other departments. As always, information is power. When sensitive information about American covert operations in Pakistan is accessible to only a tiny handful of the most senior policymakers outside the intelligence community, it narrows the policy debate and excludes a great deal of relevant expertise. In such instances, only the president can create

---

[95] One such report that received a lot attention is "Living under Drones," International Human Rights and Conflict Resolution Clinic (Stanford Law School) and Global Justice Clinic (NYU School of Law), September 2012, http://livingunderdrones.org/wp-content/uploads/2012/09/Stanford_NYU_LIVING_UNDER_DRONES.pdf. For more on this debate, see Peter Bergen and Katherine Tiedemann, "The Drone War," *New Republic*, June 3, 2009; David Kilcullen and Andrew Exum, "Death from Above, Outrage from Below," *New York Times*, May 16, 2009; Daniel Byman, "Do Targeted Killings Work?" *Foreign Policy*, July 14, 2009; C. Christine Fair, "Drone Wars," *Foreign Policy*, May 28, 2010.

[96] Ken Dilanian, "CIA Drones May Be Avoiding Pakistani Civilians," *Los Angeles Times*, February 22, 2011.

a level playing field in the policy debate between the intelligence community, military, and diplomats.

For better and for worse, that playing field was not level during the early Obama administration. America's covert activities in Pakistan enjoyed a higher priority than normal, overt U.S. interaction. Drones, CIA contractors, and the bin Laden raid – far more than KLB aid dollars, diplomatic dialogues, or American businessmen – defined the U.S. presence in Pakistan. The imbalance was striking. It effectively subordinated the State Department and Pentagon to the intelligence community when it came to making U.S. policy in Pakistan.

As long as al-Qaeda – and counterterrorism, in general – were considered the most vital U.S. interests in Pakistan, perhaps this subordination was defensible, even if it contributed to a near rupturing of relations between Washington and Islamabad. With bin Laden dead and al-Qaeda backed against the ropes, there was more reason to question the practice of privileging counterterrorism and accepting the intelligence community's de facto command over the policy process. Yet at the end of the Obama administration's first term, when senior officials drafted a formal guide, or "playbook," to establish clearer rules for using lethal drones, the program in Pakistan was specifically exempted.[97] The president and his top advisers were yet not convinced of the need to rebalance their priorities in Pakistan.

PAK-AF, NOT AF-PAK

At the same time that the Obama administration's efforts in Pakistan were handicapped by weak civilian policy tools and dominated by the counterterror agenda, they were also heavily influenced by the escalating war in Afghanistan. Even in the early days of Obama's term when he ordered a sixty-day review of "AfPak" strategy, it was clear that for many U.S. officials Pakistan was first and foremost an extension of the American mission in Afghanistan.[98]

In early 2009, when Pakistani Taliban briefly extended their control over territories just sixty miles from Islamabad, some prominent American commentators likened the situation to the rise of the Taliban in Afghanistan.[99] They

---

[97] Greg Miller, Ellen Nakashima, and Karen De Young, "CIA Drone Strikes Will Get Pass in Counterterrorism 'Playbook,' Officials Say," *Washington Post*, January 19, 2013, http://articles.washingtonpost.com/2013-01-19/world/36474007_1_drone-strikes-cia-director-playbook; Scott Shane, "Election Spurred a Move to Codify U.S. Drone Policy," *New York Times*, November 24, 2012, http://www.nytimes.com/2012/11/25/world/white-house-presses-for-drone-rule-book.html.

[98] On the Obama team's first AfPak review, see Daniel Markey, "From AfPak to PakAf: A Response to the New U.S. Strategy for South Asia," *Policy Options Paper*, Council on Foreign Relations, April 2009, http://i.cfr.org/content/publications/attachments/POP_AfPak_to_PakAf.pdf.

[99] The *New York Times* editorial, for instance, lamented that "The latest advance by the Taliban is one more frightening reminder that most Pakistanis – from top civilian and military leaders to ordinary citizens – still do not fully understand the mortal threat that the militants pose

fanned fears of an imminent collapse in Islamabad. Secretary Clinton even went so far as to suggest that the Pakistani Taliban might topple the government and get its hands on the "keys to the nuclear arsenal."[100] This faulty analysis was taken seriously only because too many Americans viewed Pakistan through the prism of the Afghan experience, where Taliban fighters had indeed taken the capital city of Kabul in the mid-1990s. By the time Obama entered the White House, many times more U.S. officials, particularly military ones, had seen action in Afghanistan than in Pakistan. They spoke and acted as if the two countries were more alike than different.

Washington's decision to draw a tighter connection between its policies on Afghanistan and Pakistan – even the symbolism associated with the "AfPak" term – was flat-out rejected by Pakistanis. How, Pakistanis asked, could Afghanistan – a landlocked, tribal society of 30 million people emerging from decades of civil war – possibly be compared to Pakistan – a nuclear-armed nation of nearly 200 million? Even if Pakistan's western border regions had a great deal in common with Afghanistan, the vast majority of the Pakistani public felt itself quite distant and distinct from its Afghan neighbor, and with good reason.

Eventually, at Pakistan's urging, Washington dropped the "AfPak" label. But the mental framework stuck. American policy discussions tended to treat Pakistan as an extension of the war in Afghanistan. In Obama's strategic review of late 2009 – recounted in scandalous detail by Bob Woodward's book, *Obama's Wars* – the lion's share of attention focused on the question of U.S. troop numbers in Afghanistan.[101] Some of this was only natural. An overwhelming majority of American troops were fighting and dying in Afghanistan, not Pakistan. And Washington had many more policy tools – military, civilian, and economic – inside Afghanistan, which offered both the prospect for greater influence and the need for greater direction.

The problem was not simply that Afghanistan drew attention and resources away from Pakistan. Beyond that, the intense focus on Afghanistan meant that unresolved differences between Washington and Islamabad over the Afghan war came to dominate the U.S.-Pakistan relationship more than ever before. At the core of the dispute was Pakistan's approach to territories like North Waziristan along the border with Afghanistan, where Taliban insurgent leaders continued to find safe haven after years of war. Washington wanted Pakistan to cut off the head of the snake that was biting NATO and Afghan forces,

---

to their fragile democracy.... And – most frightening of all – if the army cannot or will not defend its own territory against the militants, how can anyone be sure it will protect Pakistan's 60 or so nuclear weapons?" "60 Miles from Islamabad," *New York Times*, April 26, 2009, http://www.nytimes.com/2009/04/27/opinion/27mon1.html?_r=1.

[100] Ben Arnoldy, "Why the Taliban Won't Take Over Pakistan," *Christian Science Monitor*, June 7, 2009, http://www.csmonitor.com/World/Asia-South-Central/2009/0607/p06s07-wosc .html.

[101] Bob Woodward, *Obama's Wars* (New York: Simon & Schuster, 2010).

but Pakistan was unwilling to sever ties with the Haqqani network or Mullah Omar's Afghan Taliban. From an American perspective, such a shift would have improved prospects for resolving the war in Afghanistan and, simultaneously, would have set Pakistan on a path to greater stability over the long haul. That it never happened was primarily a reflection of Pakistan's own intransigence.

Pakistan: Do More

Pakistan resisted U.S. pressure despite an intensive series of diplomatic dialogues between political and military leaders in Washington and Islamabad. Publicly, Pakistani leaders denied supporting the Taliban. Moreover, they argued that Washington was asking Pakistan's army – already overtaxed by its fight against insurgents – to assume too heavy a burden along its western border. They angrily asked how America was in any position to tell Pakistan to "do more" in the fight against extremists, given the military losses and suffering Pakistan's own people had already endured. Yet by framing the question that way, Pakistan's leaders steadfastly ignored the American claim that they were guilty of fighting some groups of terrorists, such as the Pakistani Taliban, while actively or passively assisting others, like the Haqqanis.

Pakistan's refusal to cut ties with the Taliban, indeed its entire policy of supporting militant and extremist organizations, was morally reprehensible. As explained in Chapter 2, however, it was driven by a calculation that some of these groups still offered strategic benefits; namely, the prospect of Pakistani influence in Afghanistan and the ability to cause trouble for India.

Those benefits came at a cost; Pakistani leaders knew they were riding a tiger. They saw that homegrown extremists had turned against their own state. They were well aware of the fact that state-supported groups like LeT could cause terrible trouble. Even so, the alternative urged by the United States – to crack down on these groups and their many sympathizers – had the potential to be even more painful, especially in the short run.

Why? Part of the problem was that Pakistani officials never believed that Washington was fully committed to a long-term investment in Afghanistan's stability.[102] They repeatedly expressed doubts about U.S. strategy in Afghanistan, especially about Washington's plan to build the Afghan army and sustain it for years after most U.S. and NATO forces were scheduled to depart. Sooner or later, Pakistanis figured, whatever fragile edifice Washington constructed in Afghanistan would collapse. If Afghanistan fell apart after America's withdrawal and Islamabad had already turned against the Afghan Taliban, what friends (and more important, what influence) would Pakistan have left there?

---

[102] On General Kayani's doubts, specifically about U.S. long-term investment in the Afghan security forces, see Jane Perlez, "The Fight over How to End a War," *New York Times*, October 19, 2011.

Mixed Messages

Mixed, confusing signals from Washington reinforced existing Pakistani doubts about U.S. intentions and commitment in Afghanistan. This was true, above all, for the U.S. military "surge" of 30,000 additional American troops to Afghanistan, announced by President Obama at West Point on December 1, 2009.

U.S. military commanders in the field, reacting to deteriorating security and the growing momentum of the insurgency, had requested 40,000 more troops.[103] The surge came close. Obama's announcement followed on the heels of his prior decisions to more than double U.S. forces to nearly 70,000. Placing 100,000 U.S. forces in land-locked Afghanistan was an impressive commitment of American power.

The surge made waves in Pakistan. It raised the possibility – perhaps for the first time since shortly after 9/11 – that Afghanistan's insurgents had finally met their match. It is conceivable that Islamabad might have shifted its own strategy in response. Rather than hedging its bets, the Pakistanis might have jumped on the powerful American bandwagon. No point in backing losing insurgents; better to push them to the negotiating table or to seek new, less odious, Afghan proxies.

Unfortunately, strength and resolve were not the only messages the Pakistanis received from Washington. A series of leaks from within the Obama administration preceded the president's announcement of the surge. They suggested deep internal doubts about the new escalation.[104] Those doubts were also reflected in U.S. policy when the president combined his surge with a public pledge that it would only be temporary. As President Obama explained in his West Point speech, "After 18 months, our troops will begin to come home. These are the resources that we need to seize the initiative, while building the Afghan capacity that can allow for a responsible transition of our forces out of Afghanistan."[105]

---

[103] General Stanley McChrystal's request for troops was leaked to reporter Bob Woodward, who described the general's findings in "McChrystal: More Forces or 'Mission Failure,'" *Washington Post*, September 21, 2009, http://www.washingtonpost.com/wp-dyn/content/article/2009/09/20/AR2009092002920.html.

[104] On the series of leaks preceding Obama's West Point speech, starting with General McChrystal's report and including Ambassador Eikenberry's cables, see Laura Rozen, "The Eikenberry Memo and the Leak War: More Pushback against a Nudgey Pentagon?" *Politico*, November 12, 2009, http://www.politico.com/blogs/laurarozen/1109/The_Eikenberry_memo_and_the_leak_war_more_pushback_against_a_nudgey_Pentagon_.html; also David E. Sanger, *Confront and Conceal* (New York: Crown, 2012), p. 32. Bob Woodward's reporting in the *Washington Post* and his subsequent book that described the administration's internal debate in intimate detail also received great attention in Pakistan's leadership circles. See Bob Woodward, "McChrystal: More Forces or 'Mission Failure,'" *Washington Post*, September 21, 2009, http://www.washingtonpost.com/wp-dyn/content/article/2009/09/20/AR2009092002920.html; *Obama's Wars* (New York: Simon&Schuster, 2010).

[105] "Obama's Address on the War in Afghanistan," *New York Times*, December 1, 2009, http://www.nytimes.com/2009/12/02/world/asia/02prexy.text.html.

Firm timelines reflected the White House's desire to avoid an open-ended expansion of a decade-long war. They also made for good politics. Most Americans were justifiably sick and tired of the conflict, not least because it followed on the heels of the costly and frustrating war in Iraq. Congressional Democrats accepted President Obama's plans to send more forces into harm's way, but only grudgingly. All told, the White House's timed surge threaded a difficult political needle at home without rejecting the core recommendations of his generals on the battlefield.

When it came to the timetables, Obama kept his promises. U.S. troop strength reached roughly 100,000 by the summer of 2010. A year later, he declared that 10,000 troops would be home before 2012, that the rest of the surge would be recovered by September 2012, and that, "by 2014 ... the Afghan people will be responsible for their own security."[106] Given the time required to move thousands of troops into and out of Afghanistan, U.S. forces were near their peak (of between 90,000 and 100,000) for roughly eighteen months.[107]

Recognizing the obvious political constraints on the Obama administration, no one in Pakistan or Afghanistan could ever have assumed that the surge would last forever. But announcing the timeline for military departure from the outset was still a crucial blunder. It projected the wrong message to Pakistan, the Taliban leadership, and the Afghans.[108] It weakened the punch that the surge delivered to the insurgency by fostering a sense that the war's endgame was just around the corner. It offered hope to the Taliban that if they weathered one last storm, victory over the United States was within reach. Most important for the U.S.-Pakistan relationship, the mixed message about American resolve relaxed what pressure Pakistan might otherwise have felt to reconsider its own stance toward the Taliban insurgents and get onboard with Washington's program.

At the same time, Pakistani doubts about U.S. resolve were further compounded by a diplomatic initiative out of Washington. The State Department – first under Holbrooke's direction and then, after his death, under the less flamboyant stewardship of career diplomat Marc Grossman – started to explore what it termed a "reconciliation" agenda. Tentative at first, the goal was to find a diplomatic compromise that could bring the Taliban in from the cold and also end the war on terms acceptable to the United States.

---

[106] "Text of President Obama's Speech on Afghanistan," *New York Times*, June 22, 2011, http://www.nytimes.com/2011/06/23/world/asia/23obama-afghanistan-speech-text.html.

[107] For a chart showing monthly U.S. troop levels in Afghanistan, see Ian S. Livingston and Michael O'Hanlon, "Afghanistan Index," Brookings Institution, Washington, DC, September 30, 2012, http://www.brookings.edu/~/media/Programs/foreign%20policy/afghanistan%20index/index20120930.pdf.

[108] Washington's failure to conclude a strategic partnership agreement with Kabul until May 2012 – long after the timelines for military drawdown were announced – further hurt the credibility of U.S. claims that it would remain committed to Afghan security well after the surge was over. For the text of the final agreement, see "Enduring Strategic Partnership Agreement between the United States of American and the Islamic Republic of Afghanistan," http://www.whitehouse.gov/sites/default/files/2012.06.01u.s.-afghanistanspasignedtext.pdf.

In February 2011, when U.S. forces were at their peak numbers in Afghanistan, Secretary of State Clinton used a speech at the Asia Society in New York to explain the decision to talk with the Taliban. She observed that such a dialogue would proceed at the same time as the military surge as well as intensified U.S. civilian assistance and development activities. On the diplomatic initiative, she remarked, "I know that reconciling with an adversary that can be as brutal as the Taliban sounds distasteful, even unimaginable. And diplomacy would be easy if we only had to talk to our friends. But that is not how one makes peace. President Reagan understood that when he sat down with the Soviets. And Richard Holbrooke made this his life's work. He negotiated face-to-face with [Slobodan] Milosevic and ended a war [in Bosnia]."[109]

Like Obama's firm timelines for the surge, opening a dialogue with the Afghan insurgents made sense in Washington. By conjuring visions of historic diplomatic breakthroughs, it offered hope for an honorable, orderly American withdrawal from Afghanistan. The idea held wide appeal outside the United States as well. Many others – from the Afghan government in Kabul to America's European allies – were simultaneously sending out feelers to the Taliban to gauge prospects for a negotiated settlement.

Islamabad, however, responded warily. This was not a surprise. Clinton stated up front that reconciliation required a great deal of Pakistan. In her Asia Society speech, she noted that "Pakistan also has responsibilities of its own, including taking decisive steps to ensure that the Afghan Taliban cannot continue to conduct the insurgency from Pakistani territory. Pressure from the Pakistani side will help push the Taliban toward the negotiating table and away from al-Qaida."

These demands did not go down well with Islamabad. It sounded like Washington was asking Pakistan to put the screws to the Afghan Taliban so the United States could secure its own face-saving way out of the war. Supposing that strategy worked, where would it leave Pakistan? With less influence and fewer friends in Afghanistan, that's where.

Moreover, when it came to nuts and bolts of how to talk to the Taliban, Pakistan found itself betwixt and between. Washington was simultaneously asking Islamabad to turn against the Afghan insurgents and to facilitate talks with them. Pakistani officials chalked up the inconsistent demands to American hypocrisy. In September 2011, for instance, when Admiral Mullen was haranguing Pakistan for its ties to the Haqqani network, other U.S. officials were appealing to Islamabad for help in opening a communication channel to Haqqani leaders.[110]

[109] Hillary Rodham Clinton, "Remarks at the Launch of the Asia Society's Series of Richard C. Holbrooke Memorial Addresses," New York, February 18, 2011, http://www.state.gov/secretary/rm/2011/02/156815.htm.

[110] Karen DeYoung, "U.S. Goes after Haqqani network," *Washington Post*, October 14, 2011, http://www.washingtonpost.com/world/national-security/us-goes-after-haqqani-network/2011/10/14/gIQAj2i6kL_story.html.

It is at least conceivable that Islamabad might have stepped up to the plate in the way Clinton asked. But the opposite was always far more likely. Islamabad interpreted Washington's reconciliation initiative as evidence that the United States was desperate to find a quick exit from Afghanistan.[111] Rather than driving a wedge between Islamabad and its Afghan proxies, the reconciliation project ended up having a contrary effect. Islamabad sought to turn Washington's diplomatic initiative to its own advantage.[112]

Some influential Pakistani analysts and policymakers had long perceived a deal with the Taliban as an opportunity for a grand diplomatic masterstroke.[113] In one fell swoop they envisioned ending U.S. pressure to turn against the Afghan Taliban, winning greater influence over Afghanistan's future, and accelerating the U.S. military drawdown from the region. In meetings with Pakistani officials from 2010 to 2012, more than a few shared their hope that America and Pakistan might finally see eye-to-eye on the best way to win the war in Afghanistan. To put it bluntly, they wanted the United States to outsource the Afghan endgame to Pakistan.

DISTRUST AND DISAGREEMENT

Of course, this was never Washington's intention. The fact that well-placed Pakistanis believed such a deal might be on the table demonstrated just how far apart the two sides had fallen. When the United States had tried to inspire confidence, it sowed new doubt. When Washington attempted to signal resolve, Islamabad perceived desperation.

These differences persisted in spite of a series of "strategic dialogues" in which top U.S. officials attempted to explain to senior Pakistani leaders Washington's plans for Afghanistan, the pain Pakistan would feel if it undermined those plans, and the benefits Pakistan would enjoy if it got onboard with the American strategy.[114] Those conversations went nowhere. U.S. officials found their Pakistani counterparts either evasive or utterly unrealistic in their demands for American partnership. Reflecting the gulf between the two sides, the head of

---

[111] This is undoubtedly how many Afghans view the reconciliation effort. See Amrullah Saleh, "Why Negotiate with the Taliban?" *Wall Street Journal*, February 9, 2012, http://online.wsj.com/article/SB10001424052970204136404577207500541175714.html?mod=googlenews_wsj.

[112] Some argue that Pakistan has sought to do just this, in part through its strategic arrests of various Afghan Taliban leaders like Mullah Baradar in February 2010. Others suggest that arrest was much less premeditated. See, for example, Myra MacDonald, "Pakistan's Arrest of Mullah Baradar: Tactics or Strategy?" *Reuters*, February 17, 2010, http://blogs.reuters.com/pakistan/2010/02/17/pakistans-arrest-of-mullah-baradar-tactics-or-strategy/.

[113] This thesis was introduced to me most vigorously in a conversation with a senior Pakistani official in Peshawar, May 2010.

[114] On U.S.-Pakistan strategic dialogues, which appear to have covered a wide range of issues without meeting the core needs of either side, see Steve Coll, "What Does Pakistan Want?" *The New Yorker*, March 29, 2012, http://www.newyorker.com/online/blogs/comment/2012/03/classified-document-our-collective-experience.html.

Pakistan's military, General Kayani, shared a secret fourteen-page memo with President Obama in late 2010. The memo called into question U.S. motives and methods in Pakistan and Afghanistan, even going so far as to suggest that Washington was working to maintain a "controlled chaos" inside Pakistan.[115]

A year after that memo, the United States and Pakistan had reached a complete impasse. American frustration and anger over Pakistan's inaction against Afghan Taliban and terrorists in North Waziristan – along with suspicions about how bin Laden could have escaped Pakistan's attention in Abbottabad for so long – had by that point led a number of American policy analysts and politicians to argue for a purely coercive or "containment" strategy in Pakistan.[116]

In different ways, the KLB debacle, Washington's expanded counterterrorism operations on Pakistani soil, and mixed U.S. signals regarding the war in Afghanistan all set the stage for the calamitous deterioration in relations between Washington and Islamabad from 2010 to 2012. The Obama administration made its share of mistakes; there are good reasons to suspect that a more sure-footed American approach might have done more to snap Pakistan out of its dangerous, entrenched patterns.

In the end, however, Pakistan's course was set and maintained by its own leaders. For their own reasons they refused – in the face of American threats and inducements – to cut ties with terrorist organizations or to tackle head-on the broader problem of extremism in their society. Those failures ate at the core of the U.S.-Pakistan relationship. If Washington had believed Pakistan to be a trustworthy partner, there would have been no need for Raymond Davis to be spying on LeT in Lahore, no need to fly a stealthy helicopter into Abbottabad without informing General Kayani, no need for Admiral Mullen's pointed testimony before Congress. Looking to the future, unless Pakistan takes a different approach toward terrorism, militancy and extremism, cooperation between Washington and Islamabad will continue to rest on rickety foundations.

---

[115] For an account of this exchange, see David Ignatius, "Our High-Maintenance Relationship with Pakistan," *Washington Post*, July 13, 2012, http://www.washingtonpost.com/opinions/david-ignatius-pakistan-us-have-a-neurotic-relationship/2012/07/13/gJQABEDoiW_story.html.

[116] See, for instance, Bruce Riedel, "A New Pakistan Policy: Containment," *New York Times*, October 14, 2011, http://www.nytimes.com/2011/10/15/opinion/a-new-pakistan-policy-containment.html; Stephen D. Krasner, "Talking Tough to Pakistan," *Foreign Affairs* (January/February 2012), http://www.foreignaffairs.com/articles/136696/stephen-d-krasner/talking-tough-to-pakistan.

6

From the Outside-In

U.S.-Pakistan Relations in the Regional Context

The city of Peshawar stands at the door to Pakistan's semi-autonomous tribal lands, the famed Khyber Pass, and Afghanistan. For hundreds of years, it has served as an outpost and garrison, but also as a way station for invading armies, missionaries, and traders of all stripes.[1] Driving along its streets, it is easy to tell Peshawar is close to the Afghan border and the mountains; clusters of women are hidden behind burkas, and in winter men don traditional brown woolen shawls to ward off the chill. All around, three-wheeled Chinese Qingqi scooters mingle with bicycles, donkey carts, cars, and brightly painted trucks and buses.

Peshawar has always felt the reverberations of decisions made in distant capitals. In that respect, the city is much like Pakistan as a whole: seemingly distant, and yet still thoroughly connected to the wider world. In the context of Peshawar's storied history, connections with the United States are short indeed. But remote Peshawar, like the nation of which it is a part, has at times played an outsized role in U.S. policy.

In the early Cold War, American U-2 spy planes took off for missions over the Soviet Union from nearby Badaber airbase, including the ill-fated flight of Francis Gary Powers that exposed America's secret program to the world. In the 1980s, Peshawar was a meeting point and refuge for many of the Afghan fighters who formed the core of the CIA- and Saudi-sponsored mujahedeen. Osama bin Laden cut his teeth recruiting Arab fighters in Peshawar, and the city's ties to terrorism and the Taliban have persisted well after 9/11.

Before 2006 much of Peshawar was considered relatively safe. Even terrorists, the logic went, needed peace in Peshawar to do business, recuperate from

---

[1] For a short summary of Peshawar's history, from Persian and Greek to Buddhist, Hindu, Muslim, Sikh, and British rule, see Ahmad Salim, ed., *Peshawar: City on the Frontier* (Oxford: Oxford University Press, 2008), especially pp. 160–6. For the classic history of the Pashtuns and the Peshawar region, see Sir Olaf Caroe, *The Pathans* (Oxford: Oxford University Press, 1984).

the fight in Afghanistan, and watch over their families. Yet the local dynamics shifted, and Peshawar's fragile balance could not last. Peshawar found itself at the leading edge of a shocking wave of violence that would soon crest over Pakistan.

On an early morning in November 2006, as I stared out the window at the grayish brown winter landscape punctuated by farms and villages along the highway midway through a ride from Islamabad to Peshawar, the radio picked up the chilling news of Peshawar's first suicide bombing. A terrorist had strapped explosives to his chest and blown himself to pieces near a city police van. Two officers were wounded. Peshawar had entered a tragic new era.

Since then, the city has suffered terribly. Between 2006 and 2010, over 400 terrorist attacks struck the city, killing 866 civilians and wounding nearly 2,500 more.[2] Many of the city's wealthier residents have moved away to escape the violence. Extremists have also made a point of desecrating symbols of Peshawar's traditionally tolerant Sufi culture. In one of the most egregious examples of this trend, in March 2009 they bombed the mausoleum of the revered seventeenth-century Pashtun poet, Rahman Baba.[3]

Not surprisingly, Pakistan's terrorists attacked U.S. facilities in Peshawar with a special vengeance. In late summer 2008, gunmen opened fire on the vehicle of the top diplomat at the U.S. consulate as she left the gates of her home in what had been considered one of Peshawar's most secure, upscale neighborhoods. The next year, a massive suicide car bombing rocked the Pearl Continental hotel, a landmark that had served as a regular meeting spot for local journalists, international aid officials, and politicians. Washington had been in negotiations to purchase the hotel for use as an expanded consulate.[4]

In April 2010, the U.S. consulate itself – so well fortified that locals offering directions there said it looked like "Guantánamo" – was the target of a car bombing and commando-style assault that killed six but failed to breach the perimeter. These threats forced many of the U.S. diplomats and development officials who would normally live and work in Peshawar to decamp to Islamabad. But that commute also came with serious security risks. Several weeks after the U.S. raid on bin Laden's compound in May 2011, the Pakistani Taliban claimed responsibility for a suicide motorbike bomb attack on an American vehicle headed from Islamabad to Peshawar.[5]

In spite of its twenty-first-century troubles, Peshawar can still evoke the spirit of a bygone colonial era. History is strong there. The headquarters of

[2] Worldwide Incidents Tracking System, National Counterterrorism Center, http://www .wits.nctc.gov.

[3] Saba Imtiaz, "Revisiting Rahman Baba's Shrine," *Express Tribune*, June 26, 2010, http://tribune .com.pk/story/23782/revisiting-rahman-babas-shrine/.

[4] "11 Killed in Peshawar PC Blast," *Daily Times*, June 10, 2009, http://www.dailytimes.com.pk/ default.asp?page=2009\06\10\story_10-6-2009_pg1_1.

[5] "Pakistan Taliban Bomb US Consulate Convoy in Peshawar," *BBC*, May 20, 2011, http://www .bbc.co.uk/news/world-south-asia-13465910.

the paramilitary frontier forces in the imposing Bala Hisar fortress overlooks the city with a colonial stare. Sitting in its courtyard under the stars one spring evening in 2010, a Pakistani army officer recounted tales of daring raids on militant compounds along the Afghan border. Earlier that day, the provincial governor shared tea and his views on regional diplomacy in his palatial British-era residence, surrounded by manicured grounds and strolling peacocks, its interiors graced by enormous paintings of noble warriors and muskets mounted above fireplace mantels.

There is indeed a tension in Peshawar between past and present, as there is throughout Pakistan. But this is not a simple battle pitting the traditional against the modern, or Islamists versus the "West." In 2006, a provincial politician explained his reasons for a new law that would have imposed something just short of a Taliban-style "vice and virtue" ministry in the province.[6] On arriving at his office, I could see immediately that he was no bearded extremist, spouting conspiracy theories and dogma. Far from it; the politician was an articulate U.S. green card holder and former pizza chef from northern Virginia, whose sons had attended American public high schools and believed that the same curriculum should be taught to boys and girls in northwest Pakistan. Pakistan's multiple identities are at war in Peshawar. In a single politician's family, indeed in his own head, different manifestations of modernity and globalization are often in conflict.

Like the rest of Pakistan, Peshawar also has its progressives, liberals, and leftists, although in dwindling numbers. In 2010, a group of Peshawar university students proudly recounted to me how their peers had chased away Zaid Hamid, one of Pakistan's most rabid anti-Western and hyper-nationalist television pundits, when he tried to give a lecture on campus.[7] Hamid, who sports a trademark bright red hat and spins the most fantastical conspiracy theories with conviction and fervor, rose from obscurity in 2008. For several years he appealed to thousands of young Pakistanis with his strident nationalism based, in part, on an unorthodox reading of Islamic scriptures.[8]

The Peshawar university students went on to complain that outspoken critics of the United States like Hamid tend to be Pakistanis with no firsthand experience of the present insurgency along the Afghan border, and no sense of how dangerous the Taliban have become. Some even said they supported America's drone campaign, because without it they would suffer from either Taliban oppression or destructive Pakistani army operations.

[6] "Frontier Cabinet Okays Hasbah Bill," *Daily Times*, July 5, 2005, http://www.dailytimes.com.pk/default.asp?page=story_5-7-2005_pg7_5.

[7] For an overview of Zaid Hamid's rapid ascent in 2008, see Manan Ahmed, "Pakistan's New Paranoia," *The National*, March 11, 2010, http://www.thenational.ae/news/world/pakistans-new-paranoia.

[8] For a profile of Zaid Hamid, including his references to the controversial hadith on Ghazva-e-Hind, see Amber Rahim Shamsi, "Will the Real Zaid Hamid Please Stand Up?" *Express Tribune*, May 9, 2010, http://tribune.com.pk/story/11701/will-the-real-zaid-hamid-please-stand-up/.

These students and their professors are potential American allies, but they also threw darts. However bitter they were about their own government and military, they found U.S. policies in the region even more confusing and frustrating. As they marched through their own narrative of the past six decades of history, they concluded that whatever America's professed motive or agenda, the superpower had supported Pakistani dictators and abused Pakistani sovereignty. In their eyes, U.S. policy has left behind a trail of extremism, militancy, and political repression.

What they most wanted to know from me, standing before them as a visiting American lecturer, was what the future might hold. The long history of Peshawar, that quintessential frontier city, had taught them that decisions made in distant capitals like Washington could change their lives. What did the United States have in mind for Peshawar – and Pakistan – now?

I responded by retracing the steps in their historical narrative, observing that in the past Washington's interest in Pakistan has been heavily influenced by the broader regional and international context. The U.S.-Pakistan relationship has never existed in a vacuum. Formative American decisions to engage or distance from Pakistan were made in the context of Cold War developments, from Washington's early fear of Soviet advances into the Persian Gulf, to the subsequent reality of Moscow's withdrawal from Afghanistan. Later, it was the attacks of 9/11, rather than any particular concern about internal Pakistani dynamics, which rekindled U.S.-Pakistani ties.

Judging from that history, one way to think about the future course of U.S.-Pakistan relations is to think from the "outside-in"; in other words, to ask how the United States is likely to interact with Pakistan's neighbors and then consider how those relationships will influence ties between Washington and Islamabad. How will Washington assess its geopolitical interests in the wider region five or ten years from now? How will the United States balance those concerns with Pakistan-specific issues, like terrorism and nuclear weapons?

Peering just over the horizon, it is clear that no matter what happens in the endgame of the Afghan war or how present disagreements between Washington and Islamabad are resolved, Pakistan's enormous neighbors to the east – India and China – will occupy an increasing share of U.S. attention. Rather than reprising the "AfPak" framework of the early Obama administration, in which Pakistan and Afghanistan were lumped together, the future should require Washington to think in the "quadrilateral" terms of connections between China, India, Pakistan, and the United States. Together, these will be four of the world's largest countries by population, all nuclear powers, and all with established – at times conflicting – interests in the heart of Asia.

GLOBAL POWER SHIFT: CHINA'S RISE

With the benefit of hindsight, historians will frame the early twenty-first century as the beginning of a new era defined not by Iraq, Afghanistan, or al-Qaeda, but by the reemergence of the Asia-Pacific region. Its central protagonist will be China, a state that – after hundreds of years in the shadow of the West – is re-emerging to assume a role of power and leadership.

A visit to Pudong, the urban district across the river from Old Shanghai, gives a visceral sense for China's rapid ascent. Built on farmlands starting in the early 1990s, Pudong alone now boasts a population of 5 million, a gross domestic product (GDP) larger than that of Croatia, and one of the world's most dramatic skylines, especially at night when the bulbous forms of the soaring Oriental Pearl television tower are illuminated in garish hues.[9] Bankers know it as the home of the Shanghai Stock Exchange, where the daily trading volume exceeds $18 billion. Shanghai's combination of scale and wealth compares favorably to any city in the world.

After several long cab rides around the sprawling megacity in the spring of 2008, I was left with the impression that if the future is a race for bigger and better infrastructure, China has already left the United States in the dust. The city is a vast sea of concrete, asphalt, and super high-rise towers stretching on into the distance. It is hard not to come away awestruck by the immenseness of it all.

There are, of course, important caveats to China's rise. Most of China is growing, but not nearly as fast as Shanghai.[10] As of 2009, over a quarter of China's population still lived on less than $2 a day, and China's autocratic political system stifles the sorts of freedoms that typically lead to thriving societies over the long run.[11] Added to that, China's "one child" policy and the cultural preference for boy babies could eventually turn China into a nation of aging bachelors who are expected to care for their elderly parents. These are just a few of the developments that have the potential to turn China's boom into a bust in the decades to come.

That downside prospect cannot diminish the fact that so much of China is already developing at breakneck pace. On a 2011 trip to Sichuan province's Chengdu, one of China's largest inland cities, a young graduate student explained in excellent English that her parents were "semi-literate peasants." In a span of a single generation, she had moved from a world defined by a rural

[9] For the GDP of Pudong, see, "Shanghai's Pudong Sets Double-Digit GDP Growth," *Xinhua*, April 19, 2010, http://www.chinadaily.com.cn/bizchina/2010–04/19/content_9747072.htm.

[10] China's Gini coefficient, a standard metric used to measure income inequality, has worsened from 0.3 in 1986 to 0.5 in 2011. See Dexter Roberts, "China's Growing Income Gap," *Bloomberg Businessweek*, January 27, 2011, http://www.businessweek.com/magazine/content/11_06/b4214013648109.htm; Dr. Damian Tobin, "Inequality in China: Rural Poverty Persists as Urban Wealth Booms," *BBC*, June 29, 2011, http://www.bbc.co.uk/news/business-13945072; Thant Myint-U, *Where China Meets India: Burma and the New Crossroads of Asia* (New York: Farrar, Straus and Giroux, 2011), p. 130.

[11] "Poverty headcount ratio at $2 a day (PPP) (% of population)," The World Bank, http://data.worldbank.org/indicator/SI.POV.2DAY.

village to one in which she could earn a university master's degree and aspire to a well-paid corporate job in China's new globalized economy.

By the numbers as well, China's rise is very real. In the past twenty years, the Asian giant has averaged an annual growth rate of over 9 percent.[12] Even if China is unable to keep up its torrid economic expansion, its momentum may carry its GDP past that of the United States as early as 2027.[13] In recent years, China pushed the United States aside to become the top trade partner for India, Japan, and South Korea. China also has extensive investments in Africa, Central Asia, and Latin America.[14] With trade and investment come greater diplomatic influence, especially in China's case, since the authoritarian state itself controls many business decisions.

China is also busy transforming its wealth into military power. China has long maintained a huge active-duty military, with well over 2 million personnel in 2010, but those impressive numbers did not translate into a modern or especially capable force. Over the past twenty years, however, the People's Republic has expanded its defense budget to address those shortcomings. A 2011 report to Congress by the U.S. Department of Defense found that China's total military-related spending exceeded $160 billion in 2010.[15] That same Pentagon report noted that "during 2010, China made strides toward fielding an operational anti-ship ballistic missile, continued work on its aircraft carrier program, and finalized the prototype of its first stealth aircraft."[16]

As a consequence of these and other investments over the past two decades, Princeton professor Aaron Friedberg concludes that China's "PLA [People's Liberation Army] is approaching the point where it may have (or its leaders may believe that they have) a real chance of knocking U.S. forces out of the Western Pacific, at least in the opening stages of a war, using only conventional weapons and without hitting targets on America's home soil."[17] China may not be there yet, but in time its new military capabilities are likely to alter fundamentally the balance of power and influence in the region.

---

[12] Kevin Brown, "ADB Warns on China's Long-Term Growth," *Financial Times*, September 28, 2010, http://www.ft.com/intl/cms/s/0/7d660492-cad4-11df-bf36-00144feab49a.html#axzz29 Up6Ij7V.

[13] "China Overtakes Japan as World's Second-Biggest Economy," *Bloomberg News*, August 16, 2010, http://www.bloomberg.com/news/2010-08-16/china-economy-passes-japan-s-in-second-quarter-capping-three-decade-rise.html. For an assessment of what it will mean for China's economy to surpass that of the United States, see Arvind Subramanian, *Eclipse* (Washington: Peterson Institute for International Economics, 2011).

[14] For a summary of China's overseas investments, see Nargiza Salidjanova, "Going Out: An Overview of China's Outward Foreign Direct Investment," USCC Staff Report, U.S.-China Economic & Security Review Commission, March 30, 2011.

[15] "Annual Report to Congress: Military and Security Developments Involving the People's Republic of China 2011," U.S. Department of Defense, p. 41.

[16] "Annual Report to Congress: Military and Security Developments Involving the People's Republic of China 2011," p. 13.

[17] Aaron L. Friedberg, *A Contest for Supremacy* (New York: W.W. Norton, 2011), p. 224.

Even if China still has a long way to go before it catches up to the United States in terms of its overall wealth, military power, or quality of life, China's national power relative to other actors on the world stage is now indisputably greater than at any previous point in the modern era.[18] Henry Kissinger, America's high priest of Realpolitik, observes in his monumental volume, *On China*, that this development is in many ways a return toward China's traditional role as the "Middle Kingdom," or "Central Country," whose leader was "conceived of (and recognized by most neighboring states) as the pinnacle of a universal political hierarchy."[19]

Of course, China will not be the only rising Asian state. The other rising giant, India, and many of their smaller neighbors throughout the Asia-Pacific region also have expanding populations, dynamic economies, and heightened ambitions. Nor will the traditional powers – Europe, Russia, and especially the United States – simply cede their dominant roles. This will be a complex, at times competitive, and perhaps even a violent process, with existing powers looking to protect their historical clout from the growing ambitions of rising states.

America's Response

Washington has always been aware of China's strategic significance, whether in the context of Nixon and Kissinger's secret diplomacy with Mao Zedong during the Cold War or Clinton's effort to include Beijing in an expanded global free trade regime. But it was not until the George W. Bush administration that American leaders spoke of placing China at the center of their global vision and declared that China should be viewed less as a "strategic partner" and more as a "strategic competitor."[20]

That shift had its limits. The new Bush administration had no particular interest in picking a fight with China. Many of Bush's policies, especially in the realm of economics, were as conciliatory as any that came before. Yet the Bush team appreciated that the end of the Cold War and the rise of China represented fundamental shifts in the global balance of power. For this reason, the administration came into office concerned primarily about shoring up traditional alliances and managing relations with other powerful states.

In April 2001, an unexpected turn of events catapulted China to the top of the Bush administration's agenda. A U.S. EP-3 reconnaissance plane was flying in the South China Sea over waters that China considers – contrary to standard

---

[18] Michael Beckley makes an important contribution in his study of China's rise relative to the United States, concluding that America's edge is likely to endure and maybe even grow. Yet even if Beckley's argument is correct, China's absolute rise is real and Beijing will have an increasing role to play on the world stage. See "China's Century?" *International Security*, 36(3) (Winter 2011/12), pp. 41–78.

[19] Henry A. Kissinger, *On China* (New York: Penguin, 2011), pp. 2–3.

[20] Friedberg, A Contest for Supremacy, p. 94.

interpretations of international law – off-limits to foreign military planes and ships. In an over-aggressive effort at harassment, a Chinese fighter pilot flew too close to the EP-3. For him, the mistake proved fatal. Luckily, the American plane managed an emergency landing on a Chinese island and all twenty-four of its crewmembers survived, but the Chinese immediately detained them and impounded their sensitive aircraft.

Bush's secretary of defense, Donald Rumsfeld, recalls that the ensuing diplomatic crisis foreshadowed the potential for future tensions with China. He urged President Bush to take a firm stance. It was important, Rumsfeld believed, not to look like a "weak supplicant" in a way that might "embolden China's military and political leaders to commit still more provocative acts."[21]

Rumsfeld's hawkish advice was only partially heeded by the White House, but his recollection of events reveals the mind-set of the era. The incident was ultimately defused diplomatically, although Beijing did not return the U.S. EP-3 for three months. Had it not been for the 9/11 attacks and later, the war in Iraq, one would have to assume that "much of the money, manpower, and brainpower that has been directed to analyzing and responding to more immediate threats would doubtless have been directed toward Asia and the long-term challenges of a rising China."[22]

More than a decade after 9/11, China is again beginning to garner the same sort of attention it did in the early Bush administration. Some of the shift has been driven by China's own behavior. Starting in 2009, Beijing took a hard line in a number of diplomatic disputes with the United States and neighboring Asian states, including Japan, Vietnam, South Korea, and India.

In March 2009, five Chinese vessels surrounded a U.S. Navy reconnaissance ship, the USNS *Impeccable*, about seventy-five miles from Hainan Island where the EP-3 had crash-landed in 2001. In what amounted to a maritime replay of 2001, the Chinese waved flags and crossed dangerously close to the *Impeccable*, forcing it to take emergency evasive action.[23] Fortunately, the incident did not escalate further. The following year, in another naval incident, a Chinese fishing boat rammed two Japanese patrol vessels in disputed waters. Video shot by the Japanese shows that the Chinese captain clearly intended to provoke an incident. He got his wish; when the Japanese detained him, Beijing demanded his release. Then, when Tokyo was slow to act, China took the unusual step of halting exports to Japan of rare earth minerals used in the manufacture of high-tech components.[24]

[21] Donald Rumsfeld, *Known and Unknown: A Memoir* (New York: Sentinel, 2011), p. 314.
[22] Friedberg, A Contest for Supremacy, p. 3.
[23] Ann Scott Tyson, "U.S. Protests Chinese Shadowing in International Waters," *Washington Post*, March 10, 2009, www.washingtonpost.com/wp-dyn/content/article/2009/03/09/AR2009030900956.html.
[24] Keither Bradsher and Hiroko Tabuchi, "China Is Said to Halt Trade in Rare-Earth Minerals with Japan," *New York Times*, September 24, 2010, http://www.nytimes.com/2010/09/25/business/global/25minerals.html. For a broader analysis of the rise of rare earth minerals as

Some analysts interpreted Beijing's handling of these events as but one facet of a more confident, even strident, Chinese approach to foreign affairs. This, in turn, raised questions about whether China's growing power will put it irreversibly at odds with the United States and its interests.[25]

Other China watchers and policy analysts have been less inclined to see China as an especially belligerent power.[26] Geography and history bequeathed China more than a few territorial disputes, but many of these have been settled peacefully. Most important, China has worried mainly about its own economic fortunes. Its Communist Party leadership appears desperate to keep a lid on possible sources of domestic discontent. Overall, these scholars conclude, China's parochial view of the world is more likely to render Beijing irresponsibly risk averse than dangerously aggressive.[27] This too could be problematic; a wealthy, powerful China that does too little to take on the burdens of leadership would be worse than a missed opportunity; it would be a terrible abdication of responsibility.

The truth is, China itself may not be sure of its own international course. And in a very general sense, at this stage of the game, it may not matter. Whatever China's goals and intentions, it has grown so large that its actions will affect the American interest one way or another. In President Barack Obama's words:

We can't predict with certainty what the future will bring, but we can be certain about the issues that will define our times. And we also know this: The relationship between the United States and China will shape the 21st century, which makes it as important as any bilateral relationship in the world.[28]

In November 2011, Secretary of State Hillary Clinton expanded upon the president's theme when she observed, "As the war in Iraq winds down and America begins to withdraw its forces from Afghanistan, the United States stands at a pivot point.... One of the most important tasks of American statecraft over the next decade will therefore be to lock in a substantially increased investment – diplomatic, economic, strategic, and otherwise – in the Asia-Pacific region."[29]

a strategic commodity, see Keith Bradsher, "Earth-Friendly Elements, Mined Destructively," *New York Times*, December 25, 2009, http://www.nytimes.com/2009/12/26/business/global/26rare.html?pagewanted=all.

[25] Kissinger describes this strident tone as one pole in a Chinese debate about its national destiny. See Kissinger, *On China*, pp. 503–7.

[26] Andrew J. Nathan and Andrew Scobell, "How China Sees America," *Foreign Affairs* (September/October 2012); Alastair Iain Johnston, "How New and Assertive Is China's New Assertiveness?" *International Security*, 37, no. 4 (Spring 2013), pp. 7–48, http://www.mitpressjournals.org/doi/pdf/10.1162/ISEC_a_00115.

[27] Thomas J. Christensen, "The Advantages of an Assertive China: Responding to Beijing's Abrasive Diplomacy," *Foreign Affairs* (March/April 2011).

[28] "Remarks by the President at the U.S.-China Strategic and Economic Dialogue," Office of the Press Secretary, White House, July 27, 2009.

[29] Hillary Clinton, "America's Pacific Century," *Foreign Policy* (November 2011).

In short, China's rise and the U.S. response will likely represent the primary international drama for the next several decades. Relations with China will not set the parameters for everything the United States does in South Asia; the endgame and aftermath of the war in Afghanistan and the persistent challenge of international terrorism will command Washington's attention for at least the next several years. But the tide is turning, and even as these issues retain their salience, in the coming decade America's leaders will have to see them within the context of a broader global agenda over which Beijing will hold increasing influence.

LESSONS FROM THE COLD WAR

Contemplating the future of Sino-American relations immediately conjures recollections of past great power rivalries. America's Cold War with the Soviet Union defined the global strategic context for four decades after the Second World War. To be sure, the current U.S.-China relationship has some obvious and important differences from that U.S.-Soviet conflict. Unlike the United States and Soviet Union, whose economies were walled off from one another and governed by fundamentally different principles, Americans and Chinese buy, sell, lend, and borrow from each other on a massive scale. That entanglement makes violent conflict less likely. It also rules out a Cold War–style containment strategy.[30]

Even so, Americans can draw some useful historical analogies from the Cold War experience. The global competition with Moscow influenced how Washington assessed the strategic importance of South Asia. The United States came and went from South Asia, driven by what it thought was needed to contain Soviet power, not by any inherent interest in either India or Pakistan.

Cold War history also shows that both India and Pakistan viewed American support as another dimension in their own bilateral conflict. The Americans thought they were fighting communists; India and Pakistan knew they were fighting each other. Any move by Washington to help one side was understood, rightly or not, as a tilt away from the other. A 1957 review of U.S. South Asia policy by the National Security Council explained that "Pakistan's membership in SEATO [Southeast Asia Treaty Organization] and U.S. military assistance to Pakistan are interpreted by many [in India] as U.S. intervention in these issues on behalf of Pakistan."[31] According to Field Marshal Ayub Khan, Pakistan's army chief (1951–8) and first military dictator (1958–69), "The crux of the

---

[30] Ashley Tellis explores these complicating factors of the U.S.-China relationship in his overview chapter to *Strategic Asia 2011–12.* See Ashley J. Tellis, Travis Tanner, and Jessica Keough, eds., *Strategic Asia 2011–12: Asia Responds to Its Rising Powers* (Washington: National Bureau of Asian Research, 2011), pp. 17–20.

[31] "Statement of Policy on U.S. Policy toward South Asia," NSC 5701, January 10, 1957 in Department of State, *Foreign Relations of the United States, 1955–1957,* http://history.state.gov/historicaldocuments.

problem from the very beginning was the Indian attitude of hostility towards us: we had to look for allies to secure our position."[32]

If not for Moscow, Washington might have had a very different sort of relationship with both India and Pakistan. If not for Indo-Pakistani enmity, American cold warriors might never have had to pick sides between New Delhi and Islamabad. In short, America's struggle with the Soviet Union embroiled it in an otherwise avoidable regional dispute. If this past history is any guide to the future, it suggests that U.S. competition with China and unresolved disputes between India and Pakistan may again lead American leaders to pick sides in South Asia.

Picking India

During the Cold War, America usually tilted in Pakistan's favor. By the time President Clinton made his landmark March 2000 trip to South Asia, however, the opposite was true. He spent a glorious five days in India and a tense five hours in Pakistan.

Standing before the Indian parliament, Clinton delivered a soaring speech received by Prime Minister Atal Bihari Vajpayee with the words, "Mr. President, your visit marks the beginning of a new voyage in the new century by two countries which have all the potential to become natural allies."[33] In his inimitable style, Clinton then went on to charm local Indian audiences at joyous receptions around the country. Rajasthani villagers showered the beaming president in a colorful blizzard of rose petals. Clinton was in his element. The president hit the perfect note with India at precisely the time it was eager to chart a new, far friendlier path with America. Indians still recall the visit fondly.

There would be no wading into adoring crowds in Pakistan. To the contrary, fearing a terrorist attack on the first visit by any American president in over thirty years, Clinton arrived in an unmarked Gulfstream jet that trailed a decoy. Behind closed doors, Clinton warned Pakistani President Pervez Musharraf to deal with the terrorists on his soil and to re-think Pakistan's nuclear posture. He spoke of the dire threat posed by the Taliban in Afghanistan and shared his hope that Pakistan should return to civilian rule quickly.

Clinton then emerged to address the Pakistani public in a live, uncensored television broadcast. He cautioned of the "danger that Pakistan may grow even more isolated, draining even more resources away from the needs of the people,

---

[32] Mohammad Ayub Khan, *Friends Not Masters* (New York: Oxford University Press, 1967), p. 154. See also "Letter from the Officer in Charge of Pakistan-Afghanistan Affairs (Poullada) to the Special Assistant at the Embassy in Pakistan for Mutual Security Affairs (Linebaugh)," *Foreign Relations of the United States, 1958–1960*, 15, p. 804.

[33] See Strobe Talbott's narrative of the Clinton visit to India in Strobe Talbott, *Engaging India: Diplomacy, Democracy, and the Bomb* (Washington: Brookings Institution Press, 2004), p. 200.

moving even closer to a conflict no one can win."[34] Then the president rushed off, skipping the standard photo session with Musharraf to speed back the fifteen miles from Islamabad to the Rawalpindi airport along a cleared, heavily guarded highway.

With the Cold War retreating into history's rearview mirror, the Clinton administration recognized that whatever nagging differences it might have with India over nuclear nonproliferation, trade, and a number of other global issues, the relationship with New Delhi was enormously appealing. In Pakistan, however, the United States could perceive "few compelling positive interests."[35]

Clinton's successor amplified the new "India tilt." Senior members of the George W. Bush administration saw great potential in India. They believed India could play a constructive role in the global balance with China. During the 2000 election campaign, Condoleezza Rice, then Bush's top foreign policy adviser, wrote revealingly that the United States "should pay closer attention to India's role in the regional balance. . . . India is an element in China's calculation, and it should be in America's too. India is not a great power yet, but it has the potential to emerge as one."[36]

For their part, India's leaders jumped at the chance to maintain and even to enhance the positive momentum in relations with the United States. It did not hurt that New Delhi's ruling political coalition no longer included the once-dominant Indian National Congress party and therefore had little compulsion to hew to its policies of Nehruvian non-alignment. Both Washington and New Delhi signaled strong interest in turning a new page in their relationship. By avoiding the sticking points of the past, such as nuclear nonproliferation and Kashmir, they could focus on new areas of cooperation.

One of these areas was ballistic missile defense. Unlike much of the rest of the world, New Delhi chose not to castigate the Bush administration for withdrawing the United States from the Anti-Ballistic Missile Treaty in 2002. Ashley Tellis, a driving force behind improved U.S.-India relations over the past decade, explains that India's surprisingly positive response "came to reflect both an example of, and a means toward, the steady improvement in U.S.-Indian ties."[37]

When Bush's hand-selected ambassador to India, Robert Blackwill, arrived in Mumbai in early September 2001, he remarked in his first speech to an

---

[34] For a full account of President Clinton's trip to Pakistan, see Dennis Kux, *Disenchanted Allies, the United States and Pakistan 1947–2000* (Washington: Woodrow Wilson Center Press, 2001), pp. 356–8.

[35] Kux, *Disenchanted Allies*, p. 366.

[36] Condoleezza Rice, "Campaign 2000: Promoting the National Interest," *Foreign Affairs* (January/February 2000).

[37] Ashley Tellis, "The Evolution of U.S.-Indian Ties: Missile Defense in an Emerging Strategic Relationship," *International Security*, 304 (Spring 2006), pp. 113–51. On similar themes, see also Ashley J. Tellis, "The Merits of Dehyphenation: Explaining U.S. Success in Engaging India and Pakistan," *Washington Quarterly*, 41, no. 4 (Autumn 2008), pp. 21–42; Ashley J. Tellis, "India as a New Global Power: An Action Agenda for the United States," Carnegie Endowment for International Peace (July 2005).

assembly of Indian business executives that "President Bush has a big idea about India-U.S. relations. My president's big idea is that by working together more intensely than ever before, the United States and India, two vibrant democracies, can transform fundamentally the very essence of our bilateral relationship and thereby make the world freer, more peaceful and more prosperous."[38]

From New Delhi, the bullish Blackwill set to work knocking down barriers to more extensive cooperation between India and the United States. He conspired with well-placed partners back in Washington, DC, like Condoleezza Rice, then the national security advisor, and Richard Haass, the director of policy planning at the State Department. Together, they helped push policies through a bureaucracy that was unused to the idea of a transformed relationship with India, and as usual, resistant to change. The bureaucratic trench warfare left some bruised egos but demolished the obstacles that had stymied cooperation in missile defense, space, and high technology for decades. Fiercely committed to their cause, and backed by the president, these advocates paved the way for even bigger breakthroughs with India during Bush's second term.

By contrast, Pakistan was an afterthought. Well before Bush entered the White House, congressional frustration over Pakistan's military coup and nuclear program had ended U.S. assistance. The limited official exchanges that did take place were often chilly. Top Bush administration officials, enthusiastic advocates for India, cared little for Pakistan. Sharp-tongued Pakistani journalist Ahmed Rashid concludes that Pakistan and Afghanistan were "clearly not a priority on Powell's or Rice's to-do list."[39] Pakistan was neither a strong state nor a traditional ally. It had no place in the strategic vision that the new team brought to the job.

Then, on that clear blue September 11 morning, Washington's gaze was redirected by the horror of al-Qaeda's attacks. Pakistan shot to the top of the American agenda. Almost overnight, Pakistan opened its ports and airspace to U.S. forces flowing into Afghanistan. Pakistan's Inter-Services Intelligence directorate (ISI) expanded its counterterror cooperation with the CIA and FBI. Washington's regional – and some would say even its global – priorities turned upside down. Pakistan went from peripheral, near-rogue state to indispensable "front line ally" in President Bush's new "Global War on Terror." Talk of great powers and traditional allies turned to terrorism, the Muslim world, and homeland security.

Remarkably, even in the post-9/11 haze, advocates of the U.S. partnership with India kept their focus. Eager to escape the historical dilemma of picking sides between Pakistan and India, but fully aware that in the fight against al-Qaeda Pakistan was more immediately relevant than India, they worked to preserve the gains with New Delhi by "de-hyphenating" the Indo-Pakistani relationship. They argued that Washington should avoid being sucked into

[38] Celia W. Dugger, "U.S. Envoy Extols India, Accepting Its Atom Status," *New York Times*, September 7, 2001, p. A1.
[39] Rashid, *Descent into Chaos*, pp. 56–9.

the intractable Indo-Pakistani conflict. Instead, the goal should be to improve relations with India and Pakistan simultaneously and separately.[40]

Taken to extremes, de-hyphenation was a thoroughly unrealistic, artificial construct. Neither India nor Pakistan could ever lose sight of how U.S. relations with the other might tilt their own balance of power. That said, de-hyphenation was enormously successful in the one way that mattered most. It allowed the Bush administration to continue building a partnership with India even as it became increasingly entangled with Pakistan. On October 1, 2008, Bush's India team won its biggest victory of all: the U.S. Senate voted 86–13 in favor of a historic accord to open trade with India in civilian nuclear technologies.[41] The deal tossed aside decades of U.S. nonproliferation rules, all with the goal of convincing India that the United States could be a trusted friend and strategic partner. U.S.-India relations had scaled a new peak.

The early days of the Obama presidency raised some concerns in India. Indian cynics feared the new administration would lean toward China. Others worried that with no new diplomatic breakthrough on the horizon, relations with India would naturally lose steam. On Thanksgiving week, 2009, President Obama did his best to show that he would try to keep up the momentum. In enormous tents on the White House lawn, he and the first lady hosted a star-studded state dinner for the visiting Indian prime minister, the first such dinner of his presidency. India graciously returned the favor by welcoming Obama to New Delhi, where his visit got rave reviews, not least because the president arrived with a surprise gift: America's support for India's bid to become a permanent member of the United Nations Security Council.

For Obama, as for Bush, India had an infectious appeal. The main distinction between the two is that Obama was less prone to draw direct and public connections between his India policy and potential concerns about China's rising power. But there can be no doubting that a strong, bipartisan pro-India consensus reigns in Washington today.

A Future that Complicates U.S.-Pakistan Ties

The same cannot be said about Pakistan. The prevailing trends of the recent past – improved U.S. ties with India and China's assertive posture – raise serious doubts about the trajectory of U.S.-Pakistan relations.

Pakistan already feels jilted by U.S. support to India. De-hyphenation has its limits. Islamabad perceived the U.S.-India civil nuclear deal as a costly defeat. In vain, Pakistan attempted to win its own nuclear concessions from the United States to lessen the blow. When that failed, Islamabad prevailed upon Beijing to provide some of its old, second-rate nuclear power plants.

---

[40] Tellis, "The Merits of Dehyphenation," p. 23.
[41] Glenn Kessler, "Senate Backs Far-Reaching Nuclear Trade Deal with India," *Washington Post*, October 2, 2008, http://www.washingtonpost.com/wp-dyn/content/article/2008/10/01/AR2008100100533.html.

Ignoring widespread international objections, China obliged.[42] It is not hard to imagine similar patterns in the future: Washington assisting India, Beijing helping Pakistan in response.

Such a dynamic seems all the more likely because Pakistan considers China to be its closest international ally. This is nothing new. There can be no discounting the fact that Beijing has provided Pakistan with strategically critical military and nuclear technologies.[43] At times, China has also served as a significant diplomatic lifeline and buffer against outside pressure. Most egregiously, Beijing has repeatedly blocked the United Nations (UN) from placing a number of Pakistanis on official global terrorist lists, including members of Lashkar-e-Taiba (LeT).[44] China's friendship with Pakistan makes Indian aggression far less likely. For this reason alone, many Pakistanis tend to welcome a strong, assertive China – especially one that takes a tougher line against India.

Just two weeks after the killing of Osama bin Laden, when U.S.-Pakistan relations were especially tenuous, Pakistani Prime Minister Yousuf Raza Gilani embarked on a state visit to Beijing. "We are proud to have China as our best and most trusted friend," he told his hosts, "and China will always find Pakistan standing beside at all times."[45] Not a trip to Beijing goes by without Pakistanis reciting their time-worn mantra that Pakistan enjoys an "all-weather friendship" with China that is "higher than the mountains, deeper than the oceans, sweeter than honey, and stronger than steel."

By coincidence, I was in Islamabad for a research trip the nerve-jangling week after the May 2011 U.S. raid on Osama bin Laden's compound. I got my own dose of Pakistani views about China. At a mildly contentious roundtable discussion with Pakistani pundits, journalists, academics, and retired officials, one of the participants suggested that China would undoubtedly fill America's shoes if the United States ever abandoned Pakistan. Having been to Beijing a month earlier where there seemed to be a lot less enthusiasm about such a scenario among Chinese officials and scholars, I recommended that Pakistanis should pay close attention to how China's other protégé, the famine-plagued hermit kingdom of North Korea, had fared under Beijing's wing. The point was taken, but grudgingly.

Pakistanis and Chinese may claim deep, abiding friendship, but in their rhetorical excesses, both tend to mistake China's hardheaded realism for

---

[42] Glenn Kessler, "Washington Objects to China-Pakistan Nuclear Deal," *Washington Post*, June 14, 2010, http://www.washingtonpost.com/wp-dyn/content/article/2010/06/14/AR2010006 61404680.html.

[43] Rashid, *Descent into Chaos*, p. 287.

[44] In a May 16, 2012, author's interview with Hamid Gul in Islamabd, the former ISI director claimed that only Chinese assistance kept his own name off the United Nations' list of international terrorists. See also Mukund Padmanabhan, "China's 'Hold' Stopped Designation of LeT, Jaish Leaders," *The Hindu*, June 7, 2011, http://www.thehindu.com/opinion/op-ed/article2082626.ece.

[45] Chris Buckley, "Pakistan Plays China Card with Prime Minister's Visit," *Reuters*, May 17, 2011, http://www.reuters.com/article/2011/05/17/us-china-pakistan-idUSTRE74G0KT20110517.

generous altruism. In Pakistan's major wars with India as well as in more recent Indo-Pakistani crises, Beijing's assistance has been marginal. China has been more likely to counsel Pakistani restraint than to back its leaders to the hilt. China is undoubtedly useful to Pakistan, and China's rising power makes it even more attractive to its weaker neighbor, but if Pakistan were forced to rely upon Beijing as its sole patron, the professions of friendship – on both sides – would ring increasingly hollow.

Even so, for U.S. leaders, the rising Chinese dragon makes friendship with India more appealing and complicates relations with Islamabad. Why not simply accept this trend? Why not let China tend its troubled Pakistani ally while America cultivates the far more fertile Indian soil?

PAKISTAN AS SPOILER

The main problem with a firm American tilt away from Pakistan and toward India is that it encourages Pakistan to play the spoiler. To be sure, Pakistanis will make their own decisions about how to interact in the region, many of which will have little to do with what Washington says or does. Islamabad could decide, for instance, to pursue accommodation with New Delhi, or the two may fall back into hostility. Either course of action could be driven by unexpected events or by internal political and strategic considerations that the United States cannot control.

All things equal, however, if Islamabad sees no particular upside potential to cooperation with the United States, it will be more likely to devote itself to upsetting the American apple cart, starting in India. That dynamic would be all the more likely if Islamabad perceives the United States as an outright adversary, one that is undermining Pakistan's security and supporting the rise of a hostile neighbor. Under such circumstances, Pakistan would, like Iran and North Korea, seek opportunities to thwart U.S. interests.

America's fascination with India is founded on the expectation that the world's largest democracy is on its way to becoming a major global power. If India were still the impoverished backwater of the 1960s, '70s, or '80s, no one in Washington would give it the time of day. Fortunately, India overcame some important domestic obstacles to economic success in the early 1990s. It averaged a real annual growth rate of 6.6 percent from 1990 to 2010.[46] Even when Indian growth rates slipped in 2012 and early 2013, there were signs that the challenge would be met with more market reforms – like opening the country to retail giants like Wal-Mart – rather than backsliding.[47]

---

[46] "India's Annual Average GDP Growth at 6.6% in 1990–2010," *Press Trust of India*, August 18, 2011, http://www.thehindubusinessline.com/industry-and-economy/economy/article2369380 .ece.

[47] Gardiner Harris, "India Backs Foreign Investment in Retailing," *New York Times*, September 14, 2012, http://www.nytimes.com/2012/09/15/business/global/india-backs-foreign-investment-in-retail-sector.html?ref=asia.

Unfortunately, India has not yet found a way to overcome the obstacles posed by its region. On every border, it faces weak or difficult neighbors. Among them, Pakistan has already shown that it can make India bleed in ways that, if expanded and intensified, would threaten U.S. hopes for a strong, vibrant partner in New Delhi. India's long, porous borders, weak defenses, and open society will expose it to Pakistan-based terrorism for the foreseeable future. A belligerent, nuclear-armed Pakistan could keep India in or at the edge of crisis, distracting its leaders and depleting its resources from the vital business of economic development.

India's vulnerability to Pakistani disruption was painfully evident in 2001–2. After Pakistani terrorists attacked in New Delhi and Kashmir, India mobilized half a million troops along the border. But India's saber rattling spooked the international diplomats and business community as much or more than it did Pakistan. Foreign corporations and their investments fled for the exits. If Pakistan were to make these sorts of events routine, over time international investors and corporations might choose to steer clear and invest in less dangerous parts of the world. The fact that India and Pakistan are nuclear-armed only raises the stakes.

The crisis was costly in other ways as well. India's 2001–2 military mobilization alone came with a price tag of more than $1.4 billion, over 10 percent of the national defense budget.[48] Tragically, even without engaging the Pakistani army, nearly 800 Indian troops died and 900 Indian civilians lost their lives, most in land mine blasts.[49] Other Pakistan-based terror attacks have also imposed huge costs. By one estimate, the November 2008 raid by ten LeT fedayeen on Mumbai, India's financial capital, may have inflicted as much as $100 billion in business losses.[50]

Fortunately, the businesses of Mumbai bounced back quickly. India can absorb the cost of major terrorist attacks, as long as they remain sporadic. If, however, terrorism is sustained at a high level, the long-term economic costs

---

[48] "Prakaram Cost Put at Rs 6,500 Crore," *Business Standard*, January 23, 2003, http://www .business-standard.com/india/news/prakaram-cost-put-at-rs-6500-crore/176617/. For comparison, the FY2011 U.S. military budget for operations in Afghanistan was $113.3 billion, which represented 16.53 percent of the total FY2011 U.S. defense budget. See Amy Belasco, "The Cost of Iraq, Afghanistan, and Other Global War on Terror Operations since 9/11," Congressional Research Service, March 29, 2011, http://www.fas.org/sgp/crs/natsec/RL33110.pdf. For the FY2011 U.S. defense budget, see "United States Department of Defense: Fiscal Year 2012 Budget Request," Office of the Undersecretary of Defense (Comptroller), February 2011, http://comptroller.defense.gov/defbudget/fy2012/FY2012_Budget_Request_Overview_Book .pdf.

[49] "Parakram Killed More than Kargil," *Times of India*, August 2, 2003, http://articles .timesofindia.indiatimes.com/2003-08-02/india/27173886_1_indo-pak-border-mines-cross-border-terrorism; Praful Bidwai, "A Failure India Cannot Afford," *Frontline*, May 24 – June 6, 2003, http://www.hindu.com/fline/fl2011/stories/20030606003310300.htm.

[50] "Terrorist Attacks Will Further Weaken a Slowing Indian Economy," India Knowledge@Wharton, December 11, 2008, http://knowledge.wharton.upenn.edu/india/article.cfm?articleid=4339), p. 4.

would be significant, if not necessarily easy to estimate or measure. Israel's historical experience is a good case in point. By one estimate, terrorism in Israel from 2001 to 2003 resulted in a 10 percent drop in GDP per person.[51] In another case, separatist terrorism in the Basque country of Spain led to a 10 percent decline in GDP per person.[52] Net foreign direct investment also tends to drop in countries afflicted by terrorism. Between 1975 and 1991, terrorism reduced net foreign direct investment in Spain by 13.5 percent annually and in Greece by 11.9 percent annually.[53]

Pakistan's ability to play a spoiler extends beyond provoking violent crises. The decades-long Indo-Pakistani conflict blocks normal trade and commerce and hurts economic growth in both countries. Pakistani economist Shahid Javed Burki has determined that India will lose an average of 2 percent per year of GDP growth between 2007 and 2025 unless regional trade barriers are eliminated.[54] That amounts to a sizable $1.5 trillion loss (over 25 percent) in India's GDP by 2025.

Pakistan also stands in the way of India's overland access to energy-rich Central Asia and the Middle East. India simply cannot meet its projected energy demands by domestic reserves alone.[55] Indian dreams of gas pipelines from Turkmenistan and Iran may never come to fruition, but they stand no chance at all if Indo-Pakistani tensions rise.

For a nation like India, in which over 400 million people live on less than $1.25 per day and where a decade of 10 percent growth is needed to liberate roughly 40 percent of the population from poverty, such lost opportunities take on added meaning.[56] India's needs are as vast as its growing population. Economic losses from terrorism and regional conflict could determine whether

---

[51] Zvi Eckstein and Daniel Tsiddon, "Macroeconomic Consequences of Terror: Theory and the Case of Israel," *Journal of Monetary Economics*, 51, no. 5 (June 2004), pp. 971–1002.

[52] Alberto Abadie and Javier Gardeazabal, "The Economic Costs of Conflict: A Case Study of the Basque Country," *American Economic Review*, 93, no. 1 (March 2003), pp. 113–132.

[53] Walter Enders and Todd Sandler, "Terrorism and Foreign Direct Investment in Spain and Greece," *KYKLOS*, 49, no. 3 (1996), pp. 331–52.

[54] Shahid Javed Burki, South Asia in the New World Order: The Role of Regional Cooperation (New York: Routledge, 2011), p. 180.

[55] The Indian government estimates that it will need to import between 29 and 59 percent of its energy by 2031–2032. See "Integrated Energy Policy, Report of the Expert Committee," Government of India, Planning Commission, New Delhi, p. 45.

[56] According to the World Bank, in 2005 the number of poor people living on less than $1.25 per day in India was 456 million. That makes for a national poverty rate of 42 percent in 2005. Martin Ravallion and Shaohua Chen, "The Developing World Is Poorer, but No Less Successful in the Fight against Poverty," Development Research Group, World Bank Group (August 2008), http://siteresources.worldbank.org/JAPANINJAPANESEEXT/Resources/515497120149009 7949/080827_The_Developing_World_is_Poorer_than_we_Thought.pdf; "India Needs Larger Number of Creative Leaders: Former President Kalam," *IANS*, July 5, 2011, http://economic times.indiatimes.com/news/politics/nation/india-needs-large-number-of-creative-leaders-former-president-kalam/articleshow/9112459.cms.

India remains preoccupied with its own internal troubles or turns into a country that is willing and able to take on global challenges.

Could Pakistan really spoil the Indian dream? Some Indian strategists dismiss the threat. They ask, "What about South Korea?" It is true that South Korea demonstrates that extraordinary economic progress is possible even next door to a hostile, nuclear-armed dictatorship. Israel has also succeeded in spite of its hostile neighborhood. This argument, however, overlooks the tremendous costs of defending South Korea and Israel over decades. In each instance, a huge burden was shouldered by America. The question is whether India, alone or in partnership with the United States, would be able to manage a similar feat, and at what price.

Pakistan also poses a special sort of threat to India because of its historical and cultural connections. There is an often unspoken fear in India that the extreme and violent ideas that have gained so much traction in Pakistan could also win over a greater portion of India's Muslim community. Numbering nearly 180 million, India's Muslims have so far proven remarkably averse to radicalization, but if that ever changes the consequences would be dire.[57] India's Muslim community is, by-and-large, a disadvantaged minority that has suffered through bouts of communal violence and holds legitimate grievances.[58] India has already experienced sporadic instances of homegrown Islamist terrorism, some of which bore the hallmarks of Pakistani inspiration or material support.[59] Pakistan the spoiler would almost certainly intensify its efforts to exploit this point of Indian vulnerability.

Pakistan could play the spoiler in other ways as well. The analogy with Northeast Asia is instructive. The Korean peninsula is especially dangerous because it has become a possible flashpoint for conflict between the United States and China. Pakistan could turn into something similar. Imagine, for instance, if a Pakistan-based terrorist group managed to pull off a catastrophic attack in the United States. China, as Pakistan's primary backer, would find itself in the middle of the ensuing conflict. Pakistan's erratic behavior, not to mention its inadequate control over terrorists on its soil, could make it especially tough for Beijing to restrain. Even if the Pakistani pot does not boil over, China's military and nuclear assistance to Pakistan could still become a greater

---

[57] Figure on India's Muslim population from "The Future of the Global Muslim Population," Pew Forum on Religion and Public Life, January, 2011, http://features.pewforum.org/muslim-population-graphic/#/India.

[58] See "Social, Economic and Educational Status of the Muslim Community of India," Prime Minister's High Level Committee Cabinet Secretariat, Government of India (November 2006).

[59] The Students Islamic Movement of India, or SIMI, is the prime example of India's homegrown Islamist terrorism. By most accounts, it receives some Pakistani assistance. See Animesh Roul, "Students Islamic Movement of India: A Profile," *Terrorism Monitor*, Jamestown Foundation, 4, no. 7 (April 6, 2006), http://www.jamestown.org/single/?no_cache=1&tx_ttnews%5Btt_news%5D=728.

irritant in Beijing's relationship with Washington, just as it was throughout much of the 1990s.[60]

A belligerent, anti-American Pakistan could also align with other dangerous regimes like Iran and North Korea. The potential is real because in a way it has already happened. Dr. A.Q. Khan's notorious nuclear proliferation ring shared nuclear know-how with both of these pariah countries (along with Libya) in the 1990s. More recently, the Iranian regime has tried to drive a wedge between Pakistan and America. Shortly after bin Laden was killed, Iranian president Mahmoud Ahmadinejad declared, "We have precise information that America wants to sabotage Pakistani nuclear facilities in order to control Pakistan and weaken the people and government of Pakistan."[61]

So far, Iran's siren song has had little appeal among Pakistanis. Islamabad prefers not to alienate another of its well-heeled protectors, Saudi Arabia, which is engaged in a strategic and sectarian conflict with Iran. There too, however, Pakistan has the potential to destabilize the wider region. If Iran develops a nuclear bomb, the Saudis will almost certainly seek to match it, and the most likely source for Riyadh's program would be Pakistan. One need not go so far as some analysts, who claim that the Pakistani nuclear arsenal is already a virtual "Sunni" bomb, to recognize that Saudi money and influence could buy Pakistani security guarantees and even, in short order, nuclear-tipped missiles deployed on Saudi soil.[62] The sharing of nuclear technology need not stop in Riyadh, since other oil-rich Arab states would want to get into the act. If a nuclear arms race breaks out in the Middle East, an untethered and irresponsible Pakistan would be most everyone's favorite dealer.

In short, a breakdown in U.S.-Pakistan relations would hurt U.S. efforts to build up a strong India, maintain a nonviolent relationship with China, and avoid greater instability throughout the Middle East. Washington's strategic compulsions, especially the appeal of a closer relationship with India, will make it hard to live with Islamabad. But a jilted Pakistan's disruptive potential will also make it hard to live without.

BEIJING'S LONG GAME

As U.S.-Pakistan relations hit a rocky stretch in 2011, Chinese officials in Beijing and at the embassy in Washington, DC, made it very clear to anyone who would listen that China had no interest in an outright rupture between Washington and Islamabad. Part of the Chinese concern was over the prospect

[60] Shirley A. Kan, "China and Proliferation of Weapons of Mass Destruction and Missiles: Policy Issues," pp. 3–9, Congressional Research Service, April 25, 2012, http://www.fas.org/sgp/crs/nuke/RL31555.pdf.

[61] "U.S. Has Designs on Pakistan's Nukes: Iran," Express Tribune, June 8, 2011, http://tribune.com.pk/story/184086/us-plans-to-sabotage-pakistan-nuke-facilities-ahmadinejad/.

[62] Bruce Riedel, "Saudi Arabia: Nervously Watching Pakistan," Brookings Institution, January 28, 2008, http://www.brookings.edu/opinions/2008/0128_saudi_arabia_riedel.aspx.

that Beijing might find itself dragged into a conflict between Pakistan the United States. Throughout much of the late Cold War and the post-9/11 era, Beijing and Washington either stood shoulder-to-shoulder with Pakistan or worked together to promote Indo-Pakistani restraint. That state of affairs was very comfortable for China. Beijing knows it would have some tough decisions to make in the event of an unhappy divorce between Washington and Islamabad.

But what does China want from Pakistan and South Asia over the long run, particularly as its own power and influence grow? To answer this question, some proper perspective is required. From Beijing's vantage point, South Asia seems very distant. China's leaders do not wake up every morning thinking about South Asia. They worry first and foremost about internal economic and political stability, including everything from political opposition and labor unrest to restive territories like Xinjiang and Tibet. Those issues command the lion's share of their time and energy.

To the extent that China devotes attention outside its borders, its priorities begin with its eastern seaboard.[63] There China faces a range of security issues that tend to place it more or less at odds with the United States, such as Taiwan, Japan, Korea, and nearby maritime disputes. After that, Beijing contemplates global issues, such as trade and climate change, as well as defense and foreign policy matters farther afield, starting along its western and northern land borders but increasingly extending to South and Central Asia, the Middle East and even – when it comes to resource extraction and new markets – to Africa and Latin America.

Because China has so many other priorities, its relationship with Pakistan is marked by a stark asymmetry. Pakistani leaders, military and civilian, pay frequent visits to Beijing, often toting long wish lists for financial and military assistance. Top Chinese leaders rarely make it to Islamabad. From 2007 to 2013, the Chinese premier visited Pakistan only twice.[64] Over the same period, Pakistan's president and prime minister together visited China over a dozen times.[65]

As discussed, it is clear why Pakistan needs China. It is less obvious what China gets or expects to get from Pakistan. The imbalance was less pronounced in the past. Pakistan was useful to China in its early post-revolutionary days as

---

[63] Nathan and Scobell identify a similar list of Chinese priorities in "How China Sees America," pp. 33–4.

[64] On occasion China has sent some important delegations to Pakistan. In October 2012, for instance, Li Changchun, a member of the Politburo Standing Committee of the Communist Party of China led a two-day trip to Islamabad. See Qamar Zaman, "Sino-Pak Relations: Chinese Call for Boosting Partnership," *Express Tribune*, October 18, 2012, http://tribune.com.pk/story/453178/sino-pak-relations-chinese-call-for-boosting-partnership/.

[65] "High Level Visits," website of the Embassy of the Islamic Republic of Pakistan, Beijing, China, http://www.pakbj.com/pakistan_china.php?men=2; "Pakistani PM Gilani Meets Chinese State Councilor Dai Bingguo," *Xinhua*, December 24, 2011, http://news.xinhuanet.com/english/china/2011–12/24/c_131324947.htm.

an impoverished communist outcast. In the early 1960s, Pakistan International
Airlines flew to Beijing, providing a unique air link between China and the
non-communist world. If not for Pakistan's surreptitious assistance, Kissinger's
secret mission to China in July 1971 might not have been possible.[66] Also on
the diplomatic front, Pakistan has supported China in multilateral settings like
the UN, rustling up votes from other Muslim-majority states in defense of
Beijing's position on sensitive matters like Tibet and Taiwan.

For decades, China and Pakistan have also been united in their desire to cut
India down to size. Hawkish Indians are not entirely wrong to see Pakistan
as the western half of an unfriendly Chinese embrace. Military and nuclear
cooperation between Islamabad and Beijing took off in the years following
the Sino-Indian war of 1962. Over that period, China has been Pakistan's
largest arms supplier.[67] Military drills and war-gaming sessions between the
People's Liberation Army and the Pakistan Army are commonplace, and the
two have entered into co-development and production agreements for weapon
systems like the JF-17 fighter aircraft and Pakistan's main battle tank, the
Al-Khalid. These deals are less strategically valuable for China's military than
for its defense contractors, who are reaping the benefits of Pakistan's insecurity
through a range of supply contracts with the Pakistani army.

China benefits from Pakistan in other ways too. China depends on the
Pakistani military and ISI for information and analysis of events inside Pakistan
and Afghanistan. Lessons learned from Pakistan's extensive counterinsurgency
operations along its border with Afghanistan are being related to officers of
the PLA, which lacks recent firsthand experience in these areas.[68]

The Sino-Pakistani relationship also has its points of tension. Beijing fears
that Pakistan's internal problems could threaten China. Pakistan is the training
base and haven for militant anti-Chinese outfits like the East Turkestan Independence Movement (ETIM), a Uighur separatist organization operating out
of China's Xinjiang Autonomous Region. At least from China's point of view,
Islamabad has not always shown adequate commitment to killing or capturing
these groups. After the July 2011 ETIM attacks in the city of Kashgar, Xinjiang,
a local Chinese provincial official publicly suggested that the perpetrators had
trained in Pakistan.[69] This unusual Chinese outburst sounded remarkably like
Washington's routine refrain that Pakistan must "do more" against terrorists
based on its soil.

For the present, China also has countervailing interests in South Asia that
make Beijing less eager to put all its eggs in Pakistan's basket. As China's interest
in economic growth and trade has grown, it has placed a greater priority on

---

[66] Kux, *Disenchanted Allies*, pp. 190–2.
[67] SIPRI Arms Transfer Database, Importer/Exporter Trend-Indicator Value table, http://armst-
rade.sipri.org/armstrade/page/values.php.
[68] Based on author conversations, Beijing, April 2011.
[69] Michael Wines, "China Blames Foreign-Trained Separatists for Attacks in Xinjiang," *New York
Times*, August 1, 2011, http://www.nytimes.com/2011/08/02/world/asia/02china.html?_r=2
&pagewanted=all.

stability throughout South and Central Asia. Beijing has counseled restraint to Pakistan with respect to contentious issues like Kashmir. Well-placed Pakistani sources suggest that China's quiet support for nascent peace talks between New Delhi and Islamabad from 2003 to 2007 played an important part in bringing Musharraf's regime to the negotiating table, as part of a process that appears to have made more progress than any before it.[70]

Given that in 2012 China did over five times more trade with India than with Pakistan, and that Beijing and New Delhi see eye-to-eye on a number of global issues like trade and climate change, this prioritization of interests makes sense.[71] China may never choose a relationship with India over one with Pakistan, but it would prefer never to make such a choice at all. China would naturally prefer to have the best of both worlds.

In the future, however, as China extends its trade and military activity throughout the region, it is possible that Pakistani territory will be useful to China in new ways. Pakistan offers direct, albeit treacherous, land access from western China to Central Asia. The Chinese envisioned the value of this route in the 1960s, when Chinese and Pakistani workers started a nearly two-decade-long project of building the 1,300 kilometer Karakoram Highway, which (weather permitting) linked Islamabad with Kashgar.[72]

At any given time, roughly 10,000 Chinese engineers are at work inside Pakistan on a range of other projects, from infrastructure to mining. The most celebrated of these projects is the new port at Gwadar in southwest Pakistan, which was built almost entirely with Chinese investment.[73] Lacking connecting roads or rail lines, Gwadar has yet to take off in any serious way, but it does at least have the potential to connect China's western provinces to the Arabian Sea. As Robert Kaplan imagines the future in his influential book *Monsoon*, Gwadar could become "the pulsing hub of a new silk route, both land and maritime: a mega-project and gateway to landlocked, hydrocarbon-rich Central Asia – an exotic twenty-first-century place-name."[74] And Gwadar is not the

[70] Steve Coll, "The Back Channel," *The New Yorker*, March 2, 2009, http://www.newyorker.com/reporting/2009/03/02/090302fa_fact_coll.

[71] For Sino-Indian trade, see Ananth Krishnan, "India's Trade with China Falls 12 %," *The Hindu*, January 10, 2013, http://www.thehindu.com/business/Economy/indias-trade-with-china-falls-12/article4295117.ece; on Sino-Pakistani trade, see Shoaib-ur-Rehman Siddiqui, "Pak-China Bilateral Trade Crosses $12 Billion Mark for First Time," *Business Recorder*, January 28, 2013, http://www.brecorder.com/top-news/108-pakistan-top-news/103614-pak-china-bilateral-trade-crosses-12-billion-mark-for-first-time-.html.

[72] In January 2010, the highway was submerged by a lake created when a landslide blocked the nearby Hunza River. At present, the road is passable only by ferry. See "The Highest Highway, Day Three," *Economist*, October 18, 2010, http://www.economist.com/blogs/banyan/2010/10/karakoram_diary_1.

[73] Sanjeev Miglani, "In Pakistan's Gwadar Port, Chinese Whispers Grow," *Reuters*, May 26, 2011, http://blogs.reuters.com/afghanistan/2011/05/26/in-pakistans-gwadar-port-chinese-whispers-grow.

[74] Robert Kaplan, *Monsoon: The Indian Ocean and the Future of American Power* (New York: Random House, 2010), p. 71.

only grand scheme for transportation corridors that is being dreamed up by the Chinese and Pakistanis.[75] Over time, Pakistani ports and highways could turn into essential lines of communication for a new Chinese land empire.

In short, Beijing wants to maintain its "all-weather" friendship with Pakistan and it probably has designs on a long-term future in which Pakistan offers a land route to the Arabian Sea, a stepping-stone to Iran and Central Asia, and access to India's western flank. But for the time being, Beijing clearly wishes to accomplish these ends without sacrificing regional stability, finding itself at odds with Washington on yet another issue, or forfeiting a peaceful, lucrative trading relationship with India. An exclusive, narrow alliance with an isolated Pakistan, particularly one at odds with the United States, would not be China's preferred way to achieve either its short- or long-term goals.

INDIA'S INDEPENDENT STREAK

As in China, India's people and top political leaders are, at least for the moment, preoccupied with domestic development and stability. Barring a crisis, almost everything else comes second.

India has changed a great deal in recent years, but a visit is still an assault on the senses. Outside the gated preserves of tranquility in New Delhi's most posh hotels, people, animals, and vehicles all compete for space in a constant buzz of activity. There is life everywhere you look. Compared with the gleaming, modernity of China's Pudong district, most of India's landscape still feels primitive.

To read Tom Friedman's adoring descriptions of India in the *New York Times*, you might expect that India's high-tech city of Bangalore really has achieved a level of development to rival Boston, or that Chennai can be compared to Chengdu and Chicago. Friedman is right that some of India's high-tech firms have built fancy campuses for their employees, not all that much different from ones you might see in Silicon Valley. But a whiff of the acrid winter air from New Delhi's innumerable dung fires, the frustration of unremitting traffic jams in Bangalore's overcrowded thoroughfares, or the experience of several power outages during a single morning meeting on one of the city's technology campuses suggests even India's globally competitive cities have a long way to go to get their infrastructure up to par. That is to say nothing at all about India's villages, home to some 70 percent of the country's people.[76]

India is, in its own way, moving to address all of these issues. The scale of the challenge is immense. There are 1.2 billion Indians of diverse religions

---

[75] Vojay Sakhuja, "The Karakoram Corridor: China's Transportation Network in Pakistan," *BBC*, October 8, 2010, http://www.bbc.co.uk/news/business-13945072.

[76] Ministry of Home Affairs, "Provisional Population Totals: Rural-Urban Distribution," Census of India 2011, http://www.censusindia.gov.in/2011-prov-results/paper2/data_files/india/paper2_at_a_glance.pdf.

and socioeconomic strata living in twenty-eight states. Indians speak hundreds of languages.[77] Despite India's rapid economic growth and the considerable wealth amassed by many of its people, 300 million Indians still live on less than a dollar a day.

Aside from poverty, millions of Indians also grapple with internal security challenges that have practically nothing to do with foreign affairs. Naxalites, Maoist-inspired insurgents, are active in large swathes of India's east and south.[78] Prime Minister Manmohan Singh has on multiple occasions termed it the single greatest internal threat to India's security.[79]

That said, India's long history of tension and war with Pakistan is still a political hot button for many of its people and leaders. India's enormous Muslim community makes its relationship with a self-professed Islamic Republic like Pakistan a politically sensitive one. In the past, Indians were primarily worried about Pakistan's military strength. Today, there is a far greater – and justifiable – fear of Pakistan's weakness and instability, coupled with anger over Pakistan's use of terrorists. The Indian desire to punish Pakistan for events like the Mumbai attacks of November 2008 remains strong. But that desire has been tempered by the recognition that even though India may be the greater military power, any victory over Pakistan would be Pyrrhic.

India has no serious military answer to the threat posed by Pakistan-based terrorist groups. When crises have hit over the past decade, New Delhi has expected Washington to put pressure on Islamabad. For this reason, most Indian leaders would prefer to maintain good ties with a sympathetic American partner that also enjoys significant influence in Pakistan.

If U.S.-Pakistan relations break, India would lose a form of indirect leverage. The brilliant Indian strategist C. Raja Mohan, whose soft-spoken commentary carries weight with the most senior foreign policymakers in New Delhi and Washington, takes the argument one step further. He includes China's influence as a positive force in Pakistan. He writes, "There is no reason for India to wish that Washington and Beijing abandon their cooperative relationships with Islamabad. In fact, India would want America and China to exercise their influence in changing the Pakistan army's calculus in supporting international terror networks."[80]

After 2002, most Indian leaders concluded that India has much to fear from Pakistan but few solutions, military or otherwise. This led New Delhi to be receptive to diplomatic engagement with Islamabad and explains why the

77 "General Note," Census Data 2001, Government of India, Ministry of Home Affairs, http://censusindia.gov.in/Census_Data_2001/Census_Data_Online/Language/gen_note.htm.
78 "India's Naxalites: A Spectre Haunting India," *Economist*, August 17, 2006, http://www.economist.com/node/7799247.
79 Rahi Gaikwad, "Manmohan: Naxalism the Greatest Internal Threat," *Hindu*, October 11, 2009.
80 C. Raja Mohan, "The Essential Triangle," Centre for Policy Research, http://www.cprindia.org/blog/security/3373-essential-triangle.

government of Prime Minister Manmohan Singh repeatedly went back to the negotiating table, even after the 2008 terrorist attack in Mumbai and in spite of Islamabad's failure to act against the attack's Pakistan-based plotters.

Progress on opening Indo-Pakistani trade and business travel, jump-started by a return to formal peace talks in February 2011, reflected the Indian calculation that taking steps toward normalizing the relationship with Pakistan might prop open the door to dialogue about security issues later. Even if not, the agreements posed little threat to India's interests. Forging ties with businessmen across the border was perceived as a way to build stronger peace constituencies inside Pakistan.

Yet, Indian officials remained skeptical that Pakistan's diplomatic overtures would ever amount to more than tactical half-measures. New Delhi suspected that Islamabad, facing rocky times with Washington and a violent insurgency at home, simply wished to avoid additional troubles with India. That interpretation remains plausible; Pakistan's military shows little sign that it has revised its threat perception of India or slackened its drive for nuclear and conventional weapons.

A deeper Pakistani shift toward India appeared far more likely during the waning years of the Musharraf regime, when Pakistan enjoyed better relations with the United States. At that time, Washington and Beijing encouraged, and when necessary cajoled, Islamabad to seek real progress in Indo-Pakistani negotiations. This suggests that an insecure Pakistan may avoid conflict with India as a temporary tactic, but a more confident Pakistan – one that enjoys the patronage of both China and the United States – would be more inclined to seek a diplomatic breakthrough on core political and military issues like Kashmir.

Thus, Indian strategists expect that the Indo-Pakistani conflict will drag on, but many are also starting to see China as the more compelling challenge.[81] Lingering scars from India's disastrous 1962 war with China are compounded by the apprehension that Chinese military, economic, and political power could dominate the region before India even has a chance to seek its rightful place in the sun.

This fear is reasonable. China has had an enormous head start on India in economic and military terms. China outpaces India by more than three to one in terms of GDP. The People's Liberation Army is almost twice the size of the Indian military. Hawkish Indian military strategists see evidence of Chinese encirclement from Pakistan, to Nepal, to Burma, to Sri Lanka. Borrowing from a Booz Allen study conducted for the Pentagon, some describe Chinese points

---

[81] As India's former foreign secretary, Shyam Saran, put it, "India and China harbour essentially adversarial perceptions of one another." See his Second Annual K. Subrahmanyam Memorial lecture, "China in the Twenty-First Century: What India Needs to Know about China's World View," New Delhi, August 29, 2012, p. 26, http://www.globalindiafoundation.org/Second%20Annual%20K.pdf.

of expansion in the region as a "string of pearls."[82] Many subscribe to the view articulated by a prominent retired Indian diplomat who explained that Pakistan is now of concern to India only because it represents an "extension of Chinese power."[83]

Then again, there are also excellent reasons to doubt that the future of relations between New Delhi and Beijing will be defined by conflict. Trade flows between India and China are already greater in volume than flows between India and the United States.[84] With economic opportunities aplenty, neither New Delhi nor Islamabad has wanted to see diplomatic disputes get out of hand.

Leaders on both sides have even explored opportunities for closer ties in ways that rankle Washington. In 2012, New Delhi hosted the so-called BRICS group (standing for Brazil, Russia, India, China, and South Africa) for its fifth summit. In addition to seeking a balanced relationship with China, India's displays of solidarity against the established powers of the international economy signal its desire to retain what Indian policymakers and analysts call "strategic autonomy."[85] That means India will not, under any circumstances, toe the American line in the ways that other close allies, such as Great Britain or Japan, have in the past.

Indian reluctance to enter a formal alliance with Washington goes beyond the fact that the United States and India have different interests with respect to major global issues, like climate change and trade. India's desire to go its own way has deep roots in the prickly post-colonialism of Jawaharlal Nehru, the dominant prime minister for most of two decades after independence, and the architect of India's "non-alignment" stance in the Cold War. Nehru rejected formal alliances with both Washington and Moscow. He asserted, often in a

[82] A good discussion of the so-called string of pearls strategy can be found in Kaplan, *Monsoon*, pp. 10–12, 127, as well as James Holmes and Toshi Yoshihara, "Is China Planning a String of Pearls?" *Diplomat*, February 21, 2011, http://thediplomat.com/flashpoints-blog/2011/02/21/is-china-planning-string-of-pearls/. For an Indian take on the issue, see Arun Sahgal, "India and US Rebalancing Strategy for Asia-Pacific," Institute for Defense Studies and Analyses, July 9, 2012, http://idsa.in/idsacomments/IndiaandUSRebalancingStrategyforAsiaPacific_asahgal_090712.

[83] Author conversation, New Delhi, October 2010.

[84] Total trade between the United States and India in 2011 was about $57 billion, while trade between India and China in the same time period was about $74 billion. By comparison, U.S.-China trade in 2011 topped $500 billion. For details, see U.S. Census Bureau, "Trade in Goods with India," U.S. Department of Commerce, http://www.census.gov/foreign-trade/balance/c5330.html; "India-China Trade Hits All Time High of $73.9 bn in 2011," *Economic Times*, January 30, 2012, http://articles.economictimes.indiatimes.com/2012-01-30/news/30676369_1_trade-deficit-bilateral-trade-china-s-jaishankar; "U.S.-China Trade Statistics," U.S.-China Business Council, http://www.uschina.org/statistics/tradetable.html.

[85] For more on this issue, see Teresita C. Schaffer, "Partnering with India: Regional Power, Global Hopes," in Ashley J. Tellis, Mercy Kuo, and Andrew Marble, eds., *Strategic Asia 2008–9: Challenges and Choices* (Washington: National Bureau of Asian Research, 2008), p. 200.

tone that sounded irritatingly moralistic to American ears, that India had no dog in the fight between imperialists and communists.

Nehruvian non-alignment is alive and well among a surprising number of Indian leaders, even though the Cold War is long past. Indeed, in 2012, when an impressive group of Indian strategists with ties to the government released a report with recommendations for foreign policy, it was titled "Nonalignment 2.0."[86] When asked to explain the title choice, one of the report's authors said it was primarily intended to appeal to the Indian audience, for whom it would conjure up a familiar tradition of thought about India's role in the world.[87] Perhaps there was some value in that, but the title also recalled some of the very worst periods of Cold War interaction between the United States and India. To American ears, the title suggested Indian backsliding in its openness to improved ties with the United States.[88]

Many Indians oppose policies that would even hint of bringing India into America's orbit. The baffling spectacle of watching Indian Prime Minister Manmohan Singh struggle to win passage of the Indo-U.S. civil nuclear agreement in 2008 is evidence enough of this reality. American observers, many of whom thought the deal was far too generous to India, were shocked to see that if not for the prime minister's last-minute heroics, a motley political opposition could have blocked the passage of enabling legislation in the Indian parliament.[89]

India's stance on Iran offers another example of strategic autonomy in action. Indian interests in Iran, primarily its desire for Iranian petroleum, have regularly put it at odds with Washington's determined opposition to Teheran and its nuclear ambitions. But the problem between the United States and India is not just one of different goals or policy perspectives; it is also that India will not suffer the indignity of being told what to do. Mohan, the strategist, astutely notes that if "pressed publicly by the U.S. leaders to fall in line with U.S. policy (for example, on Iran), the Indian political class will be compelled to affirm its unwillingness to be dictated to."[90]

---

[86] Sunil Khilnani et al., "Nonalignment 2.0: A Foreign and Strategic Policy for India in the Twenty First Century," Centre for Policy Research, 2012, http://www.cprindia.org/sites/default/files/NonAlignment%202.0_1.pdf.

[87] Author conversation, Washington, DC, April 2012.

[88] For more on this, as well as a larger response to the "Non-alignment 2.0" paper, see Ashley Tellis, "Nonalignment Redux: The Perils of Old Wine in New Skins," Carnegie Endowment for International Peace, 2012. Tellis argues that it would be a serious mistake for India to "remain nonaligned well into the future," and that in fact, New Delhi should "enter into preferential strategic partnerships . . . with key friendly powers – especially the United States."

[89] For a revealing take on the heroics needed to push the nuclear deal through the Indian government, see Vinod K. Jose, "Falling Man: Manmohan Singh at the Centre of the Storm," *Caravan*, October 1, 2011, http://www.caravanmagazine.in/Story.aspx?Storyid=1103&StoryStyle=FullStory.

[90] C. Raja Mohan, "Poised for Power: The Domestic Roots of India's Slow Rise," in Ashley Tellis and Michael Wills, eds., *Strategic Asia 2007–8: Domestic Political Change and Grand Strategy* (Washington: National Bureau of Asian Research, 2007), p. 207.

Part of the logic of the Bush administration's civil-nuclear deal and the Obama administration's decision to support India for a permanent United Nations Security Council seat was that these steps would break down India's reluctance to partnership. That bet may pay off in time, but strategic autonomy is still India's dominant foreign policy paradigm, and there are good reasons to believe that it could remain that way well into the future.

After Obama's October 2010 trip to India, New Delhi took a number of steps that, intentional or not, reduced American expectations for accelerated partnership in the near term. Over the course of 2011, India rejected bids by American manufacturers to supply fighter jets in a mega-deal that would have amounted to well over $10 billion; abstained from the UN vote authorizing military action in Libya; and watered down UN language criticizing Syria.[91]

"Strategic autonomy" is more than warmed-over non-alignment for the twenty-first century. It also reflects India's rising power and newfound sense of confidence. Assuming India's economic growth remains strong, its leaders gradually tame some of the country's greatest development challenges, and the state translates tax revenues into increasingly potent military and diplomatic power, New Delhi will find itself less as a vulnerable supplicant playing for advantage between Washington and Beijing. Instead, it will stand tall as an independent third power, capable of charting its own course.

Under these circumstances, New Delhi may never feel the compulsion to hitch its wagon solely, or even primarily, to the United States. Unless China starts to look far more menacing than it does now, India will probably prefer to fulfill its national ambitions by working with the United States when it makes sense and, wherever possible, with China too. India will be too independent-minded and ambitious to accept eagerly the role of America's dutiful client, which is apparently the direction many Indians believe a formal alliance with the United States would take them.

PLAYING OUT THE REGIONAL GAME

What then is the answer to the question raised by the assembly of Peshawar's university students? How will the U.S.-Pakistan relationship fit within the broader regional and global context of the next decade and beyond?

First of all, a great deal will hinge upon the trajectory of relations between the United States and China. Just as the Cold War conflict manifested itself in South Asia in unexpected and profound ways, decisions in Beijing and Washington made without any particular concern for Pakistan could affect

[91] Analyst Harsh Pant lists these steps taken by India, and notes that "The decision on MMRCA [jet fighter deal] will only reinforce the perception in Washington that the much-touted strategic partnership between the US and India is more hype than substance." See Harsh V. Pant, "India's Continuing Search for 'Strategic Autonmy,'" *ISN Insights*, May 18, 2011, http://www.isn.ethz .ch/isn/Current-Affairs/ISN-Insights/Detail?lng=en&id=129264&conte-xtid734=129264& contextid735=129261&tabid=129261.

millions of Pakistanis, for better, or, more likely, for worse. The geopolitical future does not look good for ties between Washington and Islamabad.

Indeed, even leaving aside the acrimony between the United States and Pakistan born of the war in Afghanistan and the hunt for international terrorists, China's rising power – and the increasing significance of the Asia-Pacific region as a whole – will naturally draw Washington's attention away from Pakistan and toward traditional Asian allies like Japan, Korea, and Australia. Moreover, if Washington were forced to choose a partner in South Asia, its top choice would be India, not Pakistan. U.S.-India relations are warm and growing warmer for many reasons that have nothing to do with geopolitics, from business ties to cultural affinities. Pakistani fears of an American tilt toward India therefore have a solid basis.

Yet the future is complicated by the aspirations of the Chinese and Indians themselves. These rising powers have grand plans, even if they are not yet specific. Their expanding visions of regional and global influence may eventually send them into conflict with one another. In the near term, however, both are fixated on economic development and regional stability. Neither of these two Asian giants prefers to see South Asia divided into competing blocs, with India and the United States on one side, China and Pakistan on the other.

China wants to have it all in South Asia: stability across the region, trade with India, and long-term strategic investments in Pakistan. Beijing has already taken steps to try to restrain conflict between Islamabad and New Delhi, and it would prefer to avoid a rupture in relations between Pakistan and the United States. If China remains, on balance, more risk averse than aggressive in South Asia, this pattern could continue for many years to come.

India is not ready – and may never be eager – to join hands with the United States in ways that tie them. New Delhi values its autonomy and is just ambitious enough to believe it can benefit from America's largesse without any strings attached. Indians have long criticized Washington's military aid to Pakistan, but now that they worry more about Pakistan's weakness and instability than its strength, they place a greater value on the restraining influence of a viable U.S.-Pakistan relationship. Indians fear some of the implications of China's rise, but in other ways they find common ground with Beijing. New Delhi's independent streak will continue to test the patience of American policymakers; it may eventually lead them to throw up their hands and leave India to its own devices.

In the end, however, it is the threat of Pakistan as a catastrophic spoiler that makes the two-bloc scenario (United States and India versus China and Pakistan) most unappealing. Just as the violent "Kalashnikov culture" of Pakistan's frontier regions near Peshawar spilled into the settled parts of the country, disrupting traditional, civilized ways of life and threatening far greater instability and violence, so too could Pakistan's extreme ideologies, sophisticated terrorists, and well-armed militants export mayhem into the surrounding region, starting with India. An unstable Pakistan that feels jilted by the United

States would be an albatross around India's neck and a costly obstacle to America's ambition for a peaceful, prosperous region in which India plays a major, if perhaps independent-minded, role.

The threat of Pakistan as a spoiler thus provides the single most important reason that the United States must – out of fear more than affection – factor Islamabad into its broader geopolitical calculations in Asia. Fear is not a particularly firm foundation for partnership between nations, but it does sharpen the mind. Put simply, the United States will have a far easier time achieving its goals in Asia – above all managing the rise of China and cultivating better ties with a rising India – if it can also find a way to work with Pakistan.

Fortunately, it is also possible to envision a more optimistic future for Pakistan and its neighbors – one defined by economic integration rather than strategic competition. India and China, once (and possibly future) rivals, already see economic growth and development as a top priority. Despite some misgivings, their fast-growing trade ties are mutually beneficial and lend stabilizing ballast to their bilateral relationship.

Pakistan's neighbors could also exert a transformative and profoundly stabilizing influence on its economic fortunes. Indeed, the rising tide of Asian wealth may be the only external force powerful enough to lift even Pakistan's leaky boat. A fast growing economy would create opportunities for Pakistan's massive young population and dim at least some of the appeal of extremism and violence. Along the way, India, China, and the United States would also find themselves better positioned to avoid conflicts with Islamabad or each other.

7

America's Options

General Mirza Aslam Baig could not have been any more polite as he rearranged the pillows on his finely upholstered sofa to make space for his American guest. The cool, dim sitting room with its gilded décor was a welcome respite from the heat of mid-May 2012 in Rawalpindi. A decade earlier, it would have been possible to stroll the short distance from Baig's home to the official residence of Pakistan's serving army chief. The threat of terrorist attacks had, however, forced the construction of high white walls around the neighborhoods, separating Baig, a retired army chief, from his successors. The soft-spoken octogenarian settled into a nearby armchair and, after beckoning for tea and a generous array of Pakistani snacks, quietly explained that it was not he who had turned against the United States, but the United States that had turned against Pakistan.

Baig's early experiences with the United States were mainly positive ones. As a young officer in the 1950s, he joined Pakistan's newly formed Special Services Group, an elite commando unit, and trained with American forces in guerrilla warfare. Washington's goal then was to build a "stay-behind organization" of Pakistani officers that could melt into the population and resist occupation in the event of an invasion by the Soviet Union.[1]

Three decades later, similar guerrilla training and billions in U.S. and Saudi funding helped to turn the fierce Afghan mujahedeen into an effective fighting force that held the field against the Red Army. Baig had a front row seat for the anti-Soviet war. He served near Pakistan's border with Afghanistan as commander of the army's Peshawar-based XI Corps from 1985 to 1987. While there, he remembers sending many of his best officers to the United States

[1] For more on the Special Services Group and this early military cooperation between Pakistan and the United States, see Shuja Nawaz, *Crossed Swords* (New York: Oxford University Press, 2008), p. 133.

for advanced military education. In 1987, Baig was promoted to vice chief of the army staff. This made him the service's day-to-day leader while General Zia-ul-Haq served as Pakistan's president and top military commander. When Zia died in 1988, Baig immediately assumed the most powerful job in the country.

Baig's public break with the United States came shortly thereafter. In 1991, he expressed his support for Saddam Hussein's side in the Gulf War. Baig now justifies the move by arguing that Saudi Arabia was under no real threat from Saddam's forces and that America's war was nothing more than a ploy by Washington to weaken Iraq. At the time, his anger with Washington was probably also linked to the sanctions that the United States had just slapped on Pakistan for developing a nuclear bomb.[2]

From that point onward, Baig's anti-Americanism only grew deeper. Like too many of his fellow Pakistanis, the conspiracy-minded retired general doubts the official story of 9/11. He claims it was a hoax. And soon after the 2011 Abbottabad raid that killed Osama bin Laden, Baig wrote that the United States had staged the operation with a "clone" bin Laden: "This was a CIA operation, meant to fool the world and embarrass Pakistan but the fact of the matter is that the whole exercise was a fake and a lie, same as the 9/11 episode was to find an excuse to launch the crusade against the Muslim World."[3]

When pressed to consider when he first had doubts about cooperation with the United States, Baig says he should have seen trouble brewing even during the 1950s. As a young officer, he had good personal relationships with his American counterparts, but he was troubled that Pakistani intelligence reports (with highly detailed social and economic information that would be salient in a counter-Soviet insurgency) were shared with the Americans. He felt that Pakistan's leaders were too subservient, too willing to facilitate U.S. intervention in their sovereign affairs.

Looking back, Baig muses, those early missteps foreshadowed much greater Pakistani blunders in its relations with America. Washington repeatedly exploited Pakistan and interfered in its politics, but the Pakistani leaders who served as willing accomplices to America's crimes deserve a healthy share of the blame. Chief among those culprits, at least in Baig's estimation, was General Pervez Musharraf.

Baig's list of charges against Musharraf is long. He begins by proudly recounting how, shortly after 9/11, he gave Musharraf a firm dressing-down for selling out to the Americans. Baig told him that by turning against

---

[2] On the nuclear sanctions, see the discussion of the Pressler Amendment in Chapter 3. On Baig's reaction, see Ian Talbot, *Pakistan: A Modern History* (New York: Palgrave Macmillan, 2005), p. 316; Barnett R. Rubin, *The Search for Peace in Afghanistan: From Buffer State to Failed State* (New Haven: Yale, 1995), p. 115.

[3] Mirza Aslam Beg, "Confirmation: Bin Laden 'Clone' Killed at Abbottabad," *Veterans Today*, May 20, 2011, http://www.veteranstoday.com/2011/05/20/confirmation-bin-laden-look-alike-killled-at-abbottabad/.

Pakistan's erstwhile Taliban allies in Afghanistan and opening Pakistan's soil to U.S. supply routes and counterterror operations, Musharraf had committed an unforgivable crime against the nation. Bowing to American pressure was, as Baig puts it, a stain on Pakistan's honor. No self-respecting state could accept such dictates, not even from a superpower. More than anything else, Baig concludes, Pakistan needs self-respect; the country needs to show, just like revolutionary Iran, that it can stand up to any country in the world.

Not only did Musharraf sell his soul to the Americans, but he also backed the wrong horse in Afghanistan. Sooner or later, from Baig's point of view, the United States and its allies will be driven from Afghanistan just as the Russians were. "People laughed at me when I said this soon after 9/11," he recalls, "but look what is happening now. The Taliban will win. They know it. And they will dictate the terms of settlement."[4]

Baig never broke with the Taliban. By his own account, he retained indirect contact with top Taliban officials. He also remained close with Pakistani colleagues who had a hand in supporting Afghan fighters during the 1980s and 1990s, like former Inter-Services Intelligence directorate (ISI) chief Hamid Gul. Baig counted as a friend the infamous, now-deceased Brigadier Sultan Amir Tarar, who was widely known in Afghan circles as "Colonel Imam," the ISI's Taliban trainer.[5] Most believe that Tarar died in 2010, after being taken hostage near the Afghan border. A video released online by the Pakistani Taliban (TTP) shows Tarar being shot in the head as the bloodthirsty TTP leader Hakimullah Mehsud looks on.[6]

The killing was widely interpreted as evidence of the TTP's unrelenting hostility toward the Pakistani state and its agents, even longtime Taliban sympathizers like Tarar. Baig, however, tells a different story. Weaving together several unlikely conspiracies, he argues that Tarar was the victim of an elaborate American assassination plot. It is not surprising that when Baig predicts that the U.S. mission will fail in Afghanistan, there is more than a hint of *schadenfreude* in his voice.

THE STUMBLING BLOCK IN AFGHANISTAN

If American and Pakistani officials were able to put all emotions aside, let bygones be bygones, and speak honestly about their present differences, most, like General Baig, would land on Afghanistan. Boiled to its essentials, the disagreement hinges on how to deal with the Afghan Taliban and especially the Haqqani network based inside the Pakistani tribal agency of North Waziristan.

---

[4] Author conversation, May 15, 2012.
[5] Carlotta Gall, "Former Pakistani Officer Embodies a Policy Puzzle," *New York Times*, March 3, 2010, "http://www.nytimes.com/2010/03/04/world/asia/04imam.html?_r=1.
[6] The video was accessed at http://www.defenceblog.org/2011/03/pakistani-talibans-killed-colonel-imam.html.

Washington has demanded that Islamabad take greater action against these groups. Pakistan – for reasons explained throughout this book – has refused.[7]

Should differences over Afghanistan warrant jeopardizing the entire U.S.-Pakistan relationship? Stepping back from the immediacy of the Afghan war, an argument could be made that the Haqqani network, the Afghan Taliban, even all of Afghanistan are of such minor scale and importance to the United States, at least when compared to Pakistan itself, that Washington should not hold its relationship with Islamabad hostage to them. As one senior U.S. policymaker explained, the Afghan war is fading into history and as the military departs Americans will appreciate – as they have in Iraq – just how limited their interests really were in that distant, landlocked country. Why, that official asked, compound the costs of the Afghan war by allowing its endgame to drive the wedge even deeper between the United States and Pakistan?[8]

This argument has merit. It is true that U.S. interests in Pakistan extend well beyond what happens in Afghanistan or even in Pakistan's tribal borderlands. These interests begin with Washington's vital concerns about the safety and security of Pakistan's nuclear program, which are tied up with broader questions of Pakistan's stability and the trajectory of its state and society. Even the most sophisticated security precautions will offer cold comfort if the hands that rest upon Pakistan's nuclear buttons become far more belligerent or irresponsible because the military has crumbled or turned completely anti-Western in its orientation. As Chapter 2 of this book makes clear, Pakistan's jihadists do not today threaten an Iran-style revolution, but the future favors change over stasis, as the power of traditional elites and their institutions erodes day by day.

Beyond that, America's emergent interests extend to the geopolitics of the region, as explained in Chapter 6. The future may have some similarities with the Cold War past. Whereas U.S.-Soviet conflict structured U.S. policies in South Asia from the 1940s through the 1980s, the U.S.-China relationship is likely to dominate Washington's worldview of the future. Within this context, Pakistan's close ties with China and its historical animosity toward India have important implications for U.S. plans in Asia. If Pakistan breaks with the United States and reverts to its old, violent patterns with India, it would diminish or delay New Delhi's rise to global leadership. That, in turn, would undermine U.S. aspirations for a strong Indian partner in Asia. Also worrisome, a Pakistani spoiler state that relies upon Chinese patronage would represent a new point of tension between Washington and Beijing, not entirely unlike North Korea. Neither Washington (nor Beijing at this point) relishes such a prospect.

---

[7] For a revealing look at opinions of Pakistan's foreign policy establishment on U.S. and Pakistani policy toward Afghanistan, see Moeed Yusuf, Huma Yusuf, and Salman Zaidi, "Pakistan, the United States, and the End Game in Afghanistan: Perceptions of Pakistan's Foreign Policy Elite," Jinnah Institute, August 25, 2011, http://www.jinnah-institute.org/images/ji_afghanendgame .pdf.

[8] Author conversation, November 2011.

For these reasons, the United States had, and continues to have, every reason to avoid a scenario in which the Afghan war becomes a stumbling block to working with Pakistan on other important fronts. The history of U.S. relations with Pakistan is replete with shortsightedness. Washington's tendency to be driven by crisis and short-term or narrowly conceived interests is a theme that plays out again and again through Chapters 3, 4, and 5. These patterns need not be repeated.

Yet Washington would find it politically, if not strategically, impossible to look past the Afghan war in its relationship with Pakistan. As the war has taken a turn for the worse, many U.S. officials lay the blame at Pakistan's doorstep. Too many Americans and their allies have already died in Afghanistan. Too many fellow soldiers, commanding officers, families, friends, and elected representatives hold Pakistan-based insurgents responsible for their deaths. Many, echoing the words of Admiral Michael Mullen, chairman of the Joint Chiefs of Staff, see these groups as veritable arms of the Pakistani state. Few Americans leave the battlefront in Afghanistan without harboring anger toward Pakistan.

For years to come, these political realities are likely to frame the way Washington deals with Islamabad. Democratically accountable U.S. leaders face stiff political headwinds when they attempt publicly to justify assistance to, or close cooperation with, Pakistan. America would be better off if its leaders are able to brave the political storm; to seek cooperation with and even assistance for Pakistan if and when it serves U.S. interests, whatever Islamabad's perfidy in Afghanistan. Washington might be better able to manage that difficult feat if its Pakistan policies were handled through quiet consultations between the executive branch and Congress, away from the media spotlight. Yet the often tumultuous character of the U.S.-Pakistan relationship is likely to complicate that sort of under-the-radar approach.

Kick the Can Past 2014?

Since American anger over the war in Afghanistan makes it so difficult for Washington to deal with Islamabad, the relevant question is whether the United States will be better positioned to advance its long-term goals in Pakistan while U.S. forces are still heavily engaged in the Afghan war or after they depart.

Many policymakers in Washington seem drawn to the conclusion that the United States will find greater leverage in its relationship with Pakistan after 2014, when Afghan forces are supposed to assume a leading security role and the remaining international forces, mainly American, will focus on training, advisory, and counterterror missions.[9] A far smaller NATO presence in

---

[9] For more on possible endgame scenarios in Afghanistan, see Dexter Filkins, "After America," *The New Yorker*, July 9, 2012, http://www.newyorker.com/reporting/2012/07/09/120709fa_fact_filkins.

Afghanistan will mean less need for Pakistani roads, ports, and airspace as conduits for supplies, weapons, and personnel. Since the United States will then be less dependent on Pakistan's cooperation, the argument goes, it will be easier to pressure Islamabad to comply on other issues with less fear of the potential repercussions.

This argument was partially undermined over the course of 2012. Pakistan closed its roads to NATO convoys after the Salala friendly fire incident in November 2011 but NATO managed to re-route its supplies into Afghanistan by way of Central Asia for seven months until they were re-opened.[10] This Northern Distribution Network of rail, ship, and trucking routes was undoubtedly slower and more costly than the Pakistani alternative, but it demonstrated that Pakistan did not necessarily hold a trump card in its dealings with Washington. In other words, the United States *already* had more leverage with Pakistan than many in Washington (and perhaps in Islamabad) had appreciated.

The notion that Washington will be in a better negotiating situation with Pakistan after the Afghan war winds down has other problems as well. Washington's ability to threaten coercive military action throughout the region will diminish with the withdrawal of America's heavy military presence from Pakistan's backyard. Fewer troops and resources devoted to Afghanistan will also mean less concerted attention from senior American officials. Judging from the history of the past decade, Pakistan requires routine cabinet-level attention simply to deal with too-frequent crises when they break out. A more ambitious strategy would require someone on the president's national security team to champion and implement new policies. At times, it would require intervention by the president himself.

Given the wide variety of pressing domestic and international concerns that face Washington, not to mention the fact that Pakistan represents a high-risk, low-reward proposition, it is hard to believe that top policymakers will place greater, more sustained attention on Pakistan after 2014 than they have in recent years. It is revealing, for instance, that aside from Ambassador Richard Holbrooke the Obama team has filled nearly all of the top jobs in Afghanistan and Pakistan with career Foreign Service Officers or uniformed military personnel.[11] Such individuals are likely to be competent and professional, to be sure, but they also tend to lack the political clout needed to shepherd major policy initiatives. Rising political stars already view Afghanistan and Pakistan as radioactive, career-ending posts.

[10] On Salala, see Chapter 4. For a good map of what was termed the Northern Distribution Network, see Vanda Felbab-Brown, "Stuck in the Mud: The Logistics of Getting Out of Afghanistan," *Foreign Affairs* (July/August 2012), http://www.foreignaffairs.com/articles/137785/vanda-felbab-brown/stuck-in-the-mud.
[11] Ambassadors in Kabul (Ryan Crocker, James Cunningham) and Islamabad (Cameron Munter, Richard Olson), Holbrooke's replacement (Marc Grossman), and the top National Security Council staffer (Douglas Lute) all fit this pattern.

If the United States is unable to force (or induce) Pakistan to begin an about-face in its dealings with groups like the Haqqanis and LeT while a large American military contingent is in the region and top U.S. officials are focused squarely on the matter, then Washington will be less likely – and less well placed – to take another serious run at the issue later. All is not lost after 2014, but it would be little more than wishful thinking to assume that the challenge of dealing with Pakistan will get easier down the road.

Looking even further into the future, the trends discussed in Chapter 2 suggest that if Pakistan remains on its present trajectory, its population, nuclear arsenal, and terrorist networks will grow while its economy, governing institutions, and security conditions deteriorate. America's leaders cannot assume that their children or grandchildren will be better positioned to deal with Pakistan than the United States is today.

U.S. OPTIONS

In contemplating its options with Pakistan, Washington finds itself in an impossible bind. Frustration over the Afghan war endangers cooperation, but other concerns – from terrorism and nuclear weapons to regional geopolitics – make cooperation more appealing, even essential. Pakistan's pattern of political, economic, and security crises will, in one way or another, force Washington to pay attention even if American leaders would prefer to steer clear.

One possible response to the competing pressures to end cooperation and, at the same time, to recognize the persistence of Pakistan-based threats, would be to implement a strategy of "defensive insulation." Simply put, the United States would seek to protect itself from Pakistan's terrorists, nuclear weapons, and other possible dangers by erecting new layers of military, diplomatic, economic, and other barriers around the Pakistani state. U.S. partners in the region, above all India, would be bolstered as important components in the defensive scheme.

If, on the other hand, Washington and Islamabad find a way to rekindle a cooperative relationship, two models present themselves. The first would be a return to the sorts of dealings that Washington had with General Musharraf in the early post-9/11 period. That "military-first" approach would retain a tight focus on pressing issues of national security and leave most of the rest – from politics to economics – aside.

A second model, similar to what the Obama administration attempted during its first two years in office, would strive for a comprehensive partnership across military and civilian sectors. Whereas a military-first model would deal with Pakistan as it is, a comprehensive cooperation strategy would aim for the more ambitious goal of lending a helping hand to Pakistan as it navigates through massive social and political change without falling into violent revolution on the one hand or military dictatorship on the other.

DEFENSIVE INSULATION

Given the recent history of turmoil in U.S.-Pakistan relations, America's leaders must at least consider how best to achieve counterterror, nuclear, and geopolitical objectives if ties with Islamabad fray or break. Under a defensive insulation posture, Washington would address the threat of Pakistan-based terrorism at multiple levels. Some of these are consistent with past practice, even during periods of U.S.-Pakistani cooperation. Others, however, could poison the relationship and kill prospects for cooperation, perhaps for decades to come.

U.S. security and law enforcement would build upon existing efforts to interdict terrorists before they reach the United States or other important targets. Since 9/11, the United States has overhauled its homeland security as well as its domestic and international counterterror programs to better meet the threat posed by al-Qaeda and its affiliates. Between 2002 and 2011, America has increased its homeland security spending by nearly $700 billion.[12] $50 billion has been poured into aviation security alone.[13] Terrorist networks have been infiltrated and their financial flows disrupted. Of course, these jobs are never done; terrorists pose a resilient and evolving threat, and are opportunistic in their exploitation of vulnerabilities.

But defensive insulation would also require policies of coercion and deterrence that are not now a part of Washington's tool kit with Pakistan. U.S. officials could, for example, impose targeted sanctions and visa restrictions on Pakistani officials suspected of ties to terrorist organizations, steps that U.S. officials have contemplated but avoided to date for fear that they would jeopardize other forms of bilateral cooperation.[14]

As long as the terrorist threat persists, defensive insulation would feature a U.S. drone campaign inside Pakistan. To withstand a deteriorating U.S.-Pakistan relationship, that campaign might also need to grow and change. If the Pakistani military no longer clears airspace for American drones along the Afghan border, or if U.S. officials decide to send drones into other parts of Pakistan, like Baluchistan or Punjab, without Islamabad's consent, the current generation of slow, low-flying drones like the Predator would be fairly easy for

---

[12] This figure reflects the increase, in the ten years since 9/11, in federal, state, and private sector expenditures on homeland security and intelligence, not including the wars in Iraq and Afghanistan. When including opportunity costs (e.g., economic deadweight losses, airport passenger delays), the total increase in spending comes to over $1.1 trillion. For details, see John Mueller and Mark G. Stewart, *Terror, Security, and Money* (New York: Oxford University Press, 2011), pp. 2, 4, 196–7.

[13] Nancy Benac, "National Security: Ten Years after September 11 Attacks, U.S. Is Safe but Not Safe Enough," *Associated Press*, September 3, 2011, http://www.huffingtonpost.com/2011/09/03/promises-promises-us-safe_n_947688.html.

[14] Bruce Riedel, "A New Pakistan Policy: Containment," *New York Times*, October 14, 2011, http://www.nytimes.com/2011/10/15/opinion/a-new-pakistan-policy-containment.html.

the Pakistanis to shoot out of the sky.[15] Rapid advances in drone technologies could solve this problem, but the answer is not yet in America's arsenal. An ideal next-generation drone would operate around the clock and beyond the range (or detection) of Pakistan's air defenses. An armed, high-altitude stealth drone might begin to solve the problem.

Until then, a combination of unarmed high-flying or stealthy surveillance drones plus satellites could direct U.S. cruise missile strikes from outside Pakistan. They would most likely be launched from Afghanistan to reduce flight times and to make clear that they were not being directed from India (so as to avoid an unnecessary crisis between New Delhi and Islamabad). To wage its drone campaign from Afghanistan, U.S. officials would need to negotiate a long-term deal with Kabul to maintain bases on Afghan soil well after other U.S. and NATO forces depart. Defending and maintaining these bases could be a challenge once the bulk of U.S. forces leave Afghanistan, especially if the country becomes more violent or hostile to U.S. forces.

Islamabad would almost certainly see U.S. cruise missile strikes as acts of war. Cruise missiles are larger and less "surgical" than drone-launched Hellfire missiles. They would kill more Pakistani civilians. Influential anti-American groups like the Defence of Pakistan Council and voices like General Baig would have a field day. Pakistani opposition could lead Washington to limit its air strikes to only the top terrorist targets like bin Laden's successor, Ayman al-Zawahiri.

On the other hand, if international terrorist groups take advantage of a U.S.-Pakistan rift to expand their planning and training operations on Pakistani soil, Washington would have every incentive to launch air strikes and even mount helicopter-borne commando assaults in cases where extracting intelligence was worth the potential of a military standoff with Pakistani forces. In short, the United States would shift from a geographically contained drone campaign that enjoys at least the tacit consent of the Pakistani state to an unconstrained campaign operating against Pakistani wishes.[16] The gloves could come off, on both sides.

Defensive insulation would demand more than U.S. eyes and missiles in the sky. It would require intelligence gathering and covert operations on the ground to go after groups like LeT that operate inside densely populated regions of Pakistan and with the active or passive support of state authorities. Judging from the Raymond Davis affair and the CIA's ability to maintain a safe house in Abbottabad to facilitate surveillance on the bin Laden compound from the fall

---

[15] With a maximum altitude of 25,000 feet, top airspeed of 138 miles per hour, and wingspan of 55 feet, a Predator is an easy target for Pakistani air forces. For a short technical description of the Predator, see Crumpton, *The Art of Intelligence* (New York: Penguin, 2012), p. 151.

[16] On Washington's interpretation of tacit consent from Islamabad, see Adam Entous, Siobhan Gorman, and Evan Perez, "U.S. Unease over Drone Strikes," *Wall Street Journal*, September 26, 2012, http://online.wsj.com/article/SB10000872396390444100404577641520858011452 .html.

of 2010 until the May 2011 raid, Washington has already attempted a range of efforts of this sort.[17] These high-profile episodes prompted an ISI crackdown on official U.S. activities around the country.[18]

Washington will find it increasingly difficult to place spies or handlers inside Pakistan, but defensive insulation would demand it. Compared to Iran or North Korea, Pakistan is an open society where it is possible to forge working ties with Pakistani groups, individuals, or political parties who already share U.S. concerns about groups like the Taliban, LeT, and international terrorists. Pakistanis who share U.S. counterterror goals could be strengthened with U.S. money, training, and in some cases, arms. If in the future Pakistan's internal instability grows beyond the state's capacity to respond, and especially if Pakistan's army is ever divided against itself, Washington would have greater incentive to take sides in an incipient civil war.

U.S. covert operations inside Pakistan would need to grow, but the official American footprint inside Pakistan – its embassy, consulates, and USAID presence – would be downsized or even eliminated as part of a defensive insulation strategy. There would be little reason to present soft targets to Pakistani violence. A tiny skeleton staff could manage U.S. diplomacy.

Although intrusive, U.S. counterterror operations in Pakistan would not necessarily risk all-out war. The United States has implemented hard-edged strategies toward other states like Syria for decades without lapsing into war. Islamabad would face the unenviable choice of whether to retaliate against the United States, knowing that Washington will always retain the military and diplomatic upper hand.

Shifting from counterterrorism to the nuclear challenge, rather than attempting to help Pakistan improve the safety and security of its arsenal through cooperation, reassurance, and assistance (as has been the case over the past decade), Washington would shift its emphasis to deterrence. The U.S. goal would be to introduce a credible threat of overwhelming retaliation in order to make Pakistan think twice about using or sharing its nuclear weapons. That fear would help to motivate responsible, even obsessive, nuclear stewardship.

To level such a threat against Pakistan for intentionally using weapons against the United States would not be difficult. Presumably the basic point is already appreciated in Islamabad.[19] U.S. threats would be even more credible if Pakistani leaders were convinced that Washington could launch a non-nuclear

---

[17] On the CIA compound in Abbottabad, see Peter Bergen, *Manhunt: The Ten-Year Search for Bin Laden from 9/11 to Abbottabad* (New York: Crown, 2012), pp. 126–7, 131–2.

[18] See "Compliance Followup Review of Embassy Islamabad and Constituent Posts, Pakistan," U.S. Department of State and the Broadcasting Board of Governors, Office of Inspector General, May 2012, p. 7, http://oig.state.gov/documents/organization/193863.pdf.

[19] Along similar lines but in the context of non-nuclear counterterrorism, Bob Woodward reveals that the United States had in place a "retribution plan" for bombing up to 150 sites in Pakistan in the event of a terrorist attack in the United States traced back to Pakistani soil. See Woodward, *Obama's Wars* (New York: Simon & Schuster, 2010), pp. 46, 345.

attack devastating enough to eliminate Pakistan's nuclear arsenal, thereby avoiding nuclear use altogether. The existence of American plans for such an operation could be leaked or shared with Pakistani officials to make sure the threat is appreciated.

At the same time, Washington would need to frame its deterrent threats in ways likely to encourage responsible nuclear stewardship, not recklessness. In spite of U.S. claims to the contrary, many Pakistanis already fear that the United States has developed plans for its special forces to seize or destroy Pakistan's arsenal. In reality, such an operation, which would have to be mounted on a massive scale against well-fortified targets, is probably beyond U.S. means. Even so, Pakistani fears of an American raid could have counterproductive consequences. In order to elude U.S. forces, Pakistan's warheads would be moved from well-defended but easily identifiable facilities to unmarked, lightly fortified mobile vehicles. If so, the weapons would be more vulnerable to theft or accident, two of the very circumstances Washington is most eager to avoid.

The other challenge to a successful U.S. deterrence strategy lies in convincing Pakistani leaders that Washington would take similar retaliatory steps if terrorists use nuclear weapons or materials from Pakistan's arsenal. To strengthen that threat, Washington would need to be able to determine the source of a nuclear attack since even Pakistan-based terrorists might have gotten their weapons elsewhere.

That technical problem of attribution is considerable. While any nuclear explosion would leave telltale signs of its origins, only something akin to a "nuclear DNA test," which starts with the collection of samples of a country's nuclear fuel in advance, can yield conclusive results. Practical challenges abound. Even if U.S. nuclear forensics teams manage to get their hands on samples, they would need time to conduct their analyses. Time would be in very short supply after a nuclear attack.[20] According to a 2010 report by the National Research Council, the chronic under-funding and under-staffing of U.S. nuclear forensic programs reduces their ability to improve techniques, sampling procedures, and evaluation times.[21]

To deal with the possibility that deterrence might fail, Washington would also need to build and deploy defenses against Pakistan's nuclear warheads. Since Pakistan cannot yet launch a ballistic missile or long-range bomber capable of striking the United States, the only nuclear threat to the U.S. homeland would be a nuclear device, or pieces of one, smuggled in a shipping container.

America's port defenses have been improved since 9/11, as has its ability to detect the movement of nuclear cargo through other ports around the world.[22] Yet given the number of containers entering the United States and the reality

[20] Jeffrey T. Richelson, *Defusing Armageddon: Inside NEST, America's Secret Nuclear Bomb Squad* (New York: W. W. Norton, 2009), pp. 228–31.

[21] "Nuclear Forensics: A Capability at Risk," National Research Council, July 2010.

[22] The Megaports Initiative, run through the National Nuclear Security Administration, aims to improve monitoring techniques of cargo passing through American and international ports. For more, see "Office of the Second Line of Defense: Megaports Initiative," National Nuclear

that radioactive sources inside a container can be shielded in ways that make them very difficult to detect, it is clear that America's homeland defenses still need work.[23]

A breakthrough in the technologies devoted to locating nuclear weapons by satellite, plane, or drone would be enormously helpful if any of Islamabad's warheads ever go missing inside Pakistan. Today's overhead imagery can identify many things, but not, for instance, the difference between conventional and nuclear artillery shells.

As part of its nuclear security tool kit, the U.S. Department of Energy has assembled a group of technical experts known as the Nuclear Emergency Support Team (NEST).[24] In combination with U.S. Special Operations Forces, members of NEST would be on the front lines if one of Pakistan's nuclear weapons was lost or stolen. Members of the team are experts at handling nuclear devices and rendering them safe. Although NEST "stays ready to deploy [from Andrews Air Force Base, near Washington, DC] within four hours of notification" of any emergency, it does not maintain personnel in South Asia. If a small group of technical experts from NEST rotated through a nearby base in Afghanistan or one of the Gulf states, Washington would be able to respond even more quickly to a regional emergency.

For obvious reasons, if U.S.-Pakistan relations fray, Washington will have every incentive to limit the size of Pakistan's nuclear arsenal and associated delivery vehicles. Unfortunately, Pakistan will have the opposite incentive. Pakistan's military will see its nuclear program as its best guarantee against American aggression, just as North Korea does. To add weight to its ability to threaten the United States, Islamabad could conceivably attempt to build or purchase intercontinental ballistic missiles capable of reaching North America. Short of that, Pakistan would rely on shorter-range missiles targeted against U.S. ships, allies, and friends in the region.

Multilateral diplomacy has so far failed to end Pakistan's nuclear or missile development, but as part of its defensive insulation Washington would lobby China to limit its sales and transfers of technologies that might aid Pakistan's missile development. In addition, Washington would need to expand missile

---

Security Administration, September 2010, http://nnsa.energy.gov/aboutus/ourprograms/non proliferation/programoffices/internationalmaterialprotectionandcooperation/-5.

[23] See Jerrold L. Nadler, Edward J. Markey, and Bennie G. Thompson, "Cargo, the Terrorists' Trojan Horse," *New York Times*, June 26, 2012, http://www.nytimes.com/2012/06/27/opinion/the-dangerous-delay-on-port-security.html, as well as Douglas Frantz, "Deadline for Nuclear Scans of Foreign Cargo Passes By," *Washington Post*, July 16, 2012, http://www.washington post.com/world/national-security/port-security-us-fails-to-meet-deadline-for-scanning-of-cargo-containers/2012/07/15/gJQAmgW8mW_story.html.

[24] The Department of Energy's National Nuclear Security Administration maintains a variety of other technical teams to deal with a range of potential nuclear contingencies at home and overseas. See "Responding to Emergencies," National Nuclear Security Administration, http://nnsa.energy.gov/aboutus/ourprograms/emergencyoperationscounterterrorism/respondingtoemergencies.

defense systems of the sort designed to thwart an Iranian attack so they could also be directed toward Pakistan.[25]

Finally, a strategy of defensive insulation would be most effective if Washington could count on firm Indian support. Joint military plans and shared intelligence could ease the burden of containing Pakistan-based threats. In the event of a military crisis, U.S. bases, or at least temporary basing rights on Indian soil, would offer geographic and political advantages over alternatives, whether at sea, in Afghanistan, or in the Persian Gulf. An enhanced Indian missile defense system, built with American assistance, would offer another layer of protection against a Pakistani nuclear-tipped missile. Although Washington and New Delhi have already taken tentative steps in some of these directions, the United States would want to expand and accelerate the process – perhaps in ways that would initially make India's risk-averse leaders uncomfortable – in order to address Pakistan-based threats with greater confidence.

Only a Stopgap

Depending on how relations between the United States and Pakistan unfold, defensive insulation may be the only option available to Washington. This would be true if, for instance, no common ground is found on the endgame in Afghanistan, if new irritants like the Raymond Davis affair crop up, if a new slate of Pakistani leaders adopts a more hostile anti-American posture, or if clear evidence of official Pakistani complicity in offering sanctuary to al-Qaeda is uncovered. All of these scenarios would at least temporarily stymie cooperation and could raise new, more permanent obstacles. Properly crafted and implemented, a range of defenses could enable America to address many immediate security concerns, with respect to both terrorism and the nuclear threat.

None of these facts should make defensive insulation Washington's preferred approach. The strategy does nothing to address the internal dynamics that are likely to make Pakistan more of a threat to America and itself over time. Pakistan's weak civilian institutions and its failing economy (portrayed in Chapter 2) would suffer from an American strategy defined by diplomatic disengagement, bouts of unilateral military force, and an unambiguous tilt toward India. Pakistan's jihadists, not its reformers, would be best positioned to take advantage of the situation, given their greater ability to mobilize, access to illicit resources, and anti-Western ideology that would be energized by worsening relations with Washington.

By treating Pakistan as an adversary or "rogue" state without holding out the serious prospect of improved relations and without inducements to potential

[25] For a summary of current status and future plans for U.S. missile defenses in Europe, see Tom Z. Collina, "The European Phased Adaptive Approach at a Glance," Arms Control Association, June 2012, http://www.armscontrol.org/factsheets/Phasedadaptiveapproach.

allies within the Pakistani state or society, the United States would reinforce a self-fulfilling prophecy. Pakistanis who tend to support better relations with the United States would find themselves increasingly isolated. Anyone with the means to leave Pakistan would be more likely to exercise that option, resulting in a new "brain drain" that the country can ill afford.

Defensive insulation would play into the negative expectations held by much of Pakistan's public, reinforced by the history lessons about U.S. "abandonment" taught by the likes of General Baig. The more Pakistan's military leaders become convinced of hostile American intent, the more their insecurity would lead them to take the "weapons of the weak" – the nuclear warheads and terrorist proxy forces originally developed for use against neighboring India – and repurpose them for duty against the United States. By this logic, Washington's threatening actions intended to deter could actually encourage greater Pakistani recklessness and magnify the threat that the United States would then need to defend against.

As suggested by the assessment of future regional geopolitics in Chapter 6, all of the challenges of Pakistan-as-spoiler would have to be factored into Washington's calculations of the costs associated with a strategy of defensive insulation. Pakistan would be that much more inclined to foment trouble in India, to find common cause with other anti-Western regimes, and even, if the price were right, to again sell its nuclear technologies. To these threats there would be no end in sight; defensive insulation does not begin to "solve" the challenges posed by Pakistan – it only mitigates or blunts potential threats as long as the defenses are reinforced.

Chapter 6 also identifies several of the potential flaws in a U.S. strategy that depends upon an alliance-like relationship with India. First, India may not want to play ball, at least not on U.S. terms. India may instead keep its sights set on "strategic autonomy," pocketing Washington's willingness to share intelligence and support India's beefed up defenses against Pakistan without offering a matching contribution of its own.

Second, an American tilt toward India is likely to increase Pakistan's entanglement with China. Washington and Beijing would find themselves on opposite sides of another ugly regional flashpoint if a hostile Pakistan assumes a role in the U.S.-China relationship similar to that played by North Korea. At the very least, new and active diplomatic maneuvers would be needed to keep U.S.-Pakistan tensions from spiraling into a wider conflict.

Finally, one of the challenges in implementing an effective strategy of defensive insulation over the long haul would be sustaining U.S. vigilance and allocating resources sufficient to address potential threats even as those threats would appear more and more distant the longer the strategy works. This is a challenge inherent to any long-term strategy, but especially those that lack a vision of "victory" and demand a perpetual wartime footing.

Given these weaknesses, the best way to think about defensive insulation is as a stopgap solution under conditions in which greater U.S.-Pakistan cooperation proves impossible. Its long-term costs would be high, even if the savings from cuts to U.S. assistance in Pakistan might appear significant at the outset. Its side effects would include a lasting hostility with Pakistan and a difficult regional dynamic. Nor would it be a simple matter for Washington to sustain the strategy indefinitely. Pieces of the strategy, however, are necessary components to any American defense posture in a world where Pakistan's full cooperation is not – and can never be – assured. The question is whether Washington could implement a version of the strategy in ways that would improve U.S. defenses while holding out the possibility for better relations with Islamabad over time. That issue will be revisited at the end of the chapter.

MILITARY-FIRST SECURITY COOPERATION

In Beijing, Chinese government officials and policy analysts – who are all more or less affiliated with the state and work hard to toe the party line – are more than happy to lecture American visitors about how the Pakistanis hate to be lectured. Undoubtedly, projecting some of their own frustrations with the United States and perhaps reflecting more than a little time spent talking with Pakistanis like General Baig, the Chinese explain that Pakistanis worry a lot about saving face. They stress that public hectoring is precisely the wrong way to seek leverage with the politicians in Islamabad or the generals in nearby Rawalpindi. For the most part, the Chinese practice what they preach on this score. Public Chinese scolding of Pakistan is exceedingly rare; exceptions to the rule send shockwaves through Pakistan's media.[26]

Some Chinese analysts even go so far as to blame the United States for destabilizing Musharraf's military regime, which had been a trusted friend and comfortable partner for Beijing.[27] Wrong as this interpretation of Pakistani history might be, it reveals Beijing's underlying bias in favor of the "stability" born of government repression. Although China has accommodated Pakistan's civilian governments, it is whispered in Beijing and Islamabad that China always preferred Musharraf and the army.

The Chinese claim that democratic practices in Pakistan are destabilizing for some of the same reasons as they fear democracy in China. As far as it is possible to gauge views in an authoritarian country, China's South Asia analysts appeared to read the 2008 return of Pakistan's civilian rule as a passing fad more than a first step toward the consolidation of anything resembling stable

---

[26] Two recent examples are illustrative: first, following the 2011 terrorist attacks in Kashgar, Xinjiang Province, China, local Chinese officials complained about the role of Pakistan-based terror groups (see Michael Wines, "China Blames Foreign-Trained Separatists for Attacks in Xinjiang," *New York Times*, August 1, 2011, http://www.nytimes.com/2011/08/02/world/asia/02china.html?_r=2&pagewanted=all); second, Prime Minister Gilani's offer for China to assume management of Pakistan's Gwadar port was summarily rejected by Beijing. For more, see Michael Wines, "Pakistan and China: Two Friends Hit a Bump," *New York Times*, May 26, 2011, http://www.nytimes.com/2011/05/27/world/asia/27beijing.html.

[27] Author interviews in Beijing, April 2011.

democracy. All told, China's official self-perception and its prevailing biases about Pakistan combine to favor a military-to-military relationship.

The same cannot be said for the United States. Americans are inherently uneasy with undemocratic states that do not respect the sovereignty of the people. By and large, Americans also accept the dictum that democracies avoid wars with each other.[28] Even though many Pakistanis accuse Washington of preferring to deal with their generals rather than their politicians, history suggests otherwise. The dominance of Pakistan's military has marred and complicated even the best periods of cooperation with the United States dating all the way back to the earliest stages of the U.S.-Pakistan relationship described in Chapter 3. No American president likes to be charged with coddling dictators. U.S. relations with relatively liberal Pakistanis (like the renowned lawyer Aitzaz Ahsan) have also suffered as a consequence of the periods in Pakistani history when Washington's aid buttressed the ruling generals.

The Bush administration's fumbling during the Musharraf era was an excellent case in point. As Chapter 4 reveals, the White House publicly professed a commitment to promoting democracy. Privately, however, the president was determined to honor his pledge not to undermine Musharraf. This balancing act was ultimately unsustainable. As Musharraf's regime collapsed, Washington was caught betwixt and between, unable to condone the sort of ruthless crackdown that might have permitted Musharraf to maintain his grip on power and yet unwilling to offer a full-throated call for him to step aside in favor of elected civilians.

Some U.S. relationships with undemocratic regimes – including the close partnership with Saudi Arabia – withstand their inherent unpopularity in Washington because the stakes are high and appreciated by the public. Could Washington overcome its reluctance and again adopt a "Chinese-style" working relationship with Pakistan? The answer is a qualified yes.

The Bush administration chose a military-first strategy for most of its term and would have stayed the course if not for unexpected political changes wrought by Pakistanis themselves. Later, after Musharraf left the stage, it did not take long for the Obama administration to start dealing directly with Pakistan's generals. However much Obama's national security team might have wished to signal support to Pakistan's civilian leaders and take a principled stand in favor of democracy, they recognized that all major security issues were still the bailiwick of the military. Pakistan's army fiercely resisted the attempts by civilian politicians to assert control over foreign and defense policy. Washington had little to say in the matter.[29]

---

[28] This dictum is supported by political theory that traces its roots to Immanuel Kant and by a generation of scholarship on the so-called Democratic Peace. For more, see Michael W. Doyle, "Liberalism and World Politics," *American Political Science Review*, 80, no. 4 (December 1986), pp. 1151–69.

[29] Three examples from the 2008–9 period are illustrative of the massive power disparity between Pakistan's civilian government and military. First, President Zardari was overruled by the military when he tried to revise Pakistan's nuclear security doctrine through offering India a "no first

The Obama administration also maintained quiet military-to-military links and CIA-ISI ties even through some of the darkest days of 2011 and 2012. Pakistan still kept its prized F-16 jets flying with American support, even when much of Washington's military assistance was suspended and many of its personnel and contractors were forced to leave Pakistan.[30] Most revealingly, over the course of the seven months that Pakistan closed its ground supply routes to Afghanistan, U.S. planes continued to shuttle personnel and equipment across Pakistani airspace.[31]

These examples suggest that if military officials in Washington and Islamabad agree to work together without fanfare, they can make progress even on issues that are politically sensitive. Nuclear security cooperation has always fallen into this category. From the start, U.S. officials have recognized that publicizing the nature of American assistance would jeopardize cooperation since anti-American critics in Pakistan would portray it as part of a plot to compromise the nuclear program. Washington left it to Lieutenant General Khalid Kidwai, the long-serving head of the army's Strategic Plans Division, which manages the nuclear arsenal, to brief the public on security measures and to explain the nature of U.S. assistance in his own terms.[32]

This is not to suggest that a military-first strategy is already being followed by Washington. Contrary to the Obama administration's approach, a Chinese-style strategy with Pakistan would mean refraining from sharp public criticism of Pakistan's military. Instead, Washington would curry favor with the military by deferring to its authority inside Pakistan. Rather than using U.S. aid to bolster democratically elected leaders – as envisioned in the Kerry-Lugar-Berman legislation described in Chapter 5 – Washington would step back and allow the army a greater say in directing the flow of U.S. assistance dollars. When possible, funds would support military-backed construction projects, such as

use" guarantee (Michael Traub, "Can Pakistan Be Governed?" *New York Times*, March 31, 2009, http://www.nytimes.com/2009/04/05/magazine/05zardari-t.html?pagewanted=all). Second, just hours after Prime Minister Gilani announced that Pakistan's Inter-Services Intelligence directorate (ISI) would be brought under the control of the civilian Interior Ministry, the government reversed its decision under pressure from the military (M. Ilyas Khan, "Spy Agency Confusion in Pakistan," *BBC*, July 28, 2008, http://news.bbc.co.uk/2/hi/south_asia/7528592.stm). And third, the civilian government was forced to retract its public offer to send General Ahmed Shuja Pasha, head of the ISI, to India in the wake of the 26/11 Mumbai attacks when the Pakistani military objected (Jane Perlez and Salman Masood, "Pakistanis Deny Any Role in Attacks," *New York Times*, November 29, 2008, http://www.nytimes.com/2008/11/30/world/asia/30pstan.html).

[30] Eric Schmitt and Jane Perlez, "U.S. Is Deferring Millions in Pakistani Military Aid," *New York Times*, July 9, 2011, http://www.nytimes.com/2011/07/10/world/asia/10intel.html?pagewanted=all.

[31] Kamran Yousaf, "Pakistan Secretly Permitting Lethal NATO Supply via Air," *Express Tribune*, July 1, 2012, http://tribune.com.pk/story/401852/pakistan-secretly-permitting-lethal-nato-supply-via-air/.

[32] Simon Cameron-Moore, "Pakistan Seeks to Allay Fears on Nuclear Security," *Reuters*, January 26, 2008, http://www.reuters.com/article/2008/01/26/idUSISL66546.

roads and other much-needed infrastructure, which would serve the dual purpose of promoting development and enhancing the military's standing with the Pakistani public.[33]

In closed-door negotiations, the United States would use high-tech military equipment as a bargaining chip. Pakistani officers know that when it comes to blunting India's advantages in conventional weaponry, especially in the skies, the United States is their best option. Pakistan's JF-17 jets (jointly manufactured with China) do not hold a candle to upgraded U.S. F-16s.[34] This will remain true for years to come. Other U.S. equipment, like P-3 Orion surveillance aircraft, also offers anti-India defensive capabilities that Pakistan would otherwise find difficult to match. Along the Afghan border, U.S. drones have provided real-time overhead imagery to the Pakistani military, leaving Pakistanis awestruck and clamoring to have similar drones for themselves.[35]

Unfortunately, dangling the carrot of new military technologies has never been enough of an incentive to get the Pakistanis to change their fundamental security strategies. Then again, before the relationship took a nosedive in 2011, U.S. inducements did yield incremental, constructive changes in Pakistani policies. For example, by improving Pakistan's ability to wage a counterinsurgency campaign with new training and tools like helicopters and night vision goggles, troops based along the Afghan border were better able to take on militants who had challenged the writ of the state.

These enhanced capabilities were on display in March 2010, when Pakistani troops finally managed to flush Pakistani Taliban (TTP) forces from the area around the town of Khar, in Bajaur agency. That offensive was part of a broader campaign in Pakistan's tribal areas bordering the Afghan province of Kunar. A couple of months later, it was still very easy to see how well-fortified the militant stronghold along the brush-covered ridges overlooking the town had been. Back in 2006, rumors swirled that al-Qaeda leader Ayman al-Zawahiri took shelter there.[36]

The complex included fortress-like buildings as well as a warren of tunnels dug deep into the hills. The dark and dusty passageways had obviously offered refuge to militants for many years. Some of the tunnels were spacious, littered with whatever the occupants had left in their haste, from colorful bed linens to sandals. Just outside one entryway an old clock sat in the dirt, forever stopped at three thirty-five.

[33] Kamran Yousaf, "Kayani Initiates USAID Project in S Waziristan," *Express Tribune*, June 19, 2012, http://tribune.com.pk/story/395817/kayani-initiates-usaid-project-in-s-waziristan/.

[34] "The FC-1/JF-17 'Thunder' – The History and Design Philosophy," Defencetalk.com, June 20, 2004, http://www.defencetalk.com/the-fc-1jf-17-thunder-the-history-and-design-philosophy-part-1-2725/#ixzz21lQ9eUPF.

[35] Jane Mayer, "The Predator War," *The New Yorker*, October 26, 2009.

[36] Carlotta Gall, "Airstrike by U.S. Draws Protests from Pakistanis," *New York Times*, January 15, 2006, http://www.nytimes.com/2006/01/15/international/asia/15pakistan.html?pagewanted=all.

A Pakistani colonel proudly described how his forces had hammered the militants and how, as part of their wider counterinsurgency campaign, they had convinced the local tribesmen to fight on the army's side. Although U.S. military assistance did not factor into the colonel's briefing that day, a subsequent conversation back in Peshawar clarified that American training, funds, and equipment had improved the paramilitary Frontier Corps that waged those battles.[37] These were changes that Pakistan's top army officers favored, but without U.S. insistence and resources they might never have been implemented. The results served both U.S. and Pakistani interests.

If U.S. officials again aim to build trust with Pakistan's military, they could attempt to implement a policy process similar to that of the Bush administration during its early years, when Secretary of State Colin Powell could, as he put it, speak "general to general" with Musharraf.[38] At that time, Powell and his team set much of U.S. policy and also managed the diplomatic relationship. This gave Musharraf confidence that when he spoke to Powell, he understood where the Bush administration stood.

In addition to discussions at the very top of the military hierarchy, Washington could seek to maintain and expand exchanges and educational opportunities for rising Pakistani officers so as to encourage comfortable working relationships in the future. In the past, these programs have at least fostered familiarity with the United States, if not necessarily sympathy. Considering the other anti-Western influences that buffet Pakistani society and the fact that some groups like Hizb ut-Tahrir (HuT) are specifically targeting the military for infiltration and indoctrination (as described in Chapter 2), Washington could at least attempt to cultivate a greater appreciation for the potential benefits of U.S. partnership among a core of elite officers.

A military-first relationship with Pakistan could also serve Washington's broader regional interests. An improvement in Indo-Pakistani relations is unrealistic without the consent of Pakistan's generals, but at least some of them have managed to put aside their hostility with India long enough to recognize that a cold peace would be better than another hot war. Accepting this logic, Musharraf's military regime pursued a backchannel dialogue with New Delhi that made unprecedented progress, at least according to Pakistani sources close to the talks. If not for Musharraf's downfall, it seemed as if a breakthrough deal on Kashmir might have been achieved.[39] Part of the reason that President Musharraf was willing to engage in a serious dialogue with India was the simultaneous pressure he felt from the United States and China. U.S. influence in Pakistan may never again be as strong as it was during Musharraf's tenure,

[37] Eric Schmitt and Jane Perlez, "U.S. Unit Secretly in Pakistan Lends Ally Support," *New York Times*, February 22, 2009, http://www.nytimes.com/2009/02/23/world/asia/23terror.html.
[38] On the Powell-Musharraf relationship, see Chapter 4.
[39] Steve Coll, "The Back Channel," *The New Yorker*, March 2, 2009, http://www.newyorker.com/reporting/2009/03/02/090302fa_fact_coll.

but a close military-to-military relationship would offer U.S. officials access to their Pakistani counterparts and the opportunity to argue the benefits of normalized relations with India.

A good working relationship with Pakistan's generals has also proven invaluable in times of crisis.[40] The Indo-Pakistani relationship will have its ups and downs, but another military standoff remains a distinct possibility. Only the United States has had sufficient power or influence to calm the two sides. Even an increasingly powerful China will not likely enjoy enough of India's trust to play a similar role.

Retaining and expanding ties with the Pakistani military would also help Washington keep a close eye on Chinese military and economic activities inside Pakistan. Questions will persist about China's long-term intentions in the region, but it is beyond doubt that Beijing is extending its influence in Pakistan and throughout Central Asia by way of diplomacy, trade, and investment. Chinese support to Pakistan's nuclear, missile, and conventional military programs will be more apparent to Washington if U.S. officials retain working relationships with their Pakistani counterparts, even if the information is gleaned indirectly.

Finally, close ties with Pakistani generals would come in handy if China decides to pursue a more aggressive regional strategy in the future. Pakistan's generals would at least have the option to demur if China seeks to "Finlandize" their country. No matter how much they tend to profess their affection for China, Pakistanis actually have no greater interest in suffering under Beijing's yoke than Washington's. As one astute Pakistani officer explained in a moment of candor, Islamabad would much prefer to squeeze benefits from both China and the United States than to pick one over the other.[41] Recognizing this, U.S. officials have less to fear from Pakistan playing the "China card," and more to gain by offering an alternative to Beijing's dominance in the region.

Dangerous Side Effects

A military-first approach toward Pakistan suffers, however, from the crucial fact that the army has never run the country very effectively. The generals have never even managed to set Pakistan on the path to better governance, unlike celebrated strongmen in other countries such as Turkey or Singapore.

Instead, each bout of military dictatorship has eaten away at the other administrative sinews of the state, from the parliament to the police. Authority undermined, resources deprived, it is no wonder that Pakistan's civilian administration is a hollow, often corrupt, shell. Faced with the stresses of population growth, environmental degradation, and urbanization, Pakistan's civilian

---

[40] Daniel Markey, "Terrorism and Indo-Pakistani Escalation," Council on Foreign Relations Press, January 2010, http://www.cfr.org/india/terrorism-indo-pakistani-escalation/p21042.

[41] Author conversation, Washington, DC, April 2010.

authorities face a near-impossible task. Even under the best of circumstances, they would struggle to contain widespread criminality, extremism, and terrorist violence.

The weakness of Pakistan's civilian leaders is largely the consequence of an overweening military that has too often failed to accept the limits of its power or authority. Yet, the weakness is now a reality. It cannot be wished away. It explains, as described in Chapter 4, why many in Washington believed that working with Musharraf and treading lightly on the issue of democracy was their only option.

It is also the reason that the Obama administration never lived up to the hopes of Pakistan's most idealistic supporters of democracy in the early days after Musharraf was toppled. At the time, these advocates suggested that all dealings with Islamabad – starting with U.S. assistance – should be routed through elected leaders. In effect, they championed a "civilian-first" approach to Pakistan. They believed that U.S. pressure combined with the popular mood in Pakistan would force the generals to see that the tide had truly turned and accept a subordinate role to their civilian masters.[42]

This noble defense of democratic principles struck out against Pakistan's civil-military realities. First, Pakistan's generals were not about to let the civilians have their way. Second, Washington considered its security agenda in Pakistan too urgent to jeopardize with a risky bet on a new crop of politicians. Third, Pakistan's new leaders did nothing to win confidence in the United States.

The third strike was perhaps the most disappointing. When Prime Minister Gilani made his first official visit to Washington in July 2008, he managed a string of gaffes that left American audiences stunned. His performance at a Council on Foreign Relations session in front of several hundred influential journalists, officials, and analysts was literally laughable. Jeers erupted from the audience when Gilani observed without nuance or qualification that the ISI reported to the prime minister, and "Therefore they will do only what I want them to do."[43]

Until Pakistan's civilian leaders demonstrate greater capacity for statesmanship and governance, Washington will be forced to deal with the military. To be clear, this does not make the military any more effective or legitimate in running the state of Pakistan. If the military ever retakes power, it would almost certainly be bad for the country. It would also be bad for the United States.

---

[42] For example, the authors of a prominent Asia Society Task Force released in April 2009 urged Washington to "Reform the way in which the United States deals with the Pakistan military so as to help establish civilian control, and ensure that all U.S. military aid to Pakistan is fully transparent to the civilian authorities and subject to monitoring by both them and the United States." See "Back from the Brink? A Strategy for Stabilizing Afghanistan-Pakistan," April 2009, p. 28, http://asiasociety.org/files/pdf/Afghanistan-PakistanTaskForce.pdf.

[43] "A Conversation with Yousaf Raza Gilani: Transcript," Council on Foreign Relations, July 29, 2008, http://www.cfr.org/pakistan/conversation-yousaf-raza-gilani/p16877.

Yet Washington's ability to control political developments inside Pakistan is limited. If a new army chief decides to seize the reins of power, American protests are likely to fall on deaf ears, just as they did when the Bush administration counseled Musharraf against imposing a state of emergency, when the Clinton administration criticized Musharraf's coup against Nawaz Sharif, when the Carter administration warned Zia against hanging Bhutto, or when the Eisenhower administration cautioned Ayub about the dangers of heading down an undemocratic path.[44]

The next military dictator need not be any more benign or effective than Musharraf. He could be far less so. By pushing the politicians to the exits and subordinating civilian administrators, another generation of Pakistanis would fail to gain experience in self-rule. The messy – and often corrupt – process of democratic rule is rarely improved without practice. Although a military regime might offer immediate improvements in terms of security or economic growth, without a functioning political system, deeper uncertainty about the future would linger. Pakistan's military regimes have routinely implemented solid plans for seizing power, but never for managing an orderly retreat and transition.

Another military coup would also hurt the military itself. Officers who served under Musharraf, including his successor, General Kayani, learned this lesson the hard way. Distracted from its professional duties over nearly a decade, the army lost strength, unity, and the respect of the public. All of these trends would be at least as likely the next time around. And the more political a military becomes, the more prone it is to faction and breakdown. Returning to the discussion in Chapter 2, a failure of Pakistan's military would be tantamount to the failure of the state.

In a country traumatized by violence and riven by social, political, and ideological cleavages, any new Pakistani military regime is more likely to be followed by dangerous revolutionary change than by constructive reform or a bright new democratic order. Even a deeply flawed, corrupt, and compromised civilian order actually poses less of a threat to the stability of the Pakistani state than the return of direct military rule.

In spite of these grave risks, Washington could still opt to work with Pakistan's military to achieve what it considers urgent and important short-term security goals. In that case, U.S. policymakers should always remember that another bout of military rule is in no one's best interest. Behind closed doors, American diplomats would need to remind Pakistan's military leadership early and often about the many risks they run by playing politics. Beyond

---

[44] For the Bush administration's struggles, see Condoleezza Rice, *No Higher Honor* (New York: Crown, 2011), pp. 606–7. See Dennis Kux, *Disenchanted Allies: The United States and Pakistan 1947–2000* (Washington: Woodrow Wilson Center Press, 2001), for a look into the efforts by the Eisenhower (pp. 84–5, 97–101), Carter (pp. 236–8), and Clinton (pp. 356–8) administrations.

that, Washington would want to monitor the Pakistani military for signs of eroding unity and politicization, the precursors to institutional breakdown.

In public, U.S. officials would want to keep their dealings with a military regime under the radar, avoiding the example set by President Bush's tight embrace of Musharraf that hurt the White House's credibility as a supporter of democracy and did little to save Musharraf from his fate. Maintaining cooperation would be a difficult trick for any White House to pull off. Members of Congress and critics of the administration would pounce, especially if Pakistan's new military regime imposed draconian or violent measures against its opponents.

In sum, military-first cooperation may offer the best way to address short- and medium-term security concerns, but it should not be mistaken for a long-term solution. Its side effects read like a warning label on a prescription drug: American discomfort and hypocrisy, Pakistani civil-military dysfunction, and the potential for severe instability caused by the politicization of the military. For all of these reasons, it should not be Washington's preferred approach to its relationship with Islamabad. Succumbing to that temptation would represent a tragic repetition of the already costly mistakes of the past.

COMPREHENSIVE COOPERATION

The third option for Washington would be to attempt another round of comprehensive cooperation with Pakistan. Unlike a military-first approach, this would represent a more ambitious strategy of the sort advocated during the early days of the Obama administration.

Congressman Howard Berman and Senator John Kerry explained the basic logic behind comprehensive cooperation in 2009, when Congress rolled out its plan to triple nonmilitary aid to Pakistan. As they put it, their intent was to establish a "foundation for strengthened partnership between the United States and Pakistan, based on a shared commitment to improving the living conditions of the people of Pakistan through strengthening democracy and the rule of law, sustainable economic development, and combating terrorism and extremism."[45]

Comprehensive cooperation takes seriously the notion that the only way to achieve long-term security goals in Pakistan is for its people to build a stable, more healthy society. Measures short of that are, at best, stopgaps. At worst, narrow U.S. policies designed to meet immediate needs actually contribute to Pakistan's instability.

Comprehensive cooperation has few fans left in Washington. The trouble begins with frustration over Pakistan's role in fighting terrorism and the Afghan

[45] Howard L. Berman and John F. Kerry, "Joint Explanatory Statement, Enhanced Partnership with Pakistan Act of 2009," October 14, 2009, http://www.cfr.org/pakistan/joint-explanatory-statement-enhanced-partnership-pakistan-act-2009/p20422.

war, but it does not end there. Smart policy analysts ask whether Washington actually has any realistic chance of "fixing" Pakistan and, for that matter, whether Pakistanis themselves want the country to be fixed. The answer is complicated and uncertain, but prior chapters of this book offer important clues as to what would represent unrealistic American aspirations and what might still be gained from a strategy of comprehensive cooperation.

What is clear from the Obama administration's attempt to ramp up civilian assistance to Pakistan, to maintain close ties with the military, and to engage in a series of diplomatic exchanges or "strategic partnership talks" is that neither U.S. dollars nor rhetoric can turn the tide quickly in Pakistan. Billions in U.S. assistance appear to have carried little weight, either with Pakistan's leaders or its public. Worse, as Chapter 3 shows, the experience of U.S.-Pakistan interaction over decades has contributed to three strands of anti-Americanism, each of which throws up new barriers to cooperation of the sort that might once have been possible. The post-9/11 era has proven no different. If anything, comprehensive cooperation is harder to envision today than it was in 2001. Pakistan is too big, too broken, and too hostile to American influence to be brought into a cooperative, stabilizing U.S. embrace overnight.

Perhaps, however, the United States can successfully tip the scales in favor of Pakistan's reformers over its revolutionaries or build incentives that encourage greater security and diplomatic cooperation even if Washington and Islamabad never completely see eye to eye. When the bar is set just a bit lower — at tipping the scales in ongoing Pakistani political debates rather than wholesale transformation — comprehensive cooperation begins to look like a more sophisticated and realistic proposition. Even so, if the United States opts to take another crack at comprehensive cooperation with Pakistan, Washington would need to change the way it handles all aspects of the relationship, from politics and security to assistance and regional diplomacy.

On the political front, Washington would seek a more constructive role in the context of Pakistan's civil-military imbalance, quite unlike the stance prescribed by a military-first style of cooperation. This need not require a confrontational approach toward the military, which would only jeopardize cooperation in the near term. It would, however, mean staking out a principled and public position on the U.S. preference for elected civilian rule. The purpose of such rhetoric would be to convince Pakistan's own democrats that they have an ally in Washington, not a pro-military adversary.

But declaring U.S. principles won't go far enough when it comes to defending civilian rule in Pakistan. The real way for Pakistan's civilians to assert themselves against the over-dominant military is to demonstrate that they are actually capable of governing in ways that bring tangible benefits to large segments of the population. If a civilian government proved itself in this way, it would also muster public support sufficient to keep the military in its barracks.

This suggests that as part of a comprehensive cooperation strategy, Washington should pay at least as much attention to the practical performance of Pakistan's civilian leaders as to their florid rhetoric about democratic values. Washington should never be in the business of propping up repressive Pakistani leaders – military or civilian – who have little inclination for improving and reforming the country just because they spout "pro-American" rhetoric. Nor should Pakistan's idealistic reformers feel – as they often have – that America stands in their way. The aim of comprehensive cooperation would be to improve Pakistan's prospects over the long haul, not to install unpopular American mouthpieces in Islamabad.

To be sure, this is much more easily said than done. Pakistan's elites will always be better placed to forge ties with American officials, better equipped to argue their case to American audiences, and, one way or another, to shut out other voices of opposition and reform. One way to improve Washington's effort would be for U.S. officials to focus on a set of internationally accepted standards related to good governance, such as progress on the United Nations' Millennium Development Goals related to education, among others. If U.S. assistance were conditioned on progress in these areas, or if its disbursement of U.S. funds required matching Pakistani commitments, incentive structures would be improved on both sides.

Rather than doling out U.S. aid on a tight timetable as a symbolic gesture of support, Washington would make the same resources available over a longer timeframe, and only to Pakistani government agencies and nongovernmental organizations (NGOs) that demonstrate success and can make the case that their work would benefit from outside assistance. Many Pakistani reformers would appreciate a transparent aid process, one that holds Pakistani feet to the fire.

On the security front, many of the cooperative efforts that Washington would undertake in a military-first approach could also be a part of a comprehensive strategy. As in the past, American-made high-technology weapons and U.S. financial support would be used to win influence with Pakistan's generals by demonstrating the tangible benefits of partnership with America.

Unlike a military-first approach, however, U.S. officials would need to temper their dealings with the generals in ways that encourage greater involvement by Pakistani civilians in defense and foreign policy making. The balance is not an easy one to strike, particularly when Pakistan's army is primed to swat down American political interference. The process would have to be gradual and subtle. That said, comprehensive cooperation would not survive a return to military dictatorship in Pakistan, and U.S. officials would need to make that point painfully clear to their Pakistani counterparts.

Beyond the standard military-to-military cooperation, U.S. officials would also attempt to work with Pakistani civilian police forces and even with citizen groups like the Citizens-Police Liaison Committee (CPLC) of Karachi. CPLC was founded in 1990 to help address a range of citizen concerns that were not being handled by the police. The organization maintains extensive crime databases, tracking everything from car thefts to cell phone snatchings. It works directly with families of kidnapping victims to rescue their loved ones. In late 2011, one of these investigations netted the head of the Pakistani Taliban in Karachi.[46]

If Washington could establish a cooperative working relationship with CPLC, American technical and financial assistance could advance the group's crime-fighting agenda. Given the extent to which Pakistan's terrorists and militant groups have found refuge in megacities like Karachi, cooperative U.S. relationships with groups like CPLC would then offer an obvious opportunity to enhance America's counterterror reach throughout Pakistan. Obviously, such relationships would first require the consent of Pakistan's civilian and military leadership to get off the ground.

What then about U.S. aid to Pakistan? Of the three strategies considered here, only comprehensive cooperation takes up the challenge of translating U.S. taxpayer dollars into greater stability inside Pakistan. To pursue this ambitious venture, Washington first needs tangible evidence that its aid offers the prospect of bringing meaningful change.

One example from the past demonstrates how American aid to Pakistan can pay off many times over. U.S. Agency for International Development (USAID) funds helped to establish the Lahore University of Management Sciences (LUMS) in the 1980s. It is now one of the nation's best schools. That investment may not have won a great deal of public recognition, but it did indirectly nurture generations of top Pakistani students who have since gone on to leadership positions in a wide range of fields. Similarly, American contributions to India's various Institutes of Technology in the 1960s helped to build the incubators of computer wizardry that have done so much to drive India's recent economic growth.

The challenge rests in improving USAID's ability to identify new LUMS-type investments: programs that leverage resources to bring about lasting and significant change. Unless USAID retools itself, and quickly, Washington would probably have a better shot at success by channeling at least a portion of its aid dollars through other organizations with greater on-the-ground experience that can devote more time and energy to the task. One possibility would be to place U.S. aid into a trust fund managed with help from the World Bank or another international organization with a more consistent presence in Pakistan. That would offer a transparent, accountable way to ease the workload and danger for USAID staff. In addition, a trust fund would operate outside the annual U.S. budget cycle. As a consequence, the fund's programming would be less politicized and more reliable over the long run.[47]

---

[46] Author conversation with Ahmed Chinoy, CPLC chief, May 2012; for more, see "Three Alleged Taliban Militants Killed in Karachi Encounter," *The News*, December 6, 2011, http://www.thenews.com.pk/TodaysPrintDetail.aspx?ID=10806&Cat=13.

[47] For a version of this argument, see C. Christine Fair, "A Better Bargain for Foreign Aid to Pakistan," *Washington Post*, May 30, 2009, http://www.washingtonpost.com/wp-dyn/content/article/2009/05/29/AR2009052902620.html.

Another option would be to invest in a variety of "portfolio managers" that would diversify the risk to USAID and take responsibility for making the most of its money. One small but impressive example of such an organization is the Acumen Fund. As Acumen's visionary leader, Jacqueline Novogratz, explained during a visit to Washington in 2009, the fund follows a model of "patient capital," which means that Acumen is not looking to turn quick profits.[48] Instead, its goal is to use donor funds to maximize social benefits while building businesses that eventually make money. Part of the reason Novogratz came to Washington in 2009 was to see whether USAID would be willing to help Acumen expand its Pakistan portfolio. Unfortunately, Acumen has so far come away from its many conversations with USAID empty-handed.[49]

The good news is that groups like Acumen have found a number of Pakistani projects worth supporting. Progress is indeed possible in Pakistan, but not always at the speed or in the manner that Americans might hope.

In 1996, a Pakistani-born graduate of Wharton Business School, Roshaneh Zafar, founded the Kashf Foundation, Pakistan's first microfinance bank. Building on the model established by the famous Grameen Bank in Bangladesh, Kashf innovated by directing its tiny loans – up to about a $100 at a time – to women and by working in cities, where microfinance banks had never before succeeded.

Kashf's initial strategy worked, at least until 2008, when a massive bout of loan delinquency brought Kashf to its knees. As Chief Operating Officer Kamran Azim explained in 2012, newly elected civilian politicians opportunistically colluded with borrowers, telling them that they did not need to repay Kashf if they would pay a fraction of what they owed to the politicians instead.[50] Others suggest that Kashf managed the crisis poorly, and that inadequate oversight made the organization susceptible to this crisis in the first place.[51]

Either way, rather than giving up, the leaders of Kashf decided to try out a new lending process. Instead of granting tiny loans to individuals with minimal oversight, they decided to give slightly larger loans to female-owned businesses and treat the loan more like an investment, collecting additional information and collateral at the outset, monitoring progress, and providing simple business training courses to encourage effective practices. The new loans would run into the hundreds of dollars, enabling clients to buy things like sewing machines or livestock.

---

[48] Author conversation, June 4, 2009. For more, see Jacqueline Novogratz, *The Blue Sweater: Bridging the Gap between Rich and Poor in an Interconnected World* (Emmaus, PA: Rodale Books, 2009) and http://www.acumenfund.org.

[49] Author conversation with Acumen officials, Karachi and Lahore, May 2012.

[50] Author conversation, Lahore, May 24, 2012.

[51] Roshaneh Zafar addresses this issue in her essay, "The Conundrum of Microfinance Growth in Pakistan," April 2012, p. 19, http://www.kashf.org/administrator/attachment/file/Publications/TheConundrumofMicrofinanceGrowthinPakistan-RoshanehZafar.pdf.

In the winding lanes of urban Lahore, the Kashf branch office – just a small, unremarkable if slightly shabby building – is a busy place. Women arrive, usually accompanied by husbands or fathers, to apply for loans. They fill out a short worksheet designed to help Kashf personnel assess whether their business plans are viable. All of the information is then keyed into a nearby computer connected to a remote server and loan database.

Nearby, just off a dusty alleyway is the simple two-room home of a Kashf borrower. Newly married, she lives with her husband and mother-in-law. They are retailers of ladies' undergarments. The model is simple: buy wholesale and resell door to door so that modest neighbors need not venture out of their homes. She and her husband are partners and proudly explain that the business is expanding. Their success is not unusual; small-time retailers are doing well in Pakistan's cities. Despite the economy's larger structural problems, Pakistan's urban areas are growing rapidly enough that poor and lower-middle-class strivers can pull themselves up from poverty if they have a decent plan, work hard, and have access to capital. That potential for upward mobility opens peaceful and productive doors to a rising generation.

Just sixty miles to the northeast, an even more revolutionary project is under way at Jassar farm, where owner Shahzad Iqbal believes he has figured out how to improve dramatically the milk yield of Pakistan's 60 million dairy cows (the third largest herd on earth). Unfortunately, due to breeding, care, and environmental conditions, Pakistani cows now yield less than one-fifth the milk of their counterparts in the developed world. By importing bull embryos from outside Pakistan and raising them to stud, Iqbal hopes to engineer a massive genetic "upgrade" in the Pakistani bovine population. If successful, that would translate into a surge in milk production – and business opportunities – for the millions of Pakistani families that own cows.

These innovative projects are risky. But what is encouraging, even inspiring, is that there are so many similar efforts in the works focused on improving healthcare, low-income housing, primary education, and agriculture across Pakistan.[52] Many Pakistanis are working hard to improve their country, their lives, and the fortunes of their children. Some are making real progress and could, with access to greater resources and support, achieve transformative breakthroughs.

Along the Grand Trunk Road, the ancient thoroughfare traversing South Asia that links Kabul to Calcutta, about an hour to the southeast of Islamabad is Gujjar Khan, a provincial town surrounded by villages. There on a hot,

---

[52] For an example of other efforts in the healthcare sector, see the Aman Foundation, http://amanfoundation.org/v2/wp-content/uploads/Aman%20Foundation%20-%20Corporate%20Profile.pdf; in low-income housing, see Saiban, http://www.acumenfund.org/investment/saiban.html; in education, see The Citizens Foundation, http://www.tcf.org.pk/TCFStory.aspx; in agriculture, see Microdrip, http://www.microdrip.pk/aboutus.html; in drinking water, see Pharmagen, http://www.acumenfund.org/investment/pharmagen-healthcare-ltd.html.

dusty day in May 2012, Khaleel Ahmed Tetlay surveyed the scene near a small irrigation reservoir. Low cliffs of a soft clay soil in various hues of brown flanked the water. Here and there, scrub brush dotted the hills, but for the most part the soil was untethered to the land, subject to wind erosion and heavy downpours during the rainy season. Tetlay asked several of the local farmers why the banks of the reservoir were barren. They explained that goats had nibbled away their plantings. "Ah, but this should be a challenge for you, to outsmart the goats," Tetlay teased.

In his sunglasses, FDNY baseball cap, and khakis, the mustachioed Tetlay, who studied agricultural economics in the United Kingdom in the late 1970s, stood apart from the bearded villagers in their traditional cotton tunics. But it was clear that he was very much in his element. He soon shifted the conversation to the farmer who was pumping water from the reservoir to water his fields. The man proudly explained how his crops were far better off than those of his neighbors who still depended upon infrequent rains. The mini-dam that made his irrigation possible was a project of the Rural Support Programmes Network (RSPN). The wisecracking, and in fact rather wise, Tetlay was RSPN's chief operating officer.

Tetlay left his job as an economist in Islamabad and joined the first of the Rural Support Programmes (RSPs) in the 1980s.[53] The RSP was designed to help village communities identify and prioritize their needs, pool their resources, and identify and tap outside funds from the government and other donors to meet shortfalls. By nearly any measure, the model worked. Between 1986 and 1997, infant mortality in the communities of the Northern Areas and Chitral where the RSP was active dropped from 162 per 1,000 to 33 per 1,000. From 1991 to 2001, real per capita income grew by an average of 84 percent. Over that same period, poverty rates dropped from about two-thirds to one-third of the population.[54] Over time, the RSP model was replicated, with both private and state support, to encompass 108 of Pakistan's 131 districts.

Over time, Pakistan's RSPs have produced meaningful change. Standing alongside Tetlay at the irrigation reservoir was his junior colleague, Tariq Nazir. Quieter than Tetlay but quick to laugh, Nazir explained that he started

[53] Based in Pakistan's remote, mountainous regions of Chitral and the Northern Areas (now Gilgit-Baltistan), the program was intended to serve the needs of a large community of Ismailis, an Islamic sect led by His Highness Prince Karim Aga Khan IV, believed by his followers to be a descendant and spiritual successor to the Prophet Muhammad. As part of his extensive philanthropic work the Aga Khan entrusted a pioneering development worker and former civil servant, Shoaib Sultan Khan, to try out a new model of community organization in the desperately poor region. Shoaib drew inspiration from his mentor, Dr. Akhter Hameed Khan, one of South Asia's most famous grassroots organizers, advocates, and development scholars. At the core of their shared philosophy was the idea that poor people can do a great deal for themselves if mobilized and organized.

[54] Stephen F. Rasmussen et al., "Pakistan: Scaling Up Rural Support Programs," pp. 3, 10–11, http://www.microfinancegateway.org/gm/document-1.9.25816/24216_file_rural_support.pdf.

his community organizing in the area nearly two decades earlier. Back then, the same villagers who confidently walked us through a budget briefing and a tour of their newly paved street were hardly able to sit together, much less to pool their resources toward a common aim. Now, he said, the local organizations and their elected representatives are able to manage just about any sort of project.

The women of the community were also making strides. A bright-eyed group, young and old, gathered in a sparsely furnished room to explain their plans for digging a new well. In this part of the world, fetching water is women's work. The women estimated that they each spent about four hours every day walking to and from the existing well. A new well would reduce that to mere minutes, with revolutionary implications for the daily life of half the village. When asked why the well had not been selected as the village's first project, Nazir replied it was probably because the men had organized before the women. "Now the women are catching up," he added with a smile.

The benefits of organizing are social and political as well as economic. On the drive back to Islamabad, Tetlay explained that the successful community organizations represented a challenge to traditional rural politicians who, for generations, have enjoyed virtually unquestioned authority to dispense or pocket development funds from the provincial and national government. Now, grassroots leaders, including women, had a say in selecting development projects. At times, they could even circumvent politicians in soliciting money from the federal government and outside donors.

So far, however, rural politicians have chosen mainly to avoid confrontation. Tetlay likened the situation to the rise of the social welfare state in the West. "Rather than allowing the workers to unite in proletarian revolution as Marx predicted," he explained, "capitalism evolved. The capitalists met enough of labor's demands to save their system. If Pakistani politicians are smart, they will do something similar." Tetlay went on to observe that some communities were already planning town hall meetings before the next national elections, offering them an unprecedented chance to hold their local politicians accountable and to quiz their challengers.

With their demonstrated capacity to improve economic conditions and to change political dynamics in rural Pakistan, the RSPs are but one example of an organization that would benefit from a U.S. strategy of comprehensive cooperation. This is where the United States may be able to tip Pakistan's balance. Since it is the direction of Pakistani society writ large that will ultimately determine the state's stewardship of the nuclear arsenal, the numbers of militants and extremists who choose to take up arms, and the nature of Islamabad's relationships in the region as well as its global outlook, these issues are more than a matter of humanitarian concern.

Of course, Pakistan's innovative businesses and NGOs are only one piece of the development story. Decades ago, as mentioned in the Chapter 1, Washington made massive investments in Pakistan's infrastructure when it helped to build the Tarbela Dam. U.S. officials are well aware that Pakistan desperately needs more hydropower and better management of its water supply. New dams, power plants, and irrigation canals are massive and costly undertakings, but they are also precisely the sorts of projects that can transform a countryside and jump-start economies on a huge scale.

To its credit, Washington has explored the idea of helping to finance the construction of Pakistan's long-delayed Diamer Bhasha dam.[55] That project, if successful, could represent a signature "made in America" contribution with tangible as well as political benefits. When complete, the dam would generate 4,500 megawatts of electricity, roughly 1,000 more than the mammoth Tarbela.[56] To date, financing challenges have slowed land acquisition, not to mention construction.[57] Other political and diplomatic challenges await, but there is little question that Washington could tip the scales by its contributions and leverage with other international funders like the World Bank.[58]

Aside from direct assistance, Washington has failed to capitalize on the potential economic benefits of freer trade or incentivized private sector investment. Since 9/11, nearly every American report on policy toward Pakistan has advocated a reduction in U.S. tariffs on Pakistani-made textiles and garments.[59] The move would not hurt American consumers or producers. Nevertheless, Capitol Hill has never taken the issue seriously. By some estimates, congressional inaction has cost Pakistan well over a million jobs in volatile cities like Karachi.[60] A decade of job losses of that magnitude, even in such an enormous city, is no small matter. If a Pakistan-only trade deal remains impossible, perhaps a South Asia-wide plan would win more congressional support. India might profit more from such an arrangement than Pakistan, but the only real losers would be low-cost Chinese manufacturers.

Similarly, Congress has resisted calls to establish an "enterprise fund" for Pakistan that would extend loans and make equity investments in Pakistani

---

[55] Zafar Bhutta, "Raising Finance: U.S. Proposes Securitisation of Dam's Assets," *Express Tribune*, October 24, 2012, http://tribune.com.pk/story/455906/raising-finance-us-proposes-securitisation-of-dams-assets/.

[56] Saeed Shah, "U.S. Support for Pakistan Dam Could Help Stem Flow of Bad Blood," *The Guardian*, August 29, 2011, http://www.guardian.co.uk/world/2011/aug/29/us-pakistan-dam-funding.

[57] "Potentially Electrifying," *Economist*, October 19, 2011, http://www.economist.com/blogs/banyan/2011/10/new-dam-pakistan.

[58] Shahbaz Rana, "Diamer-Bhasha: WB Links Dam's Funding to Indian Agreement," *Express Tribune*, June 26, 2012, http://tribune.com.pk/story/399281/diamer-bhasha-wb-links-dams-funding-to-indian-agreement/.

[59] See *U.S. Strategy for Pakistan and Afghanistan*, Independent Task Force Report No. 65 (New York: Council on Foreign Relations Press, 2010), pp. 38–9, 48–50, and *The Next Chapter: The United States and Pakistan*, Pakistan Policy Working Group (Washington, DC: United States Institute of Peace, 2008), p. 32.

[60] "2010: US Embassy Pushed for Pakistan Textiles in Free-Trade Agreement," *Dawn*, June 7, 2011, http://dawn.com/2011/06/07/2010-us-embassy-pushed-for-pakistan-textiles-in-free-trade-agreement/.

businesses. Shortly after the collapse of the Soviet Union, similar U.S. funds for the newly independent countries of Eastern and Central Europe encouraged business growth and, in most cases, the loans were repaid in full.[61] In 2012, the U.S. embassy in Islamabad announced a new "Pakistan Private Investment Initiative," intended to deliver many of the same benefits.[62] Expanded versions of these sorts of programs would help to spur growth in Pakistan's small and medium-sized businesses, which would in turn stimulate exports and create new jobs.[63]

In short, U.S. assistance might be better used to assist Pakistani development, grow its economy, and contribute to the nation's stability in ways that also serve the American interest. Many of these efforts would be smarter than channeling millions of dollars directly into the Pakistani government, where the money provides a budgetary cushion to politicians unwilling to raise taxes or charge market rates for power and, at the same time, becomes invisible to Pakistani citizens who are already so deeply skeptical about the value of American partnership.

Finally, a comprehensive U.S. approach to cooperation with Pakistan offers the greatest diplomatic opportunity to support and encourage improved Indo-Pakistani ties, clearly the best way to stabilize Pakistan's economy and society over the long run. By hitching its wagon to the giant Indian engine of growth, Pakistan's massive population can claw its way out of poverty.[64]

The history of American diplomatic efforts to mediate between India and Pakistan suggests that subtle encouragement and nurturing of Indian and Pakistani initiatives is more likely to pay dividends than public pressure. Washington will never have enough influence to force either side to take conciliatory steps or to accept a settlement by diktat. Americans must recall that these are issues over which both Indians and Pakistanis have been willing to fight and die for decades.

The name of the game, therefore, is quiet lobbying. In Pakistan, businessmen are typically the most supportive voices for a normalized relationship with their Indian neighbors. Although in some sectors like pharmaceuticals

---

[61] For more on enterprise funds, see http://www.innovations.harvard.edu/showdoc.html?id=2364342.

[62] "New Investment Initiative Launches in Pakistan with Up to $80 Million of U.S. Funding," Press Release, U.S. Embassy, Islamabad, September 14, 2012, http://islamabad.usembassy.gov/pr_091312d.html; and for background, see Dustin Cathcart, Meredith Gloger, and Aaron Roesch, "Recommendations for the Pakistan Private Investment Initiative," John F. Kennedy School of Government, Harvard University, May 2012, http://www.innovations.harvard.edu/cache/documents/23643/2364342.pdf.

[63] See Polly Nayak, "Aiding without Abetting: Making U.S. Civilian Assistance to Pakistan Work for Both Sides," Woodrow Wilson International Center for Scholars, 2011, p. 37, http://www.wilsoncenter.org/sites/default/files/WWC%20Pakistan%20Aiding%20Without%20Abetting.pdf.

[64] On the mutual Indo-Pakistani benefits of enhanced bilateral trade see, for instance, Sayem Ali and Anubhuti Sahay, "Pakistan-India Trade – Peace Dividend," *Global Research*, Standard Chartered, June 7, 2012.

they fear Indian competition, most relish the thought of cracking into India's vast and growing market. Joint ventures with Indian counterparts would open new and lucrative vistas for Pakistanis who have tapped out their domestic market and find it difficult to work in China or the Middle East.[65]

In late 2011, Pakistan's business community supported moves by Islamabad to expand cross border trade by granting Most Favored Nation status to India.[66] In return, New Delhi moved to allow greater Pakistani direct investment in India. The positive response was immediate. For example, the Nishat group, one of the largest conglomerates in Pakistan, jumped at the opportunity, announcing that it had applied to open Indian branches of its Muslim Commercial Bank.[67]

It is in Washington's interest to support the natural inclinations of Pakistan's business community, at least with respect to deepening their ties with India. Only a strategy of comprehensive cooperation would permit this sort of involvement. Washington might, for instance, enact specific U.S. trade policies designed to promote trade and investment between all three countries, or invest in infrastructure projects like roads, ports, and rail lines, designed to link India and Pakistan.

By building a comprehensive cooperation with Pakistan, Washington would stand a better chance of avoiding scenarios – as described in Chapter 6 – in which closer U.S. ties with New Delhi translate into greater tensions with Islamabad and, in a worst case, spark conflict with Beijing as well. If the United States can find a way to work with both India and Pakistan, Washington will also be better placed to keep an eye on Chinese activities throughout the region and, if necessary, to compete with Beijing for influence. Cooperation with Pakistan's business community and civilian officials – in addition to relationships with the Pakistani military – would open windows to developments on the ground that would otherwise escape American notice.

Tipping the Balance... Slightly

The clearest shortcoming of a comprehensive cooperation strategy is that it takes two to tango. America's outreach and aid to Pakistan cannot work without willing partners on the other side. Washington can, for instance, fund the

---

[65] "Pakistan Businesses Want Trade Barriers to India Cut," *Indo-Asian News Service*, http://in .news.yahoo.com/pakistan-businesses-want-trade-barriers-india-cut-134801058.html. On the Indian business community's interest in opening to Pakistan, see Jim Yardley, "Industry in India Helps Open a Door to the World," *New York Times*, March 31, 2012, http://www.nytimes .com/2012/04/01/world/asia/private-sector-helps-propel-india-onto-world-stage.html.

[66] Zeeshan Haider, "Pakistan Grants India Most Favoured Nation Trade Status," *Reuters*, November 2, 2011, http://www.reuters.com/article/2011/11/02/us-pakistan-india-trade-id USTRE7A13VE20111102.

[67] James Crabtree and Farhan Bokhari, "Pakistani Tycoon Targets Indian Banking," *Financial Times*, July 17, 2012, http://www.ft.com/intl/cms/s/0/oaeabe48-cfdd-11e1-a3d2-00144feabdc0 .html#axzz2ot4AlElB.

construction of a Diamer Bhasha Dam, but it cannot fix Pakistan's energy regulations, or reform broken distribution and budgetary practices that today squander power production capacity that Pakistan already has. The best the United States can hope to do with a comprehensive cooperation strategy is to tip Pakistan's balance.

With potential thus measured at the margins, it will be difficult for U.S. leaders to justify the time, political capital, or resources to Pakistan that such a strategic approach would require for success. If present trends hold, it is only a matter of time before the U.S. assistance authorized by the Kerry-Lugar-Berman legislation is scaled back, or perhaps even ended altogether. The U.S. Congress is not likely to continue funneling scarce resources to a Pakistan that has proven decidedly unhelpful in Afghanistan and which has gone out of its way on several occasions to stick a high-profile finger in America's eye – for instance, by jailing the Pakistani doctor who assisted U.S. efforts to find Osama bin Laden.[68]

Moreover, even if Washington's lawmakers and the White House were somehow convinced to take another run at comprehensive cooperation, serious questions would linger about whether the United States is up to the task of turning its dialogues and dollars into constructive change. Patience would be thin from the very beginning.

GRAPPLING WITH DIFFICULT CHOICES

One problem with framing a clear set of three strategic options is that it implies U.S. officials might actually sit down, pick one approach over the others, and stick to it. As a practical matter, Washington is more likely to cobble together a set of policies to address whatever appears to be the most urgent need of the day. This scattershot approach is not unique to Pakistan; it is a reflection of Washington's bureaucratic and institutional rifts as well as competing national priorities. Pakistan's complexity also makes it especially resistant to any single strategy, not to mention that it suffers from never-ending crises that can make long-term plans and investments feel like an exercise in futility.

Yet perpetual crisis management is not a recipe for enduring success in Pakistan. It is more likely to yield confusion, frustration, and disappointment on all sides. Skeptical Pakistanis will draw their own dark conclusions about U.S. motives and policies. Other states in the region will hedge their bets, uncertain of U.S. commitments. Americans too will struggle to explain how the various pieces of U.S. policy fit together.

---

[68] Declan Walsh and Ismail Khan, "New Details Emerge on Conviction of Pakistani Who Aided Bin Laden Search," *New York Times*, May 30, 2012, http://www.nytimes.com/2012/05/31/world/asia/new-details-on-conviction-of-shakil-afridi-pakistani-doctor-who-aided-cia-in-tracking-osama-bin-laden.html.

All of these problems could be swept away if any one of America's strategic options offered the realistic prospect of a bright new future with Pakistan. The reality is that all of the options are flawed. The United States is left with difficult choices. Moreover, those choices will be circumscribed by events inside Pakistan, including the country's selection of new leaders, whether through the normal process of elections and promotions, or the drama of coups and revolutions. To these Pakistani developments, America will have no choice but to respond.

If someone like General Baig, the anti-American former army chief, ever assumes power again in Islamabad, a strategy leaning heavily toward defensive insulation would undoubtedly be Washington's best option. Pakistan would be an adversary, in league with countries like Iran and North Korea, and committed to a policy of standing up to the United States.

Fortunately, we are not living in such a world. Not quite yet. Until we are, the United States should avoid strategies that would accelerate a downward slide in U.S.-Pakistan relations by playing into Pakistan's worst fears and tendencies. Retreating to an increasingly unilateral, coercive, and India-centric approach would do exactly that.

A military-first approach to Pakistan would also do more harm than good. It is clear that Pakistan's civilian leaders are no paragons of virtue; even their commitment to democratic principles can be called into question. Yet no white knight on horseback has ever saved Pakistan from misrule for very long. Washington should not forget the debacle of Musharraf's final years or fall victim to the false hope that the next general will have a formula for governing Pakistan that his uniformed predecessors, from Zia back to Ayub, did not.

Even more frightening, the enticing short-term gains from military rule – unity of command, efficiency, reduced corruption – pale in comparison to the corrosive effects of politicizing the military, an institution whose professionalism is central to its legitimacy and whose unity is central to national stability. Whenever the Pakistani army plays politics, it plays a dangerous game that could end in bloody revolution. That would be a tragedy for millions of Pakistanis. It would endanger any security gains that Washington was seeking from military cooperation in the first place.

Finally, although USAID officials may point to ongoing development projects throughout Pakistan and eager diplomats on both sides may express their desire to reengage in dialogue after a trying couple of years, the reality is that comprehensive cooperation of the sort envisioned in the early Obama years died with bin Laden, if not before.[69] Senators and representatives in Washington are more inclined to consider legislation to end assistance to Pakistan than

---

[69] For an example of this eager rhetoric, see Secretary of State Hillary Clinton's remarks in July 2012 in "Hillary Clinton Looks for Hope with Pakistan," *Associated Press*, July 8, 2012, http://www.politico.com/news/stories/0712/78200.html.

to debate how best to improve or reform USAID's efforts.[70] Most of Pakistan's politicians also view U.S. partnership as radioactive. It is not hard to imagine that Islamabad might play to public sentiment and reject U.S. partnership and assistance programs altogether, following the example set in May 2011 by Shahbaz Sharif, chief minister of Punjab and brother of Prime Minister Nawaz Sharif.[71]

Flawed as any of America's options are, any one of them would be better than chasing the mirage of a clean escape from Pakistan and its troubles. To be sure, the United States could pull its military, intelligence, and diplomatic officials out of Pakistan. For a time, U.S. officials could even willfully ignore or neglect Pakistan, hoping that its nuclear arsenal, violent extremists, burgeoning population, and tense regional relationships would all sort themselves out without threatening important American interests. Yet nothing about Pakistan's history or likely future trajectory could reasonably lead to that conclusion. One way or another, America will be forced to grapple with the challenges posed by Pakistan, even if that means selecting from a slate of unattractive policy options.

A Glimmer of Hope

If short-term crisis management is a bad idea and each of Washington's main options is unappealing, might there still be a constructive way to deal with this mess? There is. But the prescription is neither especially neat nor entirely satisfying.

The United States should begin by recognizing that Pakistan is not a lost cause. It is more like a race that must be run as a marathon rather than a sprint. American timelines and expectations need to reflect Pakistan's scale and complexity. The next generation of Americans will come of age in a world where al-Qaeda may be history and the U.S. war in Afghanistan is but a dim memory, but by mid-century Pakistan will grow to be the world's fourth largest (and largest majority-Muslim) country, sitting nuclear-armed on the border of two other Asian giants, China and India. The threats posed by a giant Pakistani spoiler state in an increasingly important neighborhood cannot be ignored, but they may have to be managed or mitigated rather than solved.

Along the way, U.S. policymakers should seek to determine which pieces of defensive insulation, military cooperation, and comprehensive cooperation can be combined so as to maximize the strengths inherent to each approach. In

---

70 See, for instance, Manu Raju and Tomer Ovadia, "Paul May Hold Up Senate over Pakistan," *Politico*, July 12, 2012, http://www.politico.com/blogs/on-congress/2012/07/paul-may-hold-up-senate-over-pakistan-128794.html.

71 "It's Time to Say 'No' to Foreign Aid: Shahbaz Sharif," *Express Tribune*, May 17, 2011, http://tribune.com.pk/story/169730/no-to-foreign-aid-for-punjab-shahbaz-sharif/.

other words, they should ask the following question: What mixture of policies will best allow the United States to prepare for the worst, aim for the best, and avoid past mistakes?

Preparing for the worst means, for instance, investing in new technologies, including next-generation drones, that would help the United States conduct certain counterterror operations inside Pakistan even if Islamabad turns increasingly hostile; continuing to build America's homeland defenses; improving international controls on the flow of money, weapons, and people that support terrorist networks; and contemplating what sorts of military and diplomatic relationships with Pakistan's neighbors, especially Afghanistan and India, would be needed in the event that Pakistan takes a slide toward deeper instability. In sum, Washington must adopt important pieces of the defensive insulation strategy in order to protect its people and interests.

Aiming for the best means pursuing all of those steps only so far as is possible without slamming the door on U.S.-Pakistan cooperation. That will be a tricky balance. Aiming for the best also means seizing opportunities to support Pakistanis who are already working hard to promote development and peace inside their own society; encouraging Indo-Pakistani normalization as the best way to grow the Pakistani economy and enhance the nation's stability; cultivating better working relationships between military and intelligence on both sides; and bearing in mind that Pakistan's society is a remarkably youthful one, so investments in that rising generation will have the potential to take Pakistan along a different and more positive trajectory than it has traveled for its first six decades. In sum, this means pursuing comprehensive cooperation when possible, with the goal of tipping the balance toward stability inside Pakistan and improved U.S.-Pakistan ties over time.

Avoiding past mistakes means studying the history of the U.S.-Pakistan relationship and recognizing that many present dilemmas bear more than a passing resemblance to earlier predicaments. In particular, it means appreciating the dangers inherent in over-reliance on Pakistan's military and repressive, often corrupt, civilian elites without overestimating the capacity of the Pakistani reformers; avoiding statements and policies that irritate and humiliate without the prospect of delivering a powerful coercive blow; and never forgetting that Pakistani leaders will calculate their interests for themselves, often in ways that are frustratingly at odds with our own perspectives and preferences.

At present, the ideal mix of U.S. strategies should tilt toward defensive insulation. This is true for both political and strategic reasons. Politically, Washington should not waste energy attempting new and ambitious cooperative ventures with Islamabad that would only prove unpopular in both capitals. Strategically, U.S. concerns about the endgame in Afghanistan, Islamabad's persistent attachment to violent extremist organizations such as LeT, and the fact that Pakistan may lurch into greater internal instability or anti-American hostility all mean that America's leaders must, first and foremost, gird against security threats.

To be clear, however, a tilt toward defensive insulation does not mean a wholesale embrace of that strategy. Washington should also keep the door open to other strategies over the next several years. If, for instance, Pakistan's military shows itself willing to tackle threats of extremism and internal disorder (as Army Chief Kayani stated was the need of the hour in an August 2012 address to the nation), that would begin to re-open prospects for greater military cooperation.[72] Similarly, if Pakistan's elected civilian leaders choose to renegotiate the terms of their relationship with the United States rather than simply playing to the public's anti-Americanism, they should find allies in Washington willing to explore cooperative ventures that serve long-term U.S. interests.

These basic guidelines for American strategy still provide cold comfort for anyone who seeks an easy solution to Pakistan. They cannot promise success, nor even offer a full guarantee against failure. Yet this is the tragic nature of the circumstance in which the United States is trapped, much like one of Sartre's characters in *Huis Clos* described at the outset of this book, with no exit in sight. To understand the nature of the U.S.-Pakistan relationship and to calibrate our expectations, it helps to adopt a tragic sensibility. The situation may be bad, but it could always get even worse.

Yet Sartre's play does not end with despair. Instead, his characters resolve to "get on with it." The mood is reminiscent of my many conversations with Pakistanis and Americans who have devoted themselves to improving ties between Washington and Islamabad, and more broadly, to building bridges between the people of Pakistan and the United States. Sometimes, it is difficult to understand what could possibly motivate the passion and dedication these individuals bring to their cause, especially when the glimmer of hope seems so faint and far away. I believe they have realized that over the long run, a strong U.S.-Pakistan relationship offers the only way to save Pakistan from a dark and violent future, the only way to protect America from the dangers that lurk on Pakistani soil. Mindful of the tragic circumstances in which they toil, they toil nonetheless. In so doing, they offer hope to the rest of us.

[72] "Full Text of General Kayani's Speech on Pakistan Independence Day," http://criticalppp.com/archives/227063.

Index

"abandonments" by U.S. in Pakistan, history of, 2–4
Abbas, Athar, 156
Ackerman, Gary, 4
Acumen Fund, 226
Afghanistan
    border closings with Pakistan in, 107–108
    drone strikes in, 153–156
    "economy of force" operation in, 117–118
    India's relations with, 41
    as Indo-Pakistani proxy battleground, 46
    infrastructure investment in, 127n64
    insurgency in, 114–117, 125–129
    "lead nation" approach in, 126n61
    military surge in, 23–24
    opium production in, 126–127
    Pakistan's relations with, 8, 18–22, 40, 163, 169–172, 200–202, 214–222
    Pakistan-U.S. disagreement over, 202–204
    proposed U.S. withdrawal from, 204–206
    Soviet invasion of, 90, 92–93, 94n76, 103, 200–202
    Taliban in, 18–22, 40, 52, 114, 125–129, 202–204
    U.S. "AfPak" strategy and, 161–167
    U.S. surge in, 164–167
    U.S. war in, 11–16, 105–108, 111–112, 125–129
"AfPak" strategy, 161–167
Aga Khan, Karim, 228n53
agricultural programs in Pakistan, 227–229
Ahle Hadith, 54, 99–100
Ahmad, Mahmoud, 111–112

Ahmad, Salman, 60
Ahmadinejad, Mahmoud, 188
Ahsan, Aitzaz, 80–83, 103, 130, 215
Al-Huda school network, 54–55
al-Qaeda
    attacks on Pakistani military by, 69–70
    Bush administration focus on, 23, 110–118
    Christmas bomb plot of, 12
    drone strikes against, 153–156
    Khan's (A. Q.) contact with, 119
    kidnappings by, 149
    Obama administration focus on, 23–24
    in Pakistan, 11–16, 99, 158
    Salafist ideology of, 97
    U.S.-Pakistan cooperation concerning, 7–11, 108–117
al-Shibh, Ramzi, 8
al-Zawahiri, Ayman, 12, 208, 217
anti-Americanism in Pakistan
    Ahsan and, 80–83, 103, 130, 215
    Baig's discussion of, 200–202, 208, 213
    evolution of, 200–202
    historical origins of, 1–4
    jihadist groups and, 73–74, 92–103
    liberal anti-Americanism, 73, 74–83
    nationalist anti-Americanism, 73, 83–92
    perspectives on, 73–103
    policy impacts of, 184, 185–188
    polling data on, 73n3
Anti-Ballistic Missile Treaty, 180–181
Armitage, Richard, 109–110, 110n15, 111n16, 111–112n18, 114, 115, 117

Asia
　China's ascendancy in, 172–178, 188–192,
　　197–199
　India's economic role in, 186–187
　Iraq war and U.S. policy in, 117–118
　Pakistan's role in, 8, 20–22, 187–188
　U.S. policies in, 85, 110–114
assistance programs in Pakistan. *See also*
　　military assistance to Pakistan
　China and, 6–7
　Clinton's (Hillary) comments on, 140
　in Cold War era, 74–76
　comprehensive cooperation strategy and,
　　222–233
　democracy initiatives and, 140–145
　earthquake disaster assistance, 122–123
　"KLB" aid package and, 141–150
　Reagan-era programs, 112
　USAID programs and, 149n44, 145–150,
　　150n44
Aurakzai, Ali Muhammad Jan, 125–126
Avrakotos, Gus, 93–94
Awami League (AL), 78–80
Azim, Kamran, 226–227
Aziz, Tariq, 124–125
Azzam, Abdullah, 100

Baba, Rahman, 170
Baig, Mirza Aslam, 200–202, 208, 213–214,
　　234
ballistic missile defense, U.S.-Indian
　　negotiations concerning, 180–181
Baloch ethnic group, 30–32
Bangladesh
　education levels in, 33–35
　electricity infrastructure in, 36
　formation of, 78–80, 97
　HuT activism in, 57
　India and, 42, 46
　Iraq war and, 117–118
Barelvi school of Islam, 50–51
Beckley, Michael, 175n18
Berehulak, Daniel, 38–39
Berman, Howard, 141–145, 222
Beygairat Brigade, 92
Bhutto, Benazir, 31, 80
　civilian government of, 81
　criticism of U.S. by, 120
　killing of, 99, 133n77, 157
　Musharraf and, 131–133
Bhutto, Zulfikar Ali, 62
　execution of, 96, 221

　nuclear expansion under, 87–90
　political legacy of, 79n31, 80–83
　sectarian identity of, 96, 96n85
　U.S. relations with, 77n21, 77, 83, 85–86
bin Laden, Osama. *See also* al-Qaeda
　as global symbol, 99
　killing of, 5, 8, 11, 23–24, 65, 80, 139, 201
　Pakistan recruiting operations of, 169
Bismarck, Otto von, 41–42
Blackwill, Robert, 180–181
Blank, Jonah, 144
blasphemy claims, Pakistani preoccupation
　　with, 50–53
Brennan, John, 153–154
BRICS summit, 195
Brzezinski, Zbigniew, 94
Burki, Shahid Javed, 186–187
Bush, George H. W., nuclear expansion in
　　Pakistan and, 91–92
Bush, George W.
　al-Qaeda offensive under, 11–16, 23,
　　110–118, 127
　Bhutto (B.) and, 131–133
　China policy under, 175–176
　drone policy under, 153–156
　F-16 aircraft deal with Pakistan and,
　　123–124
　"freedom agenda" of, 118–122
　India's relations with, 179–182, 197
　Iraq war under, 117–118
　Musharraf and, 114–122, 215, 221
　Pakistan policy under, 23, 82, 103–104,
　　109–114, 143n22, 181–182, 215
Butt, Naveed, 57–58

Carter, Jimmy, 87, 90–91
　Pakistan policy under, 91, 95n78, 221
　Soviet invasion of Afghanistan and, 94–95
Central Intelligence Agency (CIA)
　Afghan operations of, 169
　covert operations in Pakistan and, 208–209
　drone strikes and, 153–161
　ISI relations with, 111–112, 137
Chamberlain, Neville, 129
Charlie Wilson's War (film), 93–94
Chaudhry, Iftikhar Muhammad, 80–83, 130
China
　Bhutto's (Z. A.) relations with, 77–78
　Cold War and U.S. relations in, 178–179
　ethnic groups in, 21
　global ascendancy of, 172–175, 175n18,
　　178

India's relations with, 41, 85, 190, 194–195

Pakistan's relations with, 6–10, 20–22, 38–39, 43, 70–71, 85–86, 182–184, 188–189, 189n64, 192

Soviet relations with, 84–85

terrorist attacks in, 214n26

U.S.-Pakistan relations and role of, 182–184, 188–192, 197–199, 214–215, 219

U.S. relations with, 175–178, 188–192, 211

Citizens for Free and Responsible Media, 64

Citizens-Police Liaison Committee (CPLC), 224–225

civilian rule in Pakistan

Bhutto's (Z. A.) legacy of, 79

comprehensive cooperation strategy for, 222–233

democratic initiatives and, 140–145

failures of, 32

military structure and, 215–216n29, 219–220, 220n42, 222

public opinion of, 32n8, 32, 33

U.S. relations with, 83

climate change, impact in Pakistan of, 36–37

Clinton, Bill, 91, 179–182, 221

Clinton, Hillary, 140, 161–162, 166

Cold War

China-U.S. relations and, 178–179

nuclear policy in Pakistan and, 45

surveillance aircraft in, 151

U.S.-Pakistan relations and, 1–4, 5–11, 39, 73–76, 75n9, 83–87, 103–104, 169

comprehensive cooperation strategy, 26–27, 206, 222–235

Constable, Pamela, 67

counterterror operations

Obama administration's focus on, 139, 160–161

U.S.-Pakistan cooperation on, 23–24, 117–118, 125–129, 206–214

Crile, George, 93–94

Crocker, Ryan, 19, 205n11

Crowley, Philip J., 137

cruise missile strikes in Pakistan, potential for, 206–214

Cuban Missile Crisis, 84–85

Davis, Raymond, 136–139, 149, 158, 208–209

Dawn (Pakistani English-language newspaper), 49–50

Defence of Pakistan Council (Difa-e-Pakistan) (DPC), 52, 101–102, 208

defensive insulation strategy

future of U.S.-Pakistan relations and, 235–237

overview of, 26–27, 206–214, 233–235

democracy

Bush's "freedom agenda," 11–12

Democratic Peace Theory, 215n28

Pakistan's experience with, 140–145, 215, 219–222

Deobandism, 54, 97

development projects in Pakistan, 33–35. *See also* assistance programs in Pakistan; economic growth; specific projects, e.g. Tarbela Dam

Diamer Bhasha dam project, 229–230

Dow Medical College, 25–26

drone strikes

classified information about, 160–161

defensive insulation strategy and, 206–214

in Pakistan, 11–16, 23–24, 108, 138, 151–161

Pakistan's debate over, 157–158

post-September 11 policies and, 103, 153–156

U.S. debate over, 154n66, 158–159

Dulles, John Foster, 74–76

Durrani, Asad, 48

earthquake in Pakistan, U.S. aid following, 122–123

East Turkestan Independence Movement (ETIM), 190

economic growth. *See also* financial assistance programs in Pakistan

absence of development with, 33–35

Asian regional policies and, 197–199

comprehensive cooperation strategy for, 225–231

education levels in Pakistan, 33–35

Eikenberry, Karl, 125–126, 127

Eisenhower, Dwight D., 74–76, 221

elections in Pakistan

corruption and rigging of, 47–49, 78–80, 116, 121, 132

reform agenda for, 60–62

electricity infrastructure in Pakistan, 35–38

elites in Pakistan

Al-Huda schools and, 54–55

anti-Americanism among, 80–83

caste system and, 30–32

elites in Pakistan (*cont.*)
  corruption in, 66–67
  future projections concerning, 66
  governing power of, 30
  growth of middle class and, 60–62
  leadership failures of, 37–38
  political challenges to, 68–69
  vulnerability of, 6–7
enterprise funding, proposals for, 230–231
ethno-linguistic groups in Pakistan, 30–32
extremism in Pakistan, 49–55, 66. *See also*
  al-Qaeda; specific extremist groups
  Afghan war and, 93
  ascendancy of, 97n89, 96–98, 98n91, 99
  blasphemy claims and, 50–53
  Hizb ut-Tahrir and, 55–58
  leadership failures concerning, 136–168
  Pakistan's vulnerability to, 69–70
  strength of, 6–7
  terrorist inculation and, 49–50
  U.S.-Pakistani tensions concerning, 202–206

F-16 aircraft, sale to Pakistan of, 91, 95,
  123–124
Facebook, in Pakistan, 63–64
Federally Administrated Tribal Areas (FATA),
  125–129
  drone strikes in, 103, 153–156, 158–159
  as terrorist safehavens, 117–118
flood disasters in Pakistan (2010), 68–69
Ford, Gerald R., nuclear expansion in Pakistan
  and, 90
Foreign Assistance Authorization Act, 145
Friedberg, Aaron, 174
Friedman, Tom, 192

Gates, Robert, 46
Gelb, Leslie, 148
GeoTV, censorship of, 63–64
"Ghairat (honor) Brigade," 92
Ghazi, Abdul Rashid, 131
Gilani, Yousuf Raza, 183, 215–216n29, 220
Glenn, John, 91n65, 91, 92
global economy, Pakistani vulnerability in, 6–7
Goldstone, Jack, 68n146
Grameen Bank, 226–227
Greece, terrorism in, 186
Grossman, Marc, 165
Gul, Hamid, 51–52, 58, 65, 69–70, 101–102,
  183n44, 202
Gwadar port development project, 191–192

Haass, Richard, 109–110, 180–181

Hamid, Zaid, 171
Haq, Sami ul, 52, 69–70
Haqqani, Husain, 120
Haqqani, Jalaluddin, 52, 93
Haqqani network, 19, 46, 52, 105–108
  Pakistan's support for, 155–156, 162–163,
  166–167
  U.S.-Pakistan tensions concerning, 202–206
Hashmi, Farhat, 54–55
Hashmi, Javed, 60–62
Headley, David Coleman, 14, 99, 101, 102
healthcare structure in Pakistan, 33–35, 227
Hekmatyar, Gulbuddin, 93
Hizb ut-Tahrir (HuT), 55–56, 56n103,
  57n107, 58, 69–70, 218
Holbrooke, Richard, 140–145, 147–149, 150,
  165
homeland security in the United States, 207,
  207n12, 210–211
Hoodbhoy, Pervez, 55
Husain, Ed, 57n107
hypernationalism in Pakistan, 38–39, 65,
  171

income levels in Pakistan, 33–34, 228
India
  Afghanistan's relations with, 19, 41
  Bush administration and, 179–182
  China's relations with, 41, 85, 190, 194–195
  Cold War U.S. relations and, 178–179
  economic conditions in, 186n55, 186n56,
  186–187, 192–197
  F-16 aircraft deal with Pakistan and,
  123–124
  Iraq war and, 117–118
  military mobilization in, 185–188
  Musharraf's relations with, 124–125,
  218–219
  Muslim community in, 193
  nuclear weapons in, 43–46, 181–184
  Pakistani investment in, 231–232
  Pakistan's tensions with, 6–8, 20–22,
  39–43, 124–125, 184, 193–194,
  218–219
  security vulnerabilities of, 185–188, 193
  terrorist attacks in, 14–15, 46, 99–102, 115,
  139–140, 185–188, 193
  "Twin Peaks crisis" in, 115
  U.S.-Pakistani relations and role of, 72–73,
  75, 85–86, 86n52, 182–184, 212, 213,
  231–232
  U.S. relations with, 20–22, 85, 179–182,
  184, 196–199

Indian National Congress, 180
Indo-Pakistani wars, 39, 43, 78, 85–86
    Kargil conflict and, 38, 42–43
    nationalism in Pakistan and, 89
Indus Hospital project, 25–26
infant mortality in Pakistan, 33–34, 228
infrastructure failures in Pakistan, 35–38
Inter-Services Intelligence directorate (ISI)
    China's informational reliance on, 190
    CIA relations with, 111–112, 137, 181–182,
        208–209
    civilian government and, 215–216n29
    Haqqani network and, 155–156
    LeT and, 14–15, 102
    political manipulations of, 47–49, 116
    support for Taliban in, 105–108, 202
investment in Pakistan, comprehensive
        cooperation strategy for, 225–231
Iran
    India's relations with, 196
    Khan (A. Q.) and, 119
    Pakistan's relations with, 187–188, 211
    revolution in, 98
Iraq, U.S. war in, 117–118, 201
Ismaili sect, 228n53
Israel, terrorism in, 186, 187

Jamaat-e-Islami (JI), 54
Jamaat-ud-Dawa (JuD), 52, 99–102
Japan
    Chinese relations with, 174, 176, 189
    infant mortality in, 33
    U.S. relations with, 3, 20, 198
jihadist groups in Pakistan, 73–74,
        92–103
    Red Mosque crisis and, 130–131
Jinnah, Muhammad Ali, 49–50, 66
Johnson, Lyndon B., 83–85
judiciary in Pakistan
    anti-Americanism in, 80–83
    Musharraf's conflicts with, 130
    political activism of, 47–49

Kaplan, Robert, 191–192
Karakoram Highway project, 191, 191n72
Karamat, Jehangir, 88–89
Kargil conflict, 38, 42–43
Karzai, Hamid, 40, 127
Kashf Foundation, 226–227
Kashmir
    India-Pakistan dispute over, 39–43, 77–78,
        124–125, 218–219
    insurgency in, 14, 100

Kargil conflict and, 38, 42–43
    "Twin Peaks crisis" in, 115
Kayani, Ashfaq, 105–106, 106n5, 155–156,
        158, 167–168, 221, 237
Kennedy, John F., 83–85, 86n52
Kerry, John, 133, 137, 141–145, 222
Kerry-Lugar-Berman (KLB) aid package,
        141–150, 216–217, 233
Khalilzad, Zalmay, 127
Khan, Abdul Bari, 25–26
Khan, Abdul Qadeer (A. Q.), 17–18, 87–88,
        88n56, 88n57, 90, 103, 119, 187–188
Khan, Akhter Hameed, 228n53
Khan, Ali, 56n103, 58
Khan, Ayub, 75–76, 82, 85–86, 221
    Bhutto's relations with, 77–78
    on India, 178–179
Khan, Hayat Ullah, 154
Khan, Imran, 15–16
    anti-drone protests and, 157–158
    media as tool for, 64
    popularity of, 58–60, 65
    reform agenda of, 60–62, 68, 70–71
Khan, Kamran, 65
Khan, Munir Ahmed, 88n56
Khan, Shoaib Sultan, 228n53
Khan Research Laboratory (KRL), 87–88
Khrushchev, Nikita, 83–85
Kidwai, Khalid, 216–217
Kissinger, Henry, 86–87, 90, 175
Krasner, Stephen, 122

Lahore University of Management Sciences
        (LUMS), 225
land reform, failure in Pakistan of, 30–32
Lashkar-e-Taiba (LeT), 14–15, 39, 52, 97,
        99–102
    CIA surveillance of, 137
    Mumbai attack by, 46, 99–102, 139–140,
        185–188
    Musharraf and, 114
    Pakistan support for, 69, 163, 205–206
lawyers' movement in Pakistan, 80–83,
        130–131
Libya, nuclear technology in, 18, 187–188
Lieven, Anatol, 66
living standards in Pakistan, 33–35
Lodhi, Maleeha, 60–62, 67, 111–112
Lugar, Richard, 141–145

madrassas in Pakistan, 35, 52, 97
Mao Zedong, 22, 77, 175–176
Mazari, Shireen, 38–39, 65

McChrystal, Stanley, 164n103, 164n104
McMahon, Robert J., 75
media in Pakistan, 62–65, 68–69
  journalist exchange programs and, 64
Megaports Initiative, 210n22
"Mehran men," 60–62
Mehran naval base, attack on, 69–70
Mehsud, Baitullah, 13–14, 99, 157
Mehsud, Hakimullah, 202
"memogate" scandal, 80n32, 107
microfinancing initiatives in Pakistan, 226–227
military assistance to Pakistan, 6–7
  in Cold War era, 74–76
  U.S. policies concerning, 117–118, 120
military-first cooperation strategy, 233–235
  U.S.-Pakistan relations and, 26–27, 214–222
military in Pakistan
  "AfPak" strategy and, 163
  anti-Indian ideology in, 39–43, 218–219
  Bhutto's (Z. A.) civilian control of, 79
  China's dependency on, 190
  civilian government and, 140–145,
    215–216n29, 219–222
  comprehensive cooperation strategy and
    role of, 222–233
  drone strikes supported by, 153–158
  future projections concerning, 66
  garrison mentality of, 38–39
  growth of, 29
  Hizb ut-Tahrir and, 55–58, 218
  Lashkar-e-Taiba and, 14–15, 102
  lawyers' movement against, 80–83
  media censorship by, 63–64
  media criticism of, 65
  Musharraf's relations with, 118–122, 130
  nationalist ideology in, 38–39, 92
  nuclear arsenal and, 18
  political manipulations of, 116
  power and autonomy of, 25n17, 47–49, 215
  public opinion of, 32n8, 32, 33
  Swat Valley offensive by, 139–140
  U.S. support for, 24–26, 76–77, 82,
    110–114, 118–122, 200–202, 214–222
  vulnerability of, 6–7
Mohajir ethnic group, 30–32
Mohammed, Khalid Sheikh, 11, 23, 114
Mohan, C. Raja, 193, 196
Monsoon (Kaplan), 191–192
Muhammed, Nek, 154
Mujib, Sheikh, 79n31
Mullen, Michael, 62, 105–106, 106n5, 108,
  166–167, 204

Munter, Cameron, 158–159, 205n11
Musharraf, Pervez, 15, 23
  assassination attempts against, 118–122
  Bhutto (B.) and, 131–133
  Bush administration and, 114–122, 215,
    218, 221
  Clinton administration and, 179–182
  coup against Sharif, 47–48, 221
  departure of, 29, 38
  drone strike authorizations by, 153–156,
    157
  FATA incursions under, 128
  India's relations with, 124–125, 218–219
  Iraq war and, 117–118
  Khan's (A. Q.) nuclear theft and, 88
  Lashkar-e-Taiba and, 102
  lawyers' movement against, 80–83
  media censorship by, 62, 63–64
  military relations with, 118–122, 130
  nuclear expansion under, 119
  political failures of, 31, 129–134, 221
  return to Pakistan and house arrest of,
    133–134
  self-imposed exile of, 133
  Taliban insurgency in Afghanistan and,
    125–129
  U.S. support for, 27, 76–77, 82, 103,
    105–108, 110–114, 201–202
Muslim Brotherhood, 57
Muslim Commercial Bank, 231–232
My American Journey (Powell), 110

National Command Authority (Pakistan), 44
nationalist movement in Pakistan
  anti-Americanism of, 83–92
  nuclear expansion influenced by, 87–90
  origins of, 49–50
National Research Council, 210
National Security Council (Pakistan), 121–122
The Nation (Pakistani English-language
    newspaper), 38–39
NATO forces in Afghanistan, 19, 40, 52,
    107–108, 125–126, 204–206
Nawaz, Maajid, 57n107
Naxalite movement (India), 193
Nazir, Tariq, 228–229
Nehru, Jawaharlal, 75, 195–196
Nepal, 42, 46, 194
Neumann, Ronald, 127, 127n64
The News (Pakistani English-language
    newspaper), 38
Nixon, Richard, 86–87, 175–176

No Exit (Huis Clos) (Sartre), 1, 27–28
"Nonalignment 2.0" (report), 195–196
Northern Distribution Network, NATO's use
  of, 205
North Korea
  China's relations with, 183
  Pakistan's relations with, 187–188
Novogratz, Jacqueline, 226
Nuclear Emergency Support Team (NEST),
  211
nuclear weapons
  deterrence strategy for Pakistan, 209–212
  Indo-Pakistani relations and role of, 43–46,
    185–188
  Khan's (A. Q.) role in Pakistan's
    development of, 87–88, 88n56, 90, 103,
    119, 187–188
  Pakistan's expansion of, 7–11, 69–70,
    91–92, 187–188
  U.S.-India partnership on, 181–184,
    196–197
  as "vital threat" to U.S., 16–18

Oakley, Robert, 91
Obama, Barack
  "AfPak" strategy under, 161–167
  China policies under, 177
  Davis affair and, 136–139
  democratization initiatives in Pakistan
    under, 140–145
  drone policy of, 153–154, 154n66, 156,
    158, 160–161
  election in 2008 of, 59
  India policy under, 182, 197
  Pakistan policy under, 23–24, 103–104,
    109, 205–206, 216–217, 219–222
  surge in Afghanistan and, 164–167
  U.S.-Pakistan relations and, 4, 107,
    136–151, 167–168
Obama's Wars (Woodward), 162
Omar, Mohammed Mullah, 99, 127, 162–163
On China (Kissinger), 175

Pakistan. *See* U.S.-Pakistani relations
  breakup of East and West Pakistan and,
    78–80
  China's relations with, 6–10, 20–22, 38–39,
    43, 70–71, 85–86, 182–184, 188–189,
    189n64, 192
  civilian government in, 29
  drone debate in, 157–158
  F-16 aircraft deal with, 91, 95, 123–124

floods of 2010 in, 148–149
India's tensions with, 6–8, 20–22, 39–43,
  124–125, 184, 218–219
nuclear program in, 7–8, 11, 16–18, 69–70,
  91–92, 187–188, 209–212
population projections for, 65–66
public opinion of government in, 32n8, 32,
  33
regional instability and, 169–172, 197–199
"Twin Peaks crisis" in, 115
U.S. military operations in, 169–172
vulnerability of, 6–7, 69–70
Pakistan Atomic Energy Commission,
  88n56
Pakistan Muslim League (Nawaz) (PML-N),
  31, 60–62, 132
Pakistan Muslim League (Quaid-e-Azam)
  (PML-Q), 31, 121–122, 130–131
Pakistan Peoples Party (PPP), 31, 60–62, 78,
  79n31, 107
"Pakistan Private Investment Initiative,"
  230–231
Pakistan Tehreek-e-Insaf (Movement for
  Justice) (PTI), 58–60
  reform agenda of, 60–62, 68
Panetta, Leon, 105–106, 151, 158–159
Pasha, Ahmed Shuja, 215–216n29
Pashtun ethnic group, 30–32, 40, 52–53
  in Peshawar, Pakistan, 170
  Taliban and, 125–126
"patient capital" initiatives in Pakistan, 226
Patterson, Anne, 38–39
Peace Accord of 2006 (Pakistan), 125–126
Pearl, Daniel, 38–39
Plame, Valerie, 111
politics in Pakistan
  comprehensive cooperation strategy as
    affecting, 225–231
  media culture and, 62–65
  military dominance of, 25n17, 47–49,
    219–222
  reform agenda and, 60–62
  youthful idealism and, 58–60
population projections for Pakistan, 65–66
Powell, Colin, 109–114, 117, 124, 218
Powers, Francis Gary, 169
Pressler, Larry, 91n65, 91, 92, 142
Punjabi ethnic group, 30–32
Punjabi Taliban, 53

Qadri, Mumtaz, 50–51
Qureshi, Shah Mahmood, 60–62

Raphel, Robin, 146–149
Rashid, Ahmed, 181–182
Reagan, Ronald
    Pakistan policy under, 90–91, 94–95,
        112
    Soviet Union policy under, 94–95
Red Mosque crisis, 130–131
reformist movement in Pakistan, 60–62,
    66
    regional context for, 70–71
regional instability
    China's global ascendancy and, 172–178
    as "emergent threat" to U.S., 18–22
    Pakistan-Afghanistan relations and, 6–8,
        18–22
    reformist movement in Pakistan and, 70–71
    U.S.-Pakistan relations and, 16, 169–172,
        197–199
    U.S. vulnerability to, 9–10
Rehman, I. A., 63, 64
Rehman, Sherry, 150
Reporters without Borders, 65
revolution, potential in Pakistan for, 68n146,
    68, 69
Rice, Condoleezza, 109, 120, 124, 125, 127,
    132, 180–181
Rosenberg, Matthew, 38–39
Rumsfeld, Donald, 175–176
Rural Support Programmes Network (RSPN),
    227–228, 228n53, 229

Saeed, Hafiz Muhammad, 14–15, 52, 58,
    69–70, 99–102
Salafism, 54, 98, 99–100
Salala incident, U.S.-Pakistan tensions over,
    108, 205
Sartre, Jean-Paul, 1, 5, 27, 237
Saudi Arabia
    Pakistan's relations with, 6–7, 95n78, 98,
        169, 187–188
    Salafism supported by, 100
    U.S. relations with, 215
Schmidt, John, 66–67
September 11, 2001 attacks
    Baig's skepticism concerning, 201
    drone development following, 151–156
    U.S. Afghan policies linked to, 95
    U.S.-Indian relations following, 181–182
    U.S.-Pakistani relations in wake of, 4,
        103–104, 108–117, 134–135
Sethi, Najam, 62
Shahzad, Faisal, 13–14

Shahzad, Syed Saleem, 62
Shakai Agreement (2004), 127–128
Sharif, Nawaz, 132
    censorship in regime of, 62
    coup against, 31, 47–48, 116, 221
    military relations with, 88
    re-election of, 61
Sharif, Shahbaz, 235
Shia Islam in Pakistan, 97n89, 96–99
Siachen glacier, 42
Singh, Manmohan, 124–125, 193–194,
    196–197
"Skunk Works" drone facility, 151–152
South Korea, 187
Soviet Union
    China and, 178–179
    invasion of Afghanistan by, 90, 92–94,
        94n76
    Kashmir dispute and role of, 77–78
    U.S.-Pakistani relations and, 1–4, 74–76,
        83–85
    U.S. relations with, 94–95
Spain, terrorism in, 186
Special Forces. *See* U.S. Special Forces, raids in
    Pakistan by
Sri Lanka, 42, 46, 194
state failure in Pakistan, potential for,
    68–69
Storming the World Stage (Tankel), 102
Sufi Islam in Pakistan, 54, 170
Sunni Islam in Pakistan, 97n89, 96–99
Sunni Ittehad Council, 50–51

Taliban. *See also* affiliated groups (e.g.,
    Haqqani network; Tehrik-i-Taliban
    Pakistan)
    in Afghanistan, 18–22, 40, 52, 114,
        125–129, 202–204
    "AfPak" strategy and, 161–167
    Islamic extremism and, 53–54
    Kashmir dispute and, 39
    ouster from Swat valley of, 47, 140
    Pakistan's support for, 23, 38–39, 51–52,
        99, 105–108, 127, 158–159, 161–163,
        167n112, 169, 200–202
    Punjabi Taliban group, 53
Tankel, Stephen, 102
Tarar, Sultan Amir, 202
Tarbela Dam project, 25, 229–230
tariff policies, Pakistan economic development
    and, 230–231
Taseer, Salman, 50–51

tax policies in Pakistan, 37–38
Tehrik-i-Taliban Pakistan (TTP), 13–14,
     52–53
  attacks on Pakistani military by, 69–70
  drone strikes against, 158
  expansion of, 161–162
  military campaign against, 217
  Tarar assassination by, 202
  violence in Peshawar by, 169–172
Tellis, Ashley, 180–181
terrorism
  economic costs of, 186
  as "immediate threat" to U.S., 11–16
  Pakistan safe havens for, 49–58, 114–117,
     125–129, 162–163
  Pakistan's vulnerability to, 62, 69–70,
     139–140, 169–172
  U.S.-Pakistan cooperation concerning, 7–11,
     206–214
Tetlay, Ahmed, 227–229
textile industry, Pakistan-Bangladesh
     comparisons of, 36
Tora Bora raid, 114–117
trade-related issues
  comprehensive cooperation strategy and,
     230–231
  India-China relations and, 194–195,
     195n84
  India-Pakistan tensions and, 186–187
Truman, Harry S., 75n9
trust fund for Pakistan investment, proposals
     for, 225
"Twin Peaks crisis," 115

Uighur separatist groups, 21, 190
Ul-Haq, Abrar, 60
Ummah Tameer-e-Nau (UTN), 51n82
United Nations' Millennium Development
     Goals, 224
United States. *See also* U.S.-Pakistan relations
  assistance programs in Pakistan by, 23–24
  China's relations with, 175–178, 188–192,
     197–199
  competing priorities in Pakistani strategies
     for, 233–235
  defensive insulation strategy in Pakistan
     and, 206–214
  drone strike debate in, 158–159
  economic sanctions against Pakistan by,
     91–92
  F-16 aircraft deal with Pakistan, 91, 95,
     123–124

financial assistance programs in Pakistan
     from, 74–76, 112, 122–123, 140,
     145–150
  flawed assumptions concerning Pakistan in,
     29
  Indian relations with, 20–22, 85, 179–182,
     196–197
  nuclear weapons accidents in, 44–45
  politics of Pakistan policies in, 202–204
  port defenses in, 210n22, 210–211
  strategic options in Pakistan for, 26–27, 206
  vulnerability of, 7–11
U.S. Agency for International Development
     (USAID), 23–24, 149n44, 145–150,
     150n44
  comprehensive cooperation strategy and,
     225–231
USNS *Impeccable* incident, 176
U.S.-Pakistan relations
  Afghanistan war and, 92–103, 202–204
  "AfPak" strategy and, 161–167
  anti-Americanism in Pakistan and, 73–103
  in Bush administration, 23, 82, 103–104,
     109–114, 143n22, 181–182
  China's role in, 182–184, 188–192,
     197–199
  Cold War and, 178–179
  comprehensive cooperation strategy for,
     222–233
  covert operations cooperation and, 208–209
  crisis-oriented policies in, 109–110
  Davis affair and, 136–139
  defensive insulation strategy for, 206–214
  distrust and disagreement in, 165n108,
     167–168
  drone strikes and, 11–16, 23–24, 138
  future options for, 182–184, 235–237
  historical background, 1–4, 72–73, 76n15,
     103–104
  Iraq war and, 117–118
  "KLB" legislation and, 141–150, 216–217
  military-first cooperation strategy and,
     214–222
  missed opportunities in, 108–117
  in Musharraf era, 105–108, 118–122
  mutual vulnerability in, 5–11
  nationalism in Pakistan and, 91–92
  nuclear expansion in Pakistan and, 90,
     209–212
  Obama administration and, 136–168
  overview of U.S. options in, 26–27
  political climate in U.S. and, 202–204

U.S.-Pakistan relations (*cont.*)
    potential state failure and, 10–11
    pragmatism in, 24–26
    recent failures in, 22–26
    reformist movement in Pakistan and, 70–71
    regional context for, 20–22, 169–172, 197–199
    successes in, 122–125
    surge in Afghanistan and, 164–167
    U.S. withdrawal from Afghanistan and future of, 204–206
    Zia's Islamization of Pakistan and, 96–99
U.S. Special Forces, raids in Pakistan by, 155–156
U.S. State Department, Pakistan aid policies and, 145–150

Vajpayee, Atal Bihari, 124, 179
Vietnam War
    Afghan war compared with, 93
    U.S. Pakistan policy and influence of, 85, 110

Wahhabi Islam, 54, 99–100
Wall Street Journal, 38–39
Waseem, Mohammad, 76–77

water shortages in Pakistan, 36–37
Weinstein, Warren, 149
Wilson, Charlie, 93–94, 95
Woodward, Bob, 162, 164n104, 209n19
World Bank, 225, 229–230
World Health Organization, 25–26

youth culture in Pakistan
    media technology and, 64
    politics and, 58–60, 65
    resistance to nationalism in, 92
YouTube, in Pakistan, 64, 92

Zafar, Roshaneh, 226–227
Zardari, Asif Ali, 32, 64, 80, 80n32, 133, 215–216n29
Zardari, Bilawal, 80
Zia-ul-Haq, Muhammad, 2, 49–50
    censorship in regime of, 62
    death of, 51, 81
    execution of Bhutto (Z. A.) and, 80
    Islamic extremism and, 53–54
    Islamization of, 96–99
    military relations with, 200–201
    nuclear expansion under, 90
    U.S. support for, 76–77, 82, 93–95, 112

Made in the USA
Monee, IL
31 May 2022

97298038R00152